20·12

Fireworks® 4

Waterford Institute of Technology

fast & easy
web development

Lisa Lee

PRIMA
TECH

A D   W.I.T.   HING

To the memory of Jos Claerbout, http://www.spies.com/~jos

A Division of Prima Publishing

Prima Publishing and colophon are registered trademarks of Prima Communications, Inc. PRIMA TECH and Fast & Easy are trademarks of Prima Communications, Inc., Roseville, California 95661.

Publisher: Stacy L. Hiquet
Associate Marketing Manager: Heather Buzzingham
Managing Editor: Sandy Doell
Acquisitions Editor: Lynette Quinn
Project Editor: Cathleen D. Snyder
Technical Reviewer: Kyle Stephan
Copy Editor: Geneil Breeze
Interior Layout: Shawn Morningstar
Cover Design: Prima Design Team
Indexer: Sharon Shock

ISBN: 0-7615-3519-5
Library of Congress Catalog Card Number: 2001086176
Printed in the United States of America
00 01 02 03 04 DD 10 9 8 7 6 5 4 3 2 1

Acknowledgments

Thanks to Marta Justak for introducing me to the folks at Prima Tech, and to Lynette Quinn, my Acquisitions Editor, and Cathleen Snyder, my Project Editor, for being such great people to work with. Thanks to all the folks at Prima Tech who contributed to this book and to my family, friends, and co-workers for their patience and support.

Special thanks to all the Macromedia Evangelists who do such a great job supporting Macromedia's Fireworks forum. Thanks to Linda Rathgeber, Brian Baker, Kevin French, and Kleanthis E for sharing their Fireworks tips and tutorials with the world on their Web sites. Also, thanks to all the Fireworks support folks, especially Mark Haynes and John Dowdell, for posting all kinds of helpful information about Fireworks to Macromedia's Fireworks news forum. Also, a big thank you to Matias Duarte for being such a phenomenal Fireworks graphics designer and an inspiration to me.

About the Author

Lisa Lee is the author of Fireworks Fast & Easy Web Development, Adobe Photoshop 6 Digital Darkroom, and several books about how to use software with Macintosh and Windows computers. She has also been the technical editor for books about Macintosh, WebTV, Palm, and Handspring hardware and software. Over the past decade she has worked at companies such as Microsoft and Apple to help create user-friendly products for the Macintosh, Internet, and the Web. She has over six years of Web design experience using Macs, Windows, and Linux systems. You can download additional Fireworks tutorial files and see her latest artistic designs and Web projects by visiting her Web site at http://www.flatfishfactory.com/FW4/fireworks4.htm.

Contents

Introduction

Fireworks 4 Fast & Easy Web Development is designed to help intermediate or advanced computer users and graphics designers become familiar with some basic and advanced features of Fireworks 4. Using a step-by-step, visual approach, you'll get familiar with the Fireworks workspace and learn how to design some simple and sophisticated Web graphics.

Although many of the tasks in this book are fairly easy to follow, I don't recommend this book to a new computer user or someone who is not familiar with graphics applications or Web design. However, you can use this book side by side with any number of other books about Mac OS, Windows, Web design, Flash, Dreamweaver, UltraDev, and Fireworks. I used a G4 Macintosh computer running Mac OS 9 and a PC running Windows 2000 to create the examples for this book.

If you're looking for a complete reference of Fireworks features, or explanations about why Macromedia supports a particular JavaScript routine in Fireworks, you won't find that information in this book. This book contains a selected set of examples that show you how to design some basic Web graphics using the drawing, editing, layers, and masks tools in Fireworks. It also shows you how to put together more sophisticated Web graphics, such as complex rollovers, animated GIFs, sliced images, and pop-up menus. All the examples are included on the CD-ROM located at the back of this book. You can use them to follow along with the examples in each chapter.

Who Should Read This Book?

Although this book is designed for intermediate and advanced Web designers, I'd like to think it would be helpful to anyone who wants to learn how to create Web graphics with Fireworks 4, including beginners. If you're adventurous and learn quickly, or you prefer following a visual, step-by-step approach to learn new things, you'll probably appreciate this book. The examples in this book show only some of the many different ways you can design interactive Web graphics. I encourage you to visit Macromedia's Fireworks forum and navigate Macromedia's Web tutorials to extend your knowledge about Fireworks.

I wrote this book for those who are, of course, new to Fireworks, but are generally familiar with Web design concepts and Web-related languages, as well as those who are experienced Web designers. You don't have to be an artist to create simple buttons, rollovers, and animation, but it helps if you have surfed Web pages and can tell the difference between a button and an animation, or static text versus a link. Learn how to put together elegant, image-driven Web pages without having to manually create or modify HTML and JavaScript code to add those graphics to a Web page. If you are familiar with Windows or Macintosh computers, as well as graphic applications and Web design, this book is for you!

How This Book Is Organized

I tried to organize this book so you could learn all about Fireworks features from cover to cover or use it as a reference book to find out how to use a particular feature. This book is divided into four main sections: Getting Started, Designing Graphics, Designing Interactive Web Graphics, and Combining Web Graphics with Web Pages. Each part of this book introduces you to a particular set of features in Fireworks and shows you how to use each one, step by step, in a task-based format. The goal of each part of this book is to show you how to use the most commonly used graphics and interactive Web graphic features in Fireworks.

The first chapters of this book familiarize you with the Fireworks workspace. You can find out what all the menus, tools, and windows can do. The second part of the book shows you how to work with bitmap and vector graphics in Fireworks. You can try out the drawing tools, create a mask, organize layers of image objects, dabble with colors, and create animation. After you've designed or opened some graphic objects, you can move on to the third part. You can take the examples you just created or use the Fireworks files provided with this book to design buttons, navigation bars, and pop-up menus using behaviors, objects, URLs, hotspots, and slices. When you're ready to put your art on the Web, Part IV shows you how to use Dreamweaver to add your Web graphics to a Web page. You can work with Fireworks and Flash, using Dreamweaver as a command-central HTML editor application for all your Web development.

A CD-ROM is located on the inside back cover of this book. It contains the project-related files for the examples shown in most of the chapters in this book, along with 30-day trial copies of Fireworks 4, Dreamweaver 4, Dreamweaver UltraDev 4, and Flash 5. You can access the files on the CD-ROM by viewing the HTML file, located on the root level of the CD's directory. Or, you can double-click on a folder icon to access the project files or the 30-day trial installer applications.

Almost all the screenshots in this book were created with the Macintosh version of Fireworks 4. If you plan to use Fireworks 4 on a Windows computer, both versions of Fireworks are nearly identical. You can also share the same Fireworks file between the Windows and Mac versions. Tasks that use keyboard shortcuts combine Windows and Macintosh keys. For example, Ctrl/Command + C represents Ctrl + C if you're using Windows, and Command + C if you're using a Mac. In general, for keyboard combinations, Windows uses the Ctrl key, while the Mac uses the Command key. Also, Windows uses the Alt key, while the Mac uses the Option key.

Conventions Used in This Book

TIP
Tips offer hints, explain more about a special feature, or tell you how to use a shortcut to boost your productivity and make work fun.

NOTE
Notes provide additional information about a feature, or extend an idea about how to use a feature.

CAUTION
Cautions warn about pitfalls and potential problems that you might encounter. Most cautions apply to both Windows and Mac versions of Fireworks 4.

Whether you have a Windows or Macintosh computer, have fun learning how to use Fireworks 4 and Dreamweaver 4, fast and easy!

Getting Started with Fireworks 4

Web site development tools have evolved rapidly over the past few years. Macromedia provides an entire suite of applications to help you create everything from HTML and line art to Web and motion graphics. Dreamweaver and Dreamweaver UltraDev are Macromedia's Web site design applications. Both support HTML 4.0 and JavaScript in addition to style sheets and other standard browser language features. Both also permit you to hand-code your own Web pages. UltraDev also allows you to create database-backed Web sites. Macromedia's Flash 5 enables you to create scalable, scriptable motion graphics that are optimized for the best Web playback performance. Fireworks is a dedicated Web graphics application that can work together with Dreamweaver and Flash to bring great-looking graphics to any Web site.

Macromedia Fireworks 4 enables you to design bitmap or vector graphics for the Web. You can use the built-in tools to create your own graphics, or you can import Illustrator (EPS), Photoshop (PSD), Flash (SWF), GIF, JPEG, or PNG graphic, photo, or animation files into Fireworks. You can also design interactive Web graphics with Fireworks, such as buttons, navigation bars, image maps, drop-down menus, animated GIFs, static graphics, and so on. The more sophisticated features in Fireworks enable you to automate tasks with JavaScript. Then, when you're ready to add your images to a Web page, you can integrate your Web graphics into other Web site design applications such as Dreamweaver 4, Flash 5, Microsoft FrontPage, and Adobe GoLive.

1

Installing Fireworks 4

Before you can use Fireworks 4, you must check your computer to make sure that it meets Macromedia's requirements for running Fireworks 4. You might also want to make sure that your computer has enough memory and disk space to work with Dreamweaver or any other Web development applications, since you'll probably want to use Fireworks with a Web development application. If your computer meets the minimum requirements, you can install Fireworks from the CD-ROM included with this book, purchase the Fireworks 4 CD-ROM, or download the 30-day trial version from Macromedia's Web site. Fireworks 4 is available for both Windows and Macintosh computers. After you install it on your computer, you can also install Dreamweaver 4 or UltraDev 4, if you wish.

In this chapter, you'll learn how to:

- Use the Fireworks installer application
- Get help with Fireworks

System Requirements

Opening and editing graphic and image files requires more memory and disk space than working with traditional text or HTML files. Graphic files are larger than text files because each graphic image has to store color information in addition to pixel information. The bigger the graphic image, the larger the graphic file, and the more memory you'll need to work with that image. In comparison, text files are considerably smaller than graphic files, although you can combine text with graphics to create some intriguing Web art.

The bottom line is that a faster computer makes a big difference if you want to increase your productivity when working with graphic images. Usually a faster computer means one with more memory and a larger hard disk.

Macintosh Requirements

The minimum requirements for using Fireworks on the Macintosh platform are a Power Macintosh computer, running Mac OS 8.6 or 9.x, with 64 MB or more of physical memory, 100 MB of free hard disk space, a mouse or digitizing tablet, a CD-ROM drive, and a monitor that can display at least 256 colors.

Macromedia recommends using a screen resolution of 1024 × 768 with millions of colors on a Power Macintosh G3, G4, or higher computer, running Mac OS 8.6 or 9. My Macintosh system is configured with 256 MB of memory and more than 10 GB of free hard disk space. Also, if you plan to use Type 1 PostScript fonts, you'll need to install Adobe Type Manager 4.

NOTE

Most newer model Macs only enable you to display 256, thousands, or millions of colors. Any of these settings will work fine with Fireworks. You can set the color depth and desktop size from the Monitors control panel. To find out more about setting the color depth and resolution of the computer monitor, see Chapter 7, "Working with Colors, Layers, and Masks."

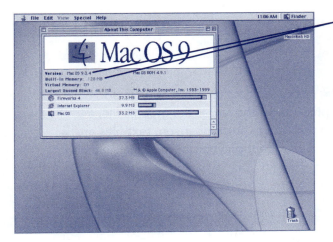

1. Choose About This Computer from the Apple menu to find out the version of Mac OS installed on your computer. You'll also see the amount of memory installed on your system.

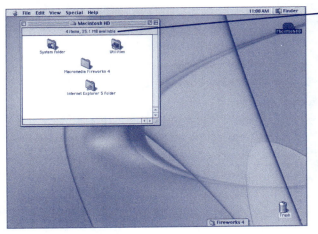

2. Open any Finder window to view the amount of hard disk space available.

NOTE

If you plan to install Dreamweaver 4, UltraDev 4, or Flash 5 on a Macintosh or Windows computer, make sure that your computer has enough memory and disk space to accommodate these applications, too.

CAUTION

Make sure that the Contextual Menu Extension is in your Extensions folder in your System folder. Apple installs it with Mac OS version 8.6 through the latest 9.x version. However, if you move this extension out of the System folder, Fireworks may freeze when it starts.

Windows Requirements

The minimum requirements necessary to use Fireworks on a Windows-based system are a Pentium 120 computer with 64 MB of memory, 100 MB of free hard disk space, a mouse or digitizing tablet, a CD-ROM drive, and a monitor capable of displaying at least 256 colors.

Macromedia recommends using a Pentium III PC running Windows 95, 98, 2000, Millennium Edition (Me), or NT 4.0 (with Service Pack 3); and a screen resolution of 1024 × 768, displaying millions of colors.

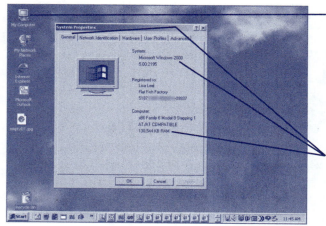

1. To find out which version of Windows you are using, how much memory is installed, and the processor type of your PC, right-click on the My Computer icon and choose Properties. This example shows the Properties window for Windows 2000.

2. Click on the General tab and view the amount of memory at the bottom of the window. The version of your Windows software appears at the top of the window.

Using the Fireworks Installer

If you're already familiar with how to install Fireworks on your computer, skip ahead to the "Finding Help" section to learn about the built-in tutorials and lessons in Fireworks. The Fireworks installer application is similar to other installer applications for Macintosh or Windows computers. The Macintosh installer uses the standard Easy Install, and the Windows installer only has one default installation for Fireworks.

If a previous version of Fireworks is already installed on your computer, install Fireworks 4 in its own, new folder. You can run older and newer versions of Fireworks on your Mac or PC, as long as you don't install more than one version of Fireworks into an existing Fireworks folder on your hard drive. Be sure to label each separate version of Fireworks, so you can easily find each version.

Installing Fireworks on a Macintosh Computer

You can download the Fireworks installer application from Macromedia's Web site (http://www.macromedia.com/software/fireworks), or you can start it from the CD-ROM included with this book. Start up your Macintosh, then insert the Fireworks CD-ROM into the CD- or DVD-ROM drive.

For best results, you might want to start up your Mac with all extensions off. Even though the Fireworks installer does not add any extension files to your System folder, some extensions might conflict with the Fireworks installer. For the most problem-free installation, start up your Mac with all extensions off by holding down the Shift key at startup. Then run Apple's Disk First Aid application to check your hard disk for any potential problems. Start the application, select a hard drive icon, and then click on the Verify button to check the selected drive. If no errors are found, perform the following steps to install Fireworks 4 onto your Macintosh computer.

1. Double-click on the Fireworks 4 Installer icon. When the Macromedia splash screen appears, click on Continue.

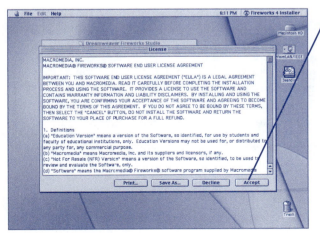

2. Read the License Agreement. Click on Accept if you agree to the terms of the license agreement, and the Fireworks 4 Installer window will appear. Click on Decline if you do not agree, and the installer application will quit.

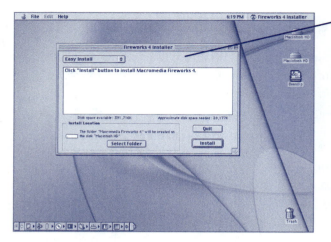

3. The Fireworks 4 Installer window displays information about the type and suggested hard drive location for the installation. Only two installation types are available: Easy Install or Uninstall. However, you can specify where on your hard drive you want to install Fireworks.

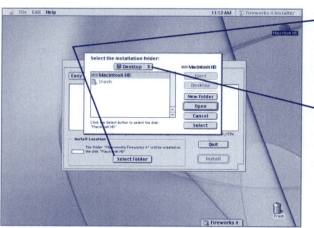

4. If you want to change the location of the Fireworks installation, click on Select Folder. A dialog box will open, asking you to select the installation folder.

5. Select a folder name to choose where you want to install Fireworks 4 on your hard drive.

NOTE

If you want to create a new directory, click the New Folder button. Type a name for the folder, then click on the Create button. The Fireworks 4 installer puts all the files in one folder, so if you aren't particular about where Fireworks is installed, you don't need to create a new folder for the installation.

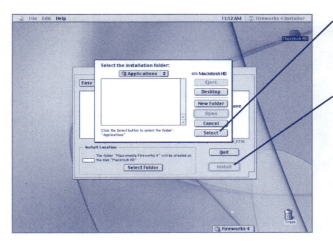

6. Click on the Select button to choose the folder. The main install window will reappear.

7. Click on the Install button to start the installation. When prompted, type your name and serial number for Fireworks and then wait for the files to copy to your hard drive.

NOTE

If you have any virus protection software, or to reduce any potential problems during installation, open the Extensions Manager control panel and choose the Mac OS 8.x or 9.x Base set. Restart your computer, and then run the Fireworks installer application.

Installing Fireworks on a Windows Computer

If you want to install Fireworks on a Windows PC, insert the CD-ROM into the CD- or DVD-ROM drive. The Fireworks installer should automatically start. If it doesn't,

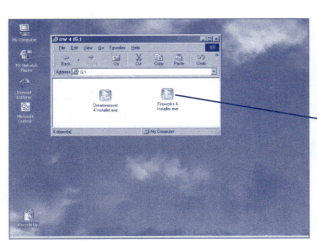

double-click on the My Computer icon on the desktop. Double-click on the icon for the CD-ROM or DVD-ROM drive, and then double-click on the Fireworks Installer executable icon.

1. Double-click on the Fireworks 4 Installer icon. The Macromedia Fireworks installer splash screen will appear. Click once to continue.

2. Read the message on the Welcome screen. Then, click on Next to continue to the next screen.

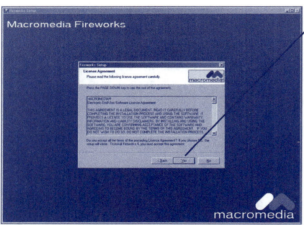

3. Read the License Agreement. Click on the up or down scroll arrow to navigate through the text in the License Agreement. Click on Yes if you agree with the terms of Macromedia's license agreement.

4. Next, the Fireworks 4 Destination/Location window will display information about the suggested hard drive location for the installation. If you want to change the location of the Fireworks installation, click on the Browse button and navigate to the folder in which you want to install Fireworks. If you want to create a new folder on your hard drive, type a name for the new folder and click on the Select button.

5. Click on the Next button to continue. Review the installation information. I chose the default installer settings when I installed Fireworks on my Windows 2000 computer. Click on the Next button to view the Fireworks Setup window.

6. Review the installer settings in the Fireworks Setup window. Click on Back if you want to change any of the settings. Otherwise, click on the Next button to install Fireworks on your computer.

7. When the installation completes, the installer will display a window asking whether you want to review the release notes, which are in HTML format and are located on your hard drive. Click on the check box to deselect the option if you do not want to review the release notes. Finally, click on the Finish button to complete the installation.

NOTE

Be sure to have small fonts selected in your Windows Display Properties settings. To adjust the font size, click on the Start menu, choose Settings, Control Panel, then double-click on Display. Click on the Settings tab in the Display Properties dialog box, then click on the Advanced button. Choose Small Fonts from the Font Size drop-down menu in the General tab of the dialog box. Click on the OK button to save your changes.

Removing Fireworks

You can use the Fireworks 4 installer application to remove or uninstall Fireworks from your computer. If you have a Windows computer, you can use the Add/Remove Programs option in the Control Panel to uninstall Fireworks 4 from your hard drive. If you are using a Macintosh computer, insert the Fireworks CD into your CD- or DVD-ROM drive. Start the Fireworks application and then perform the following steps to remove Fireworks from your Macintosh computer.

1. Choose Uninstall from the pop-up menu in the Fireworks 4 Installer window.

2. Click on Uninstall to remove the Fireworks application from your hard disk.

Finding Help

Several different kinds of help resources are built into Fireworks. Most of these help systems require that you have a browser application such as Internet Explorer 5 or Netscape 4.7 already installed. The built-in help information brings the information in the Fireworks 4 manual to your desktop. You can learn how to build a Web site with Fireworks and Dreamweaver by following the Web tutorial. You can also choose from six lessons that introduce you to all the major Web graphic features available in Fireworks.

Building a Web Site with the Tutorial

When you first start Fireworks, a Welcome window appears. You can click on What's New, Tutorial, or Lessons to learn more about Fireworks anytime you want. Each of the electronic help systems is also accessible from the Help menu in Fireworks 4. The tutorial is designed to familiarize you with the Fireworks production workflow. You can learn how to create vector shapes and text, import and edit bitmap images, align objects, create buttons, add links to buttons, use the History panel, create rollovers, and export the image and its HTML. To access the built-in tutorial help information, follow these steps.

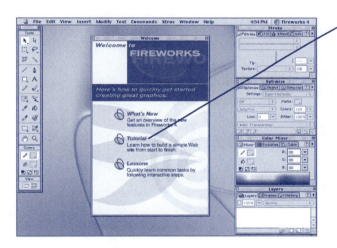

1. Click on Tutorial in the Welcome window. If the Welcome window is not open, choose Welcome from the Help menu, and then click on the Tutorial link in the Welcome window.

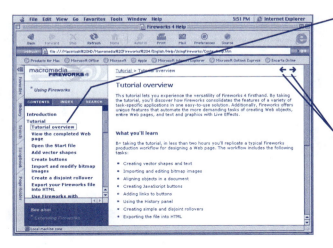

2. You can read through the HTML files or use the tutorial files installed with Fireworks 4 to follow along with the tutorial information in the browser window.

3. Click on the Next or Previous arrows to navigate through the Tutorial.

> **TIP**
>
> You can download additional tutorials from Macromedia's Web site, at http://www.macromedia.com/software/fireworks.

Learning Web Design with Lessons

Macromedia includes six lessons that give you a tour of Fireworks features. You can view an introduction to the Fireworks workspace, or learn how to create animation, slices, rollovers, and pop-up menus. You can also learn how to automate repetitive tasks, such as changing a color across images in a Fireworks document or finding a specific shape across several Fireworks files. The following steps show you how to access the lessons, which are installed with Fireworks.

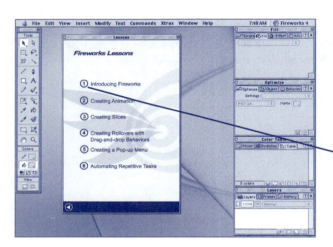

1. Choose Lessons from the Help menu or from the Welcome window.

2. Click on a number to start a lesson.

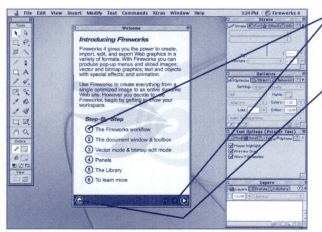

3. Click on a lesson number or an arrow icon to navigate back and forth through the lesson pages.

4. Click on the Home icon to return to the lesson menu.

TIP

Forget how to do a particular task in Fireworks? Choose Using Fireworks from the Help menu to access Fireworks help pages. You can view Fireworks information organized by content or in index form, alphabetized from A to Z.

Using the Help Menu

Macromedia did a great job of including a healthy dose of built-in and Web-based help in Fireworks. If you can't remember how to design a particular Web element in Fireworks, help is just a menu away. The following steps provide a brief tour of the help options available in the Fireworks Help menu.

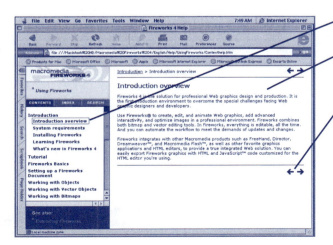

1. Click on the Help menu to view the list of Fireworks help resources.

2. Choose Using Fireworks to view HTML-based help files.

3. Click on a topic in the Help window.

4. Read about that topic in the right panel of the browser window.

5. Click on the previous or next arrow to navigate the help files.

> **TIP**
>
> If this is your first time using Fireworks 4, choose Using Fireworks from the Help menu. Wait for the browser application to start, then click on the Introduction overview text to find out more about Fireworks.

> **NOTE**
>
> Although Apple provides Balloon Help to every application, Macromedia doesn't provide any balloon help for Fireworks.

Searching for Help Topics

In addition to viewing Fireworks help information by contents or as an index, you can also search for a help topic. Click on the Search button in any browser Help window. A secondary search window will appear in front of the main browser window. The following steps show you to search for a help topic.

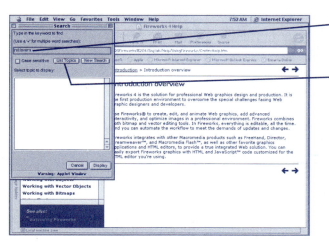

1. Type a word or words for which you want to search.

2. Click on List Topics to start the search. If the search yields any matching items, they appear in the bottom half of the Search window. You can use the scroll bar to scroll through the list of results.

> **TIP**
>
> If no results appear, try using fewer words to broaden your search. If too many results appear, try adding a word to limit the list of found items.

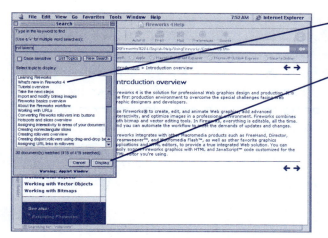

3. Click on any item in the search results list to view the related information.

4. Click on the Display button to review the information in the browser window.

TIP

To change the default browser used with the Help system, choose Preview in Browser from the File menu and then pick your default browser.

Using the Fireworks Manual

If you don't have the luxury of extra window space or the use of a second computer, you can look up a topic in the printed manual. Most of the information in the manual is also available in the Using Fireworks HTML-based help files. You can also download a printable PDF file of the Fireworks manual from Macromedia's Web site.

NOTE

Although the manual is included if you purchase Fireworks from a computer retail shop, you won't get one if you download the 30-day trial version or opt for the download purchase and decide not to pay the $10 for the CD-ROM and the manual.

Fireworks Support Resources

Software isn't perfect. If trouble strikes and your troubleshooting efforts don't yield any quick solutions, never fear; Fireworks support is online. If your computer has Internet access, you can read the most popular tech notes, keep current with the latest news about Fireworks 4, download updates, and more. If you have a question, or want to see what kinds of questions other Fireworks users are asking, visit Macromedia's Fireworks forum at news://forums.macromedia.com/macromedia.fireworks. To find out more about troubleshooting Fireworks or if you want to learn new Web techniques, choose Fireworks Support Center from the Help menu. Alternatively, you can use your browser to access the Fireworks 4 support Web site at http://www.macromedia.com/support/fireworks. Several user-sponsored Web sites also offer Fireworks tutorials. A list of Fireworks tutorial sites is available from Macromedia's Web site at http://www.macromedia.com/support/fireworks/ts/documents/web_sites_fireworks.htm. I also have several tutorials available on my Web site at http://www.flatfishfactory.com/FW4/fireworks4.htm. The following items highlight different support areas available on Macromedia's Web site.

- **What's New**. Read the latest news about Fireworks 4.

- **TechNotes**. Read detailed information about specific Fireworks features. Each technical note has a unique identification number, so you can keep track of your favorites. You can also determine which TechNote is the most current.

- **Macromedia Exchange**. Macromedia encourages users to create and share custom commands and other tools. Visit the Dreamweaver Exchange to check out the latest commands and behaviors that you can use to extend Fireworks or customize the way you work. Visit Macromedia's exchange forums at http://www.macromedia.com/exchange to find out more about how to extend Fireworks.

- **E-mail**. After you've registered Fireworks, you can send your questions to the Macromedia technical support group in an e-mail message at http://www.macromedia.com/support/email/complimentary.

- **Discussion groups**. If your browser is configured to read newsgroups, you can read messages posted by other Fireworks users or post one yourself. This can be an excellent way to find out how other users accomplish various tasks. Macromedia sponsors a dedicated Fireworks forum at news://forums.macromedia.com/macromedia.fireworks.

2

Exploring Fireworks 4

Fireworks 4 has many of the same tools, menus, and panels as Dreamweaver 4 and Flash 5. Macromedia has been working closely with its customers to not only make it easy to create and work with graphics in Fireworks, but also to make the Web design experience as easy as possible. This chapter gives you a brief tour of the Fireworks 4 workspace, including a look at how the menu commands are organized.

In this chapter, you'll learn how to:

- Use the workspace
- Navigate the menus

Fireworks is a dynamic Web graphics application because it enables you to import or design both bitmap and vector graphics in the same document. For example, you can use any of the built-in tools to create vector graphics such as lines, shapes, and animation, or you can import a bitmap image from a digital camera or scanner. You can modify an image object's stroke or fill characteristics and adjust its color, hue, saturation, or tonal levels. If you want to create interactive Web graphics, you can organize image objects into layers and frames, or control playback using the Frame Controls located at the bottom of the document window.

In addition to having access to a full suite of drawing, editing, and interactive Web graphic tools, you can also optimize your images and view up to three different results side-by-side in the document window. When you're ready to combine your Web graphics with a Web page, you can export the images and HTML code from Fireworks. Then you can add them to a Web page using Dreamweaver 4, UltraDev 4, or another Web design application such as FrontPage or GoLive.

A Brief Tour of the Workspace

Double-click on the Fireworks application icon to start Fireworks 4. First, you'll see a Fireworks 4 splash screen, and then you'll see the Fireworks workspace. The workspace consists of four basic elements—the document window, menu bar, toolbox, and panels. You can click on a tool in the toolbox to create an image object in the document window. Or, you can import an image using the File, Import menu command. As you make changes to image objects in the document window, any related windows, including panels, will update automatically.

Viewing an Empty Workspace

When you first start Fireworks, the Welcome window appears. Click on its Close box to dismiss it. You can't do much without opening a document window in Fireworks. But, the menu bar, toolbox, and panels can be a bit overwhelming. This section provides a brief tour of the workspace. You'll learn more about the menus, toolbox, and panels in the next chapter.

- **Menu bar.** The Fireworks menu names are similar to those on the Macromedia Flash 5 and Dreamweaver 4 menus. However, most of the menu commands in Fireworks are unique. Click on a menu in the menu bar to view a list of menu commands. If an arrow appears on the right of a menu command, that command has a submenu.

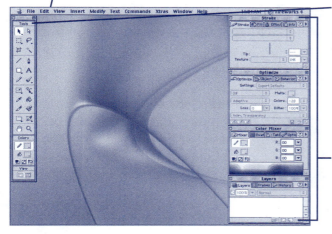

- **Toolbox**. The toolbox is divided into three sections: Tools, Colors, and View. In turn, the Tools section consists of four parts: selection, drawing, editing and Web tools. The toolbox can also be called the Tools panel. Choose Tools from the Window menu to open or close the toolbox.

- **Panels**. You can choose from 19 different panels to work with in the Fireworks workspace. Panels can be grouped into the same window, or you can separate a panel that's grouped with other panels. Each panel has a close and collapse/uncollapse box located in the left and right corners of the title bar. You'll also find a Help button (question mark icon) located in the upper-right corner of the panel, right beside the Panel Options pop-up menu button. The bottom of each panel has one or more icons that enable you to add, delete, or edit items in that panel. For more information about panels, see Chapter 3, "Getting Familiar with Tools, Objects, and Panels."

NOTE

The Windows version of Fireworks has an additional status bar at the bottom of the workspace. You can turn this feature on or off by choosing Status Bar from the View menu.

Creating a New Document

You can create a new document in Fireworks, or you can open an existing Fireworks document. A Fireworks document consists of a canvas, which is the area where you design graphics, plus all the Frame, mini-launcher, and other window controls located at the top and bottom of each document window. If you open the document window beyond the size of the canvas, the canvas boundary will be surrounded by a light gray color.

To create a new document, choose New from the File menu. You can set the canvas size, resolution, and color in the New Document dialog box. However, if you're copying and pasting an existing image into Fireworks, the dimensions of the canvas automatically will be entered into the New Document dialog box. The following list explains each setting in the New Document dialog box.

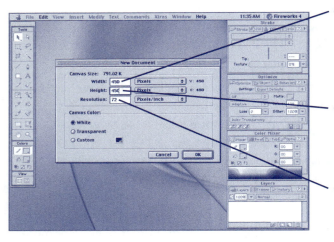

- **Width**. Type a number in the Width text box to define how wide the canvas will be. I've used pixels as my measurement for width, but you can also use inches or centimeters.

- **Height**. Type a number in the Height text box to define the height of the canvas. The Height text box works like the Width text box.

- **Resolution**. Type the resolution for the document. Measurements can be in pixels/inch or pixels/centimeter.

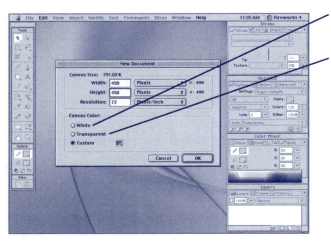

- **White**. Select this option to set the canvas color to white.

- **Transparent**. Select this check box if you do not want the canvas to have a background color. A gray-and-white checkerboard pattern represents transparency in the Fireworks document window.

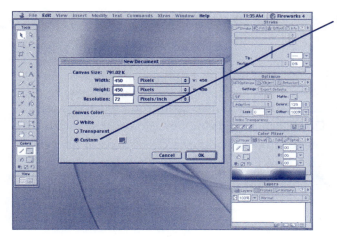

● **Custom**. Use this option to select a custom color for your canvas. You can choose a canvas color from the pop-up color window, or you can click on the color wheel icon in the upper-right corner of the Color pop-up menu to choose a color from the Windows or Mac color picker window.

NOTE

You can change the canvas size after creating a new document. Click on the Modify menu and choose the Canvas Size menu command. Type the number of pixels, inches, or centimeters for the canvas. If you want to extend the canvas in a specific direction, click on an anchor button to tell Fireworks to extend the canvas in a specific direction.

You can also change the canvas color after creating a new document. Click on the Modify menu and choose Canvas Color to view the current setting in the Canvas Color window.

Working with a Document Window

The Fireworks document window has the same size, hide, and close controls as most Windows and Macintosh applications. In addition to being a work area, each document window contains four tabs, and a status bar area located at the bottom of each window. If your document uses more than one frame, you can navigate those frames by clicking on the Frame Controls located in the lower-left corner of the document window. The following list provides a brief tour of the controls in a document window.

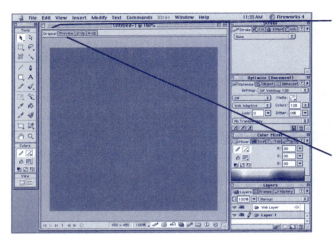

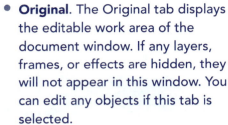

- **Original**. The Original tab displays the editable work area of the document window. If any layers, frames, or effects are hidden, they will not appear in this window. You can edit any objects if this tab is selected.

- **Preview**. This tab works with the settings in the Optimize panel to display a preview of how the original image will look if you export it.

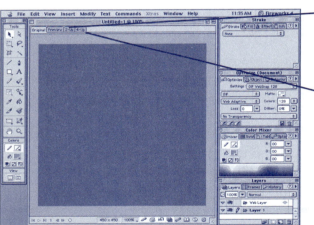

- **2-Up**. The 2-Up tab displays the original window image side-by-side with the same image displayed with settings from the Optimize panel.

- **4-Up**. This tab displays the image in the original window alongside the same image with up to three different settings from the Optimize panel. Select a preview panel, and then choose different settings in the Optimize panel to compare optimization settings.

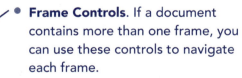

- **Frame Controls**. If a document contains more than one frame, you can use these controls to navigate each frame.

- **Page Preview**. This displays the dimensions of the document window. If you click on this area, the width, height, and resolution information are displayed.

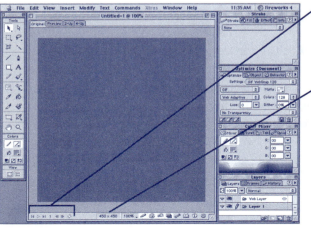

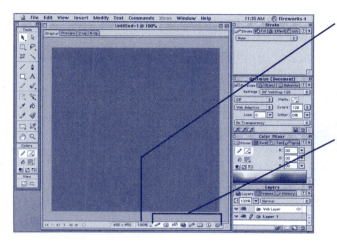

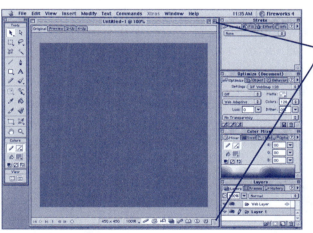

• **Magnification**. Choose from 11 different magnification settings for the document window. Larger numbers zoom in on the document, while smaller numbers shrink the contents of the document window.

• **Mini Launcher**. Each document window includes eight shortcut icons for the Stroke, Color Mixer, Optimize, Layer, Tool Options, Library, Styles, and Behaviors panels. You can open or close any of these panels by clicking on its shortcut icon in a document window.

• **Size controls**. You can grow or shrink a document window by clicking and dragging that window's Grow box. On a Mac, click on the Collapse/Uncollapse box located in the upper-right corner to hide or show a document window. On a Windows computer, you can use the minimize/maximize or grow boxes as you would in other Windows applications.

TIP

Click and drag any panel tab to create a separate floating window for that panel.

Working with Vector and Bitmap Modes

You can familiarize yourself with the workspace by using a tool from the toolbox to create an object in the document window. If you're already familiar with the Flash 5 or Fireworks 3 workspace, you should feel pretty comfortable working with the drawing tools in Fireworks 4.

One thing that's different about creating graphics in Fireworks is that each document can be used in two different modes: Vector Mode and Bitmap Mode. When you create vector objects, you'll notice that you can customize the stroke, fill, effect, and object settings independently of each other. Bitmap objects, on the other hand, are pure pixel-based images. You can't assign a stroke or fill setting to a bitmap object, or an object created in Bitmap Mode.

Each image object you create in Vector Mode is a vector graphic, also called a path. You can work with two types of image objects in Fireworks: bitmap or vector graphics. You can create bitmap objects when a document is in Bitmap Mode. Bitmap graphics, or bitmap objects, are pixel-based images, such as an image file created with a digital camera. Because each bitmap has a fixed number of pixels, you cannot increase the size of a bitmap image without decreasing the clarity of the image. On the other hand, vector graphics are designed to be scalable. Macromedia Flash and Fireworks are both designed to work with vector graphics. Although it would be nice to think all vector images scale accurately, don't be surprised if you don't always get the results you expect when scaling or transforming a vector image object in Fireworks. The following list highlights some of the unique characteristics of vector and bitmap tools.

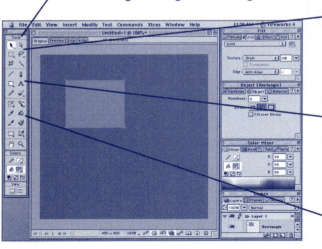

- **Toolbox**. The toolbox is a central location for all the vector and bitmap selection, drawing, editing, Web design, color, and view tools available in Fireworks.

- **Selection tools**. The Pointer tool enables you to select a vector object. You can use the Lasso, Marquee, Crop or Magic Wand tools to select all or part of a bitmap object.

- **Drawing tools**. The drawing tools allow you to choose a rectangle (or other shape), pen, pencil, or brush to create paths or bitmap objects in the document window.

- **Editing tools**. These tools allow you to modify the shape of a path.

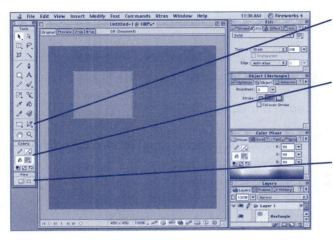

- **Web design tools**. The Web design tools let you add a hotspot or slice up an image.

- **Color tools**. With the color tools, you can choose a different stroke or fill color from the pop-up color menu, or you can select a custom color.

- **View modes**. The view modes allow you to view the document window with or without any hotspots or slices. Press the 2 key as a shortcut to toggle between these two view states.

Drawing with the Rectangle Tool in Vector Mode

You can create a vector object or a bitmap object with the Rectangle Tool. To put the document into Bitmap Mode, choose the Empty Bitmap command from the Insert menu. Then choose the Rectangle, Rounded Rectangle, Ellipse, or Polygon tool from the toolbox. Click, drag, and release the tool to create a bitmap object in the document window. However, each document opens in Vector Mode. The following steps show you how to draw and select a rectangle in Vector Mode.

1. Select the Rectangle/Shape Tool or press R on the keyboard. Press the R key several times to cycle through the different shape tools that live with the Rectangle Tool.

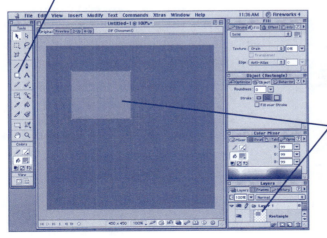

2. Click and drag the mouse in the document window. A light blue outline will appear as you drag the mouse. The light blue border identifies the edges of the shape being created.

3. Release the mouse button to create a rectangle. A new layer will appear in the Layers panel. A thumbnail image of the rectangle will appear in that layer.

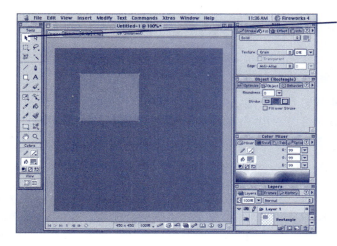

4. You can choose the Pointer Tool (V) to select or move any object in the document window. Click once on the rectangle to select it. If an image object is selected, it will be surrounded by a light blue line with a grow handle in each corner. Click and drag the object to move it to a new location in the document window.

Drawing with the Pencil Tool in Bitmap Mode

You can create a vector object or a bitmap object with the Pencil Tool. Each document is in Vector Mode by default. A striped line appears around the canvas area of the document window if a document is in Bitmap Mode. The following steps show you how to select and draw a bitmap object with the Pencil Tool.

1. Choose Empty Bitmap from the Insert menu.

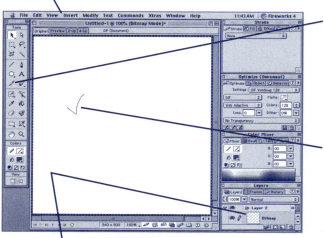

2. Select the Pencil Tool or press Y on the keyboard. Click and drag the mouse in the document window. As you drag the mouse, you will see the stroke color appear as a single-pixel line in the document window.

3. Release the mouse to create a path. A light blue line will appear over the line you just drew. The light blue line and any points on that line define the path you just created with the Pencil Tool.

4. A new layer will appear in the Layers panel, containing a thumbnail image of the bitmap object you just created.

Navigating the Menu Bar

Before I go into more detail about how to design graphics in Fireworks, take a quick look at some of the menu commands. Many of the drawing and design tools are easily accessible from the panels. However, some commands are only available in menu form. This section describes how menu commands are grouped together and how you can use them.

Opening and Closing Files with the File Menu

Many of the menu commands you'd hope to find in the File menu are here in Fireworks. You can create a new document, open existing Fireworks files, close windows, import and export files, print, and quit Fireworks. The following list summarizes the menu commands located in the File menu.

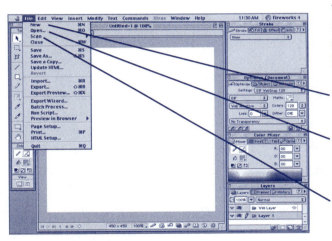

- **New**. Use this menu command to create a new Fireworks document.

- **Open**. With this command, you can open native Fireworks files, PNG, GIF, or JPEG image files.

- **Scan**. You can use the Scan command to download images from a digital camera or scanner using any installed TWAIN plug-ins with Fireworks.

- **Close**. Use this menu command to close the active window in Fireworks.

- **Save commands**. The save menu commands enable you to save a file in the native Fireworks PNF file format.

- **Import**. Fireworks 4 can import Photoshop files, including those from Photoshop 6. It can also import Freehand, Illustrator (EPS), and Wireless Bitmap (WBMP) files.

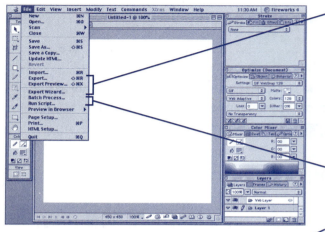

● **Export commands**. Export, Export Preview, and Export Wizard can help you choose or view your graphics before they leave Fireworks. Be sure to save your original graphics as PNG or Fireworks files so you can continue to work on them after exporting all or part of that file.

● **Batch commands**. Use these menu items to run a command or JavaScript script, or to batch process several files.

● **Preview in Browser**. You can use this menu command to choose the default browser you want to use to view your Fireworks graphics.

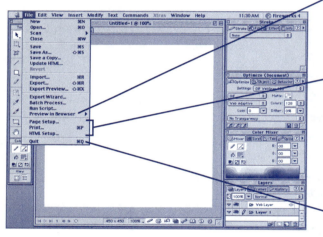

● **Print-related commands**. Page Setup and Print commands work similarly to other Windows or Macintosh applications. If you have specific preferences for your HTML files, choose HTML Setup to view and change any of these settings.

● **Exit/Quit**. Exit the Fireworks application by choosing this menu command.

Finding and Changing Objects with the Edit Menu

The Fireworks Edit menu contains the standard Copy, Paste, and Undo menu commands. The Find and Replace and crop menu commands are also located in this menu. If you want to view or change your preferences or keyboard shortcuts, you can access their respective windows from the Edit menu, too.

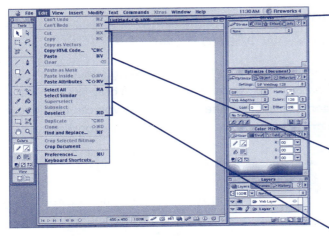

- **Undo commands**. Reverse or reapply an Undo command by choosing one of these Undo commands. You can also press Ctrl/Command + Z or Ctrl/Command + Y as a shortcut to undo or restore an undo in the document window.

- **Copy and Paste commands**. Cut or copy an image from any document window and then paste it into a new layer or frame using these commands.

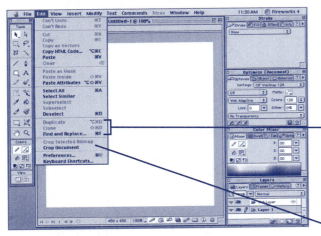

- **Select commands**. Choose from Select All, Select Similar, Superselect, Subselect, or Deselect menu commands. Alternatively, you can use one of the selection tools to perform many of the same tasks on image objects in the document window.

- **Find, Replace, and Copy commands**. You can invoke the Find and Replace panel from the Edit menu, and you can duplicate or clone an image object using the copy commands.

- **Crop commands**. Use the Crop commands to complete the crop created using the Crop Tool in the toolbox.

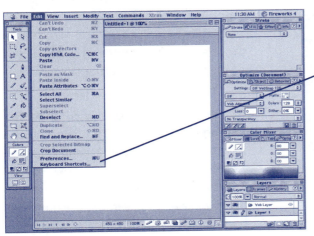

- **Preferences and Keyboard Shortcut commands**. Using these commands you can access all the Fireworks preferences settings or keyboard shortcuts. For more information about preferences and keyboard shortcuts, see Chapter 4, "Customizing Preferences and Keyboard Shortcuts."

Customizing a Document's Appearance with the View Menu

Choose from a variety of document view settings to help you design your graphics. You can add rulers, guides, and grids to the document window to help lay out your graphics. You can also access zoom, fit, and gamma setting commands to help you view your art close up or far away.

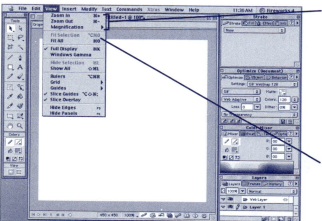

- **Zoom commands**. Using these commands, you can toggle between the magnification settings located in the pop-up menu at the bottom of a document window. Press Ctrl/Command + = to zoom in and Ctrl/Command + - to zoom away from the contents of the document window.

- **Fit commands**. Use one of these commands to choose the magnification setting to display a selected object or the entire document without altering the size of the document window.

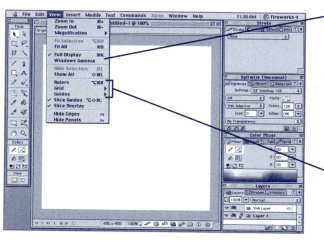

- **Display and Gamma commands**. These commands allow you to toggle between wire-frame or full display mode. Image objects can be drawn faster if the document is in wire-frame mode. Choose between Windows or Macintosh gamma settings from the View menu, too.

- **Rulers, Guides, and Grid commands**. Using these commands, you can add or remove rulers, guides, and grids to or from the document window. You must select Rulers to add horizontal and vertical guides in the document window.

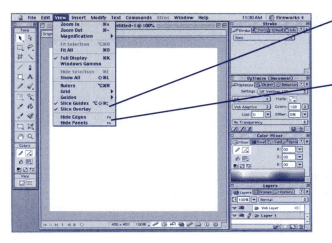

● **Slice commands**. The slice commands enable guides that identify the boundaries of a slice or slice overlay.

● **Hide commands**. Click on the hide commands, or press F9 to hide path edges or F4 to hide the toolbox or any open panels.

Adding Objects with the Insert Menu

Many commands in the Insert menu are also replicated with tools or icons in the toolbox or panels. For example, you can create a slice by drawing directly in the document window, or by selecting an image object and choosing Slice from the Insert menu. Another example is the new document icon in the Layers and Frames panels. You can click on this icon to add a new layer or frame to your document, or choose Layer or Frame from the Insert menu. The Insert menu contains a list of all the different kinds of objects you can add to a Fireworks document.

● **New Button**. The New Button command enables you to design a button, and up to five different states for that button, in the Button Editor window. The button is created as a symbol. All symbols are stored in the Library panel.

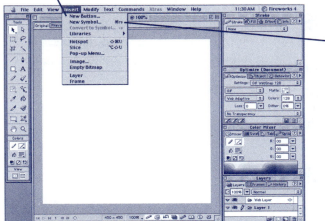

● **New Symbol**. Using this command, you can create a graphic, animation, or button symbol. A symbol is a representation of an image object stored in the Library. You can use symbols to create animation stored in a comparatively smaller file size than if you created the animation with individual vector or bitmap images.

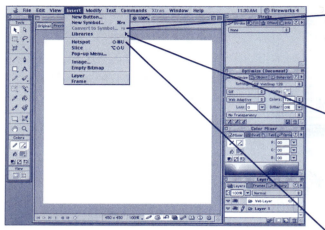

- **Convert to Symbol**. Choose this menu command to convert a bitmap or vector object into a graphic, animation, or button symbol. Symbols are stored in the Library panel.

- **Libraries commands**. Choose from the Animations, Bullets, Buttons, and Themes that are installed with Fireworks 4. You can also choose a custom library file by choosing Other from the Libraries menu.

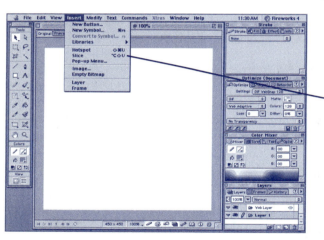

- **Hotspot**. Use this command to add a hotspot to the selected image object in the document window. A hotspot can be used to create a simple rollover or image map.

- **Slice**. The Slice command allows you to convert a selected image object into a slice, breaking up a larger image into smaller pieces. This enables you to create sophisticated Web effects, such as pop-up menus, image swapping, and different rollover state behaviors.

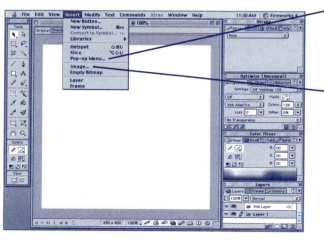

- **Pop-up Menu**. This command opens the Pop-up Menu Wizard window. You can create pop-up menu Web graphics using this menu command.

- **Image commands**. These commands enable you to import an image into the document window. You can choose Empty Bitmap to add a placeholder image to the document window.

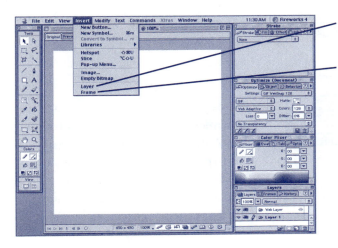

- **Layer**. Choose this command to add an empty layer to the Layers panel.

- **Frame**. You can create an empty frame in the Frames panel by selecting this menu command.

Transmogrifying Objects with the Modify Menu

Fireworks has a complete set of commands that enable you to customize an object you've created. Try not to be too overwhelmed by all the menu commands tucked away in the Modify menu. Using these commands, you can transform a selection or an image object in many ways.

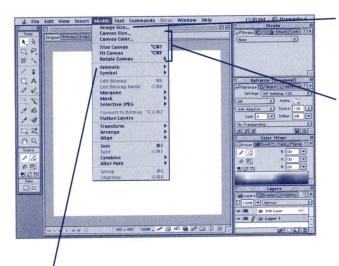

- **Image Size**. Use this menu command to change the width, height, or resolution of an image from the Image Size window.

- **Canvas commands**. You can enlarge or shrink the canvas size from the Canvas Size window. Set the anchor point for the current canvas contents to direct which way the canvas size changes. You can also choose Canvas Color to change the color of the canvas, and you can select various commands to trim, fit, or rotate the canvas.

- **Animate commands**. Select an image and turn it into an animation by choosing Animate Selection. Fill in the settings in the Animate window and then use frames and layers to put together a Web animation.

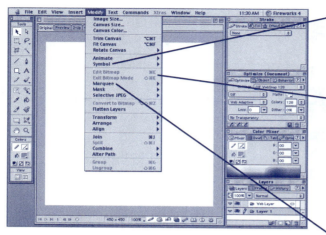

- **Symbol commands**. You can Edit, Tween Instances, and Break Apart symbols by choosing one of these menu commands.

- **Bitmap commands**. Using the bitmap commands, you can convert a vector graphic to a bitmap image, or exit Bitmap Mode. You can also click on the X icon at the bottom of the document window to exit Bitmap Mode.

- **Marquee commands**. These commands work with a selection tool. Choose from Select Similar, Select Inverse, Feather, Expand, Contract, Border, Smooth, Save Selection, and Restore Selection.

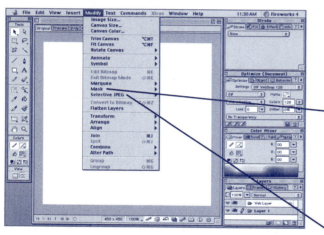

- **Mask commands**. The mask commands apply mask behaviors to a selected image object. A mask is a counterpart to an image object and can act as a cutout to show or hide part of an image.

- **Selective JPEG commands**. Using these commands, you can save or restore a highlighted object as a selective JPEG mask. Choose the Settings command to adjust the selective quality of the selective JPEG settings.

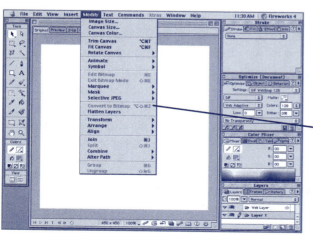

- **Convert to Bitmap**. Select a vector graphic and choose this menu command to convert it to a bitmap image.

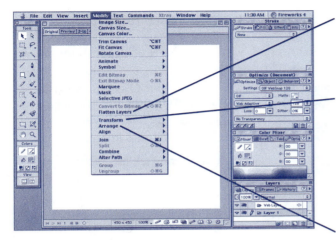

- **Flatten Layers.** If a document contains more than one layer, this command flattens the contents of all those layers into one single layer.

- **Transform commands.** Use the commands in this menu to scale, skew, distort, flip, or rotate an object. The Free Transform command enables you to apply several different kinds of transformations without having to select each separate menu command.

- **Arrange commands.** Each object in the document window is created in its own layer, and new objects are added on top of older ones. Use the Arrange commands to change the order of object layers in a document.

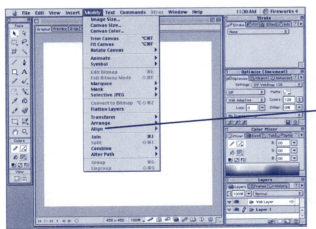

- **Align commands.** The Align commands in Fireworks work similarly to those in Flash. You can adjust the left, right, center, top, bottom, or center horizontally, or distribute widths or heights of image objects using these menu commands.

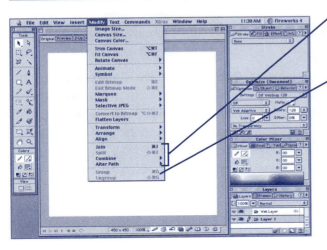

- **Path commands.** Use these commands to merge or modify multiple selected objects.

- **Group commands.** Each object contains its own unique attributes or settings. If you want to group two objects together, they will continue to retain their unique settings, but will move together whenever you click and drag one object or the other.

Stylizing Fonts and Paths with the Text Menu

If you plan to add text to your Web graphics, you'll find many of the settings in the Text menu are also easily found in the Text Editor window. You can choose from any font, font size, or font style installed with Windows or the Mac OS. You can also align text, change text orientation, and convert text to paths. The following list shows you where to find these text commands in the Text menu.

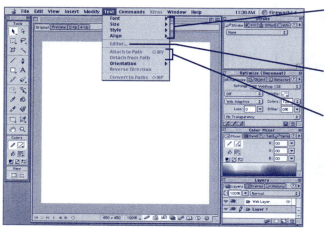

● **Font commands**. Pick a font, font size, or font style from these commands. You can also align text.

● **Editor**. Choose the Editor command to open the Text Editor window.

● **Path commands**. After you've typed some text into a document window, hold down the Shift key and select the text and an image object. Choose Attach to Path to attach the text to the path.

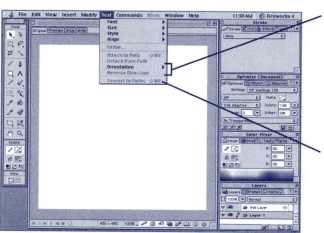

● **Orientation commands**. Using these commands, you can rotate, or change a text object's alignment from horizontal to vertical. You can also choose the Skew Vertical and Skew Horizontal commands if you want to distort a text object.

● **Convert to Paths**. Select any text you type into the document window and choose this menu command to convert it to paths.

Extending Fireworks with the Commands Menu

Most things that you can do in Fireworks are scriptable. What does this mean? If you perform a particular task over and over, or if you want to apply a specific set of commands to an image object, you can do this fairly easily by creating a command and then choosing it from the Commands menu. Fireworks also contains a set of commands that you might find helpful. Click on the Commands menu to view the four sets of included commands.

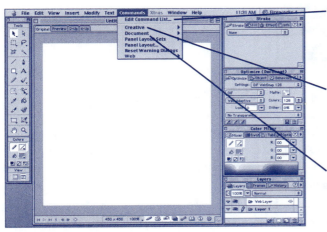

- **Edit Command List**. This command opens the Edit Command List window, which allows you to rename or delete a command.

- **Creative commands**. You can choose Convert to Grayscale, Convert to Sepia Tone, or Create Picture Frame using this command menu.

- **Document commands**. This menu contains scripts that enable you to center an object in the document, distribute objects to layers, hide other layers, lock other layers, reverse all frames, and reverse frame range.

- **Panel Layout Sets commands**. These commands reorganize the way your panel windows appear in your workspace. You can choose from a 1024 × 768, 1280 × 1024, or 800 × 600 panel layout.

- **Panel Layout**. Choose this command to save your own custom panel layout for your workspace.

- **Reset Warning Dialogs**. Select this command to reset all the "Don't Show Again" warning dialog boxes so that they will all appear if invoked.

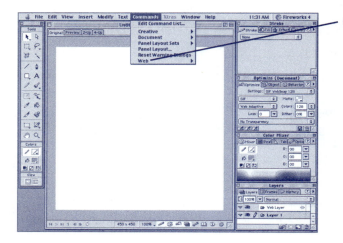

• **Web commands**. From this menu, you can access three commands that enable you to create a shared palette, select blank ALT tags, and set ALT tags.

Adding Effects with the Xtras Menu

Macromedia uses the term Live Effects synonymously with Xtras. Both are similar to effects, or filters, in Photoshop. In Fireworks, Live Effects enable you to toggle on or off any effect applied to an object at any time, and give you the flexibility to experiment with different looks with different image objects to help you design Web graphics more dynamically. More Live Effects are available in the Effects panel. However, before you can apply an effect to a vector object, you must convert it to a bitmap.

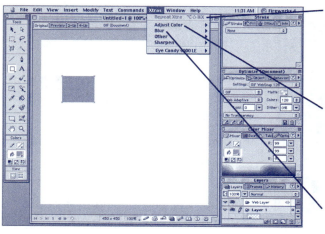

• **Repeat command**. After an effect is applied to an image, you can repeat the effect by choosing this menu command, or by pressing Ctrl/Command + Shift + Alt/Option + X.

• **Adjust Color commands**. You can choose Auto Levels, Brightness/Contrast, Curves, Hue/Saturation, Invert, or Levels from the Adjust Color menu.

• **Blur commands**. Using the commands in this menu, you can Blur, Blur More, or add a Gaussian Blur to an image object.

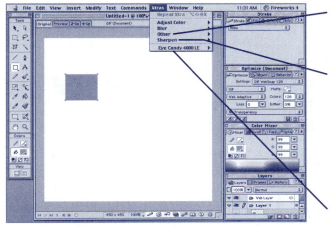

Other commands. Using this menu, you can convert an image to Alpha, or choose the Find Edges menu command.

Sharpen commands. The Sharpen commands (Sharpen, Sharpen More, and Unsharp Mask) apply an algorithm to a set of pixels in the bitmap and attempt to make an image sharper by emphasizing certain pixel patterns over others.

Eye Candy commands. Apply Bevel Boss, Marble, or Motion Trail effects to a bitmap image using these menu commands.

Opening Panels Using the Window Menu

You can access any of the Fireworks panels from the Window menu. In addition, you can duplicate the currently open window by choosing New Window, or you can cascade or tile any open window. In case you're not sure which documents you've opened, the name of each open file appears at the bottom of the Window menu.

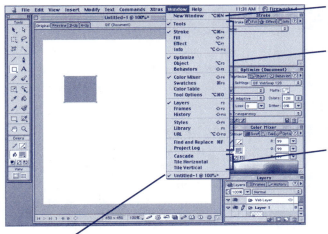

New Window. Choose this command to duplicate the active window.

Window panels commands. Use these commands to open or close any of the 20 Fireworks panels. Press the appropriate shortcut key to show or hide any panel.

Organize windows commands. You can use these commands to choose from three different ways to lay out any open windows in the workspace.

Open document windows. Use these commands to select any open document window and bring it to the foreground of the workspace.

Finding Information with the Help Menu

Last but not least, the Help menu is always there, ready and waiting to give you a hand. Macromedia includes three different kinds of help files with Fireworks. You can view the manual from a browser, learn about Fireworks by following the lessons and tutorials, or visit one of the many Web resources available for Fireworks and Dreamweaver.

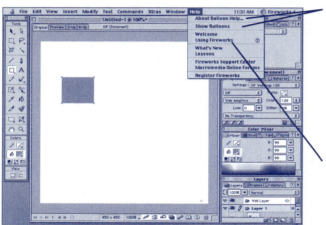

- **Mac OS balloon help commands**. If you're using a Windows computer, you won't see these menu commands. If you're a Mac user, you'll find general Mac OS balloon help information, but no Fireworks-specific help. You can show or hide balloon help messages by selecting these menu commands.

- **Built-in HTML help files**. Use this command to access the Fireworks manual on your computer by viewing it in a browser window.

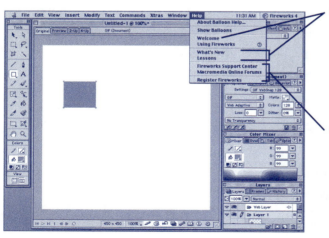

- **Built-in tutorials and lessons**. Follow Macromedia's built-in examples to learn how to create a Web site with Fireworks and Dreamweaver and get familiar with the basic Web graphics features in Fireworks 4.

- **Links to Macromedia's Fireworks Web pages**. If your computer has Internet access, you can go directly to Macromedia's support pages, or Macromedia's Fireworks Web site.

3

Getting Familiar with Tools, Objects, and Panels

Macromedia bundles a full set of selection, drawing, and color tools in the Fireworks toolbox. By default, the toolbox window opens on the left side of the workspace. However, you can click and drag this window to place it anywhere you want.

This chapter walks you through all the fancy tools in the toolbox. The first section explains what each tool does and identifies its shortcut key(s). That's followed by a brief demonstration of the drawing and selection tools, concluding with a section on how to set up a document with guides and grids.

In this chapter, you'll learn how to:

- Use the toolbox tools
- Work with guides and grids
- View and use the panels

Overview of the Toolbox Tools

The toolbox is divided into three main sections: Tools, Colors, and View. The Tools section is further divided into five sections: selection, drawing, editing, Web layout, and Hand and Zoom tools. Although you can only use one tool at a time, you can view 22 different tools at any time, with a total number of 39 tools available. You can also access color and view tools from the toolbox. The color tools enable you to pick the stroke or fill color of an object. The view tools allow you to show or hide the Web layer in the document window. The following sections give a brief explanation of each tool in the toolbox, along with its shortcut key, if one exists.

Selection Tools

You can choose between a simple pointer, marquee, magnifying glass, or hand to select and move objects. Each selection tool enables you to select one or more objects in the document window in a unique way. However, you can only use the Pointer Tool to select a vector object, even though you can use any of the selection tools with a bitmap object. You must select an object before you can edit, move, or delete it.

Some tools have a small triangle located in the lower-right corner of their button. This small triangle indicates that additional tools can be selected by pressing the tool button.

- **Pointer/Select Behind/Export Area (J)**. These tools enable you to select a vector or bitmap object in the document window. Hold down the Shift key to select more than one object.

- **Subselection (A or 1)**. The Subselection Tool selects an individual anchor point in a vector object.

- **Rectangular Marquee/Elliptical Marquee (M).** These tools allow you to select a rectangular or oval-shaped bitmap area of the document window.

- **Lasso/Polygon Lasso (L).** These tools enable you to select any part of a bitmap image in the document window. Press the Shift key and click on a pixel you want to add to the selected area, or press the Alt/Option key to remove a pixel from the selected pixels.

- **Magic Wand (W).** The Magic Wand Tool lets you select specific colors or color ranges in a bitmap image.

- **Hand (H).** This tool enables you to move the canvas area within the document window. You can also use this tool in the Preview, 2-Up or 4-Up windows.

- **Zoom (Z).** The Zoom Tool allows you to enlarge or reduce the magnification of any part of the document window.

TIP

Try to learn and use the keyboard shortcuts for the tools you use most frequently, to increase your productivity using the selection and drawing tools. On your keyboard, press the letter listed beside the name of the tool to select a tool from the toolbox.

Drawing Tools

Drawing tools enable you to create vector and bitmap objects in Fireworks. The Pen, Pencil, Brush, Rectangle/Shape, and Line tools can be used to create a scalable vector object or a pixel-based bitmap image. The document must be in Vector Mode before you can use the drawing tools to create vector objects, or in Bitmap Mode if you want to create bitmap objects. The tools work the same way in either mode. Almost all of the examples in this book use the drawing tools to create vector objects.

You can draw shapes or create objects with the Pen, Brush, and Pencil tools. Each drawing tool has a unique set of tool options located in the Tool Options panel. You can also assign a unique stroke, fill, or style to each vector graphic. Remember, though, that stroke, fill, and style settings can't be applied to a bitmap graphic.

- **Line (N)**. The Line Tool enables you to draw a straight line. Click once in the canvas area of the document window to create the starting point of the line. Click a second time in another location in the canvas to create the end point of the line.

- **Pen (P)**. The Pen Tool draws with a slightly different pen stroke than the Pencil or Brush tools. Click on the canvas to create a point. Then click on another location on the canvas to create a second point. The Pen Tool creates a line connecting the first point to the second point. Continue to click until you return to the first point to create a closed path object, or double-click on the last point of a path to create an open path object.

- **Rectangle/Rounded Rectangle/Ellipse/Polygon (R)**. These tools create shapes in the document window.

- **Text (T)**. The Text Tool enables you to add text and choose any font, style, or size for the text selected in the document window.

- **Pencil (Y).** The Pencil Tool draws single pixels in the document window.

- **Brush/Redraw Path (B)**. These tools draw a slightly wider stroke than does the Pencil Tool.

TIP

The Pencil Tool draws freeform without the use of the Freeform Tool. Use the Freeform Tool to reshape any objects created by the Brush, Pen, Line, or Rectangle/Ellipse/Polygon tools. To find out more about the Freeform Tool, see Chapter 8, "Modifying Vector and Bitmap Graphics."

Editing Tools

Fireworks provides a full set of editing tools so that you can tweak your graphics to look the way you want. Skew, scale, distort, and rotate objects with the Transform Tool, or clean up paths with the Freeform and Path tools. You can also change or find out more about an object using the Paint Bucket, Eyedropper, or Eraser tools to fine-tune your work.

- **Transform tools (Q).** Choose either the Scale, Skew, or Distort tool from the toolbox. Each Transform Tool enables you to change the shape of the selected object in the document window. In this example the Scale Tool is selected.

- **Freeform/Reshape Area/Path Scrubber Plus/Minus (F).** These tools reshape existing freeform (unstructured) shapes created with the Pencil Tool.

- **Eyedropper (I).** The Eyedropper Tool selects the stroke or fill color from the document window.

- **Paint Bucket (K).** The Paint Bucket Tool fills a selected area with the stroke color.

- **Rubber Stamp (S).** This tool creates a duplicate of a selected image part and uses the duplicate as a pen stroke in another part of the same image.

- **Knife/Eraser (E).** In Bitmap Mode, dragging the Eraser Tool over the document window deletes that portion of the image. In Vector Mode, the Eraser Tool becomes the Knife Tool. Use the Knife Tool to disconnect points in an object's path.

NOTE
Some tools share the same keyboard shortcut. Press the shortcut key several times to cycle through the different tools.

Web Layout Tools

There are two primary Web layout tools in Fireworks: the Slice and Hotspot tools. The Slice and Hotspot tools create Web objects in the document window. Each Web object appears in the Web Layer of the Layers panel.

The Hotspot Tool can add rollover and link functionality to an image object. Slices enable you to break up an image into several images. You can create rectangular- or polygonal-shaped hotspots or slices using these tools.

- **Rectangle Hotspot/Circle/Polygon Hotspot (U)**. These tools enable you to create a hotspot, such as a rollover link, in the document window.

- **Slice/Polygon Slice (G)**. These tools enable you to create a slice in the document window.

TIP

You can customize keyboard shortcuts for each tool in the toolbox. Click on the Edit menu and choose Keyboard Shortcuts to access the tool commands in the Keyboard Shortcuts window. For more information about how to change keyboard shortcuts, see Chapter 4, "Customizing Preferences and Keyboard Shortcuts."

Color Tools

Color helps define the overall design of Web graphics, and can also affect each object in a design. The color tools can help you create precise colors, as well as explore colors combined with textures, gradients, and other stroke or fill settings. Unlike selection and drawing tools, color tools work the same way in Vector or Bitmap modes. The following list highlights some of the most commonly used color tools located in the toolbox (or Tools panel).

- **Stroke Color.** This tool enables you to select a color for the next shape or pen stroke in the document window. The stroke color works with the fill color to enable you to define the colors of a vector object.

- **Fill Color.** This tool selects the color to be used to fill the next shape created.

- **Default Brush and Stroke (D).** This tool resets the stroke color to black and the fill color to white.

- **No Stroke or Fill (3).** This tool removes the fill and stroke colors.

- **Swap Brush or Fill (X).** This tool reverses the fill and stroke colors, exchanging the fill color with the stroke color.

NOTE

The Windows version of Fireworks allows you to dock or undock a tool to the toolbar. To view the toolbar, choose Main from the Window, Toolbars menu. Move the toolbar into the top or bottom of the application window to dock it. Or, click on the title bar of the toolbar and drag it away from its docked location to undock it.

View Tools

You can view the document window with or without hotspots or slices (Web objects). Click on either the Hide or Show Slices button in the View section of the toolbox to hide or show the Web layer in the document window. Alternatively, you can press the 2 key on the keyboard to select either the Hide or Show Slices buttons.

- **Hide Web Layer (2).** This tool hides slice and hotspot layers in the Web layer of the document window.

- **Show Web Layer (2).** This tool exposes the slices and hotspots from the Web layer of the document window.

NOTE

All objects in the layers and Web Layer are stored in the Layers panel. To hide an object or layer, click on the eye icon in the Layers panel. If the eye icon does not appear beside an object or layer, that object is hidden. You can select a hidden hotspot or object in the Layers panel and view that object's outline in the document window.

Working with Drawing and Selection Tools

Although Fireworks has Vector and Bitmap modes (the mode changes depending on what type of object you're working on) and each tool has its own unique settings, you can use the same drawing process to create a vector or bitmap image. There are many ways to design Web page graphics and patterns with Fireworks tools. A good place to start is by selecting a drawing tool from the toolbox, and then creating a vector drawing. This section shows you how to create a few simple vector objects and modify them with commands such as the Join and Punch commands located in the Modify menu.

Drawing with the Pen Tool

The Pen Tool enables you to create straight or curved lines by plotting each point of an open or closed path object. As you add points to create a path, you can press the Backspace/Delete key to remove any previous point in the path. You can also choose Show Pen Preview from the Tool Options panel to view each point or the next line or curve as you create a path. Select the Show Solid Points check box to view solid points (blue versus white squares) in a path. The following steps show you how to draw straight and curved lines with the Pen Tool.

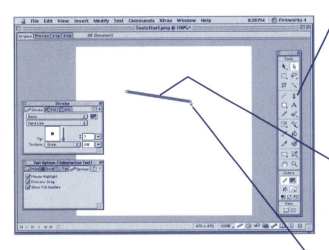

1. Click on the Pen Tool in the toolbox. Alternatively, press the P key to select the Pen Tool. You can adjust the Stroke settings in the Stroke panel. For this example, the Stroke settings for the Pen Tool are set to Basic, Hard Line, with a tip of 7 pixels wide and 0% opacity.

2. Click once on the canvas in the document window. A light blue point will appear. Click a second time to add the next point in the path, creating a straight line. You can click to add any additional points to the path.

3. Double-click the last point of the path to end that path.

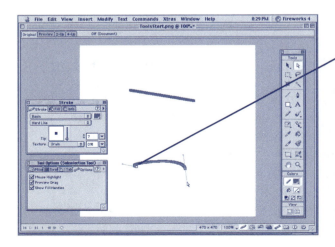

4. Click and drag the Pen Tool on the canvas in the document window. The light blue point will appear with a line extending from both sides of that point. The angle of that line determines the angle of the curve. Release the mouse button to view the first point and the angle of that point.

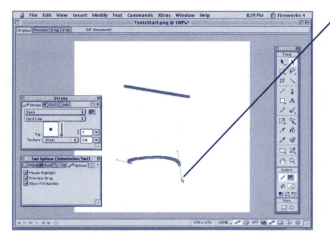

5. Click and drag the mouse a second time in the document window. A connecting line from the first point will appear. As you click and drag the second point, the angle of the curved line will change. Release the mouse button to create a curved path.

Choosing Objects with Selection Tools

You can select any vector object with the Pointer Tool, or select a point in a vector object with the Subselection Tool. Use the Magic Wand, Marquee, or Lasso tools to select a bitmap object in the document window. Click on a selection tool, or press the keyboard shortcut to select a tool in the toolbox, and then click on an object to select it. Or, if you're using the Marquee Tool, click and drag the cursor around an object to select it. The following steps show you how to select one or more objects in the document window using the Pointer Tool.

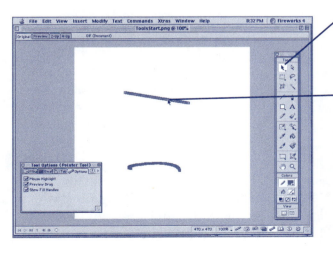

1. Click on the Pointer Tool in the toolbox or press the V key to select the Pointer Tool.

2. To select an image object in the document window, click on it. Hold down the Shift key and click on any other objects if you want to select a group of objects. Click on the Subselection Tool (white pointer icon) to select an individual object within a group of objects.

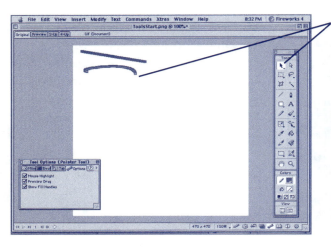

3. Click and drag an object to move it in the document window. You can also select an object by clicking on that object's layer in the Layers panel.

4. Press the Delete key to remove a selected object from the document window. The object and its layer will be removed from the document. Choose Undo Delete from the Edit menu to bring the object back into the document window, or press Ctrl/Command + Z.

NOTE

When a keyboard command is used in this book, both Windows and Mac keys are combined. For example, in Step 4, press Ctrl + Z if you're on a Windows PC. If you're on a Mac, press Command + Z.

Creating Paths with the Brush Tool

You can draw freehand images in the document window using the Brush Tool. The Brush Tool can be customized to edit vector and bitmap images. Adjust the settings in the Stroke panel and the Tool Options panel to experiment with different brush strokes. The following example shows you how to create a path with the Brush Tool and then change the brush stroke.

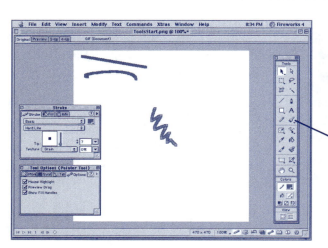

1. Click on the Brush Tool in the toolbox or press the B key. For this example, the Stroke settings for the Brush Tool are Basic, Hard Line, with a tip of 7 pixels wide, and 0% opacity.

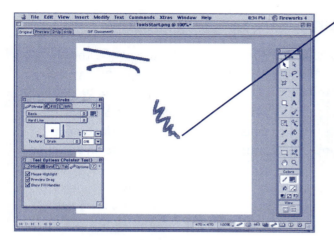

2. Click and drag the mouse on the canvas area of the document window to create a path.

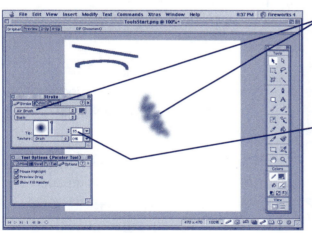

3. Select the path created by the Brush Tool in the document window. Then, click on the pop-up menu in the Stroke panel to choose a different kind of brush.

4. Type a larger tip size in the text box located on the right side of the Stroke panel. The brush stroke will change in the document window.

NOTE

The Brush Tool might seem similar to the Pencil Tool. However, any changes you make to the brush size remain and will be applied each successive time you chose this tool. The Pencil Tool, on the other hand, defaults to a single-pixel width each time you select it from the toolbox.

Combining and Editing Paths

Fireworks enables you to group, join, and intersect two or more paths. These commands are all located in the Modify menu. The following steps show you how to apply the Group, Join, and Intersect commands to path objects created with different shape tools.

Applying the Group Command

The Group command enables each selected object to retain its own unique settings while being grouped with other objects. Grouping objects enables you to easily move a complex graphic image around in the document window. Here's one example of how you can apply the Group command to two objects.

1. Create and select two or more paths in the document window.

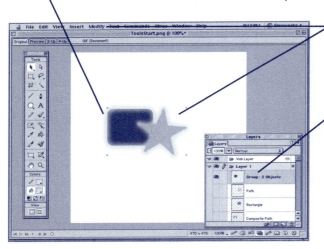

2. Choose the Group command from the Modify menu. The selection area for the grouped objects is designated by four corner points.

3. View the single grouped object in the document window. The grouped objects will also appear as one object in the Layers panel.

Creating a New Object with the Join Command

The Join command enables two or more vector objects to share the same settings. The settings of the last selected object are shared with the other selected objects. The resulting object in the Layers panel is a Composite Path. Joining objects enables you to group two paths as one. Here's how:

1. Create and select two or more paths in the document window. In this example, the selected objects overlap each other. However, you can also apply the Join command to objects that don't overlap each other.

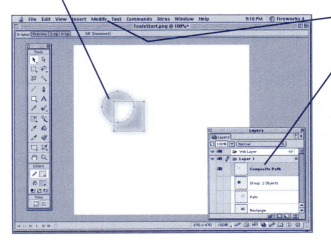

2. Choose the Join command from the Modify menu.

3. View the joined objects in the document window. The joined objects will also appear as a single Composite Path object in the Layers panel.

Combining Objects with the Union Command

The Union command merges the selected objects together, forming a new object. Perform the following steps to apply the Union command to two closed-path vector objects.

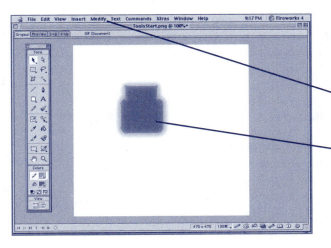

1. Create and select two or more overlapping paths in the document window.

2. Choose the Union command from the Modify, Combine menu.

The merged objects will appear as a single object in the document window. Both objects share a single path and appear as one path object in the Layers panel.

Using the Intersect Command

Overlapping areas between two objects can be merged together to form a new object if you apply the Intersect command. The following steps show you how.

1. Create and select two or more paths in the document window.

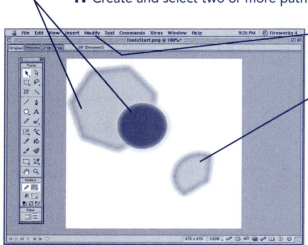

2. Choose the Intersect command from the Modify, Combine menu.

The intersection of the two objects will appear in the document window. The characteristics of the bottom object define the resulting object.

CAUTION

You can always ungroup a group of objects. However, it's not as easy to reverse the Join or Intersect commands after you've applied them. You might want to create a backup copy of a work in progress to preserve any graphics that might take time to recreate.

Punching through Objects

You can use the shape tools as cookie cutters to create new vector graphics. What do I mean by cookie cutter? Place one object over the other, just as you would place a cookie cutter over cookie dough. Except in Fireworks, choose the Punch command to create a new path. It won't taste like a cookie, but the Punch command makes a cleaner shape than if you tried to draw it freehand. The following steps show you how to punch one vector object through another.

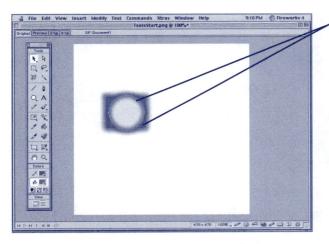

1. Create two or more objects in the document window.

2. Place the objects in the document window so that one overlaps with the other. Place the object you want to modify below the shape with which you will modify it. Then select both objects.

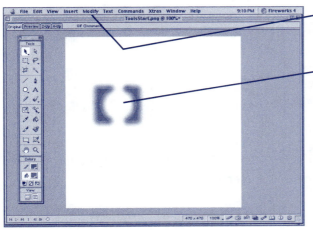

3. Choose Punch from the Modify, Combine menu.

The shape of the top object will create a hole in the object below it.

Expanding and Insetting Paths

You can increase or decrease the thickness of a path's stroke using the Modify, Alter Path commands. Choose Simplify to remove points on a path. Conversely, you can select the Expand Stroke or Inset Path commands to grow or shrink a path's stroke size. The following steps show you how to apply these commands to a path.

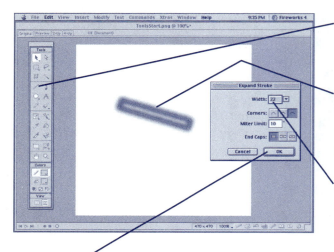

1. Select a drawing tool, such as the Line Tool (N), from the toolbox and create a path.

2. Select a path and then choose Expand Stroke from the Modify, Alter Path menu. The Expand Stroke dialog box will open.

3. Type a number in the Width text box to set the pixel width of the path. Adjust any of the other stroke settings if you want.

4. Click on the OK button to save your changes and apply them to the path in the document window.

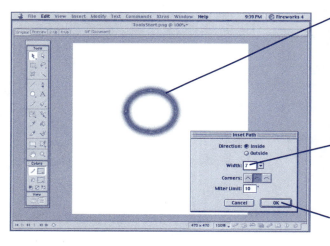

5. Create another path in the document window.

6. Select the path and then choose Inset Path from the Modify, Alter Path menu.

7. Type a value into the Width text box to reduce the stroke size of the selected path.

8. Click on the OK button to save your changes.

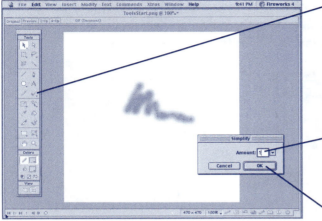

9. Select the Brush Tool (B) from the toolbox. Create a path in the document window.

10. Choose Simplify from the Modify, Alter Path menu.

11. In the Amount text box, type a number that is less than the number that currently appears in the box.

12. Click on the OK button to save your changes and return to the document window.

Working with Guides and Grids

If you prefer to design using geometric layout aids, you can work with guides, rulers, and grids to create the perfect Web page layout for your graphics. By default, guides and grids are not visible in the document window. When these features are active, an object will snap to a guide or grid when you move it within the canvas area.

The Rulers, Guides, and Grid commands are all located in the View menu. If any of these features are active, a check mark appears to the left of the menu command. If the feature is turned off, there is no check mark beside the menu command. Guides, grids, and rulers can be used to help lay out graphic objects on the canvas.

Viewing Rulers and Adding Guides

Adding rulers to a document window can help you create objects that need to be a specific height or width, or determine the ratio of the size of one object to another. The ruler settings measure the number of pixels in the document window. Rulers begin in the upper-left corner of the document window and extend horizontally and vertically across the top and left side of the document window, and are independent from the size of the canvas. You can also use rulers combined with the Guides feature to lay out image objects in the document window. The following steps show you how to add rulers and guides to a document window.

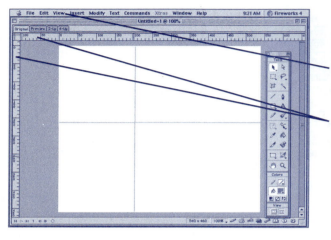

1. Open a document or create a new document window.

2. Click on the View menu and choose Rulers.

Rulers will appear on the left and top borders of the document window.

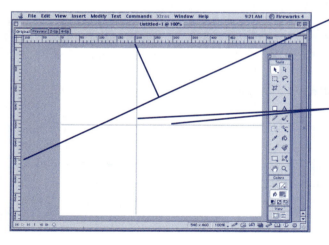

3. If Show Guides is checked in the View, Guides menu, you will see guide lines appear as you move the mouse in the document window.

4. Click in the top or side ruler and drag the mouse into the document window to add a guide. Although guide lines will appear in the document window, you can't print or export them along with your graphics.

NOTE
Remember, you must select Rulers to add guides to a document window.

Activating the Grid

In addition to rulers and guides, you can also view a grid within the boundaries of the canvas. Grids are visible in the document window. However, they cannot be printed or exported from Fireworks. You can use the grid to lay out image objects in the canvas area. The following steps show you how to activate the Show Grid menu command.

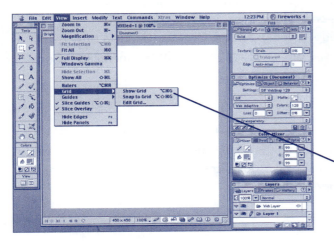

1. Open a document window in the Fireworks workspace.

2. Click on the View menu and choose Grid, Show Grid. A grid pattern will appear in the document window.

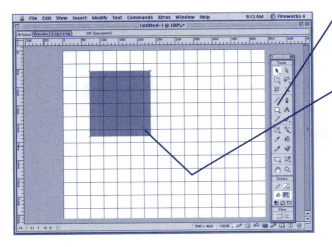

3. Choose a shape or drawing tool from the toolbox and create a vector in the document window.

4. Use a selection tool to select the object and move it around in the document window. Choose the Snap to Grid command from the View, Grid menu if you want Fireworks to help move the object's alignment to the nearest grid lines.

NOTE

When the Snap to Grid or Snap to Guides command is active, the snap distance is set to five pixels. You can adjust the snap distance to a value between one and 10 pixels. Unlike the Snap to Grid feature in Finder on a Macintosh, objects won't snap as sharply to a guide or grid in a Fireworks document.

Adjusting Guide and Grid Settings

You can customize the guide and grid settings. On a Mac, choose Edit Grids from the View, Grids menu, or choose Edit Guides from the View, Guides menu. The Grids and Guides dialog box will open. You can view and change settings for both grids and guides from a single dialog box. Simply click on the Grids or Guides tab to view the different settings. On a Windows computer, the Grids and Guides settings are located in separate dialog boxes: a Grids dialog box and Guides dialog box.

Guide Settings

Many of the settings in the Grids and Guides window (Mac) or Guides and Grids windows (Windows) are also available in the View, Guides menu. You can adjust the guide settings for image objects, as well as for slices, from the Guides panel of the Grids and Guides dialog box. Here's how:

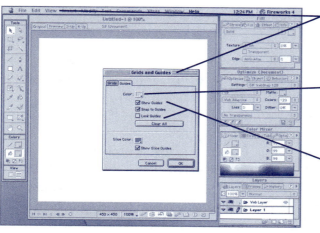

1. Select View, Guides, Edit Guides. The Grids and Guides dialog box or the Guides dialog box will open.

2. Click on the Color pop-up menu to choose a different guides color. The default color for guides is bright green.

3. Click on the Show Guides, Snap to Guides, or Lock Guides check boxes if you want to select or deselect these features.

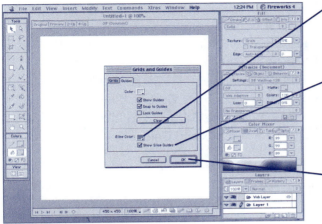

4. Click on the Slice Color pop-up menu to change the color of the slice guides.

5. Check the Show Slice Guides check box if you want the horizontal and vertical edges of a slice to be visible in the document window.

6. Click on the OK button to save your changes.

Grid Settings

You can adjust the color and size of the grid from the Grids panel of the Grids and Guides dialog box (or the Edit Grid dialog box, if you're using Windows). Here's how:

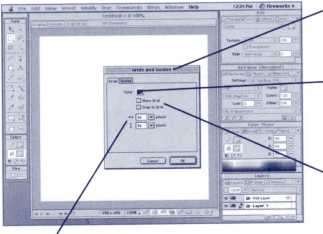

1. Choose Edit Grid from the View, Grid menu. The Edit Grid dialog box will open.

2. Click on the Color pop-up menu to select a color for the grid lines that appear in the document dialog box. The default color for the grid is black.

3. Click on the Show Grid or Snap to Grid check boxes if you want to select or deselect each of these features.

4. Type a number into the vertical or horizontal text box to set the width and height of the grid in pixels.

5. Click on the OK button to save your changes.

> **TIP**
>
> If you plan to use a particular guide or grid setting with another Fireworks document, you can create a JavaScript command in the Commands menu. To create a command, choose your guide or grid settings, then select the task from the History panel. Select the Save as Command menu item from the History panel's pop-up menu. Type a name for the command, then click on the OK button. The command will appear in the Commands menu. Select this command to automatically change your guide or grid settings for a document.

Working with Panels to Design Graphics

Fireworks groups all its panels into four main windows located on the right side of the screen. However, you can customize the location of each panel. Click and drag any panel away from a group of panels if you want to move a panel to a new location in the workspace. You can also re-group panels by clicking and dragging the tab of one panel and releasing it in the tab area of a second panel. The main document window also consists of four tabbed sections, which cannot be pulled apart.

A Brief Tour of the Panels

There are a total of 20 panels in Fireworks. Each panel can be opened or closed by choosing the corresponding menu command from the Window menu. The toolbox, which was explained earlier in this chapter, is a panel. However, since it has the unique function of storing a core set of drawing-related tools, I have not grouped it with the remaining 19 panels covered in this section. The following list provides a brief explanation of how each panel works.

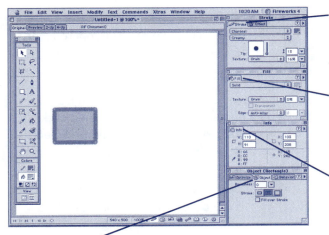

- **Stroke panel (Ctrl/Command + Alt/Option + F4).** Use this panel to set the type of stroke, plus the stroke's tip size, opacity, texture, and color.

- **Fill panel (Shift + F7).** Use the tools in this panel to assign a fill color, pattern, texture, or gradient to a vector object.

- **Info panel (Alt/Option + Shift + F12).** Use this panel to view the location of the cursor, as well as red, green, and blue color values for the cursor location.

- **Object panel (Alt/Option + F2).** The contents of this panel change depending on the type of object that's selected in the document window. View object information for vector objects, vector and bitmap masks, slices, and hotspots in this panel.

- **Layers panel (F2).** Web and object layers are all located in the Layers panel. You can view or select any object in a document from this panel.

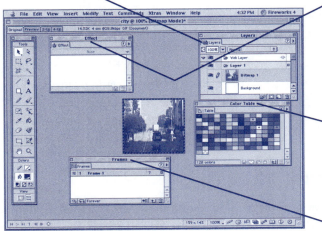

- **Effect panel (Alt/Option + F7).** The Effect panel enables you to apply a filter or an effect to a vector or bitmap object. Click on the eye icon to turn any effect on or off from the Effect panel.

- **Color Table.** Using this table, you can view colors for an 8-bit formatted file, such as a GIF file. If a document contains multiple slices, you can view the color table for a specific slice.

- **Frames panel (Shift + F2).** Frames enable you to create animation. Each frame can store a unique or shared set of objects and layers.

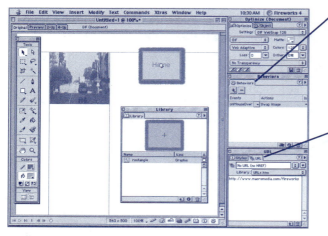

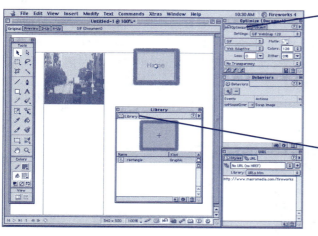

- **Behaviors panel (Shift + F3)**. Using this panel, you can assign a rollover behavior to a slice or hotspot Web object. You can also share behaviors created in Macromedia's Dreamweaver 4.

- **URL panel (Alt/Option + Shift + F10)**. From the URL panel, you can add a Universal Resource Locator (*URL*) to create a link for a slice or hotspot Web object. You can also assign a URL from the Object panel.

- **Optimize panel**. Reduce the image quality or file size of a document by choosing different file formats, transparency, and other optimization settings from this panel. Click on the Preview, 2-Up, or 4-Up tab to view different optimization settings.

- **Library panel (F11)**. The Library panel contains button, graphic, and animation symbols that you can click and drag into any frame or layer. Once a symbol is added to a document it becomes an instance, or an instance of that library symbol.

Changing Tool Options

If you've used any of the tools in the toolbox, you might already be familiar with the Tool Options panel. You can view and change a tool's settings from the Tool Options panel. The settings that appear in the Options panel change, depending on the tool selected in the toolbox, or the object selected in the document window. The following steps show you how to use the tool options for the Paint Bucket Tool.

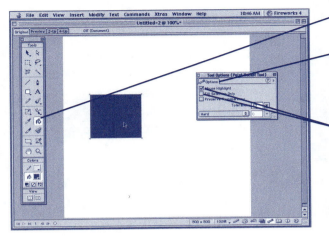

1. Select a tool from the toolbox.

2. Choose Tool Options from the Window menu, or press Alt/Option + Shift + O to open the Tool Options panel.

3. Select or clear a check box to toggle a feature for the selected tool.

> **NOTE**
>
> For more information about the Options panel, see Chapter 5, "Creating and Designing Graphics."

Changing Object Strokes

You can use the settings in the Stroke panel to customize the Pencil, Brush, Pen, and other path tools. You can also save, edit, or delete a stroke by clicking on the pop-up menu that appears at the top-right corner of the panel.

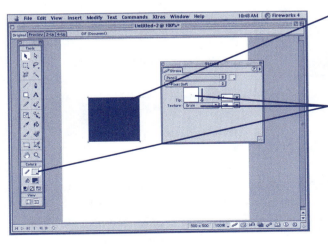

1. Click on an object in the document window, or select a tool from the toolbox. In this example, I've selected a shape in the document window.

The stroke color will appear in the Colors section of the toolbox. The Stroke panel will show the selected tip and texture.

2. Click on the top pop-up menu to choose a different stroke.

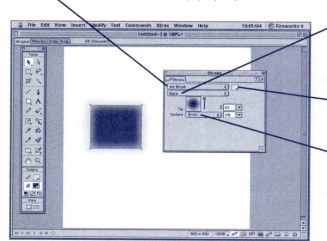

3. Adjust the type of stroke by choosing Basic or Textured from the second pop-up menu.

4. Click on the color pop-up menu to change the color of the stroke.

5. Choose a texture from the Texture pop-up menu.

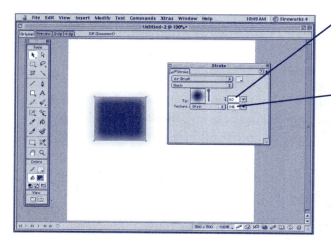

6. Type a number into the text box located in the middle of the panel to set the tip size of the stroke.

7. Type a number into the text box located in the lower-right corner of the panel to adjust the stroke's texture value.

NOTE

For more information about the Stroke panel, see Chapter 5, "Creating and Designing Graphics."

Viewing Object Information

The Info panel displays location and color information for any object selected in a document window. You can click on the pop-up menu in the right-hand corner of the Info panel to view RGB, CMY, or HSB color information. You can also view the width and height of an object, as well as the X and Y axis in pixels, inches, or centimeters from the pop-up menu.

1. Choose a selection tool from the toolbox.

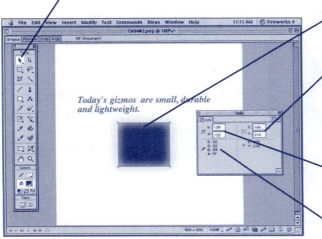

2. Select an object in the document window.

3. View the X and Y axis information about the object's location. The X and Y coordinates indicate the current location of the cursor in the document window.

4. View the width and height of the object.

5. View the color information about the selected object.

Assigning a Fill Color to an Object

You can add a fill color to vector objects using the Paint Bucket Tool, or by selecting an object and choosing a solid, pattern, or gradient fill from the Fill panel. You can create a custom fill pattern by adjusting an object's opacity setting and texture, and by choosing between a hard, anti-aliased, or feathered edge for the fill. The following steps give you a brief tour of the Fill panel.

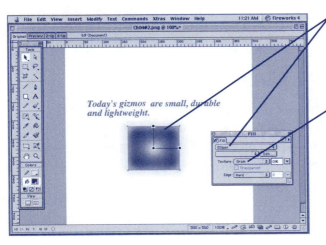

1. Click on an object and then select the type of fill you want to use. In this example I've selected the rectangle object.

2. Choose a texture from the Texture pop-up menu.

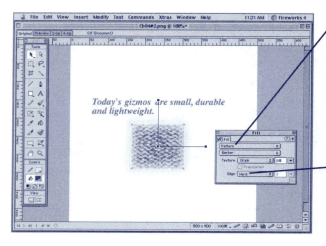

3. Click on the top pop-up menu and choose Pattern if you want to use a PNG, GIF, or JPEG image to fill the selected object. Click and drag the slider control or type a number in the Texture text box to adjust the amount of the texture applied to the object.

4. Click on the Edge pop-up menu to choose the type of edge you want to apply to the fill area of the object. Choose between Hard, Anti-Alias, and Feather edges.

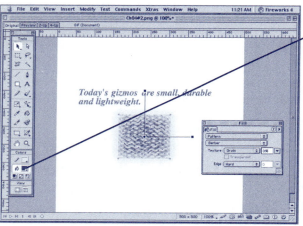

5. View the Fill color in the Colors section of the toolbox. Click on the color square to view a pop-up menu of available colors and choose a new fill color.

NOTE

For more information about the Fill panel, see Chapter 8, "Modifying Vector and Bitmap Graphics."

Adding an Effect to an Object

The Effect panel enables you to quickly change the appearance of an object without permanently altering the original path shape, stroke, fill, or color. Use the Effect panel to add one or more effects to an image file. Click on the check box to add or remove the effect from the selected image.

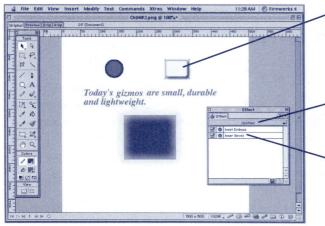

1. Select an object in the document window. If any effects have already been applied to that object, they will appear in the Effect panel.

2. Click on the pop-up menu and choose an effect.

3. View the effect. The newly added effect will appear in the Effect panel.

NOTE

Live Effects is one of the coolest features in Fireworks 4. You can add as many effects to an object as you want. You can reselect that object at any time and edit each effect's settings, or you can turn each one on or off from the Effect panel. For more information about effects, see Chapter 9, "Applying Effects."

Working with Color

You can change the color of an object from several different panels in Fireworks, including the Optimize, Color Table, Swatches, and Color Mixer panels. Use the Swatches panel to choose a new color as you create graphics. View the list of colors in the preview window using the Color Table panel. The following sections give you a brief tour of the Color Table, Swatches, Color Mixer, and Styles panels.

Choosing Colors with the Color Mixer Panel

You can open the Color Mixer panel by choosing its icon (an artist's palette) from the bottom of the document window, by choosing Color Mixer from the Window menu, or by pressing Shift + F9 on the keyboard. You can choose a new stroke or fill color from the Color Mixer panel. Open the Color Mixer panel and follow these steps to change the stroke or fill color of an object.

1. Click on the Stroke or Paint Bucket Tool button in the Color Mixer panel. The selected tool button will appear highlighted.

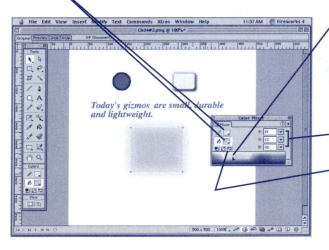

2. Choose a color from the pop-up menu of the color well. You can also click in the color bar located at the bottom of the Color Mixer panel to select a stroke or fill color.

3. View the color values in the panel.

4. Click on the Swap Colors button to switch brush and fill colors. These same colors will also appear in the toolbox.

TIP

You can pick an exact color from another application by clicking and dragging the Stroke or Fill color well over another application window on your desktop. For example, if you have a browser window open behind your Fireworks document window (with a Web page in plain view), click and hold the mouse button over the Stroke (or Fill) color well. The color pop-up window will open. Then, drag the cursor over an area of the Web page. You will see the color in the pop-up menu change to match the color of the Web page below the cursor. Release the mouse button to select a color, or note the hexadecimal value of the color in the pop-up window.

NOTE

You can choose a color in the Color Mixer panel by clicking on a color in the color wheel, or by typing in a color value in the R, G, or B text boxes. To find out more about how to work with color, see Chapter 7, "Working with Colors, Layers, and Masks."

Working with Swatches

Once you've selected a stroke or fill color from the color well, you can add it to the Swatches panel. Simply click on the stroke or fill button in the toolbox or Color Mixer panel, then select the Swatches panel. Move the cursor to the bottom of the Swatches panel until the eyedropper icon becomes a paint bucket icon. Then click once to add the stroke or fill color to the bottom row of colors in the Swatches panel. You can use the Swatches panel as a place to store frequently used colors. You can also view or choose a new color while creating or editing an image object. Here's how:

1. Choose Swatches from the Window menu. Alternatively, you can press Ctrl/Command + F9 to open the Swatches panel. Select a stroke in the image window.

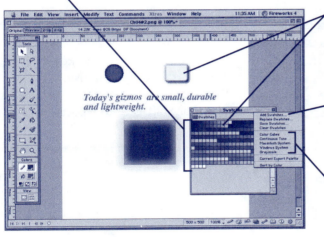

2. Click on a vector object in the document window. Then click on a different color in the Swatches panel to change the color of the selected object.

3. Click on the panel options button to view the pop-up menu commands for the Swatches panel.

4. Choose a different set of swatches or colors from the Swatches panel pop-up menu.

NOTE

For more information about editing colors, see Chapter 7, "Working with Colors, Layers, and Masks."

Interpreting the Color Table

The Color Table displays the color of a selected image in the Preview pane of the document window. Each color has a tiny symbol in it to indicate whether it has been edited, locked, or made transparent; has multiple attributes; or is Web safe.

1. Select a GIF file format from the top pop-up menu in the Optimize panel.

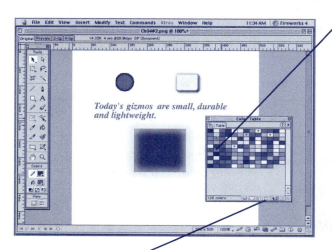

2. Choose Color Table from the Window menu. The Color Table panel will open. Click on the pop-up menu for the Color Table panel and then choose Rebuild Color Table. Click on a color in the color table.

TIP

Hold down the Command key (or the Ctrl key if you're using Windows) to select multiple colors, or Shift-click to select a range of colors.

---

3. Click the Lock icon to prevent changes to the color.

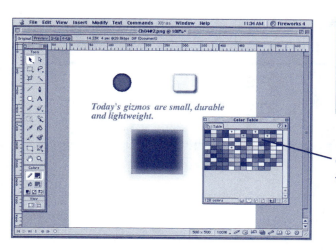

NOTE

When you lock a color, it cannot be changed or removed if you switch to another color panel.

---

4. Select a color from the panel and then double-click it to edit it.

5. Click on the pop-up menu in the Table panel. You can choose the Save Palette command if you want to store a particular color table on your hard drive and apply it to another Fireworks document.

NOTE

If you've added a slice object to a document, you won't be able to view any colors in the Color Table panel. Select the slice object to view the color table for that slice object.

Working with the Styles Panel

Give an object a nice, new look by applying a style from the Styles panel. Choose Styles from the Window menu to open the Styles panel, or press Shift + F11 on the keyboard. After the Styles panel opens, perform the following steps to apply a style to a vector graphic.

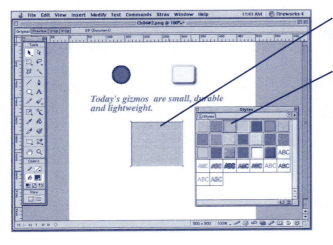

1. Select an object in the document window.

2. Click on a style icon in the Styles panel.

3. The selected object's stroke and fill options will change to match the selected style. Wasn't that easy?

NOTE

For more information about the Styles panel, see Chapter 8, "Modifying Vector and Bitmap Graphics."

Creating a Rollover with the Behaviors Panel

Objects, hotspots, slices, and images can all have their own unique behaviors. One of the most common types of behavior to add to a Web page is a rollover. A rollover can have one of several behaviors. For example, when you click on a hotspot or slice, the rollover can load a new Web page URL into the browser window or swap an image. To open the Behaviors panel, choose Behaviors from the Window menu, or press Shift + F3. The following sections show you how to create a simple rollover and work with the Behaviors panel.

Assigning a URL to Hotspot or Slice

Open the URL panel if you want to add a link to a URL to a slice or hotspot Web object in the document window. Although you need to create a slice or hotspot before you can use this panel, you'll need to read Chapter 10, "Introduction to Slices, Hotspots, and Image Maps" to find out how to create Web objects. The following steps show you how to assign a URL to a hotspot or slice.

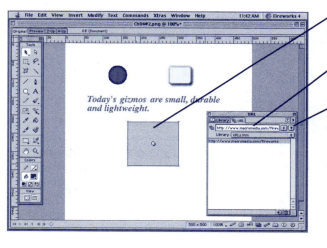

1. View the current URL for a selected Web object in the URL panel.

2. Type a new URL in the text field.

3. Alternatively, you can click on the Plus button to add an existing URL to the selected object.

Viewing Behaviors

You can create, edit, and view object behaviors, such as rollover triggers and actions, in the Behaviors panel. Each behavior you add to a hotspot or slice will be associated with some JavaScript code that will be exported along with any images when you're ready to put your graphics on a Web page.

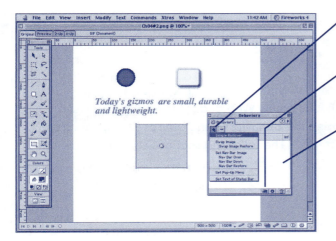

1. Click on the Plus button to add a behavior to a selected hotspot or slice.

2. Toggle the visibility of grouped behaviors on or off.

3. Double-click an item to view its behavior information.

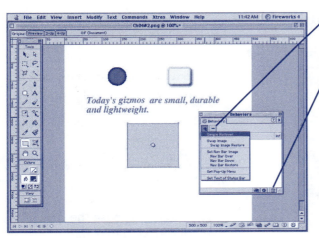

4. Click on the Minus button to remove a behavior.

5. Select a behavior and then click on the Trash icon to delete it.

NOTE

For more information about the Behaviors panel, see Chapter 12, "Making Buttons with the Button Editor."

Checking out the Library Panel

In the Library panel, you can create buttons and rollover behaviors, and track symbols and instances with animation. For more information about symbols and instances, see Chapter 12, "Making Buttons with the Button Editor." Choose Library from the Window menu to open the Library panel, or press F11. The following steps give you a brief tour of interface elements in the Library panel.

1. View the selected symbol in the top window of the Library panel.

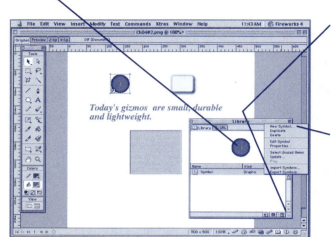

2. Click and drag the lower-right corner of the panel window to enlarge the Library panel. Adjust the panel window so you can view all the columns providing information about the library objects.

3. Click on the Library panel pop-up menu to view the list of available commands for this panel.

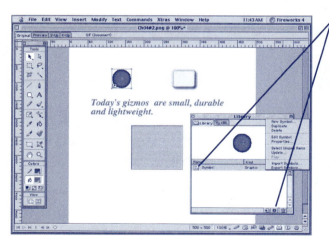

4. Select a symbol from the window list at the bottom of the panel. Then click on the i icon to view the symbol properties.

NOTE

To create a symbol, choose New Symbol from the Insert menu. Type a name for the symbol and click on a radio button to choose the type of symbol you want to create. Then create a vector object, or copy and paste a bitmap object into the symbol window.

Using Find and Replace

Can't find a word, or aren't sure whether certain words are all formatted with the same font? Use Find and Replace to locate and replace graphics or text across files in a project. Press Ctrl/Command + F or choose Find and Replace from the Window menu to open the Find and Replace panel.

Filling in the Find and Replace Panel

You can use the Find and Replace tools to update several documents in the same project, or to simply search and replace text within one file.

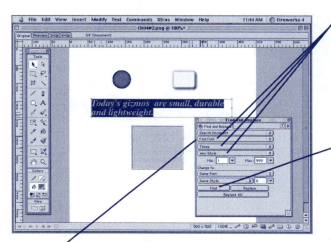

1. Define the search criteria using a pop-up menu or by typing a word or words into the text edit field. In this example, I've selected to search for a font. Select a font, then type a minimum or maximum font size into the appropriate text boxes.

2. Click on the Find button to start the search.

3. Click to choose a different search criteria from the second pop-up menu in the Find and Replace panel. Choose to search and replace a font, color, text, URL, or non-Web216, non-Web safe color.

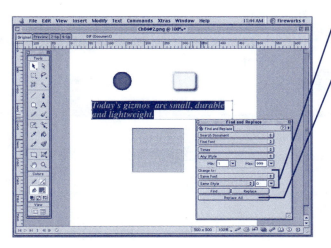

4. Select the desired replacement criteria. Then click on the Find button.

5. Click on Replace All to replace all project files.

NOTE

For more information about the Find and Replace panel, see Chapter 16, "Exploring Automation," and Chapter 18, "Creating Commands and Updating Projects."

TIP

There are two ways to search and replace information in Fireworks. If you select a range of files, use Replace All to replace all instances across all files. You can also search a specific selection of text or image, and Fireworks will only replace within the selected range of items.

Tracking Tasks with the Project Panel

Log and review changes made to files using the Project panel. Choose Project from the Window menu to open the Project panel. The following steps show you how to track a task in the Project panel by using the Find and Replace panel.

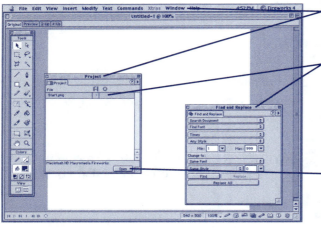

1. Choose Project Log from the Window menu to view the Project panel.

2. Select an item in the Project panel. The items that appear in the Project panel are generated by find and replace tasks performed in the Find and Replace panel.

3. Click on Open to view a selected log entry.

NOTE

For more information about the Project panel, see Chapter 16, "Exploring Automation."

Arranging Document Windows

If you open too many menu windows, but you want all windows to be one click away, choose Cascade from the Window menu. Fireworks will arrange the document windows so that each is partially visible within Fireworks.

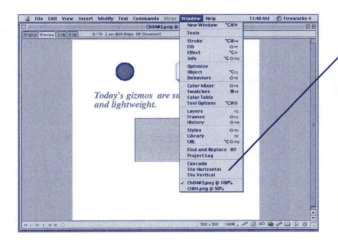

1. Open several document windows.

2. Choose Cascade from the Window menu. Alternatively, choose Tile Horizontal or Tile Vertical to arrange windows horizontally or vertically in the workspace.

TIP

Click and drag any panel tab to create a separate floating window for that panel.

Working with the Layers and Frames Panels

Each document window has the same tabs, tools, and window controls. Each document window is also an integral part of the Layers, Frames, and History panels. The following list provides a brief tour of the controls available in the document window. The following sections show you how to use a document window with the Layers, Frames, and History panels.

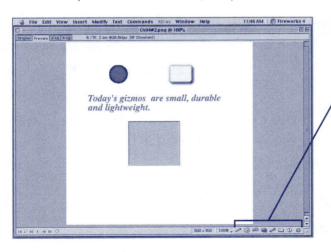

1. Choose a shortcut from the mini-launcher located in the lower-right corner of a document window.

2. Click on the Preview tab to view the current objects as they would appear if they were to be exported from Fireworks.

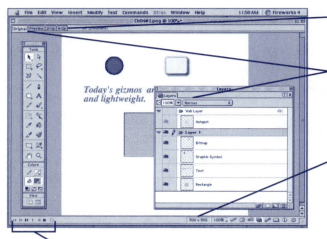

3. Compare additional renderings with the original in the 4-Up tab.

4. Choose the Original tab if you want to edit any of the objects in the document window. Click on a layer to select an object in the document.

5. View the width and height of the document.

6. Use the Frame Controls to view different layers of the document.

Organizing Layers

Layers can be added as you add images, objects, text, or effects to a document window. Use layers to protect objects that you do not want to edit on the active layer. The following steps show a selected set of features in the Layers panel.

1. Choose Layers from the Window menu, or press the F2 key to open the Layers panel. You can also choose the Layers shortcut from the mini-launcher area of the document window. Drag and drop an image file onto the Fireworks document window to add a layer to the current document.

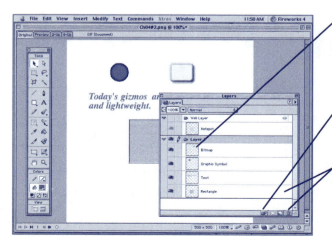

2. Select a layer to make it active in the document window, or double-click on a layer to change its name and view layer options.

3. Click on the folder icon in the Layers panel to create a new layer.

4. To delete a layer, first select it and then click on the Trash icon.

Working with Frames

When you use frames, you can create complex Web pages or animation, or just experiment with them. Click on Play to view document window frames. Click on the other control buttons to step through or jump to the beginning or end of the Web pages.

1. Click on a frame in the Frames panel to view the frame's contents in the document window.

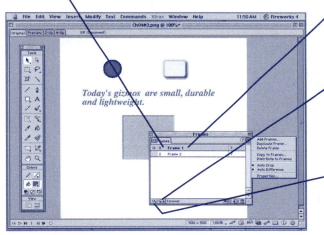

2. Double-click on a frame in the Frames panel to view delay and the Include when Exporting check box.

3. Turn looping on and off by choosing no looping, or 1, 2, 3, 4, 5, 10, 20, or Forever from the GIF Animation Looping pop-up menu.

4. Change frame settings by clicking and dragging the onion skinning icon along the left side of the frames you want to view from the Frames panel.

NOTE

The features in Step 2 are also accessible from the Properties menu command in the Frames pop-up menu.

Changing a Document's History

Every step or click is tracked in the History panel. You can create one-step commands by selecting a group of tasks from the History panel. Press Shift + F10, or choose History from the Window menu to open the History panel. The following steps show you how to view and revert to a previous document state using the History panel.

1. Select one or more steps in the History panel.

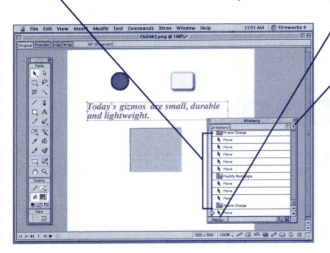

2. Click on Replay to view the selected steps.

3. Choose the Save as Command menu item from the History panel's pop-up menu to change one or more selected steps into a command. All commands are created with JavaScript code and are located in the Commands menu.

4

Customizing Preferences and Keyboard Shortcuts

Fireworks preferences affect editing tasks, folder settings, and the general appearance of images. Fireworks 4 preferences consist of General, Editing, Launch and Edit, Folders, and Import preferences settings. You can adjust the way the cursor selects objects in the document window, adjust the default settings for images imported into Fireworks, change the number of undo steps supported by the Undo command in the Edit menu, or assign specific folders for Fireworks plug-in files.

Macromedia also includes a full-featured Keyboard Shortcuts window in Fireworks 4. You can view, edit, or add shortcuts for menu commands, toolbar tools, or other miscellaneous commands in Fireworks. In this chapter, you'll learn how to:

- Use general preferences
- Use editing preferences
- Set folder preferences
- Change import preferences
- View and change keyboard shortcuts

Using General Preferences

You can open the Preferences window by choosing Preferences from the Edit menu. The Preferences window consists of five different sets of preferences: General, Editing, Launch and Edit, Folders, and Import. Choose one of these settings by clicking on the pop-up menu in the Preferences window. General preferences are used to set the number of undo steps, the default colors for drawing elements, and the scaling method, or *interpolation,* of an image. The following sections show you how to adjust each of the General settings in the Preferences window.

Setting Undo and Color Defaults

In the General Preferences window, you can view or change the default settings for undo or redo steps, and the default colors for brush strokes, fills, or highlights. If you change the number of undo steps, though, you will need to quit and restart Fireworks to use the new undo setting. The following steps show you how to adjust the undo and color default settings in the General Preferences window.

1. Click on Edit and choose the Preferences menu command.

2. Choose General from the pop-up menu.

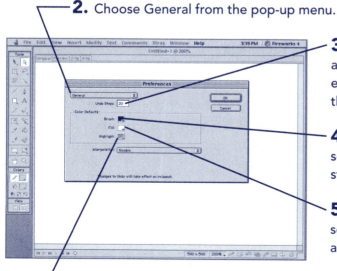

3. In the Undo Steps text box, type a number between 0 and 100. In this example, I've typed the number 20 in the text box.

4. Click on the Brush pop-up menu to select the default color for pen or brush strokes.

5. Click on the Fill pop-up menu to select the default fill color for tools such as the Paint Bucket.

6. Click on the Highlight pop-up menu to select the default highlight color for text and graphics.

Setting Interpolation

Interpolation preferences are located at the bottom of the General Preferences window. You can choose from four different processes that affect the way an image appears when you adjust its size in the document window. Choose one of the four possible scaling methods to interpolate pixels when an image is made smaller or larger.

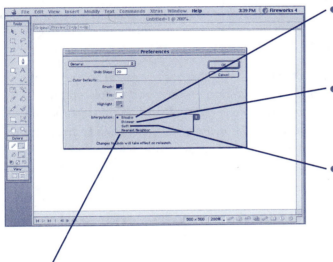

- **Bicubic interpolation**. The default scaling method, bicubic interpolation generally produces the highest-quality, sharpest image.

- **Bilinear interpolation**. Although not as sharp as bicubic interpolation, bilinear interpolation creates sharper results than soft interpolation.

- **Soft interpolation**. Soft interpolation eliminates sharp details and adds a soft blur to the scaled image, and is useful if other methods of scaling are not productive.

- **Nearest Neighbor interpolation**. Similar to zooming in or out of an image with the Magnify Tool, nearest neighbor interpolation creates jagged edges and sharp contrasts with no blurring.

NOTE

Try scaling images with the default setting. If the scaled image looks too distorted or grainy, try bilinear or nearest neighbor interpolation. Get the best results by starting with the highest quality source image you can capture or scan with a digital camera.

Using Editing Preferences

You can view or change many of the default settings for visual cues and window behaviors when editing images with Fireworks 4. The Editing Preferences window consists of three main sections of settings. You can click on a check box in the top two sections of the Editing Preferences window to turn a specific setting on or off. The two text boxes at the bottom of the window enable you to adjust the distance for clicking or dragging objects to guides or grids in a document window.

Setting Image Editing Preferences

In the Preferences dialog box, select Editing from the pop-up menu to view and change the image editing preferences. The editing preferences enable you to choose between two types of pointers when using a tool, and adjust other visual cues and behaviors related to image editing. If a check box is checked, that setting is active; if it is not checked, the setting is no longer active. The following list provides a brief explanation for each check box item that appears in the Editing Preferences window.

- **Precise Cursors**. Select this box to change the icon pointer to a crosshair pointer for any tool.

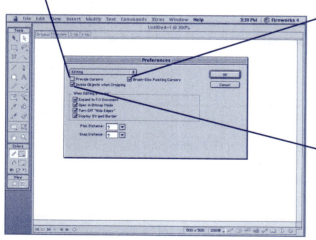

- **Brush-Size Painting Cursors**. Select this box to adjust the size and shape of the Brush and Eraser tool pointers so that you can draw or erase with more accuracy. This setting can be helpful if the Brush Tool has been configured to use multiple tips.

- **Delete Objects when Cropping**. This option automatically deletes any part of the image outside the bounding box when you are using the cropping tool. Use the Crop Document command in the Edit menu or the Canvas Size command in the Modify menu to activate this feature.

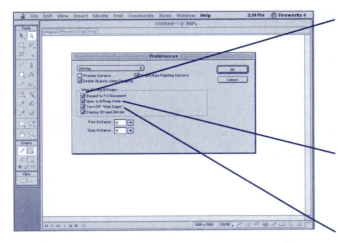

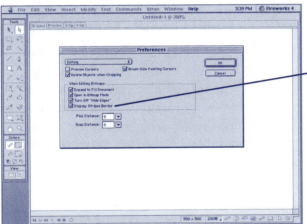

- **Expand to Fill Document**. Selected by default, this option changes the entire document window into Bitmap Mode when a bitmap object is selected. If this option is not selected, only a highlighted bitmap object is editable.

- **Open in Bitmap Mode**. This setting forces any image files to open in Bitmap Mode. If this feature is off, image files open in Vector Mode.

- **Turn Off "Hide Edges."** This setting turns off Hide Edges automatically when entering or leaving a document in Bitmap Mode.

- **Display Striped Border**. When this check box is selected, a candy-striped border surrounds the canvas area of the document window if a bitmap object is in Bitmap Mode.

TIP

A blue and black striped bar will surround the canvas area if a document is in Bitmap Mode. Click on the Exit Bitmap Mode button (a red button with a white X) in the document window to exit Bitmap Mode. Similarly, a black and yellow striped mask appears if a mask object is selected in the Layers panel. Click on the Exit Bitmap Mode button in the document window to deselect the mask object in the Layers panel and return to Vector Mode.

Changing Distance Settings

Editing preferences enable you to adjust how the cursor and selected image objects behave as you interact with them in the document window. You might need to adjust these settings if you need to see an image object as you select it, or if you want objects to snap to a guide or grid a little more quickly. You can type a number into the text box to change a distance setting, or click on the pop-up arrow to choose a different setting. The following lists shows you how to use the Pick Distance and Snap Distance editing preferences.

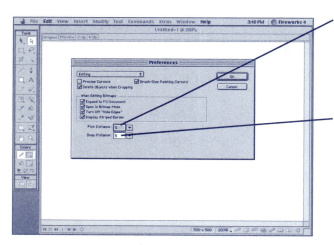

● **Pick Distance.** This option enables you to determine how close the cursor has to be for you to click on an image object. You can adjust this setting between 1 and 10 pixels.

● **Snap Distance.** This option works with the Snap to Grid or Snap to Guides commands located in the View menu. Adjust the snap distance between the object you are moving and the closest grid or guide lines. The snap distance can be set between 1 and 10 pixels.

TIP

Try the default Pick and Snap settings before adjusting them in the Preferences window. The default setting is 5.

NOTE

Although you can type any number into the distance settings text boxes, the slider control for the Pick Distance or Snap Distance text boxes only recognizes values between 1 and 10.

Setting Launch and Edit Preferences

Choose Launch and Edit from the pop-up menu in the Preferences window to access the source file behavior settings. Use the source files preference settings to tell Fireworks how to edit or optimize PNG files from other applications, such as Macromedia Dreamweaver or Director. The Launch and Edit preferences are recognized by Dreamweaver in most cases, and you'll be asked to locate the source PNG file if Dreamweaver cannot find it. The following list shows you how to select an editing and optimization preference for Fireworks PNG files.

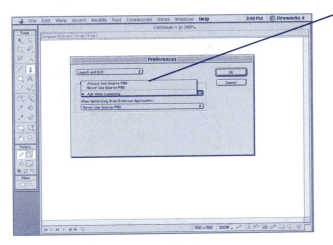

- **When Editing from External Application**. This option opens the original Fireworks PNG when using Fireworks to edit image files within another Web editor such as Dreamweaver or FrontPage. Choose either Always Use Source PNG, Never Use Source PNG, or Ask When Launching from the pop-up menu. In this example, I've selected Ask When Launching. This option enables me to choose whether to modify the source or current file each time I want to edit or optimize an image.

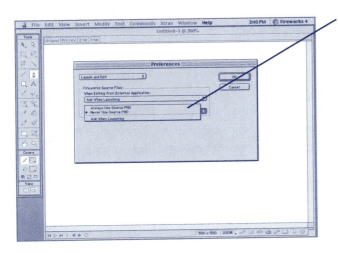

- **When Optimizing from External Application**. This option consists of three settings: Always Use Source PNG, Never Use Source PNG, and Ask When Launching. Choose Always Use Source PNG if you want the original PNG file to open in Fireworks. Choose Never Use Source PNG if you want to only update the selected file, and not its source PNG file.

NOTE

A Design Note is created for each image file (including each slice) exported from Fireworks. Dreamweaver reads the Design Note whenever you open a Fireworks image in Dreamweaver. The path to the source PNG file is stored in the Design Note for a file exported from Fireworks.

TIP

If you choose the Never Use Source PNG option, you can only work with a copy of the original image file. If you do not plan to use the original PNG file to continuously update Web sources, choose this option in the Editing Preferences window.

Using Folders Settings

With the Folders preference settings, you can configure Fireworks to access additional Photoshop plug-in, texture, and pattern files, or to specify where you want Fireworks to store its temporary cache files. Although some Photoshop plug-in files cannot be used as Xtras or effects in Fireworks, you can select particular folders to choose plug-ins, as well as textures and patterns you want to use with Fireworks. Files and folders can be located on a local hard drive, network volume, CD-ROM, DVD-ROM, or external drive.

Setting Plug-Ins

Photoshop plug-in files are part of Adobe Photoshop. These files enable you to apply effects to images in Photoshop. However, most plug-in files also work as Live Effects in Fireworks. If you already have Photoshop installed on your hard drive, you can configure Fireworks to use the Photoshop plug-in files to extend your library of Live Effects. Here's how:

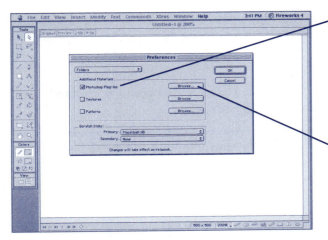

1. Default Photoshop plug-ins are located in the Fireworks Xtras menu. Select Photoshop Plug-ins in the Folders Preferences window to enable Fireworks to locate the folder of plug-in files on your computer.

2. Click on Browse to locate the files.

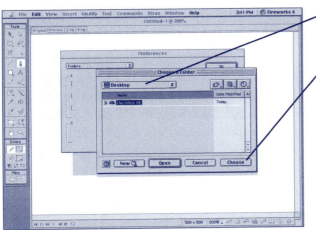

3. Navigate to the plug-in folder.

4. Click on the Choose button to set the plug-in folder.

Setting Textures

The Textures check box works together with the Browse button to enable you to load additional textures stored in a PNG file on your hard drive. The folder you select in this preference setting will appear in the Textures pop-up menu in the Fill panel, and also in the Textures pop-up menu in the Stroke panel. The following steps show you how to select a textures folder from the Preferences window.

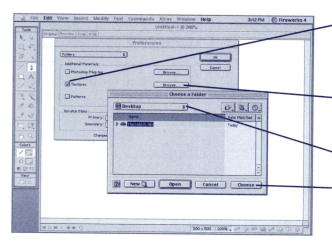

1. Select the Textures check box to enable Fireworks to locate the selected folder on your computer.

2. Click on the Browse button to locate the files on the hard drive.

3. Navigate to the textures file.

4. Click on the Choose button to set the PNG file containing the textures.

Setting Patterns

If you want to use your own custom patterns, you can configure Fireworks preferences to read a PNG file containing patterns. The folder selected in this preference setting will appear in the Pattern list of the Fill panel. After you've performed the steps below, click on the top pop-up menu in the Fill panel and choose Pattern to load the patterns selected in the Preferences window. The following steps show you how to choose a Patterns folder from the Preferences window.

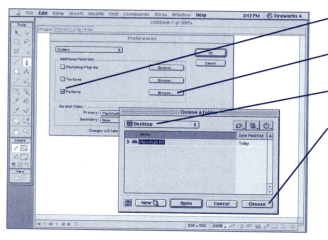

1. Select the Patterns check box.

2. Click on the Browse button.

3. Navigate to the patterns file.

4. Click on the Choose button to set the PNG file containing the patterns.

Setting Scratch Disks

The primary scratch disk is a temporary folder, usually on a hard disk, created by Fireworks. It is used to store data as you edit an image file. These cache files are removed from your hard disk when you exit Fireworks. The following list shows you how to choose a primary and secondary scratch disk in the Preferences window.

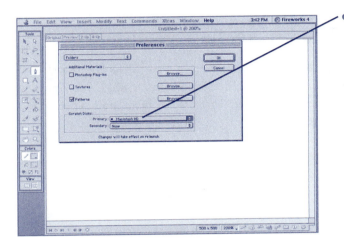

- **Primary**. Choose the main scratch disk on which you want Fireworks to store temporary cached data for image files.

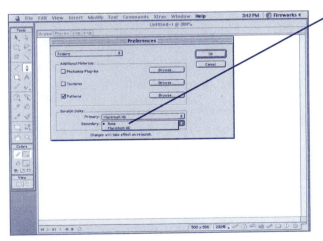

- **Secondary**. Select an additional disk for storing cached data, should the primary disk be full.

TIP

If you're not sure which hard drive to select for the primary or secondary scratch disk, use the default settings. If Fireworks 4 generates error messages indicating that it is running low on memory (for example, if you're working on several images at the same time), try choosing a different primary disk that contains more available space, or select a secondary scratch disk.

Using Import Preferences

Import preferences enable you to define the way a Photoshop file is converted as it is opened or imported into a Fireworks file. You can convert layers to objects or frames, or adjust the way text is handled. The following sections show you how to use the Photoshop File Conversion settings in the Import Preferences window.

Setting Photoshop File Conversion Settings

Open a Photoshop file, also called a PSD file, in Fireworks. Fireworks can translate many native Photoshop features, such as layers, masks, and text, when you open or import a Photoshop file in Fireworks. The following list explains the Layers options in the Import Preferences window.

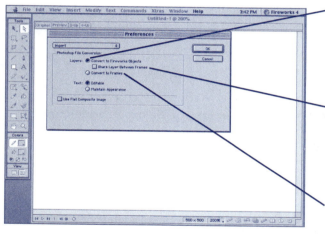

- **Convert to Fireworks Objects**. When you select this option, each layer in a Photoshop file is imported into Fireworks as a separate bitmap object in its own layer.

- **Share Layer Between Frames**. If a Fireworks file contains more than one frame, this setting copies any layers imported from a Photoshop file into each frame in the Fireworks file.

- **Convert to Frames**. This option creates a separate frame for each layer in the imported Photoshop file. This preference setting can be helpful if you plan to import files to create animation.

CAUTION

Make sure that Fireworks has enough allocated memory before you try to import a large Photoshop image file. Check the number of colors and size of the image file and compare it to other image files opened by Fireworks 4. On a Mac, you can increase the amount of memory allocated to an application. To change the amount of memory allocated to Fireworks, first make sure you quit the Fireworks application. Select the Fireworks application icon and then choose Get Info from the File menu. Choose Memory from the Show pop-up menu, and then type a larger number in the Preferred Size text box.

On a PC running Windows, you might need to exit some applications or increase the amount of virtual memory. Right-click on the My Computer icon and choose Properties. For Windows 98, click on the Performance tab and choose the Virtual Memory button to access the settings for virtual memory. If you have Windows 2000, click on the Advanced tab, click on the Performance Options button, and then choose the Change button for Virtual Memory.

Text Preferences

When you import a Photoshop file into Fireworks, you can affect the way text is managed before the file is converted. Fireworks 4 converts any text in a Photoshop 6 file into a bitmap image, so you won't be able to edit text in Fireworks if you import it as part of a Photoshop file. The following list explains the text options and how to use the Use Flat Composite Image check box in the Import Preferences window.

- **Editable**. If you choose this option, text is imported as editable text blocks. However, imported text might not look exactly the same as it did in Photoshop. If the Photoshop file requires a font that is not installed on your computer, it will appear "blocky" as well.

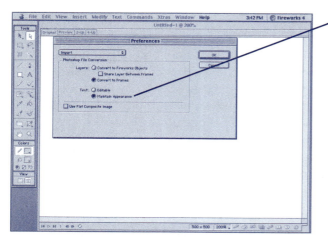

- **Maintain Appearance**. If you select this option, imported text objects are converted to bitmap images. This preference setting maintains the appearance of a font but prevents you from editing that text in Fireworks. On the plus side, if the Photoshop file uses a font you do not have, the text will appear correctly in Fireworks.

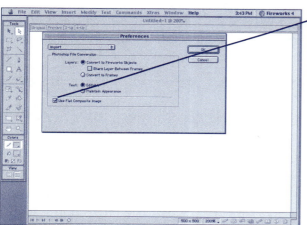

- **Use Flat Composite Image**. When this box is selected, any layers in a Photoshop file are ignored, and only a single, flat composite image is imported if the Photoshop file contains a composite image.

Changing Keyboard Shortcuts

One of the big productivity-boosting features in Fireworks is the availability of all kinds of shortcut keys for toolbox tools, menus, and other special tasks in Fireworks. A keyboard shortcut enables you to press a single key, or combination of keys, to select a menu command or tool in an application. If an item is selected in the document window, you can use keyboard shortcuts to copy or move the selected object instead of clicking and dragging the mouse.

Macromedia has a full-blown Keyboard Shortcuts window that you can open by choosing Keyboard Shortcuts from the Edit menu. You can create new sets of keyboard shortcuts, export a set as HTML, or delete keyboard shortcut sets. You'll find similar keyboard shortcuts windows in Flash 5 and Dreamweaver 4, too. If you're more familiar with Fireworks 3, Photoshop, Illustrator, or FreeHand shortcuts, Macromedia lets you switch to other keyboard shortcuts so that you don't have to relearn or change the way you work in Fireworks 4.

Adjusting Menu Command Shortcuts

Windows and Macintosh computer users commonly use shortcuts for menu commands. You can copy and paste text by pressing Ctrl/Command + C and Ctrl/Command + V. In fact, the keyboard shortcuts for these commands are the same for both Windows and Macs. Fireworks menu command shortcuts work similarly. On a Windows computer, you press the Ctrl key instead of the Command key, which you would use on a Mac. For example, press Ctrl + C to copy a selected object in Windows, or press Command + C to do the same task on a Mac.

Macromedia includes a standard set of keyboard shortcuts with Fireworks 4. After you open the Keyboard Shortcuts window, you can view each menu bar item in the Commands window list. If you want to save your changes, click on the OK button. Otherwise, you can exit without saving any changes by clicking on the Cancel button. The following list shows you how to work with menu command shortcuts and keyboard shortcut sets in the Keyboard Shortcuts window.

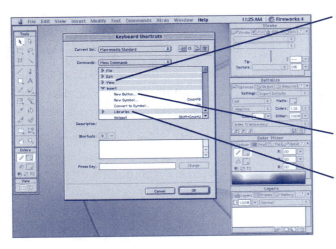

• **View menu commands**. A list of menu commands appears in the window list located below the Commands pop-up menu. Click on the triangle icon to view a list of menu commands.

• **Select a menu command**. Click on a menu command to view its shortcut.

• **Submenus contain additional commands**. Uncollapse a triangle to view additional menu commands for submenus.

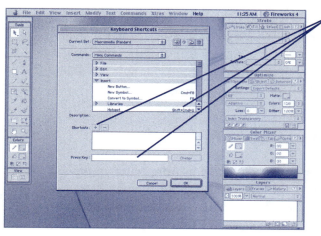

- **Edit a shortcut**. Select a keyboard command from the Commands window list, and click on the Plus button to add a new shortcut. Press the Command key along with another key to create a new shortcut. The key combination will appear in the Press Key text box. If the shortcut you entered is already being used, Fireworks will tell you which menu command it is assigned to. A list of shortcuts for the selected command will appear in the Shortcuts window list.

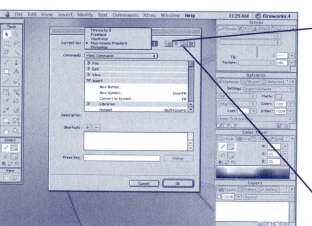

- **Duplicate a set**. Click on the Duplicate Set button to create a copy of a shortcut set. You cannot edit any of the sets Macromedia installs with Fireworks 4. If you change a shortcut for one of these sets, Fireworks will ask you to create a new copy of a set, which you can change as much and as often as you like.

- **Export a set**. Click on the Export HTML icon to export the shortcuts as an HTML file.

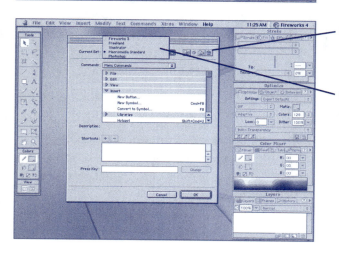

- **Delete a set**. Click on the Trash icon to remove the currently selected set from the Keyboard Shortcuts window.

- **Switch sets**. Click on the Current Set pop-up menu to select a different keyboard shortcut set.

> ## CAUTION
>
> If you're using Mac OS 9, you might have difficulty accessing shortcuts that require you press a Function key combined with an Option key. The best workaround for this limitation in Mac OS 9 (due to the Keyboard control panel settings), is to create a duplicate keyboard shortcut set in Fireworks and choose a different keyboard shortcut. For example, you might want to choose a different keyboard shortcut for the Stroke or Effect menu commands in the Window menu.

Changing Toolbar Shortcuts

In addition to being able to change menu command shortcuts, you can change the shortcuts for tools. Click on the Commands pop-up menu and choose Tools. The items in the window list will change. You can view the toolbar tools and their keyboard shortcuts in the window list. Click on a tool to view, edit, or add a shortcut.

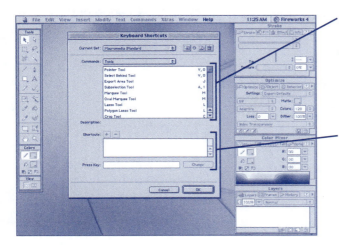

- **Select a tool**. Click on a tool name in the Commands window list to view the tool's shortcut. If a tool has more than one shortcut, it will appear in the Commands window list as well as in the Shortcuts window list.

- **Add a shortcut**. Click on the Plus button to add a shortcut. Press a number or alphabet character on the keyboard. It will appear in the Press Key text box. Click on the Change button to change the shortcut. The new shortcut will appear in the Shortcuts and Commands window lists.

Setting Miscellaneous Shortcuts

But wait, there's more! Fireworks has several special keyboard shortcuts, affectionately grouped under the Miscellaneous category in the Commands pop-up menu. These commands enable you to copy or move the selected image object in the document window. For example, you can clone, fill, float, nudge, paste inside, play animation, or go to the previous frame using shortcut keys. Add, edit, or view these shortcuts in the same way you would the menu command or tool shortcuts.

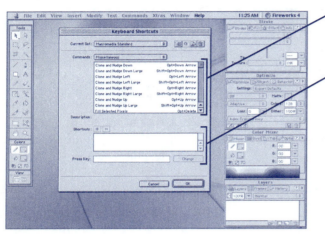

- **View shortcuts**. Click on a command to edit its shortcut information or to add a new shortcut.

- **Add a shortcut**. Click on the Plus button to add a new shortcut to the selected command. Press a combination of keys that you want to use for the selected command. These keys will appear in the Press Key text box. Click on the Change button to add the shortcut to the Commands and Shortcuts lists.

PART II

Designing Graphics with Fireworks

Fireworks has a deceptively simple workspace. If you're familiar with graphics applications, you can probably design graphics in Fireworks with little or no help. However, it won't take long before you realize that Fireworks is also very different than other graphics applications.

One of the first things you'll notice is that Fireworks treats vector objects differently than bitmap objects. Fireworks has a Vector Mode (no striped line surrounds the canvas) for creating and editing vector objects, and a Bitmap Mode (designated by a striped line that surrounds the canvas), for working with photos and other bitmap images. Both objects can co-exist in the same document, and can be combined together in a layer as a grouped object or mask. However, Fireworks contains different sets of tools to enable you to work with each type of image.

You can design your own graphics or import images, such as photos or line art, created in other applications. Then, you can work with colors and a full suite of editing tools, and apply filters and effects to design your Web graphics. The following chapters show you how to create, open, import, and edit graphics in Fireworks. There's a chapter dedicated to color and effects, too.

5

Creating and Designing Graphics

One of the more difficult tasks involved in designing a Web page or a Web site is prototyping different sets of graphics for all the buttons, banners, and images that can be used to define a Web site. You can create several prototypes of different images and Web page graphics in one document using frames, or separate each set of images into its own document.

Fireworks enables you to work with both bitmap and vector graphics in the same document. Each graphic you import or create is placed in its own layer, located in the Layers panel. You can combine objects and their layers by grouping them. You can also place one object over another, or select part of an object to create an image mask. This chapter shows you how to use selection tools with vector and bitmap graphics to design new image objects. You'll also learn how to work with layers, masks, and frames. In this chapter, you'll learn how to:

- Create vector and bitmap graphics
- Work with layers
- Create mask objects
- Design animation
- Use the Animation Wizard

Creating Bitmap and Vector Graphics

The canvas area in a Fireworks document can be in either Vector or Bitmap Mode. Vector Mode enables you to create and edit vector paths and objects. You can design line art or use the Shape, Stroke, and Fill tools to create banners and buttons. When bitmap objects are present, the document changes to Bitmap Mode if all or part of the canvas is selected. In Bitmap Mode, the selected area is treated as a group of pixels. If you want to apply an Xtra, or convert a vector object to a bitmap object, you must first change the vector object to a bitmap object by choosing the Convert to Bitmap command from the Modify menu.

Working with Vector Graphics

To create, edit, or delete vector objects, the document window must be in Vector Mode. First, you need to understand what makes a vector graphic special. You can generate a graphic image on a computer in several ways. One way is to draw each line and curve as a vector, based on a mathematical formula, which enables the computer to quickly calculate how that line or curve will look at any particular size.

You can also create custom-shaped vector paths with the Pen Tool. Although the Pen Tool is the only true vector drawing tool, each shape or path you create with a drawing tool shares the same object, stroke, and fill settings. The Pencil, Rectangle, and Brush tools are vector tools when a document is in Vector Mode, but can also be bitmap tools when a document is in Bitmap Mode. Because each of these objects has similar characteristics and can only be created in Vector Mode, I will refer to objects created using these drawing tools as vector objects or vector graphics throughout this book.

Each line or curve has a stroke associated with the line itself. The fill color defines the area inside a closed path. You might have already noticed that an open path vector object doesn't change if you assign a different fill value to it from the Fill panel. Together the line or curve, along with its points, plus the stroke and fill define the vector graphic, which can also be called a path, object, vector, or any combination of those three words. The easiest way to tell whether an object is a vector is to click on it. If you see a path with at least two points defined in the framework of the object, then it's a vector graphic (except for text objects). If a box surrounds the object, it's probably a bitmap image. You can also open the Object panel to determine whether an object is a vector (or path) or a bitmap. The following list highlights several characteristics of vector objects.

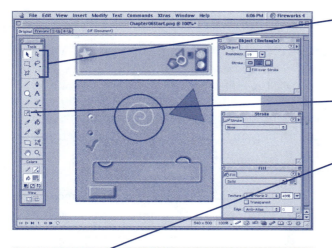

- **They are editable**. You can make a curve curvier, straighten or add a line to a path, or change the stroke or fill color at your whim.

- **They are scalable**. If you change the little star to a big star, it still looks like a star.

- **They can be altered using command options**. Select a vector object in the document window and then click on the Modify menu. You can choose the Transform, Alter Path, Combine, Mask, and Group commands to change the way a vector object appears or interacts with another image object.

- **Their object attributes can be customized.** Vector objects can have customizable object, stroke, and fill settings. Click on the pop-up menus in the Stroke or Fill panels to view lists of strokes, textures, fills, gradients, patterns, and colors. You can also extend those settings by creating and adding your own stroke and fill settings.

NOTE

Another way to check to see whether an object is a vector or bitmap image is to scale it. Click on an object to select it and then choose the Scale Tool to change the boundary of the object in Transform mode. Click and drag a corner of the object away from the center of that object to grow it. Release the mouse button to view the scaled image. If the resized image retains the clarity of the original, it's a vector graphic.

Selecting a Vector Object

The easiest way to select a vector object is with the Pointer Tool. Press the V key to select the Pointer Tool. If you place the cursor over a vector object, its path will turn red, and each of the path points will become visible.

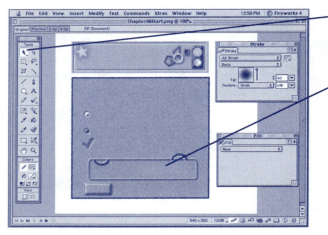

1. Choose the Pointer Tool from the toolbox. Click on an image object to select it.

2. Click and drag an object to move it to a new location in the document window.

TIP

If you need to select an object located on a layer below another object, choose the Select Behind Tool in the Pointer submenu of the toolbox.

Selecting a Vector Path

You can select or edit the lines or points on a vector path by choosing the Subselection Tool from the toolbox. The Subselection Tool looks like the Pointer Tool, except that it's a white cursor instead of a black one.

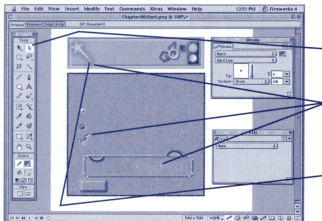

1. Select the Subselection Tool from the toolbox.

2. Click on an object in the document window. Its points will be highlighted in the document window.

3. Click on a point to select it.

Setting an Object's Stroke

When you create an object, you can adjust how the stroke overlaps with the fill area. Click on the Window menu and choose Object, or press Alt/Option + F2 to open the Object panel. The following steps show you how to change the object's stroke settings.

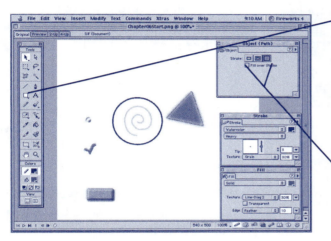

1. Click on a shape or drawing tool in the toolbox, and create an object in the canvas area of the document window.

2. Choose Object from the Window menu to open the Object panel, or press Alt/Option + F2.

3. Click on a Stroke button to determine whether the object stroke is set inside, center, or outside the object's path.

Applying Effects to Objects

You can add an effect from one of seven different groups of effects. You can correct colors, blur an image, or sharpen an image by choosing one of these effects from

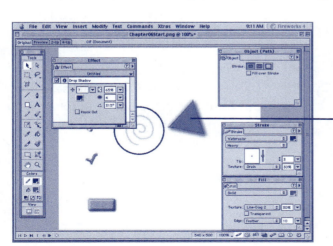

the pop-up menu in the Effect panel. In addition, you can modify an image with a bevel, emboss, shadow, or glow effect. The following steps show you how to add an effect to an object.

1. Click on an object in the document window.

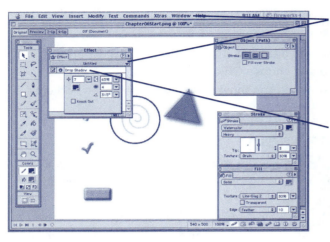

2. Choose Effect from the Window menu or press Alt/Option + F7. Click on the pop-up menu located at the top of the panel to view the list of available effects.

3. Choose an effect to apply to the selected object. The effect will appear in the Effect panel.

Converting Vector Objects to Bitmap Images

You can convert a vector object into a bitmap object by choosing the Convert to Bitmap command. If you're working with fonts and do not want to include the original font with the Fireworks document, you can convert the vector image of the font into a bitmap.

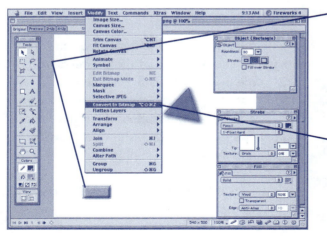

1. Select a vector object in the document window. You should be able to see the paths that make up that object. In this example, I selected the rectangle button object at the bottom of the document window.

2. Click on the Modify menu and choose Convert to Bitmap. The selection box for the selected object will change to four points on each corner of the bitmap object.

NOTE

You can also convert a vector or bitmap object into a graphic, animation, or button symbol. A symbol enables you to create one image object and place it in different layers or frames within the same document, without duplicating the original object. You can view all symbols in the Library panel. Click and drag a symbol to the document window to create an instance, or alias (or shortcut, for you Windows folks), to the symbol.

To create a graphic symbol, choose New Symbol from the Insert menu. Type the name for the graphic symbol, and then select the Graphic radio button in the Symbol Properties window. Click on the OK button and an empty symbol window will appear. Use the drawing tools to create a vector or bitmap object, or copy and paste an object from the document window.

Working with Bitmap Graphics

Bitmap images are made up of a group of pixels instead of being drawn based on a vector algorithm. In addition to adding vector objects in Fireworks, you can add pixel-based, or bitmap, images just as easily. You can import digital pictures or convert vector graphics into bitmaps. The following sections show you how to modify a bitmap object.

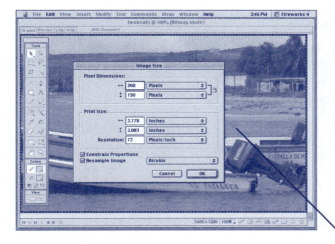

Resizing a Bitmap Image

Choose the Image Size command in the Modify menu to adjust the number of pixels that make up a bitmap image. The Image Size command resizes the entire canvas in the document window. To adjust the size of a specific object, choose the Scale Tool from the toolbox or choose Scale from the Modify, Transform menu.

1. Select a bitmap object in the document window.

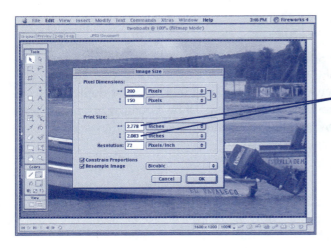

2. Click on the Modify menu and choose Image Size. The Image Size window will appear.

3. Type a different width or height in the appropriate text box.

Applying the Feather Command

The Feather command can be applied to vector or bitmap objects. It enables you to blend the edges of the image object with the canvas or background object. The following steps show you how to apply the Feather command to a bitmap.

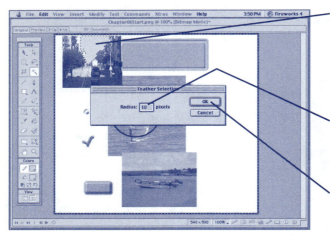

1. Select pixels in the bitmap image with the Marquee or Magic Wand Tool.

2. Choose the Feather command from the Modify, Marquee menu.

3. In the Feather Selection dialog box, type the number of pixels to apply with the Feather command.

4. Click on OK, and view the feathered edges of the selected image.

Using the Marquee Commands on Bitmap Images

Click on the Modify, Marquee menu to view a set of Marquee commands. If you select part of a bitmap image with the Marquee, Lasso, or Magic Wand selection tools, you can modify the way Fireworks interacts with the selected area by choosing one of these commands. The following steps show you how to apply the Inverse Select command. You can use this command to select everything except the selected area in a bitmap image.

1. Choose the Marquee or Magic Wand selection tool from the toolbox.

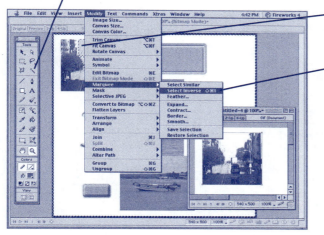

2. Select an area of a bitmap image in the document window.

3. Choose the Modify, Marquee menu and click on Select Inverse. A dotted line will appear in the document window, indicating that the previously selected area has been reversed.

4. Press Ctrl/Command + C or choose Copy from the Edit menu. Create a new document by pressing Ctrl/Command + N, or by choosing New from the File menu. Click on the OK button in the new document dialog box.

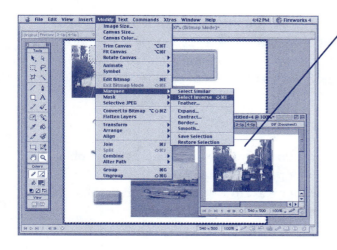

5. Press Ctrl/Command + V or choose Paste from the Edit menu to view the inverse selected image in the document window.

Selecting Colors with the Magic Wand

You can select a specific range of colors with the Magic Wand Tool. You can use the Magic Wand Tool to select a single color or a range of colors. Hold down the Shift key while clicking on a color in a bitmap image to select a range of colors with Magic Wand Tool. Here's how:

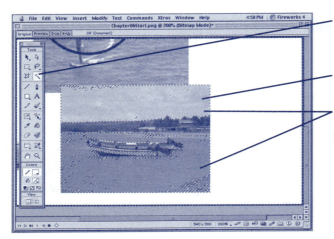

1. Select the Magic Wand Tool from the toolbox.

2. Click on a color in a bitmap image.

3. Hold down the Shift key to select any additional colors in the bitmap.

Combining Text with Image Objects

Text objects can be vector or bitmap objects. When you choose the Text Tool and add text to the document window, that text is created as a text box. You can modify the text as often as you like as long as it's a text block. Once you choose Convert to Bitmap from the Modify menu, you will no longer be able to use the Text Editor window to modify that text object. The text you type in the document window can be sized to fit in a specific area of the canvas. You can also group text with a path object to customize how the text flows in the document window.

Adding Text to a Document

Click on the Text Tool to add text to a document. Text is added as a text object. However, you can convert it to a vector path or bitmap object, too. Use the Text Editor window to type, format, and apply text to a document window. The following steps give you a brief tour of how to add text to a document.

TIP

If you add a single character to document, depending on the character, the object may or may not be a grouped object. Choose the Convert to Paths command from the Text menu, and then choose the Ungroup followed by the Join command from the Modify menu if you want to combine the character or text object with another vector object.

1. Select the Text Tool (T) from the toolbox.

2. Click in the document window. The Text Editor window will appear.

3. Type some text in the Text Editor window.

4. Click on OK to add that text to the document window. When text is selected, a bounding box will surround it.

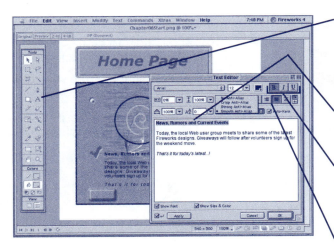

5. Now try adding more text to this document. Select the Text Tool and click in the document window. Type some text in the Text Editor window.

6. Select some of the text in the Text Editor window.

7. Format the text by choosing the Bold, Italic, or Underline buttons in the Text Editor window.

8. Click on the left, center, or right align buttons to change the text's alignment.

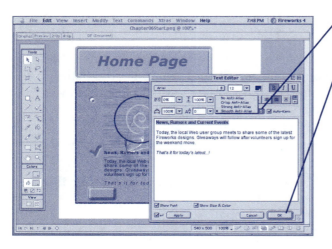

9. Click on the pop-up menu to adjust the anti-alias effect on the font.

10. Click on OK to save your changes and view the text in the document window.

Attaching Text to a Path

To attach text to a path, you can select some text in addition to a path. Then, choose the Attach to Path command from the Text menu to change the flow of the text to match the shape of the selected path. The following steps show you how to use the Attach to Path command.

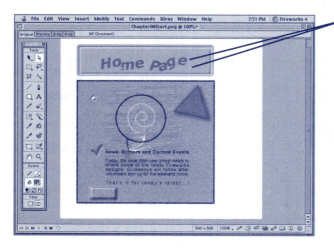

1. Create and select two or more paths in the document window.

2. Choose the Attach to Path command from the Text menu. The text will be grouped along the shape of the selected path.

Creating a Circle of Text

You can attach text to a shape if you want the text to flow along with the outside of that shape. The following steps show you how to use the Attach to Path command to create text shaped around a circle.

1. Create and select two or more paths in the document window.

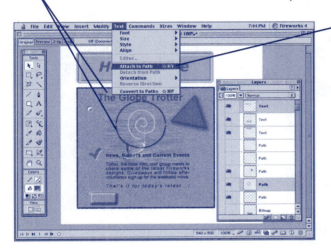

2. Choose the Attach to Path command from the Text menu.

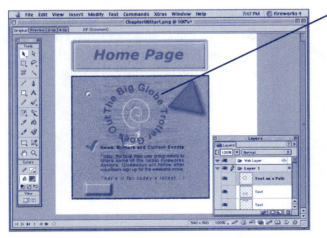

The text will be redrawn along the selected path.

Changing Text to a Path

To change text from an editable bitmap to a vector path, choose Convert to Path from the Text menu. After a text path is modified, you can't convert it back into an editable bitmap. For example, if you perform the following steps, you won't be able to double-click on the text to modify it in the Text Editor window.

1. Click on the Text Tool and type some text in the document window.

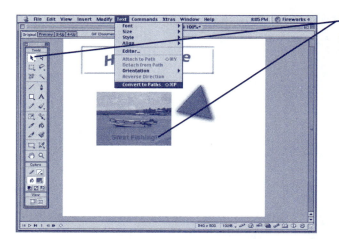

2. Choose the Pointer Tool from the toolbox and select the text object.

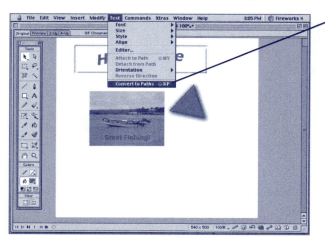

3. Select the Convert to Paths command from the Text menu. The text path will appear in the document window.

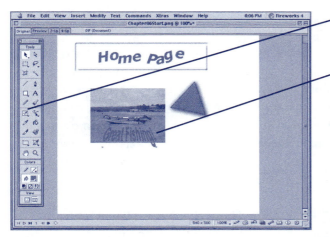

4. Click on the Scale Tool (Q) to transform the text path.

5. View the effect in the document window.

CAUTION

Not all fonts convert to paths with great-looking results. Once you apply the Convert to Paths command to a text object, you will no longer be able to use the Text Editor window to adjust spacing or formatting options. If you don't like the way a font looks after choosing this command, press Ctrl/Command + Z to undo the Convert to Path command.

Working with Layers

Although layers in Fireworks seem similar to layers in Photoshop, they are actually quite different. Each object added or created in Fireworks is created as an object on a layer. What appears to be a layer folder in Fireworks is more accurately an individual layer in the document.

I'm going to use the terms *layer folder* or *layer set* to describe a layer, and I'll refer to a vector, bitmap, or text object as an *object layer*, or *object*. You can group objects together, delete them, and organize them into layers. For example, you might want to place a background image in one layer and button graphics in another layer. Then you can share the background image across all frames (for example, if you're creating an animation) as you design your Web graphics. The following sections give you a brief description of how to create and work with layers.

A Tour of the Layers Panel

A layer is represented by a folder icon in the Layers panel. Keep in mind that if you want to share objects across the same layer as you create new frames, you must be careful about which objects you place in each layer. Each layer determines whether its object contents are shared across frames. For example, you can only double-click on a layer to choose the Share Across Frames option. You can't share a single object across frames; you must share a layer and all visible objects within that layer. Each image object appears as a separate list item in the Layers panel. The following list takes you on a brief tour of the Layers panel.

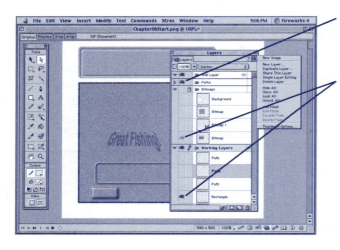

- **Show all layers in layer folder**. Hide any visible objects in a layer by clicking on the eye icon for a layer.

- **Show/hide layer**. Click on the eye icon to make an object or layer visible or invisible in the document window.

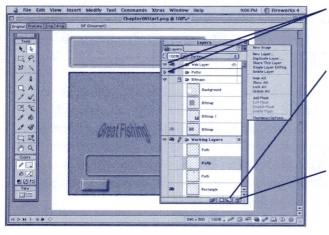

- **Collapse/uncollapse layer folder**. Click on a triangle to show or hide the contents of a layer set.

- **Create a new bitmap**. Click on this button to create a new, empty bitmap object. Select this button if you want to create a bitmap object with the Pencil, Brush, or Rectangle/Shape tools.

- **Delete a layer**. Select an object or layer, then click on the Trash icon to delete it.

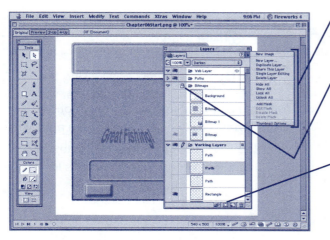

- **Layers menu commands**. Click on the right arrow button to view a list of menu commands for the Layers panel.

- **Edit/lock layer**. Once you've customized an object's settings and location, click in this column to lock the layer in the Layers panel.

- **Layer mask**. Click on an image object and choose the mask button to turn that object into a mask.

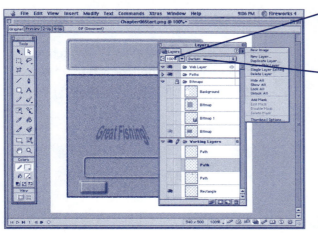

- **Adjust layer opacity**. Select an object or layer and set the transparency or opacity setting using this feature.

- **Layer blending mode menu**. Place one object over another, then choose a blending mode from the pop-up menu to combine the color from the object in the top layer with the color settings of the object below it.

Creating a New Layer

Click on the folder icon located at the bottom of the Layers panel to add a new layer to a document. There are several different ways you can add an object to a document. For example, you can apply a drawing tool, or copy and paste an image into a document to add an object to it. Whenever you create a vector path or object using the drawing or shape tools in the toolbox, a new object is created in the Layers panel. When you copy and paste an object into a document, a new object also is created in the Layers panel. You can also create a new object by importing an image into the document. The following steps show you how to add a vector and bitmap object to a document.

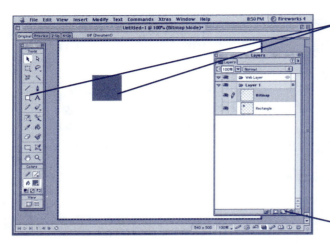

1. Create a shape or draw a path in the document window.

2. Open the Layers panel using the Window menu or the shortcut at the bottom of the document window. A vector path or object will appear in the Layers panel. In this example, the rectangle vector object appears in the Layers panel.

3. Click on the New Bitmap Image icon to create a new bitmap object in the Layers panel.

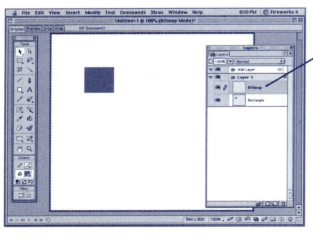

The document window will switch to Bitmap Mode, and a new bitmap object will be highlighted in the Layers panel.

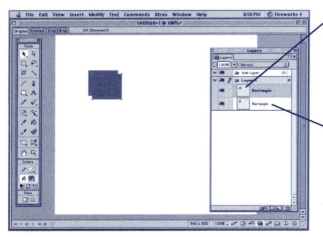

4. Click on an object or layer in the Layers panel. Drag and drop the object or layer over the New Bitmap Image icon located at the bottom of the Layers panel.

A copy of the selected object or layer will be created in the Layers panel.

Organizing Layers in the Layers Panel

Organizing layers and objects is as simple as creating a new layer and moving objects into it. You can hide or show any object, or hide or show all objects in a layer. The following steps show you how to organize objects by creating new layers in the Layers panel.

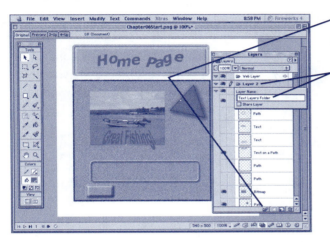

1. Click on the folder icon to create a new layer.

2. Double-click on the layer name, and then type a name for the folder in the resulting text box. Click in the Layers panel to exit the text box window.

3. Select an object in the Layers panel.

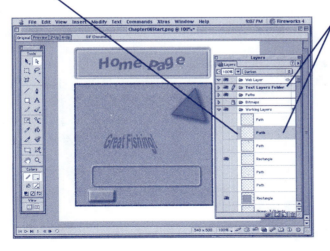

4. Click and drag the selected object and drop it into the layer folder in the Layers panel. The selected image object will appear below the layer folder.

Flattening Layers

If you use Photoshop, the Flatten Layers command might seem familiar to you. Don't be fooled! The Flatten Layers command in Fireworks performs a slightly different task than the command in Photoshop. You can combine objects that reside in different layer folders into a single layer by choosing the Flatten Layers command from the Modify menu. You might want to flatten layers as a first step to reorganizing objects in a document. The following steps show you how.

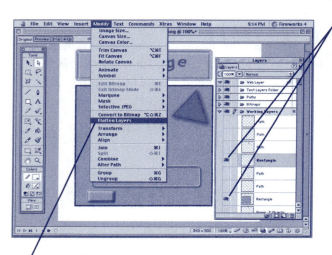

1. Click on one or more eye icons to make any layers or objects you want to flatten visible in the document window.

2. Click on the Modify menu and choose the Flatten Layers command.

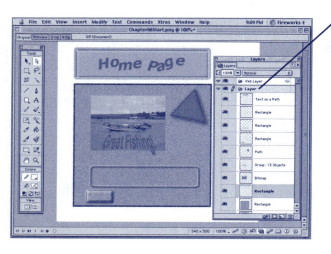

All visible layers and objects are reorganized, or flattened into a single layer in the Layers panel.

Creating Masks in Fireworks

When I first heard the term mask, I thought of a Halloween mask. As it turns out, masks in graphics applications, including Fireworks, work similarly. A mask consists of two objects: a foreground object and a background object. The foreground object, which is used to define the mask, overlaps the background object. The background object can be shown or hidden by the masked area of the foreground object.

Confused? If you've used an application like Photoshop, you might be wondering how the traditional white-masked image compares to the masks in Fireworks. Well, they're different. Color can be used to create part of a mask in Fireworks.

Although traditionally, the color white represents the masked area of an image and black represents the non-masked area, you can choose any color for an object mask. One way to apply a more traditional mask is to create an empty mask. A black empty mask will hide the masked object; an empty white mask will show it. You can also group two or more objects together to create a mask using the Group as Mask command.

Creating a Mask with a Vector Object

You can add a bitmap mask to a vector or bitmap object by selecting an object and then clicking on the mask icon in the Layers panel. A second thumbnail will appear

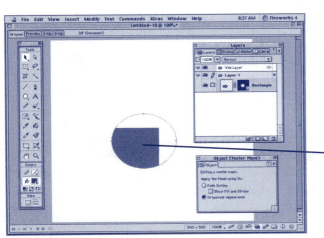

in the selected object layer, and the border of the canvas will show a black-and-yellow striped canvas. You can also create a mask with two vector or bitmap objects. The following steps show you how to create a group mask with two vector objects.

1. Create two vector objects in the document window. Place one object on top of the other. The object in the top layer will become the mask for the object below it.

2. Select the Group as Mask command from the Modify menu.

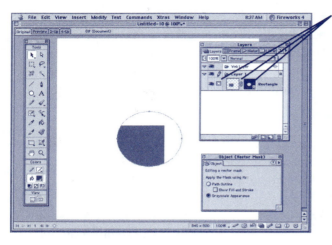

The thumbnail image of the mask will appear in the Layers panel. Notice that the mask thumbnail uses the foreground, or top vector object, and the object thumbnail on the left uses the bottom, or background object. A link icon will appear between the two thumbnail images, indicating that the mask is applied to the object. Also, a mask icon will appear beside the thumbnail image of the object in the Layers panel.

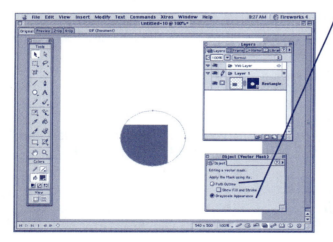

3. Choose Object from the Window menu. Choose the Path Outline or Grayscale Appearance setting for the mask, and click on the Show Fill and Stroke check box to view the fill and stroke settings for the unmasked object.

NOTE

Another way to create a mask is to apply it to a second object using the Paste Inside command from the Edit menu. Create an object and then click on the mask icon in the Layers panel. Create a second object and then select it. Choose the Copy command from the Edit menu, click on the mask object, and then choose the Paste Inside command from the Edit menu. The new object will contain the mask image and the object you copied and pasted into the masked object.

Creating a Mask with a Bitmap Object

If you don't want to combine vector objects to create a mask, you can combine two images, or an image with a vector object or path, to create a custom mask. The following steps show you how to combine a bitmap object with a vector object to create a bitmap mask.

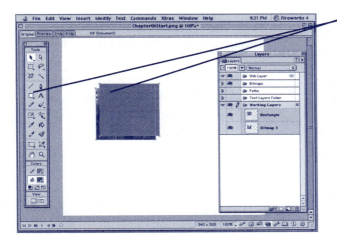

1. Create a vector object and then add a bitmap image to the document window.

2. Select both objects using the Pointer Tool (V).

3. Choose Group As Mask from the Modify menu.

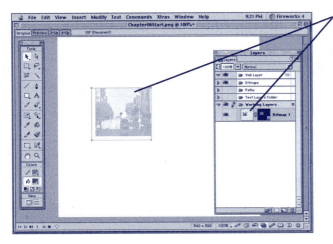

The bitmap mask will be created in the document window and in the Layers panel. The bitmap image will appear through the shape of the vector object placed on the layer above the bitmap object.

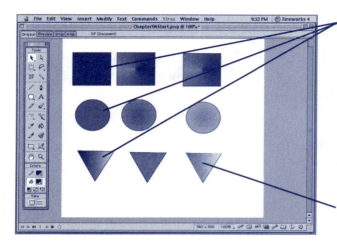

4. Now, create a shape object with a solid fill.

5. Duplicate the first shape. Select a gradient for the second object and place it over the first object.

6. Select both objects, and choose Group as Mask from the Modify menu.

The masked image will display the gradient combined with the fill color from the first object.

NOTE

Another way to create a mask is to apply it to a second object using the Paste as Mask command from the Edit menu. Create two objects, then select the second object and choose the Copy command from the Edit menu. Click on the mask object, and then select the first object. Choose the Paste as Mask command from the Edit menu. The copied object will become the mask for the first object.

TIP

You can change the way a bitmap mask is applied by adjusting its settings in the Object panel. Select a bitmap mask from the document window or Layers panel. Then, choose either an alpha channel or grayscale appearance option for that mask from the Object panel.

Opening a Photoshop Mask

If you'd rather work with a Photoshop mask, you can open a Photoshop PSD file containing a mask in Fireworks. However, because Fireworks does not enable you to view alpha channels, you won't be able to view or select a Photoshop mask.

If you plan to share masks between Photoshop and Fireworks, copy and paste the mask image into its own document and then open it in Fireworks. You can create a new mask out of the Photoshop mask and add it to your library of Web graphics. The following steps show you how to open a Photoshop file containing a channel mask in Fireworks.

1. Choose the Open command from the File menu.

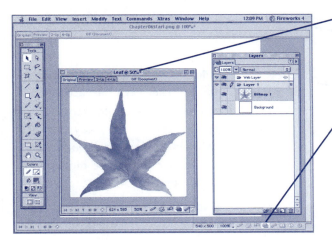

2. Navigate to the hard drive and locate the Photoshop file you want to open. Double-click on the file to open it. The file will open into a new window in Fireworks.

3. Click on the Layers shortcut in the document window.

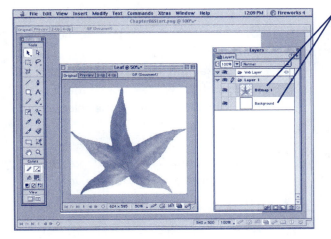

4. View the objects (formerly layers in Photoshop) for the Photoshop document in the Layers panel.

Creating a JPEG Selection Mask

A JPEG selection works a little differently than a vector or bitmap group mask. The JPEG selection mask enables Fireworks to optimize a specific area of a JPEG image. Since most JPEG images are bitmaps, the document will most likely be in Bitmap Mode when you're creating this type of mask. The following steps show you how to create a JPEG selection mask in Bitmap Mode.

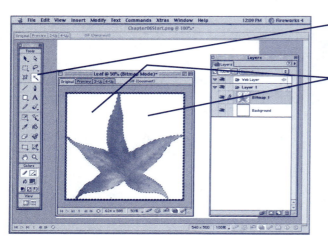

1. Select the Magic Wand Tool (W) from the toolbox.

2. Click in the white area of the image file. When you click on a bitmap object, the document will switch to Bitmap Mode. Hold down the Shift key and click in each white section of the image window. Each section will be highlighted, or selected, as you click in it.

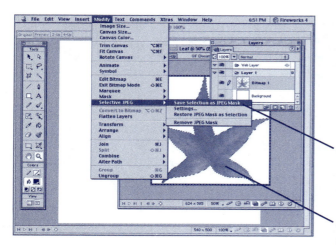

3. Click on the Select Inverse menu command from the Modify, Mask menu. In this example, I want to select the inverse of the white color so that I can make the bitmap image the selective JPEG mask.

4. Choose the Save Selection as JPEG Mask from the Modify, Selective JPEG menu.

5. The masked area will appear with a highlighted color, indicating that the selective JPEG settings will apply to the mask area of that image file.

> **TIP**
>
> Choose the Restore JPEG Mask as Selection command to view the special selected area after you open a file or deselect the marquee area in the document window.

> **NOTE**
>
> If you want to remove a JPEG selection mask, choose Remove JPEG Mask from the Modify, Selective JPEG menu. The JPEG selection must be selected to access this menu command.

Disabling a Mask

After you've created a mask, you can temporarily disable it so that you can edit an individual object or simply view the two objects that define a mask. The following steps show you how to disable a mask and remove the JPEG select area from an image.

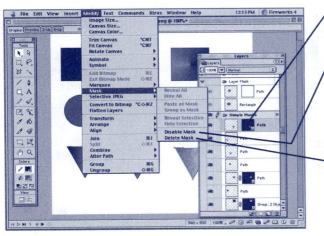

1. Click on a mask thumbnail object in the Layers panel.

2. Choose Disable Mask from the Modify, Mask menu. A red X will appear over the mask thumbnail icon beside the layer icon image in the Layers panel.

3. Choose the Delete Mask command from the Modify, Mask menu to remove a mask from a layer. A dialog box will appear, asking you if you want to delete the mask or apply it to the object.

Choose Apply if you want to permanently change the object in the document by applying the mask to it, or choose the Discard button to only remove the mask from the document. The selected objects will revert to their original, separate layers.

Designing Animation with Frames

Fireworks isn't designed to create a feature-length animation or even an animated short. A typical Web animation can consist of as few as two frames of animation, or as many as several dozen frames. The key to creating a smooth-playing animation for the Web is to keep a low number of frames, so that people visiting your Web site won't have to wait for all the animation files to download to their browsers to view your animation. The following sections show you how to create animation with Fireworks' Live Animation feature, in addition to familiarizing you with the many magical features of the Frames panel.

A Tour of the Frames Panel

Although frames are most conveniently used to create animation, they can also be used to prototype several Web design layouts. The following list highlights all the elements that make up the Frames panel.

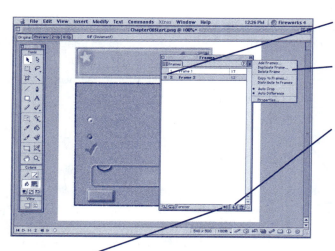

• **Window list**. This list displays all frames for the open document.

• **Panel Options menu**. The Panel Options menu contains all the frames-related menu commands.

• **New/duplicate frame**. Click on this button to create a new frame, or drag another frame over it to create a duplicate of that frame. The copied frame will appear just below the original in the window list.

• **Distribute to frames**. Relocate an object to another frame using this nifty command.

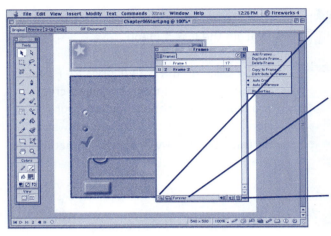

- **Onion skinning setting**. View additional frames in the document window by choosing a menu option from the onion skinning menu.

- **Set looping speed**. Click on the GIF Animation Looping pop-up menu to set the number of times a movie will replay after you click on the Play button.

- **Delete a frame**. Select a frame and then click on the Trash icon to delete the frame from the document.

Working with Frames

Interacting with the Frames panel is somewhat similar to working with the elements in the Layers panel. In fact, if you're using the Frames panel, you'll also probably have the Layers panel open nearby. Each frame is made up of any visible layers in the Layers panel, so you can't really do much with a frame if there aren't any objects or layers in the Layers panel. The following sections walk you through some common tasks performed with the Frames panel.

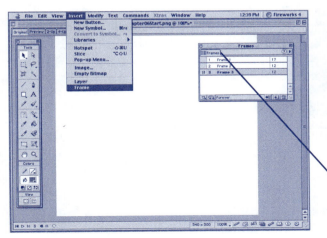

Adding a Frame

Create a key frame of text or a graphic object, then add frames to animate or build interactivity with your Web site. You can create a new, empty frame if there are no layers containing shared objects in the document. Here's how:

1. Choose the Frames tab in the Layers panel, or choose Frames from the Window menu to view the Frames panel.

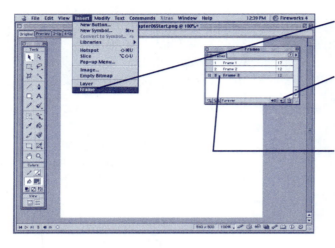

2. Alternatively, you can choose Frame from the Insert menu.

3. Click on the New/Duplicate Frame button on the Frame panels to create a new frame.

The new frame will appear in the Frames panel.

Duplicating a Frame

You can also select a layer and drag it to the New/Duplicate Frame button in the Frames panel to copy the contents of the frame into a new frame. Here's how:

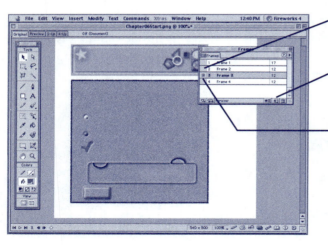

1. Select a frame from the window list in the Frames panel.

2. Click and drag the frame to the new document icon.

A new frame will appear, containing the same data as the original frame.

Sharing Objects across Frames

An efficient way to place objects across frames is to move any objects common to all frames into one layer in the Layers panel. Then, share that layer across all frames. The following steps show you how to share one or more objects across all frames.

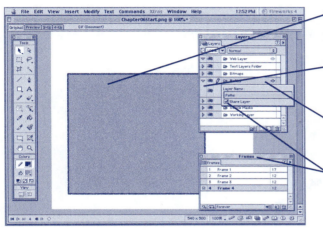

1. Create an object in the document window.

2. Place the object in a layer in the Layers panel.

3. Double-click on the layer to view the layer's name.

4. Check the Share Layer check box. Any objects placed in that layer will be shared across any new or existing frames in that document.

Reordering Frames

You can change the order of the frames viewed in the document window by simply clicking and dragging a frame within the Frames panel. Here's how:

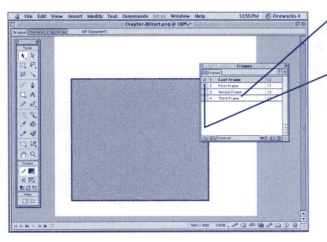

1. Select a frame from the window list in the Frames panel.

2. Drag the selected frame to a new location in the frames list. After you release the mouse button, the selected frame will appear in its new location in the Frames panel.

Adding Objects to a Frame

One way to add objects to frames is to share them. You can also use the Copy and Paste commands to add images to frames. The following steps show you how.

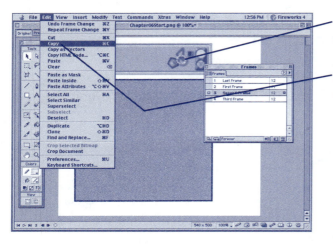

1. Select an object in a frame from the document window.

2. Choose the Copy command from the Edit menu.

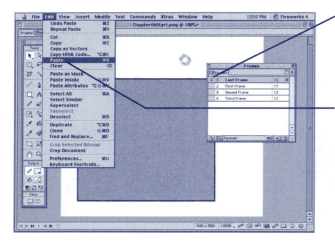

3. Click on the New/Duplicate Frame button in the Frames panel, or choose the Frame command from the Insert menu to create a new Frame.

4. Select the new frame from the Frames panel, then choose the Paste command from the Edit menu. The copied object will appear in the document window of the new frame.

Changing the Loop Setting

You can set the number of times an animation plays back, sort of like a rerun setting. Click on the Loop Setting pop-up menu in the Frames panel to view the different looping options. Here's how:

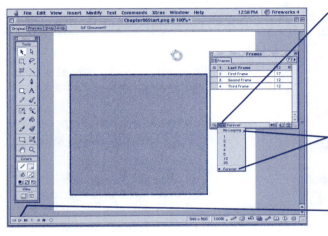

1. Click on the GIF Animation Looping pop-up menu in the Frames panel. A list of commands will appear.

2. Choose from No Looping, 1, 2, 3, 4, 5, 10, 20, and Forever in the Looping menu.

3. If you plan to create an animated GIF file, choose Forever. Otherwise, choose No Looping.

4. Click on the Play button to view the frames in the document window.

Setting Frame Delay

You adjust the timing of each frame in an animation by typing in a new delay value in a frame's properties window. Here's how:

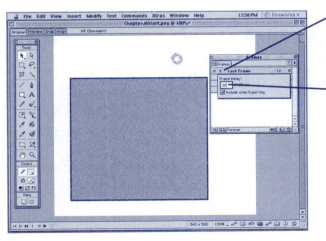

1. Double-click on the right column of a frame in the Frames panel. The Frame Properties window will open.

2. Type a value in the Frame Delay text box. Then, press the Enter/Return key to save your change and exit the Frame Properties window.

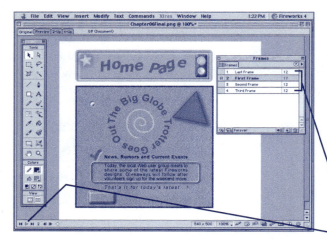

Previewing Frames

Flip through the frames in a document by clicking on the Play button in the Frame Controls. The controls in the document window enable you to preview an animation frame-by-frame or view it in real time. Here's how:

1. Create several frames with at least one image in each frame.

2. Click on the Play button to preview the animation in the document window.

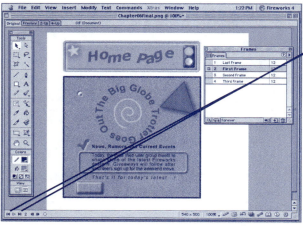

3. Click on the First Frame button to jump to the first frame of the document. Click on the Last Frame button to jump to the last frame in the document.

4. View the current frame number between the Last Frame and Previous Frame buttons.

5. Click on the Previous Frame button to step back to the previous frame.

6. Click on the Next Frame button to step forward to the next frame.

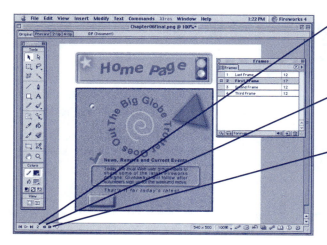

Using the Copy to Frames Command

Don't want to share an object in every single frame? You can copy objects to specific frames by choosing the Copy to Frames command from the panel options menu in the Frames panel. Here's how:

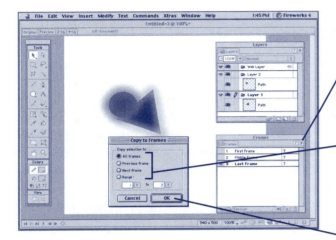

1. Select one or more objects in the document window.

2. Choose the Copy to Frames command from the panel options pop-up menu in the Frames panel.

3. Click on the All Frames, Previous Frame, Next Frame, or Range radio button to select the frames you want to copy.

4. Click on OK to save your changes.

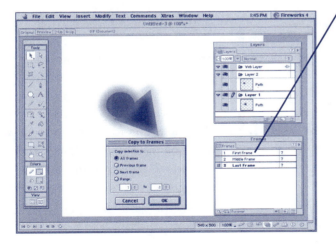

5. Click on a different frame in the Frames panel. The objects in the selected frame will appear in the document window.

Working with Layers and Frames

Now that you've read all about how to use frames, take a look at how you can distribute objects across different frames. You can also find out about a shortcut you can use to copy several frames all at once.

Distributing Objects across Frames

There are a couple of different ways you can add an object to a frame. One way is to manually copy and paste an object into each frame. Alternatively, you can share an object in one layer across all frames. If you want to randomly distribute objects across frames, choose the Distribute to Frames command from the Frames pop-up menu. The following steps show you how to distribute one object across three frames of animation.

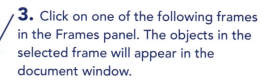

1. Select one or more objects in the document window.

2. Choose the Distribute to Frames command from the Frames panel pop-up menu. If the selected object is not in the next frame, it might disappear from the selected frame and re-appear in the following frame.

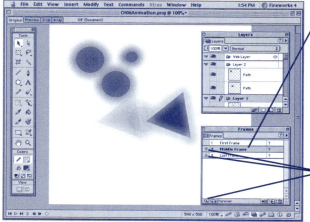

3. Click on one of the following frames in the Frames panel. The objects in the selected frame will appear in the document window.

4. Choose the onion skinning feature to view two or more frames at a time in the Frames panel.

Duplicating Frames and Layers

Hold down the Shift key to select more than one frame in a document. You can duplicate multiple frames in a single click-and-drag step in Fireworks. Here's how:

1. Use the Pointer Tool to select one or more frames from the Frames panel. In this example, three frames are selected.

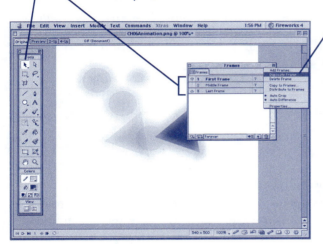

2. Click on the Frames panel pop-up menu and choose the Duplicate Frame command. The new frames will appear in the window list of the Frames panel.

Creating an Animated GIF

If you want to create animation in Fireworks, you will want to use layers and frames to design it. Designing animation is similar to creating a static, nonmoving graphic image, except with one or more frames containing many of the same objects, but with some of those objects moved to new locations on the canvas.

The following sections explain how to create a simple animation. The most commonly used file format for animation on the Web is an animated GIF.

Creating the First Frame

You have to start somewhere. Each Fireworks document contains a single frame, so thank the folks at Macromedia for creating your first frame of animation. The following steps show you how to add objects to the first frame of your animation.

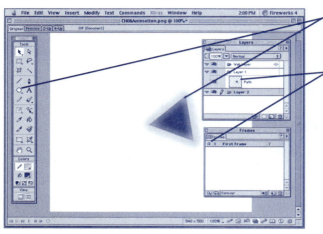

1. Create an object in the document window.

The object will appear in the Layers panel in the first frame of the document.

2. Choose a drawing tool and create additional objects, or import or open an image and copy and paste it into the document.

Making the Final Frame

Create or duplicate the first frame in the document to add the last frame of the animation. I'm assuming that the objects in the first frame of my animation will also be in the last frame. The following steps show you how to create the final frame of this simple animation.

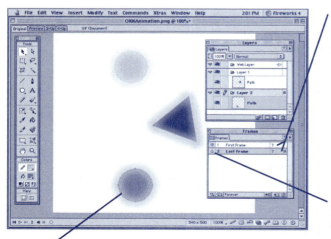

1. Create two or more frames with at least one image in each frame. This example contains two frames.

2. Select the last frame of the animation from the Frames panel.

3. Copy new objects to the document window to create the last frame of the animation. Alternatively, you can copy and paste images from the first frame of the document to create objects in the last frame.

Previewing an Animated GIF

View the animation in the document window. As you view it, decide whether you want to add, move, or remove any of the objects in the animation. The following steps show you how to preview your animation.

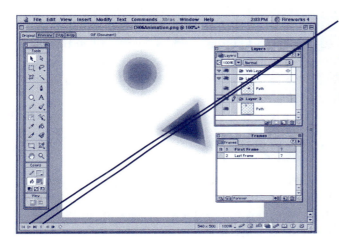

1. Click on the Play button in the Frame Controls. The frame number will change in the lower-left corner of the document window as each frame changes in the document window.

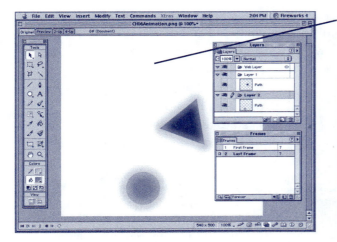

2. View the animation in the document window.

NOTE

To save the file as an animated GIF, choose animated GIF from the left pop-up menu in the Optimize panel. Then, export the file as an animated GIF. Drag and drop the exported file into a browser window to view it.

Creating Live Animation

You can create an animation in Fireworks in many different ways. You can create an animation from an animation or graphic symbol, or from a vector or bitmap object. Then you can put each frame together by hand, copy and paste frames of animation from other applications, or simply open an animated GIF file. The folks at Macromedia added an Animate window so that you can view several animation settings for one or more selected objects in a single window. Simply fill in the settings you want to use and Fireworks will generate the contents for each frame of animation, including the frames. The following sections show you how to use the built-in Animation Wizard to create a simple animation.

Defining Animation Settings

First, take a quick look at the basic steps you'll need to follow to create an animation object, or, in this example, an animation instance. One of the magical features of the Animate Selection command is that is automatically converts a vector or bitmap object into an instance of a symbol.

If this is the first time you've heard of an instance or a symbol, symbols are stored in the Library panel. You can simply drag a symbol to add an image object, called an instance, to a document window. Using symbols to design animation reduces the overall file size of the animation, and can optimize playback performance of

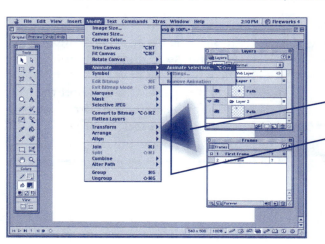

the animation, too. The following steps provide a brief overview of what you need to do to invoke the Animate window and get familiar with its settings.

1. Click on any text or image object.

2. Choose the Animate Selection command from the Modify, Animate menu to open the Animate window.

3. View all the animation settings available to you in the Animate window.

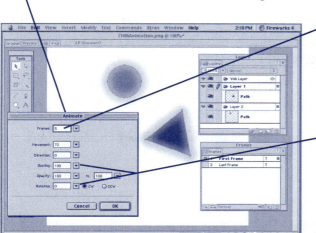

4. Set the number of frames. Type a number into the Frames text box, or click and drag the slider control beside the Frames text box to define the number of frames in the animation.

5. Scale and rotate the object by typing a number into the respective text boxes. Click on the OK button to generate the frames of your animation. When you first create an animation with the Animate Selection command, a dialog box will appear when you click on the OK button to create the frames for the animation. It will ask you if you want Fireworks to automatically create new frames for the animation. Click on the OK button.

NOTE

You can also create an animation instance by choosing New Symbol from the Insert menu. Type the name for the animation symbol, and then select the Animation radio button in the Symbol Properties window. Click on the OK button and an empty symbol window will appear. Use the drawing tools to create the first frame of the animation symbol, or copy and paste an object from the document window.

TIP

Access the Frames, Scaling, Opacity, and Rotation text boxes, as well as the Transform commands, from the Object panel, in addition to the Animate window.

Editing Animation Settings

Don't expect your first crack at animation to produce a polished-looking classic. It's okay to experiment with your animation. The following sections show you how to modify a variety of animation settings.

Opening the Animate Window

You can open the Animate dialog box after you create an animation. Here's how:

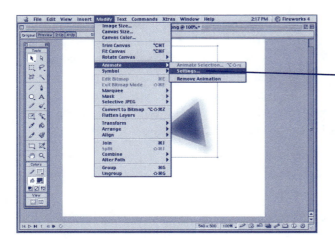

1. Open a document containing an animation. Select an animation instance.

2. Click on the Modify menu, choose Animate, and then select the Settings menu command. The Animate dialog box will open.

Modifying Animation Settings

When you select an animation instance, the selected object displays a small amount of visual information about that animation. For example, the light blue line extending from animation represents the directional flow of the animation. Each dot on the line represents a frame of animation. This visual information can help you determine whether you want to modify an animation symbol. Whenever you open the Animate dialog box, it's an open invitation to change any setting you want. The following steps show you how to adjust the settings in the Animate dialog box.

1. Select an animation instance, and then choose Settings from the Modify, Animate menu.

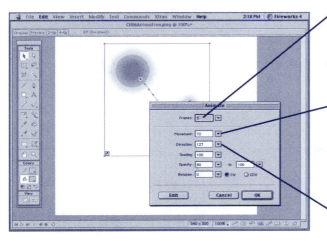

2. Type a different number in the Frames text box. You can enter a maximum number of 250. However the default value, shown in this example, is 5.

3. Adjust the distance (in pixels) the object moves across frames by increasing or decreasing the value of the movement number in the Movement text box. Choose a value between 0 and 250.

4. Set the direction (in degrees) of the image object by typing a new value between 0 and 100 in the Direction text box.

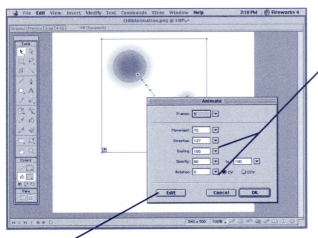

5. Change the Scaling, Opacity, or Rotation settings by typing a new value in the respective text box. If you change the Scaling setting in the last frame of the animation, you can create a zoom effect with the animation. Similarly, if you choose a lower opacity setting for the first or last frame of the animation, you can create a fade in or fade out effect. Type a number in the Rotation text box to define the angle of rotation, and then choose either a clockwise (CW) or counter-clockwise (CCW) direction for the rotation. The rotation will begin at the first frame of the animation and end on the last frame.

6. Click on the Edit button to edit the selected animation.

> **TIP**
>
> Click on an animation instance to select it. If the animation contains more than one frame of animation, you'll see a light blue line extending from it. Each dot represents a frame in that animation instance. Click on a dot to skip to a particular frame in the animation.

Creating an Animation with Symbols

One way to slim down the file size of an animation is to convert a vector object into a symbol. The following steps show you how.

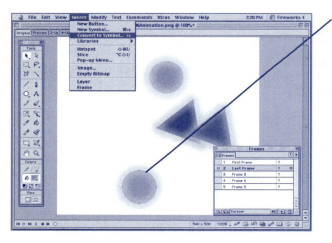

1. Create a vector object using the Rectangle/Shape Tool or a drawing tool from the toolbox.

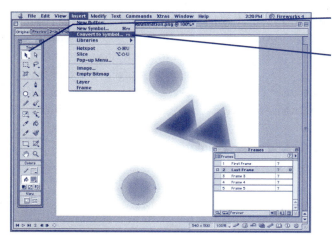

2. Select the object.

3. Choose Convert to Symbol from the Insert menu. The Symbol Properties dialog box will open.

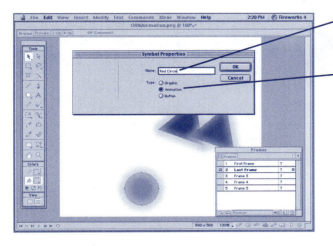

4. Type a name for the symbol in the Name text box.

5. Click on the Animation radio button.

6. Click on the OK button to save your changes. The Animate dialog box will appear.

7. Type your settings for the animation and then click on the OK button in the Animate dialog box.

8. A small arrow icon will appear in the lower-left corner of the animation instance when it is selected. The arrow icon indicates that the object is a graphic, animation, or button symbol, not a vector object.

Editing an Animation Symbol

You can use individual vector or bitmap objects to create animation. Another way of creating an animation is with symbol animation. You can edit the contents of a symbol animation after you've created it. First, double-click on a symbol object to open its Symbol window, where you can apply tools and menu commands to the selected symbol object. The following steps show you how to apply a fill color and a transform tool to a symbol object.

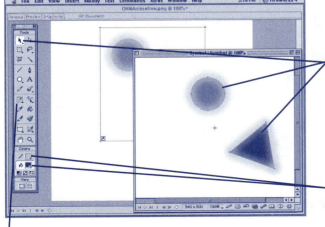

1. Use the Pointer Tool (V) to select a symbol in its Symbol window.

2. Choose a new fill or stroke setting for the symbol.

3. Use a Scale, Distort, or Skew tool to exaggerate an animation.

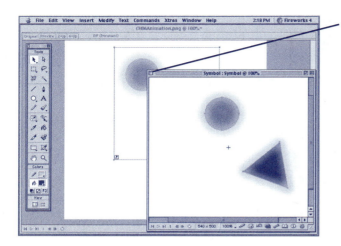

4. Click in the Close box of the symbol window to save your changes.

Using the Remove Animation Command

You can delete an animation instance by selecting it and pressing the Backspace/Delete key. Its symbol will still remain in the Library panel, enabling you to add it back to the document if you want. If you created an animation instance using the Animate Selection menu command in the Modify, Animate menu, you can remove the animation settings from an object. The following steps show you how to use the Remove Animation menu command.

1. Click on the animation instance in the document window.

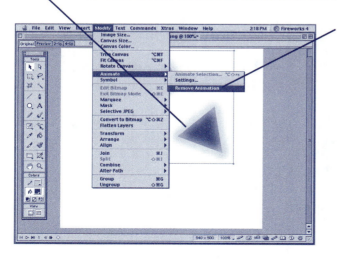

2. Choose Remove Animation from the Modify, Animate menu.

Adding In-Between Frames

Fireworks can generate in-between instances within a frame. In-between images are only placed between the two main instances; they are not redrawn in the traditional sense of an in-between image in animation. The following steps show you how to create in-between frames between two symbols.

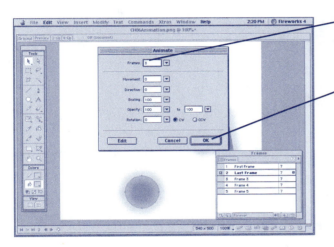

1. Create an animation instance. In this example, I've created an object that contains three frames of animation.

2. Click on the OK button to save your changes to the Animate dialog box.

3. Select a frame from the Frames panel.

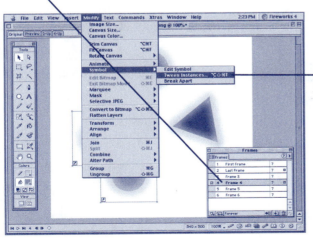

4. Click on an animation instance in the document window.

5. Choose Tween Instances from the Modify, Symbol menu.

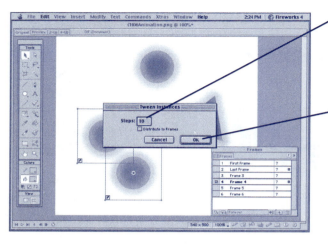

6. Type a number in the Steps text box in the Tween Instances dialog box to set the number of in-between frames for the selected symbols.

7. Click on the OK button to save your changes and generate the in-between frames.

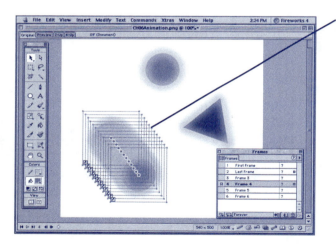

The in-between frames will appear in the document window.

6

Opening and Editing Files

Fireworks enables you to open or import files created with Adobe Photoshop, Adobe Illustrator, or Macromedia's FreeHand or Flash. You can use the Open command to create a new window for the file you want to open. Or, you can choose the Import command if you want to open the selected file into an active document window. Use the Open or Import commands to add image objects to any Fireworks document.

In this chapter you'll learn how to:

- Open images from a digital camera
- Open GIF, JPEG, animated GIF, and other files
- Open a Photoshop PSD file in Fireworks
- Work with Photoshop layers and masks in Fireworks

If you're using Fireworks to create Web graphics, you'll probably be doing two things with the Fireworks document. First, you'll be saving it as a native Fireworks file (a PNG file), and exporting it as a GIF or JPEG Web graphic file. Saving the PNG file enables you to continue to edit layers and frames in a document. If you choose the Save command from the File menu, you'll discover you can only save PNG files in Fireworks. Choose the Save command to preserve all the stroke, fill, layer, frame, and object settings in a Fireworks file. When you export an image, most of this information will be removed from the exported file. Although you can preview and edit a GIF or JPEG file in Fireworks, PNG files offer you full editing access to frames, layers, and objects.

After you save a Fireworks file as a PNG file, you will probably export it as a GIF, JPEG, or animated GIF. You can export an object, image, or document in a particular file format so that you can post the image file or files to a Web server. You can export an image in a variety of file formats, including GIF or JPEG. For more information about exporting files, see Chapter 17, "Exporting Fireworks Files." After a file is exported, you can open it with Fireworks.

Importing Images from a Digital Camera

Digital cameras commonly are used to quickly capture images destined to be published on a Web page. If you have a camera, check to see if it came bundled with a CD-ROM containing software for your Windows or Macintosh computer. Some cameras include a CD containing a Twain plug-in, also known as a Photoshop-compatible plug-in file. This software enables you to control a camera and download its images directly into Fireworks. The following sections show you how to use the Scan menu commands to bring digital bitmap images into Fireworks.

Selecting a Source File

You can put almost any picture on a Web page. The tough part is getting the picture into your computer. After you install the Mac or Windows software for your camera, check to see if you can access a Twain plug-in from within Fireworks. Many scanners also come bundled with a Twain plug-in file, so if want to scan images into Fireworks, look to see if your scanner comes bundled with this type of software.

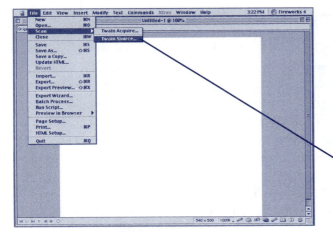

If your camera or scanner can interact with Fireworks, you will be able to view, download, and resize pictures from your digital camera, or scan an image into a Fireworks document. The following steps show you how to select a Twain plug-in from the Fireworks File menu.

1. Choose Scan from the File menu, and then choose Twain Source. A dialog box titled Select a Source will appear.

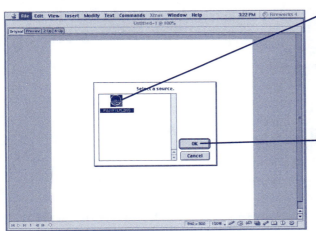

2. Click on the Twain file for the camera with which you want to work. In this example, I've selected the FUJIFILM_DSS file so that I can download images from my Fuji MX 2700 2 megapixel digital camera.

3. Click on the OK button to save the selected source information.

NOTE

After a bitmap file is imported or opened in Fireworks 4, you will probably need to resize or edit it. Click on the Stop button (the red circle with a white X in the middle) in the document window to switch the image out of Bitmap Mode so that you can resize or edit the image object.

Connecting the Computer to the Camera

Before you download digital pictures to your computer, put a fresh set of batteries into your camera, or recharge them. Connect the cable, which should have been included with your camera, to your computer and your camera. Some cameras also require you to choose Download or Computer mode in order to communicate with a computer. Power on the camera and then perform the following steps to begin downloading images from a digital camera to your computer. The next two sections provide additional steps to show you how to get those pictures on your hard disk.

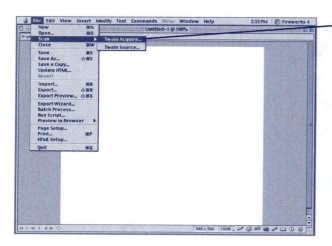

1. Choose Scan from the File menu, and then choose Twain Acquire. The filter you selected in the Twain Source window will be accessed when you choose the Twain Acquire command.

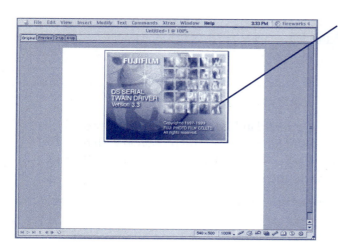

2. If the plug-in software successfully communicates with Fireworks, a splash or Welcome screen will appear.

3. Wait for the computer to successfully connect to the camera.

Viewing Images in Fireworks

After you select Twain Acquire from the File, Scan menu, you should be able to view the images stored on the digital camera in Fireworks. The camera images will appear as thumbnail-sized buttons in a window within Fireworks. The following steps show you how to view digital images in Fireworks.

1. Any images on the digital camera will appear in a window created by the camera's plug-in software. Click on a thumbnail image in the camera window to select it.

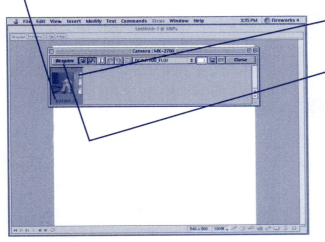

2. Double-click on a thumbnail image if you want to view it at full size.

3. Click on the Acquire button if you want to copy the file from the camera to your computer.

NOTE

JPEG image files are the standard file format used by digital cameras. Several types of JPEG compression offer high- to low-quality images. You can use Fireworks to download JPEG images from a camera, then adjust the compression level in a JPEG image to create great-looking images that are stored in a relatively small file size.

Downloading Images to the Computer

Downloading an image from a camera to a computer can take a few seconds, if not longer. That's why you should recharge the camera's batteries, or put in a new set of batteries, before performing this operation.

A faster way of bringing digital pictures into your computer is to remove the Compact Flash, Smart Media, Sony Memory Stick, or IBM Micro Drive from the camera and insert it into a media card reader. If you have a laptop, insert the media card into a PC card adapter. The following steps continue the steps from the previous sections and show you the final steps for downloading an image to your computer.

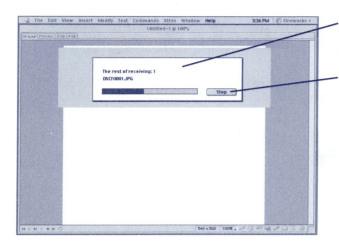

1. Wait for the image to download to your computer.

2. Click on the Stop button if you want to cancel the download.

3. When the download completes, the image will appear in its own window in Fireworks.

Saving an Image

After a file has successfully downloaded to your computer, you can view and edit it in a Fireworks document window. Before you make any changes to the picture, save a copy of the original. Here's how:

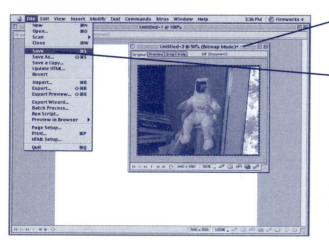

1. Click on the window containing the image you want to save.

2. Choose the Save command from the File menu.

3. Pick a folder or other location where you want to save the file on your hard drive. Then, type a name for the image file and click on the Save button. The file will be saved as a native Fireworks file, which is an enhanced version of the PNG file format.

Opening Files with Fireworks

You can open any file you save or export from Fireworks. You can also open GIF, JPEG, animated GIF, or PNG files created by other applications, such as Macromedia Flash or Adobe Photoshop, in Fireworks. Supported file formats include PNG, GIF, JPEG, and animated GIF files, as well as line art created in Macromedia FreeHand or Adobe Illustrator. The following sections show you how to open a native Fireworks file, as well as a GIF, JPEG, animated GIF, Adobe Illustrator and EPS file with Fireworks.

Opening Native Fireworks Files

In the previous section you created a Fireworks file by opening a new document and downloading a digital image into it. Now, quickly review the steps to open it. If you already know how to do this, skip ahead to the next section. The following steps show you how to open a Fireworks PNG file.

1. Choose Open from the File menu.

2. Select a file from the Open dialog box. In this example, I chose the final tutorial file that Macromedia installs in the Tutorials folder of the Fireworks folder. Fireworks files display the Fireworks application logo and usually have file names that end with .png.

3. Click on Open, or double-click on the file name to open the file.

4. The Fireworks file will open in a new window in the Fireworks workspace.

TIP
Open a copy of a file without changing the original version by first selecting a file in the Open File dialog box, then checking the Open as "Untitled" check box.

Viewing a Fireworks File

A Fireworks file can contain bitmap, vector, or text objects. These are the simple files; they're easy to edit and easy to figure out. Open the Object, Stroke, Fill, Layer, and Optimize panels, and you can get a pretty good idea how that file was created and how you can edit it. Fireworks files can also contain frames and masks, in addition to Web layout elements, rollover behaviors, and other Web object elements. These Web-related features are covered in Part III, "Designing Interactive Web Graphics." The following steps show you how to view the layers and frames in a Fireworks document.

1. Choose Frames from the Window menu.

2. View the Frames panel in the workspace.

3. Click on the Frame Controls in the document window to view each frame of animation.

4. Click on the Window menu and choose Layers, or click on the Layers shortcut at the bottom of the document window. The Layers panel will open in the workspace.

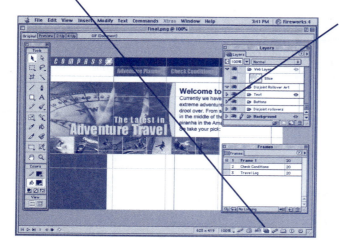

5. Click on a triangle to view the contents of a layer set.

Opening GIF and JPEG Files

The two most common kinds of graphics files used with Web pages are GIF and JPEG files. You can create and export GIF and JPEG files in Fireworks. Even if you didn't create them with Fireworks, you can open and view them. Here's how:

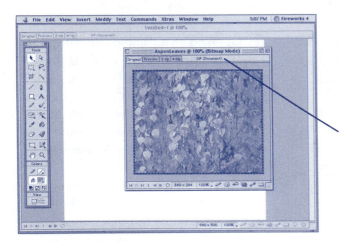

1. Click on the File menu and choose the Open command. Navigate your hard drive and locate the GIF file you want to open. Click on a file's icon and then click on the Open button.

The GIF file will open into its own window in Fireworks.

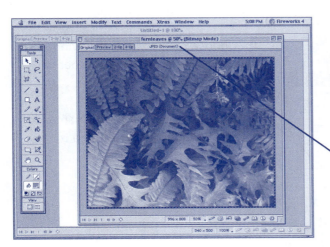

2. Opening a JPEG file is similar to opening a GIF file. Choose Open from the File menu, or press Ctrl/Command + O. Navigate your hard drive from the Open File window and double-click on a file to open it.

The JPEG file will open in Fireworks.

NOTE

If an image is too large to be viewed on your computer's desktop, Fireworks will scale the image to a lower magnification so that you can view the entire image in the document window.

Opening Animated GIF Files

An animated GIF is a single file that stores two or more frames of images. If you drag and drop an animated GIF into a browser window, you'll see animation play back, although you might only expect to see a static graphic image. The following steps show you how to open and view an animated GIF file in Fireworks.

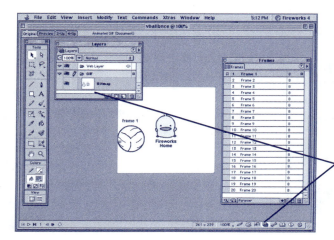

1. Opening an animated GIF file is similar to opening a GIF or JPEG file. Choose Open from the File menu, or press Ctrl/Command + O. Navigate your hard drive from the Open File window and double-click on a file to open it. The animated GIF will open in a new window.

2. Click on the Layers icon in mini-launcher located at the bottom of the document window to open the Layers panel. View the layers for each frame of the animated GIF file.

3. Choose Frames from the Window menu, or press Shift + F2 to open the Frames panel.

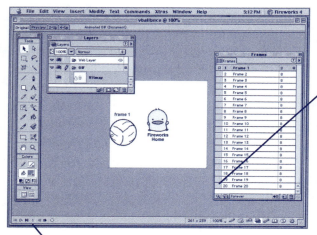

4. View the total number of frames for the animation. Click on a frame to view its contents.

5. Click on the Frame Controls to navigate to the previous or next frame of animation in the file.

TIP

You can select multiple files located in the same folder and open them as an animation in Fireworks. Choose the Open command from the File menu and navigate to a folder containing the image files. Hold down the Shift key and click on the files you want to include in the animation. Here's the important step: Check the Open as Animation check box. Then, click on the Open button. Fireworks will open a new file, placing each image into a separate frame.

Opening and Importing Line Art

If you design line art with Adobe Illustrator, Macromedia FreeHand, or Flash 5, you can save or export line art from these applications as an Adobe Illustrator (AI) or Encapsulated PostScript (EPS) file and open it in Fireworks. If you open an EPS file, it will open as a bitmap image. Opening an Illustrator file opens the entire file as a grouped object. Choose the Ungroup command to view or edit each vector object in Fireworks.

Importing a file containing line art is similar to opening a file containing line art. Choosing the Import command brings the contents of the file into the active document, while selecting the Open command creates a new window for the file. The following sections show you how to open an EPS and Adobe Illustrator file in Fireworks.

Opening an EPS File

If you design line art with FreeHand or Flash, you can save the line art as an EPS file and then open and edit it in Fireworks. An EPS file is an Encapsulated PostScript file. This file format was created by Adobe, a software publisher also known for creating PostScript technology. Fireworks tries to open EPS files as vector images first. If it can't, the EPS file is opened as a flattened bitmap image. The following steps show you how to open an EPS file in Fireworks.

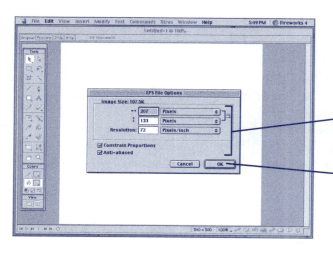

1. Choose Open or Import from the File menu. Navigate the hard drive and locate a file ending with .eps. In this example, I've selected SampleFile.eps.

2. Adjust any of the File Option settings, if necessary.

3. Click on the OK button to open the file.

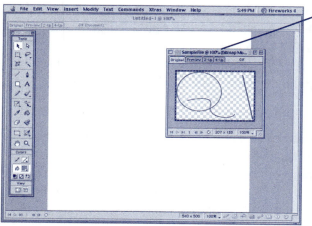

The EPS file will open in Fireworks.

Opening an Adobe Illustrator File

You can also open line art saved as an Illustrator file in Fireworks. When you open an Adobe Illustrator (AI) or FreeHand (FH8) file, you can choose from several different conversion settings, and then view or edit each vector object in Fireworks. Each vector object is accessible from the document window and the Layers panel when you open a FreeHand file. By default, Illustrator files open as a grouped object in Fireworks. If you want to edit each object, you must select the group object, then choose the Ungroup command from the Modify menu. The following steps show you how to open an Illustrator file in Fireworks.

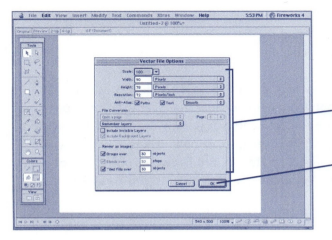

1. Choose the Open or Import command from the File menu. Navigate the hard drive and locate a file ending with .ai to open an Adobe Illustrator file.

2. Adjust any of the File Option settings, if necessary.

3. Click on the OK button to open the file.

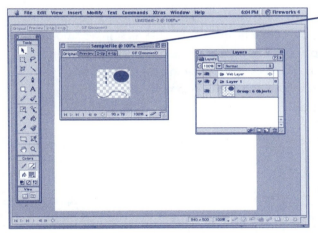

The Illustrator file will open in Fireworks.

Opening and Importing Photoshop Files

Although most Web graphics are saved as GIF, JPEG, or PNG files, many designers use Adobe Photoshop to create and edit images, too. Photoshop enables designers to create complex vector and bitmap images comprised of masks, channels, and layers for print media as well as for Web graphics. Fireworks can also open PSD files created by ImageReady.

If you are using Photoshop to create Web graphics, an image file might contain layers and masks, which you might also want to edit in Fireworks. To do this, you must save that file as a native Photoshop file, which uses the PSD (Photoshop Document) file format. Fireworks 4 enables you to import native Photoshop (PSD) files, preserving layers, masks, and channel information.

Importing a Photoshop file into Fireworks is similar to opening a Photoshop file in Fireworks. The main difference between these commands is that the Open command creates a new window and the Import command brings each layer of the file into the active document as a bitmap object. Choose either command, and Fireworks will automatically convert Photoshop layers and masks into Fireworks objects. The following sections show you how to open a Photoshop (PSD) file in Fireworks.

Opening PSD Files

Native Photoshop files are saved with a file name ending with the .psd extension. A Photoshop image file can contain a single layer or sets of layers, in addition to masks. You can open a Photoshop file in Fireworks to use an image or bitmap graphic along with your other Web graphics. The following steps show you how to open a native Photoshop file. The file used in this example was created in Photoshop 6 and contains several layers of images.

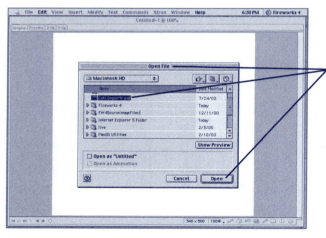

1. Click on the File menu and choose Open.

2. In the Open File dialog box, navigate to the document you want to open. Double-click on the document's icon to open it, or click once on the file's icon and then click on the Open button.

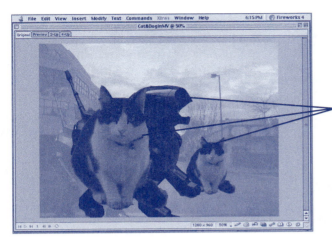

The Photoshop file will open in Fireworks. Fireworks will automatically arrange any layers or masks when it opens a Photoshop file.

All images in all layers are made visible in the document window when a Photoshop file is opened in Fireworks.

NOTE

If the Photoshop file contains large image files, like the one used in this example, it might take a minute or two for Fireworks to open it. Be sure to have plenty of memory and disk space available if you plan to edit the bitmap images or add more images to this file.

Viewing Photoshop Layers in Fireworks

Masks and layers stored in a Photoshop file are converted into objects in the Layers panel in Fireworks. You can click on the Layers shortcut icon located at the bottom of the document window to open the Layers panel. Fireworks removes any layer sets from the PSD file and opens all layers into one layer set in the Fireworks document. The following steps provide a brief tour of the layers of a Photoshop file open in Fireworks.

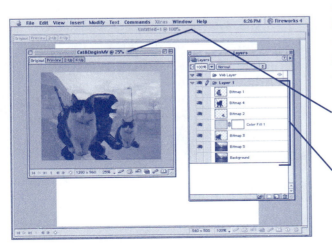

1. Click on the window containing the Photoshop file.

The layers for the Photoshop file will appear in the Layers panel.

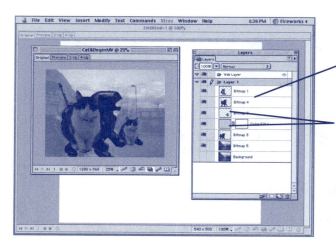

NOTE

Layer names in the Photoshop file are converted to generic names.

Adjustment layers and transparencies in layers are preserved in the Fireworks document, but are now image objects accessible in the document window or the Layers panel.

NOTE

You might also notice a slight change in colors after opening the Photoshop file in Fireworks. To reduce color fluctuation, try embedding the RGB color management information (look for a check box in the Save File dialog box) in the Photoshop file when you save it in Photoshop.

Reorganizing Photoshop Layers

You can reorganize layers in a Photoshop file just as you would reorganize layers in a Fireworks file. Click on the folder icon in the Layers panel to create a new layer, and then click and drag each layer into the layer set folder to group images together. However, don't forget that in Fireworks, objects in a shared layer folder will automatically appear across frames. The following steps show you how to organize layers in a Photoshop file opened in Fireworks.

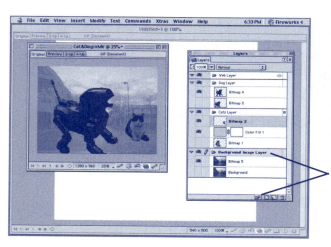

1. Click on the new folder icon to create a new Layer folder.

2. Select an image layer and drag it to the new layer folder. You can only drag one layer at a time to a new location, even though Fireworks lets you Shift-select multiple layers at a time.

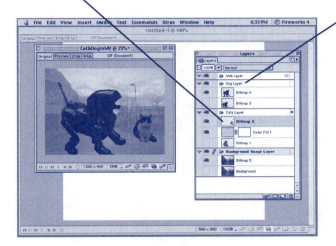

3. Double-click on the name of a layer to rename it. Type a new name and then press the Enter/Return key.

Editing Photoshop Layers

You can rotate, scale, distort, skew, flip, or apply one of the bitmap editing tools to any bitmap object in a Photoshop layer. The following steps show you how to scale an image created in Photoshop with Fireworks.

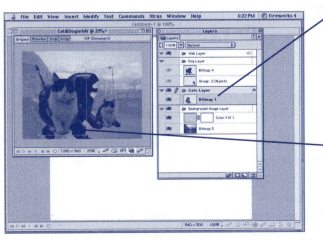

1. Click on a layer in the Layers panel to select the image object.

2. Alternatively, you can click on the frontmost object in the document window. A light-blue border will surround the object, indicating that it is selected.

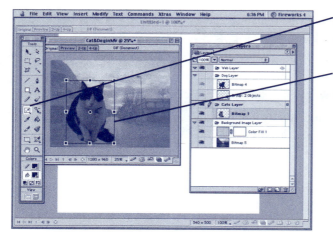

3. Click on the Scale Tool (Q) in the toolbox.

4. A bounding box will appear around the selected object.

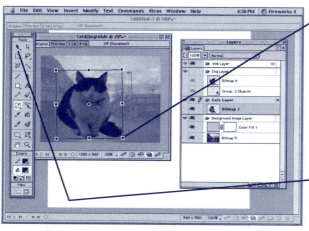

5. Click and drag a corner handle and pull the bounding box outward to enlarge the image. Drag the bounding box inward to shrink the image.

6. Click and drag the handle on the top of the object to grow the image vertically but not horizontally.

7. Click on a selection tool to complete the Scale command.

Grouping Photoshop and Fireworks Layers

You can select two layers and group them together into a single layer in the Layers panel. You can apply the Group command from the Modify menu to retain the proximity information between two or more objects. If you want to separate grouped objects, choose the Ungroup (Shift + Ctrl/Command + G) command from the Modify menu. The following steps show you how to apply the Group command.

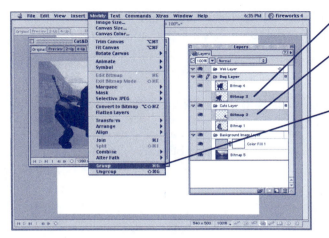

1. Select a layer in the Layers panel.

2. Hold down the Shift key and select a second layer.

3. Choose the Group command (Ctrl/Command + G) from the Modify menu.

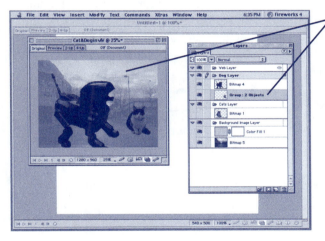

The two layers will be renamed as one layer in the Layers panel, and the bounding box for the two objects will resize into a larger bounding box for one object in the document window.

Opening and Importing Masks

A mask enables you to create an image where the viewable image is editable, and the pixels around it are protected, or uneditable. Think of a mask as a digital stencil. Instead of using a stencil, you can choose a selection tool to cookie-cut part of an image and move it to its own file, or add it to another image file.

Fireworks enables you to create a mask out of a single vector or bitmap object, or by grouping overlapping objects. You can also open Photoshop files that contain masks in Fireworks. However, Fireworks cannot distinguish between a quick mask, channel mask, or layer mask. If you plan to work with masked images using

Photoshop and Fireworks, you should save each masked image as a separate PSD file. The following sections show you how to open, view, and edit masks in Photoshop and Fireworks.

Viewing a Photoshop Mask in Fireworks

When you open a Photoshop image file in Fireworks, such as a GIF or JPEG file, the background color from that file is opened as a separate object from the image object. For example, when I opened the image used in this example, a background object opened along with the bitmap object. You'll see this same behavior if you open a Photoshop file containing a mask. Because Fireworks does not enable you to view a

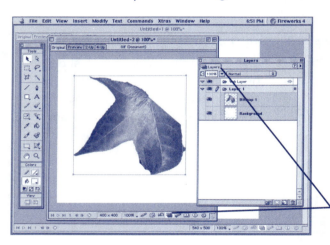

document's channel information, an image mask appears simply as bitmap object in Fireworks. The following steps show you how to open, view, and select a Photoshop mask in Fireworks.

1. Choose Open (Ctrl/Command + O) from the File menu. Navigate the hard drive and open the Photoshop file containing the mask.

2. Click on the Layers shortcut icon in the document window. The Layers panel will open.

3. Select the masked image in the document window.

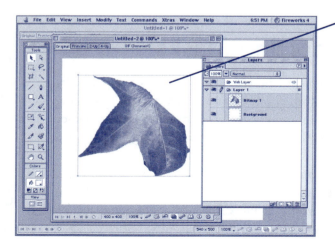

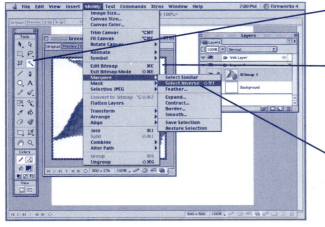

4. Click on the Magic Wand Tool (W) in the toolbox.

5. Click in the white areas of the document window. These pixels will eventually not be included in the mask you will create.

6. Choose Select Inverse from the Modify, Marquee menu. The white areas of the image will no longer be selected, but the bitmap object will be selected. In this example, the bitmap image of the leaf defines the mask in the Photoshop file.

NOTE

Importing a file containing a mask is similar to opening a file containing a mask. Choosing the Import command brings the contents of the file into the active document as objects. Selecting the Open command creates a new window for the file.

Editing a Photoshop Mask in Fireworks

The following steps are a continuation of the previous steps. If I've lost you somewhere in-between here and there, here's what happened. The Photoshop file I opened contained an image, plus a mask of that image. When I opened that file in Fireworks, the image appeared but not the mask. But I want to work with a mask, so I'm going to create a new one in Fireworks. Here's how:

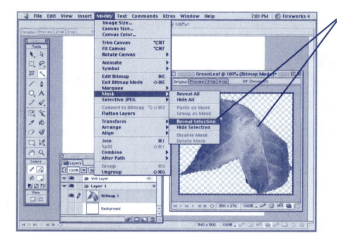

1. With the image selected in the document window, choose Reveal Selection from the Modify, Mask menu.

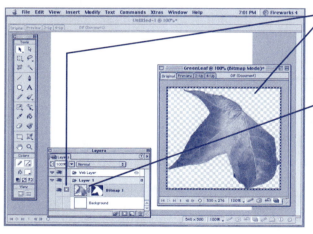

The masked image will appear in the document window and in the Layers panel, and a mask icon will appear beside the layer.

2. Click on the link icon to disable the mask.

Creating a Vector and Bitmap Object Mask

Now that you've created a bitmap mask in the previous sections and a vector mask in Chapter 5, "Creating and Designing Graphics," create a mask by combining a vector object with a bitmap object. The following steps show you how.

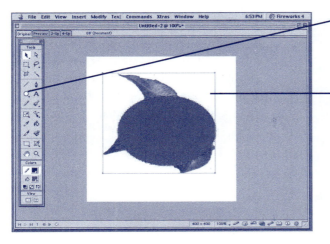

1. Open a Fireworks file containing a bitmap image and then create a vector object in the document window.

2. Click on the Pointer Tool (V) in the toolbox. Then, hold down the Shift key and select each object. Place the vector object on top of the image object.

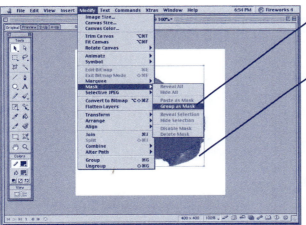

3. Select the Group as Mask command from the Modify, Mask menu.

The bounding boxes in the document window will change into a single selected object. Notice that the resulting image doesn't look much different than before you chose the Group as Mask command. Try it again. Choose the Undo command until the masked objects are ungrouped in the document window.

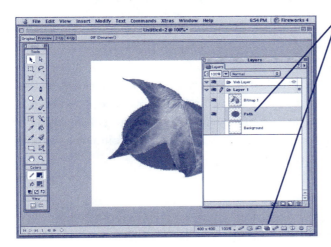

4. Click on the Layers shortcut located in the mini-launcher area of the document window. The Layers panel will open.

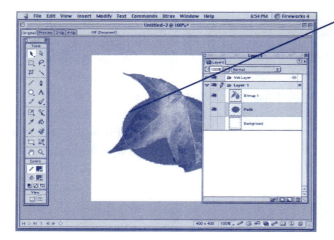

5. Click and drag the path object and place it below the bitmap object. The vector object will appear below the bitmap object. The object in the top layer will become the mask for the object in the layer below it.

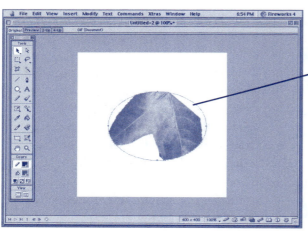

6. Choose Group as Mask from the Modify, Mask menu.

7. View the mask image in the document window.

Opening a Fireworks Mask

Choose the Save command (Ctrl/Command + S) from the File menu to preserve the mask created in the preceding section. You can open a Fireworks file containing a mask just as you would a Fireworks file containing other objects and settings. The following steps show you how to find out whether an opened file contains a mask.

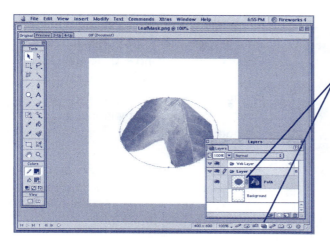

1. Choose the Open command from the File menu.

2. Press F2 or click on the Layers shortcut in the document window to open the Layers panel. The object in the Layers panel contains a vector object and a mask object. The link icon indicates that the mask is active.

Editing a Fireworks Mask

After you've created one mask, you can create many more. You can modify a mask in the same way that you can modify any other image object. You can apply effects, adjust colors, and combine it or group it with other objects. The following steps show you how to apply Transform commands and add a mask to a mask.

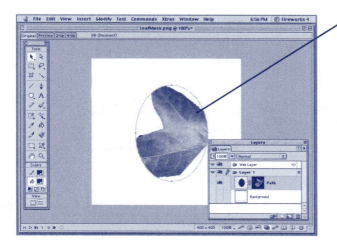

1. Select the mask in the document window.

2. Choose one of the flip or rotate commands from the Modify, Transform menu.

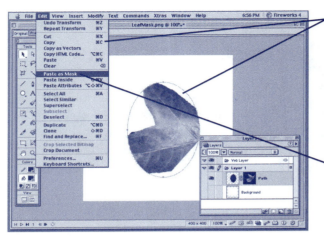

3. Select the mask object and then choose Copy from the Edit menu, or press Ctrl/Command + C. To view this effect a little more easily, you can change the fill color of the selected mask in the document window, or change its rotation.

4. Choose the Paste as Mask command from the Edit menu. A Fireworks dialog box will appear, telling you that a mask already exists.

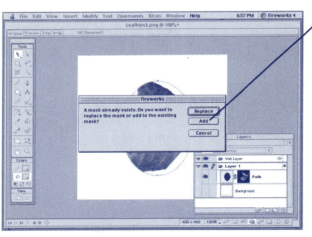

5. Click on the Add button to add the mask from the Clipboard to the document window.

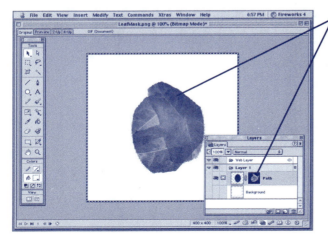

6. View the modified mask in the document window. Notice that the mask in the Layers panel has also changed.

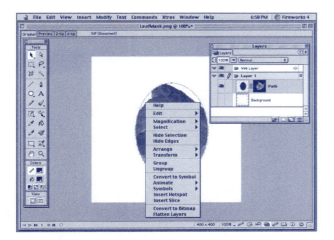

7. You can also modify a mask by choosing a menu command from the mask object's context menu. On a Mac, hold down the Control key and click on the mask object in the document window. If you have a Windows computer, right-click on the mask. A contextual list of menu commands will appear for the selected mask object.

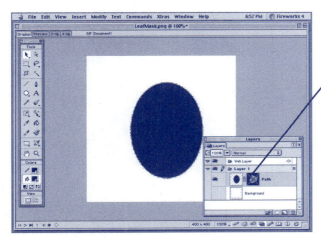

8. Choose Disable Mask from the Modify, Masks menu.

A red X will appear over the mask in the Layers panel.

7

Working with Colors, Layers, and Masks

Desktop and laptop computers are becoming more affordable, and most are built with display cards or graphic chip sets capable of displaying thousands or millions of colors. Not only are Web designers creating Web sites with these robust computer systems, people visiting and viewing Web sites are also using these newer computer systems. This means that you'll probably be designing colorful Web graphics—not that there's anything wrong with black and white or grayscale colors.

In this chapter you'll learn how to:

- Adjust color settings on your computer
- Work with the Color Table, Swatches, and Color Mixer panels
- Adjust colors for mask and layer objects

You can add or modify the colors of bitmap or vector objects. If you're working with a vector object, you can customize its stroke and fill colors independently, or blend or feather the colors if there are any overlapping areas. The primary color tools in the toolbox are the Stroke and Fill color wells, accompanied by Default, No Stroke or Fill, and Swap buttons. The Magic Wand and Paint Bucket tools can be used to select and modify colors for bitmap objects.

You can also view or change color settings for graphic objects using the Color Mixer, Color Table, or Swatches panels. Color can also be affected by settings in the Layers panel, such as blending modes, transparency/opacity settings, and where an object is located in a layer. Grouping objects into a mask or pasting into a mask can be another way of altering the color of a graphic or text object. This chapter shows you how to select, apply, and correct colors for vector and bitmap objects, as well as how to work with color in combined with layers and masks.

Setting up and Working with Colors

Before you begin fine-tuning any colors in a Fireworks document, you might want to check your computer and make sure you've selected the optimal color settings for your Windows or Mac OS. If you haven't already set your computer to a 1024 × 768 desktop displaying thousands or millions of colors (24- or 32-bit color), you should definitely configure these settings before you start working with color in Fireworks.

In addition to the color settings you can choose in the Windows or Mac OS, the accuracy of the colors on your computer's monitor can vary depending on the type of display card and monitor you're using. If you plan to share files with other Web designers, you might want to customize the software settings for the monitor and the display card, in addition to the settings mentioned in this chapter. Don't be surprised if you're unable to achieve color nirvana between two different brands of monitors or display cards. Despite all the latest technological achievements, precise color calibration is not standardized across monitor and display card manufacturers. The following sections show you how to check and configure your computer's color settings so that you can work with the color-related tools in Fireworks.

Adjusting Color Settings on Your Computer

Before you begin experimenting with colors, be sure you're seeing the right ones on your computer screen. The colors you see on your computer monitor are generated by a combination of graphics hardware and software installed on your computer. Your computer can only display the amount of color that the display card is capable of storing in its memory. Of course, you'll also need to make sure that the software settings for the resolution of your desktop and the color depth of the operating system are set up correctly.

The following sections show you how to view your display card and monitor settings on Macintosh and Windows computers.

Viewing Mac Display Card Settings

If you're using a Macintosh computer, open the Apple System Profiler application to view the display settings. You won't be able to change any of these settings; you can only view them. Here's how:

1. Click on the Apple menu and select Apple System Profiler. The Apple System Profiler application will start, and the window will open to the System Profile page.

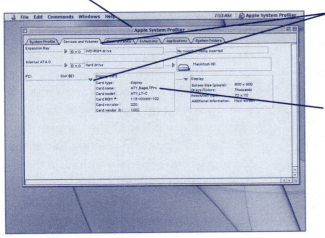

2. Select the Devices and Volumes tab, then click on the triangle icon for the PCI section of the window to view the Display Card and Display settings.

The card name appears in the Display Card section of the PCI information. Most current Macs, such as the iMacs, G4 desktops, iBooks, and PowerBooks ship with an ATI graphics chip set. Some of the newer G4 Desktop Macs use the Nvidia graphics chip set.

The resolution of the screen appears in the Display section of the window.

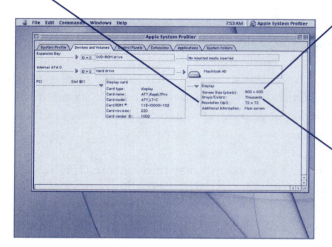

The current desktop size in pixels is the first item in the list of Display information. Although this desktop is set to 800 × 600, Macromedia recommends using a 1024 × 768 or larger desktop size.

3. View the number of colors, or the color depth of the desktop. In this example, thousands of colors are viewable on the screen.

Setting the Color Depth on a Mac

Access the color depth and resolution settings for your Macintosh monitor from the Monitors control panel, conveniently located in the Apple menu. If you're using a pre-Mac OS 9 version of the Mac OS, look for the Monitors & Sound control panel. The following steps show you how to adjust the color depth and resolution for your Mac.

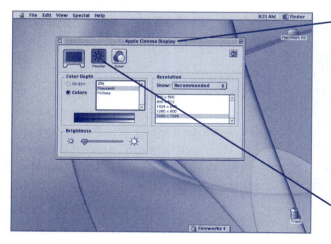

1. Click on the Apple menu, choose Control Panels, and then select Monitors. The Monitors control panel window will open. The name of the Macintosh computer or the name of the monitor will appear in the title bar of the Monitors control panel window. In this example, the Monitors control panel window is titled Apple Cinema Display.

2. Select the Monitor button to view the Color Depth, Resolution, and Brightness settings for your Macintosh computer.

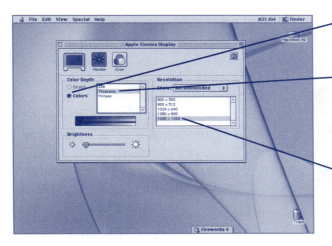

3. Click on the Colors radio button to select a color (versus grayscale) palette.

4. Click on Thousands or Millions in the Color Depth list to set the number of colors the Mac OS will display in any application, including Fireworks.

5. Click on a resolution in the Resolution list to set the size of the desktop. In this example, I chose 1600 × 1024.

NOTE

The Monitors control panel might also be titled the Monitors & Sound control panel, if you're using Mac OS 8.6.

Choosing ColorSync Settings

ColorSync is the color management software included with Mac OS. You can configure the Mac OS to work with specific color settings for viewing colors onscreen, printing, or exporting color documents to other applications. The following steps show you how to choose ColorSync settings.

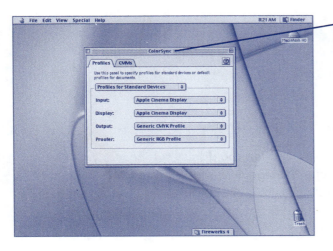

1. Click on the Apple menu, choose Control Panels, and then select ColorSync. The ColorSync control panel window will open. In this example, version 3.0.2 of the ColorSync window is shown.

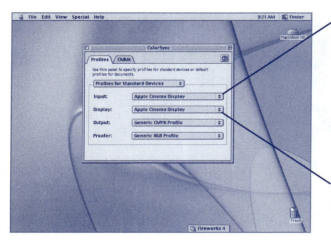

2. Click on the Input pop-up menu to choose a device. If you're using a PowerBook, choose a PowerBook display setting. If you're using a desktop system, choose a profile that matches the type of monitor connected to your Mac. In this example, I chose the Apple Cinema Display setting.

3. Click on the Display pop-up menu and choose a device setting.

4. Choose Profiles for Standard Devices to view the profiles for RGB, CMYK, Gray, and Lab settings in ColorSync.

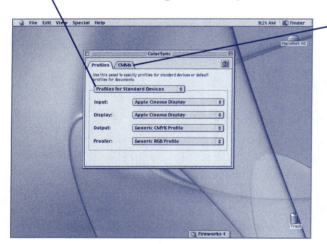

5. Click on the CMMs tab to view or select a preferred CMM setting. By default, Automatic is selected in the Preferred CMM pop-up menu. However, you can manually choose Heidelberg or Apple CMM if you want.

Viewing Windows Display Settings

If you're running Windows 2000, you can view the display settings for your computer by opening the Computer Management window. The following steps assume that all the display-related software is already installed on your computer. These steps show you how to view the display card and display settings on a computer running Windows 2000.

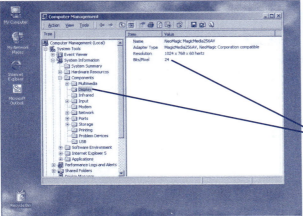

1. Click on the Start button, choose Programs, and then select Administrative Tools. Finally, select Computer Management from the Administrative Tools menu. The Computer Management window will open.

2. Click on the Display folder in the left pane of the window. The bits per pixel setting appears at the bottom of the right pane. In this example, Windows 2000 is set to display 24 bits of color.

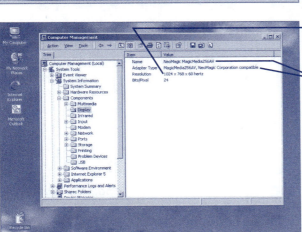

3. View the size of the desktop in the Resolution setting in the right pane.

4. The type of display card is displayed beside the Name and Adapter Type items.

NOTE

You cannot modify your computer's display and resolution settings in the Computer Management window. See the next section to find out how to change the display settings on a Windows 2000 computer.

NOTE

If you're using Windows 98, click on the Start button. Then choose Programs, Accessories, System Tools, and select the System Information menu item. The Microsoft System Information window will open. Click on the Plus button to expand the Components item in the window list. Then, click on Display to view the display information for your computer.

Changing the Number of Colors

If you need to change the display or resolution settings on your Windows computer, simply right-click on your desktop and choose the Properties menu command. The Display Properties window will open. Click on the Settings tab to view or change the display colors or screen area settings. Here's how:

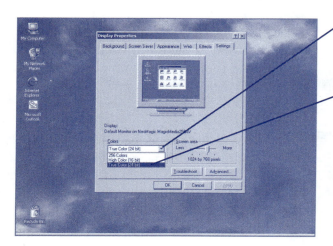

1. Click on the Colors drop-down menu to view the number of colors available for Windows 2000, 98, or NT.

2. Choose 24- or 32-bit color from the Colors drop-down menu. Even though your monitor might not be able to display the full range of 32-bit color, you will be able to select and edit a wider range of colors in 32-bit mode than in 24-bit mode.

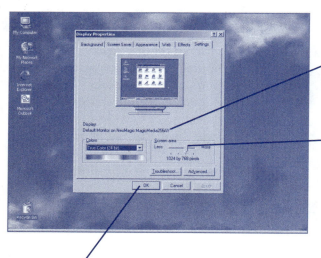

NOTE

The display card appears below the Display text in the Display Properties window.

3. Click and drag the slider control to select a screen area or desktop size for your computer. If you choose a different Screen Area setting, Windows will ask whether you want to test that setting. Click on the OK button. If the new settings appear on your screen, you can click Apply to save the new settings for your Windows system.

4. Click on the OK button to save your changes to the Display Properties window.

Working with Color

Now that you have set up your computer to display thousands or millions of colors, it's time to take a tour of the color tools in Fireworks. If you've used other graphics applications before, the color well, containing the stroke and fill colors, should look pretty familiar to you. Working with color in Fireworks involves selecting, choosing, and applying a color to a selected vector or bitmap object.

Color can be used for designing print media and Web graphics. CMYK is the color model most commonly used to create print media. RGB is the standard color model used for Web graphics and digital image files, such as those created by digital cameras and scanners. If you take a look at the colors on a Web page, you'll notice colors are represented by hexadecimal RGB values. Because Fireworks was designed to help you create Web graphics, any document you open is automatically converted into the RGB color model. You can easily view the hexadecimal RGB value of a stroke or fill color from the Info or Color Mixer panels, or from the color well pop-up menu. You can also view the color values for another color model, such as CMY, HSB, Grayscale, RGB or Hexadecimal by choosing a color model from the Color Mixer panel's pop-up menu.

Most browsers, such as Internet Explorer and Netscape Communicator, support the hexadecimal RGB color model. Hexadecimal values start at 0, representing black, and end with F, representing white. Each red, green, or blue value for a hexadecimal color is made of a double-digit value. Each double-digit can be one of the following range of numbers and alphabet characters: 0,1,2,3,4,5,6,7,8,9,A,B,C,D,E, or F. For example, the color black would be represented as #000000 in hexadecimal.

Although there are slight color differences between Windows and Mac platforms, you can be sure the colors you create in Fireworks will appear as the same color when viewed in a browser. If you plan to print some of the graphics you create for a Web site, you will need to use a different application, such as Photoshop, to convert the RGB color model to CMYK and prepare Fireworks graphics for print media. The following sections show you how to use the Color Mixer, Swatches, and Color Table panels. Each set of steps assumes that you've already opened the corresponding panel from the Window menu.

Picking a Stroke Color with the Color Mixer Panel

Choose Color Mixer from the Window menu to open the Color Mixer panel. You can also click on the shortcut icon (it looks like an artist's palette) for the Color Mixer panel located in the mini-launcher area of the document window. The Stroke and Fill color wells in the Color Mixer panel might give you a sense of déjà vu if you've already used these same color wells in the toolbox. If you also use Photoshop 6, the bottom portion of the Color Mixer panel might remind you of the bottom portion of the color palette in Photoshop.

When you change the stroke or fill color in the Color Mixer panel, toolbox, Stroke panel, or Fill panel, the color well in any of the other panels automatically gets updated with the latest selected color. Of course, if you click on an object, that object's stroke and fill color settings will appear in all those panels, too.

1. Add a few shape or path objects to the document window. Click on the Pointer Tool (V) and then select an object. Click on the Stroke color well in the toolbox. A pop-up color menu will appear.

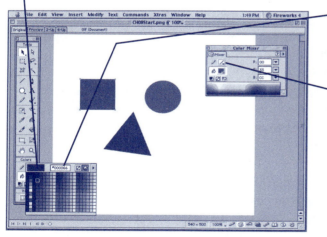

2. Drag the mouse over a color to view its hexadecimal value in the text box. Click on a color to select it.

The selected color also will appear in the Stroke color well in the Color Mixer and Stroke panels.

TIP

Another way to change a stroke or fill color is to type a color value into the text box in the Color Mixer panel. Choose Hexadecimal from the Color Mixer pop-up menu. Then, type each hexadecimal value of the color into the text boxes in the Color Mixer panel to change the selected stroke or fill color.

> **NOTE**
>
> You can also use the Color Mixer panel to translate color values between different color models. For example, if you know that a particular color is RGB, type that value into the Mixer panel, choose Hexadecimal from the Mixer pop-up menu, and then view the hex value for that same color.

Picking a Fill Color

You can select a fill color using the same steps you used to choose a stroke color. However, because the fill color covers the entire area of the selected object, there are a few different issues to consider when picking a fill color. First, you'll need to decide whether you will be using a texture. For instance, a lighter fill color might look better with a particular texture than a darker color. You can also apply a texture to a gradient or pattern. Try to decide how you want to work with color as you select different options in the Fill panel.

If you plan to use a gradient fill, a two-color gradient will use the stroke and fill colors as the default colors for the gradient. You can always edit the gradient colors after you've applied the gradient, but it helps to visualize the stroke and fill colors before applying a gradient to an object. The following steps show you how to select a fill color from the Color Mixer panel.

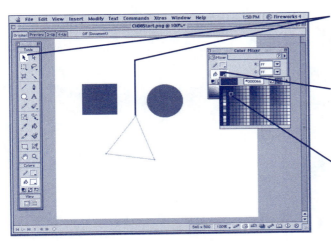

1. Add a few vector objects to the document window. Click on the Pointer Tool (V) and then select an object.

2. Click on the Fill color well in the Color Mixer panel. A color menu will appear.

3. Drag the mouse over the color squares to view any particular color. Click on a color square to select that color. The fill color of the selected object will change to the color in the color well.

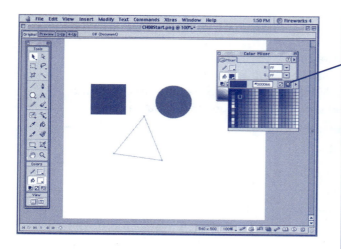

TIP

If you prefer to choose a color using the Mac OS or Windows color picker windows, choose the color wheel button located in the pop-up color menu for the stroke or fill color. The color picker window for Windows or the Mac OS will open in the Fireworks workspace. To find out more about how to use the color picker, see the section titled, "Adding Colors to the Swatches Panel" later in this chapter.

Working with Swatches

In addition to the color wells located in the toolbox and the Color Mixer panel, you can also select and change the color of an object from the Swatches panel. When the cursor hovers over a color in the Swatches panel, the cursor icon will change to an eyedropper icon. You can sample colors, view the hexadecimal value of a color, or load and save custom sets of swatches from the Swatches panel. The following steps give you a brief tour of the Swatches panel.

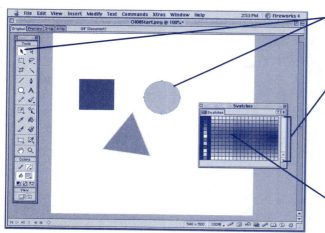

1. Add a few shape or path objects to the document window. Click on the Pointer Tool (V) and select an object.

2. View the range of colors in the Swatches panel.

3. Click on a color in the Swatches panel to change the fill or stroke color of the selected object.

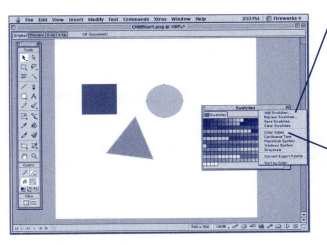

4. Click on the pop-up menu button to view the menu commands for the Swatches panel. You can add, replace, save, clear, or sort the colors in the Swatches panel by choosing the corresponding menu command.

5. Select a different color palette, such as Color Cubes, Continuous Tone, Macintosh System, Windows System, or Grayscale to change the color palette in the Swatches panel.

NOTE

You can change a vector object's stroke or fill colors using the Swatches panel. However, you cannot change the canvas color of a document from the Swatches panel.

TIP

If you want to change the color in a bitmap object, you'll need to select the Magic Wand Tool and then select a group of pixels in the bitmap object. Pick a color from the Fill color well, then apply that color to the selected pixels in the bitmap using the Paint Bucket Tool.

Viewing Colors in the Color Table Panel

Each document contains a unique set of colors used to define stroke or fill, colors for a vector object, or pixel color values in bitmap objects. The colors utilized by a GIF or PNG document can be viewed from the Color Table panel. The document must be in 8-bit file format before you can view and edit its color settings from the Color Table panel. For example, you must choose a GIF or PNG file format from the Optimize panel in order to view colors in the Color Table panel. If you choose JPEG, no colors will appear in the Color Table panel. If the document is in one of the preview modes (such as Preview, 2-Up, or 4-Up), its color table will automatically update as you select different settings in the Optimize panel, or if you select a different slice object in the document window. The following steps assume you have selected GIF or PNG in the Optimize panel. Perform these steps to learn how to view document colors in the Color Table panel.

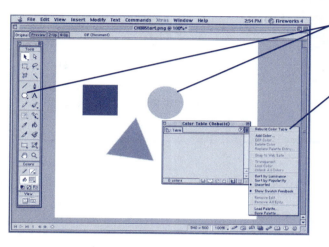

1. Add a few vector objects to the document window. Click on the Pointer Tool (V) and then select an object.

2. Choose Rebuild Color Table from the pop-up menu in the Color Table panel. The colors for the active document will appear in the Color Table panel.

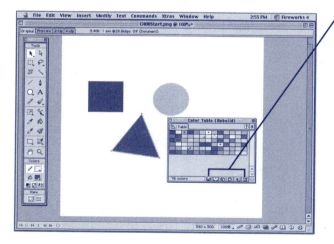

When you click on a color in the Color Table panel, the six tools located at the bottom of the palette will become active. You can apply more than one tool to any color square.

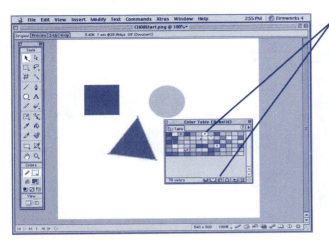

If you apply a tool to a color, an icon will appear in the selected color square. Each tool is associated with a unique symbol. For example, the Lock button displays a small white square in the lower-right corner of the color square. The Snap to Web Safe button displays a white diamond shape in the color square, and the Transparent button displays a gray-and-white checkerboard pattern. Select a color square and then click on a tool button in the Color Table panel. In this example, I chose the Web Safe button to change the selected color to the nearest Web-safe color.

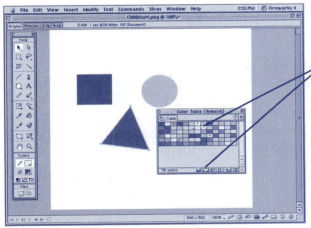

Another tool you're likely to use is the Transparent button located in at the bottom of the Color Table panel. You can click on a color in the Table panel and then select the Transparent button, and that color will appear transparent when you export the document.

Working with Gradient Fill Colors

Gradient colors share the same color palette as stroke and fill colors. The thing that makes gradients unique is that you can blend two or more colors together to create a gradient. Gradients enable vector objects to display multiple fill colors. You can also create custom effects by combining gradients with textures. Or, you can create a three-dimensional sphere by applying a linear gradient to an ellipse vector object. You can adjust the opacity of two or more gradient objects to create sophisticated graphics, and you can customize a gradient after you've applied it to a vector object. The following steps show you how to apply and edit gradient colors.

1. Add a few shape or path objects to the document window.

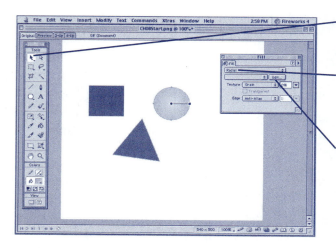

2. Select the Pointer Tool (V) from the toolbox, then click on an object.

3. Choose Fill from the Window menu to open the Fill panel. Choose a gradient to apply to the selected object.

4. Click on the Edit button to view the gradient colors for the selected object.

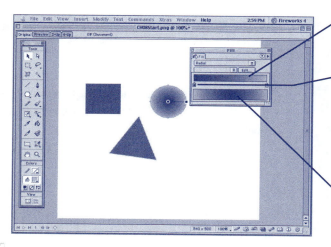

5. View the gradient colors in the top section of the gradient pop-up window.

6. Click on an existing square to select a new gradient color for the square. Click below the top section of the gradient window to add a new gradient color to the selected object.

The applied gradient pattern, along with its colors, will appear at the bottom of the pop-up gradient window.

TIP

If you're simply creating a three-dimensional object, you can choose a white to black radial gradient to create a 3D lighting effect on an object and apply the color of that object as a mask.

Correcting Colors

There are many different ways to correct colors in Fireworks. The following sections show you how to view the hexadecimal value of a color, work with several different tools to adjust an object's stroke or fill colors, lock colors, make colors transparent, or make them Web safe. You can design Web graphics without having to worry about whether a particular color will appear correctly in a browser. However, after you've finished an object or image, you might need to match colors across different objects or with other objects stored in a different graphics file.

If you're working with a bitmap image in a single document and you want to correct a blue, green, or off-color hue, you can apply a filter effect from the Effect panel or the Xtras menu. You can find out more about how to apply effects and filters in Chapter 9, "Applying Effects."

Identifying the Current Color

Before you start changing colors, check to see what the current object's color value is and then compare it to another object's color value. If you're designing a graphic for the Web, it's best to view a color value as a hexadecimal value instead of in another color model, so you can be sure that the color you select is the one used in the HTML code. The following sections show you how to use the Eyedropper Tool combined with the stroke and fill colors and the Info panel to view object color values. You'll also learn how to view and change the canvas color.

Using the Eyedropper Tool

The Eyedropper Tool in Fireworks enables you to pick a color in the document window and make that color a stroke or fill color. This behavior is similar to the way an eyedropper tool works in other graphics applications. In Fireworks, if you place the Eyedropper Tool over a color in the document window, you can view the color value in the Info panel. If you click on that color, the Eyedropper tool selects that color as the stroke or fill color. The following steps show you how to view a hexadecimal color value in a bitmap image.

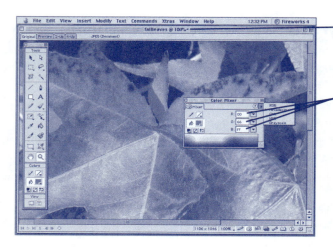

1. Open an image file or create a few objects of varying color in the document window.

2. Select the Eyedropper Tool (I) from the toolbox. If you move the cursor over the document window, it changes from an arrow to an eyedropper icon. Move the cursor over an object and view its RGB hexadecimal value in the Info panel. Click on the stroke or fill color in the toolbox, then click on a color in the document window to change the current stroke or fill color.

3. View the current stroke or fill color in the Color Mixer panel. Click on the pop-up menu and choose a different color model if you want to view the color value for a different color model in the Color Mixer panel.

You can view color values from one of five different color models in the Color Mixer panel: RGB, Hexadecimal, CMY, HSB, or Grayscale. The following list provides a brief summary of each color model.

- **RGB**. The RGB color model consists of three channels: red, green and blue. Each channel has a value ranging from 0 to 255. 0-0-0 represents the values for the color black, and 255-255-255 represents the values for the color white.

- **Hexadecimal**. Hexadecimal values are based on the red, green, and blue values of the RGB color model, except that each value is represented by 00, 11, 22, 33, 44, 55, 66, 77, 88, 99, AA, BB, CC, DD, EE, or FF. For example, black is represented as 00-00-00, and white is FF-FF-FF.

- **CMY**. CMY is an acronym for cyan, magenta, and yellow. Black is also used to define this color model. Each channel can have a value between 0 and 255. In this color model, 0-0-0 represents the color white, and 255-255-255 represents the color black.

- **HSB**. HSB is an acronym for hue, saturation, and brightness values. In this color model, hue and saturation each have a value between 0 and 360 degrees. Brightness has a value between 0 and 100%.

- **Grayscale**. The grayscale model is based on a percentage of black. It consists of values between 0 and 100, where 0 represents white and 100 represents black.

TIP

If you're working with a bitmap image, you can use the Magic Wand Tool to select the color you want to change in the bitmap image. Pick a different fill color from the color well in the toolbox, and then select the Paint Bucket Tool from the toolbox. Click in the selected area of the bitmap image to apply the new color.

Viewing the Stroke or Fill Color

You can view the currently selected stroke or fill color by clicking in the Stroke or Fill color well in the toolbox or the Color Mixer panel. A color menu window will open, displaying a rainbow of color squares. Be careful not to drag your cursor over a different color square or you might inadvertently select a new stroke or fill color. The hexadecimal value of the selected color appears at the top of the Color pop-up menu. The following steps show you how to view stroke and fill colors.

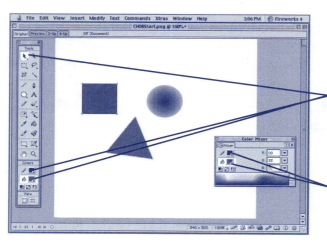

1. Open an image file or create a few objects of varying color in the document window.

2. Choose the Pointer Tool (V) and select an object. Click in the Stroke or Fill color well in the toolbox to view the object's stroke or fill color.

3. Alternatively, you can click on the Stroke or Fill color well in the Color Mixer panel to view the current stroke or fill color.

Working with the Info Panel

You can view a color's RGB hexadecimal values in the Info panel. Move the cursor over an object color to view its color information. The Info panel updates its information as you move the cursor within the document window. The following steps show you how to interpret the color information in the Info panel.

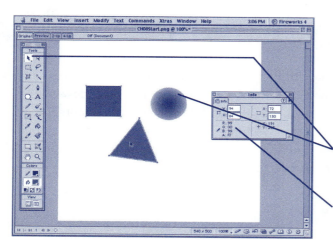

1. Open an image file or create a few objects of varying color in the document window.

2. Choose Info from the Window menu to open the Info panel.

3. Select the Pointer Tool (V) and move it over a color in the document window.

4. The color's red, green, and blue hexadecimal values will appear in the Info panel.

Viewing the Canvas Color

Although the canvas color might appear to be the background color of a Web page in Fireworks, it's possible to change this color in Dreamweaver or any other HTML editor. You can create custom background images in Fireworks, in addition to foreground graphics. However, you'll probably want to create each in a separate document. You can choose a specific canvas color, or no canvas color (a transparent background), from the Canvas Color dialog box. If you choose a canvas color, you can preview object colors against the background color as you design your Web graphics. The following steps show you how to view and change the canvas color of a Fireworks document.

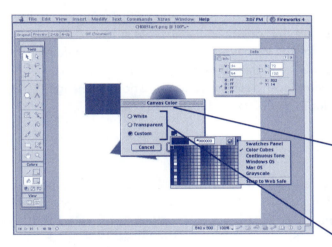

1. Open a Fireworks document or create a new document by choosing New from the File menu. If you choose New from the File menu, the canvas color settings will appear at the bottom of the New Document window.

2. If you want to modify the color in an existing document, choose Canvas Color from the Modify menu. The Canvas Color dialog box will open.

3. Click on the Custom radio button to choose a custom canvas color. Alternatively, you can choose either the White or Transparent option.

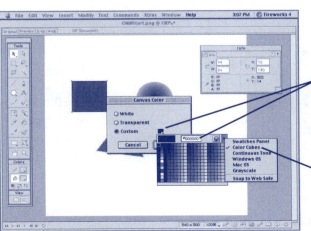

4. Click on the color well to view and select a different color for the canvas. The current color is displayed at the top of the Color pop-up menu.

5. Click the pop-up menu to select a different color palette.

6. View the canvas color in the document window.

> **NOTE**
>
> If you have a Web site that contains Web pages with varying background colors, you might want to put images containing transparencies inside a table, create a custom transparent image for each page, or redesign the color of your Web site to a single background color. Fireworks transparency settings are only designed to work with a single background color.

Tweaking the Color Palette

After you've identified the current color of an object, as well as the color to which you want to change it, you can select that object and change its stroke or fill colors. Because you're creating graphics for the Web, you can work with a Web-safe color palette and change colors without worrying about picking a color that won't appear correctly in a browser. The following sections show you how to change several settings for a specific color in an object or document.

Changing Colors

You can type the exact value of a color for an object into the Color Mixer window or into the Color pop-up menu for a stroke or fill color. You can use the Eyedropper Tool combined with the Info panel to view different color values. Then, select the object you want to edit and type in the new color value. The following steps show you how.

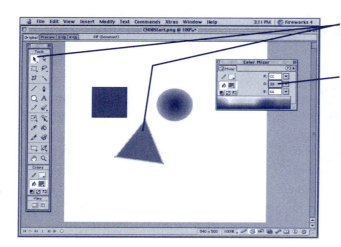

1. Open a document and use the Pointer Tool (V) to select an object.

2. Click in one of the R, G, or B text boxes in the Color Mixer panel. Type in a new value to change the stroke or fill color. In this example, I've changed the fill color.

Locking a Color

After you've picked a color for a particular object, you can lock it if you don't want that particular color to change. Choose Color Table from the Window menu to open the Color Table panel. The tools at the bottom of this panel enable you to adjust several color-specific settings. The Lock color button is represented by (you guessed it!) an icon of a lock. The following steps assume the Color Table panel is already open, and that you've rebuilt the color table. Perform the following steps to lock a color in the Color Table panel.

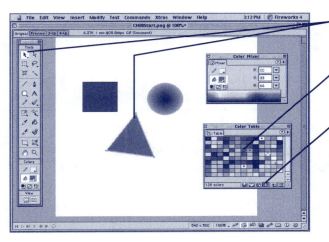

1. Open a document and use the Pointer Tool (V) to select an object.

2. Select a color in the Color Table panel.

3. Click on the Lock Color button located at the bottom of the Color Table panel. A small white square will appear in the lower right corner of the selected color square.

Creating a Transparent Color

Most Web graphics are laid out over a background image or background color of a Web page. In Fireworks, you can set the canvas color to be the same color as the background color of a Web page. If you want a particular area of the background color or pattern to show through a particular color area of an image object, you can make the object's color transparent. The following steps show you how to make a color transparent, using the Color Table panel.

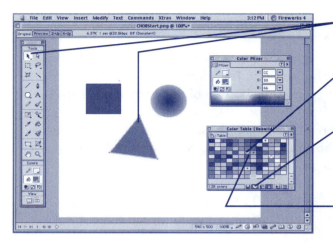

1. Open a document and use the Pointer Tool (V) to select an object.

2. Select a color in the Color Table panel.

3. Click on the Transparent button, located at the bottom of the Color Table panel.

A gray-and-white checkerboard pattern will appear in the selected color square, indicating that color will appear transparent when you export the file.

TIP

Be sure to export an image that contains transparent colors as a GIF or PNG file. JPEG images do not support transparency. Your first clue will be that you can't view a color table in the Color Table panel for a JPEG image.

Checking for Web-Safe Colors

You can adjust colors to make them Web-safe. Web-safe means that a color value exists in the set of colors supported by the latest, most popular browser applications. When you select this button in the Color Table panel, Fireworks will change the selected color to the closest-matching Web-safe color. The following steps show you how to change a color into a Web-safe color.

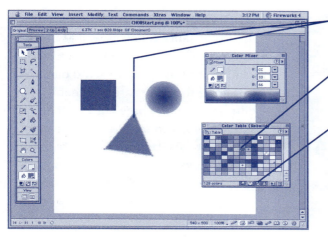

1. Open a document and use the Pointer Tool (V) to select an object.

2. Select a color from the Color Table panel.

3. Click on the Snap to Web Safe button, located at the bottom of the Color Table panel. A diamond icon will appear in the center of the selected color square, indicating that color has been changed to the nearest Web-safe color.

Comparing Gamma Settings

Colors created on a Mac won't look exactly the same on a Windows computer, and vice versa. Each computer platform supports its own custom gamma settings. The result is that a dark orange color created for a Mac browser will appear as a brighter, bolder orange color in a Windows browser. If you don't want your Web graphics to look too drastically different between the two platforms, you can preview the Windows Gamma settings on a Mac and vice versa. Here's how:

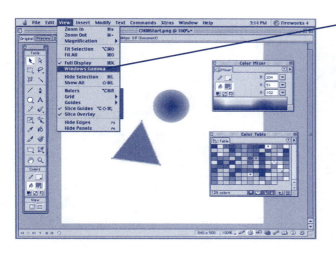

1. Click on the View menu. If you are using a Macintosh computer, choose Windows Gamma. If you are using a Windows computer, choose the Macintosh Gamma menu command.

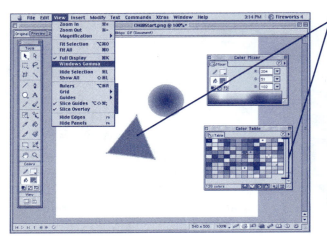

2. Fireworks will adjust the colors in the Color Table panel, as well as the colors for each object in the document window, to the newly selected gamma setting. If the colors are noticeably different than the previous gamma settings, you can try to adjust the colors to be more similar. To do this, choose Curves, Levels, or Hue/Saturation from the Effect, Adjust Color pop-up menu in the Effect panel. Try to choose colors that look similar with the Windows and Mac gamma settings.

TIP

If you want to maintain two separate sets of image files for Mac and Windows browsers, you can add JavaScript code to check for a Mac or Windows browser, then load the appropriate graphics.

Saving Colors

You can save a color palette as a file on your hard drive. Once you save a color palette, you can load it and use it with another document. This can come in handy

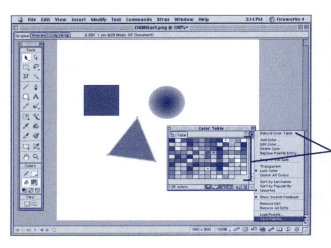

if you plan to use a common set of colors across several Web pages, but you don't want to spend a lot of time adjusting the colors for each object on each page. The following steps assume you have selected GIF or PNG from the Optimize panel.

1. Click on the pop-up menu in the Color Table panel. Choose Rebuild Color Table to update the color table for the document.

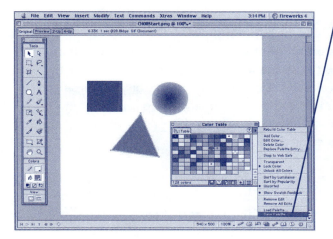

2. Select Save Palette from the Color Table panel's pop-up menu. Type a name for the color palette and then click on the Save button. Fireworks will create a file on your hard drive. Choose the Load Palette command from the Color Table pop-up menu if you want to use this palette or another palette with the active document.

Correcting Bitmap Image Colors

Most of the objects you create with the Rectangle/Shape, Pencil, Brush, Line and Pen tools are created as vector objects. This means that you can make these objects larger or smaller without having to worry about pixelating the appearance of the object. You can also change the stroke and fill colors for a vector object without having to use a bitmap object selection tool like the Magic Wand. *Pixelation* is a term that evolved from working with bitmap objects, which in this case will most likely be images from a digital camera or a scanner.

If you try to grow a bitmap object, you'll start to see some of the pixels in the image grow along with the image. As the image grows larger, each pixel used to define that image also grows larger. That's because each bitmap image is comprised of a fixed set of pixels. When you try to make a bitmap object larger, Fireworks tries to pick the nearest colors surrounding each pixel to create a larger image. However, if enough color information is not available in that image object, those pixels will appear more square or blocky-looking than other pixels in the image.

Working with color and bitmap objects in Fireworks involves a slightly different set of steps than working with color and vector objects. First, you'll need to use a selection tool, such as the Rectangle Marquee or Magic Wand, to select specific colors in a bitmap image. Then, you'll need to select and apply the Paint Bucket Tool. Whenever you edit a bitmap image, the document switches to Bitmap Mode (as opposed to Vector Mode). You must exit Bitmap Mode to select or edit any vector objects. The following sections show you how to work with color and bitmap objects.

Changing to an Exact Color Value

Although there are several different kinds of selection tools in Fireworks, the simplest way to choose a pixel is to use the Magic Wand Tool. You can select a single color by clicking on that color in the document window, or you can select multiple colors by holding down the Shift key and then clicking on two or more different colors. The following steps show you how to change the color of a bitmap object to a specific hexadecimal color value.

1. Open a new window and create several vector objects. Select each object and then choose Convert to Bitmap (Ctrl/Command + Alt/Option + Shift + Z) from the Modify menu. Now each object is a bitmap (not a vector) object.

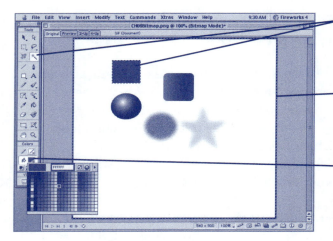

2. Click on the Magic Wand Tool (W) in the toolbox. Click on a color in the document window.

The window will switch to Bitmap Mode. The striped pattern will surround the canvas area of the document.

3. Click in the Fill color well in the toolbox and then click inside the text box located at the top of the Color pop-up menu window.

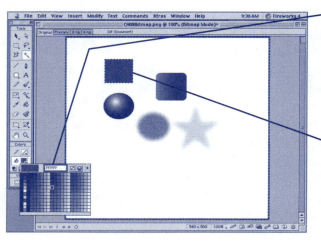

4. Delete the previous value from the text box. Type a new hexadecimal value into the text box and press the Enter/ Return key. In this example, I've typed FFFFFF, the color white, for the new color.

5. The fill color will change to the new color. Click on the Paint Bucket Tool (K) and click inside the selected area created by the Magic Wand. The object's color will change to the new color.

Adjusting Hue and Saturation

The Hue/Saturation filter can be selected from the Xtras, Adjust Color menu, or from the Effect, Adjust Color pop-up menu in the Effect panel. The Hue/Saturation dialog box enables you to adjust the Hue, Saturation, and Lightness values, and select a check box for the Colorize and Preview settings. The hue setting represents the red, yellow, green, or blue color for the selected object or pixels. You can choose a hue value between –180 and 180. The saturation setting adjusts the purity of the selected colors and is represented by a value between –100 to 100. The lightness setting is represented by a value between –100 to 100, and affects the lightness of colors in the selected object or group of pixels. The following steps show you how to adjust the settings in the Hue/Saturation dialog box for a bitmap object.

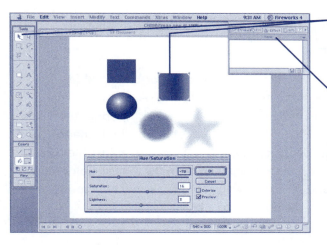

1. Open a document containing several bitmap images. Click on the Pointer Tool (V) and select a bitmap object.

2. Choose Effect from the Window menu or press Alt/Option + F7 to open the Effect panel. Then, choose Hue/Saturation from the Effect, Adjust Color pop-up menu. The Hue/Saturation dialog box will open.

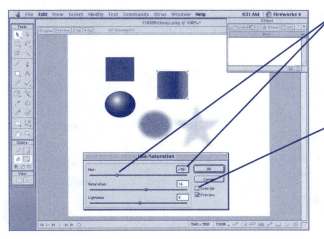

3. Click and drag a slider control to adjust the hue, saturation, or lightness level of the selected object. Alternatively, you can type a new value into the appropriate text box.

4. Check the Colorize check box to apply an additional hue/saturation filter to the selected object.

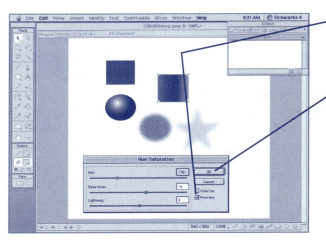

5. Check the Preview check box if you want to view the object changes as you make them.

6. Click on the OK button to save your changes.

Setting Brightness and Contrast Levels

You can adjust the brightness or contrast values in a vector or bitmap object by choosing the Brightness/Contrast menu item from the Xtras, Adjust Color menu, or from the Effect, Adjust Color pop-up menu in the Effect panel. The brightness and contrast values each range from –100 to 100, and affect the highlight, shadow, and midtone values in the selected object or pixel area. You can also adjust the tonal range of an image by choosing the Curves command from the Adjust Color menu in the Xtras or Effect pop-up menu. The following steps show you how to adjust the settings in the Brightness/Contrast dialog box for a bitmap object.

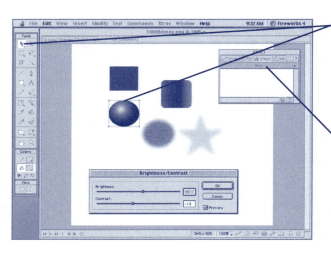

1. Create a new document and import a bitmap, or open an existing document that contains several bitmap images. Click on the Pointer Tool (V) and select a bitmap object.

2. Choose Effect from the Window menu or press Alt/Option + F7 to open the Effect panel. Then, choose Brightness/ Contrast from the None, Adjust Color pop-up menu. The Brightness/Contrast dialog box will open.

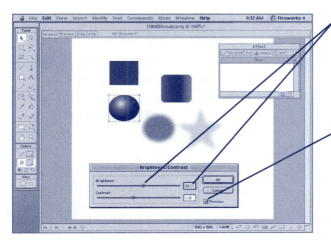

3. Click and drag the slider control, or type a value between –100 and 100 into a text box to set the brightness or contrast level in the Brightness/Contrast dialog box.

4. Check the Preview check box if you want to preview your changes in the document window.

5. Click on the OK button to save your changes.

Locating a Brighter or Darker Color

If you're not sure about the color values you see in Fireworks, you can choose the color wheel button in the Color Mixer pop-up menu to view colors from the Mac or Windows color picker window. You can view the current color and a new color in the color picker window. You can also view lighter or darker colors relative to the current and new color. The following steps show you how.

1. Open a document containing several bitmap images. Click on the Pointer Tool (V) and select a bitmap object, or select the Eyedropper Tool (I) from the toolbox.

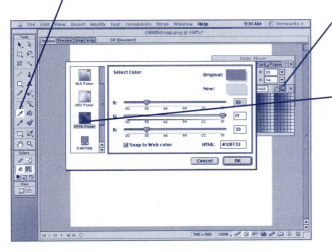

2. Click on the Fill color well in the toolbox or Color Mixer panel. Then, select the color wheel button.

3. The operating system's color picker window will open. On a Mac, you can choose a color model from the left window list in the color picker window. In this example, I've selected the HTML Picker color model, so that I can view the hexadecimal value for each color. If you're using a Windows computer, the default color picker only displays RGB color information.

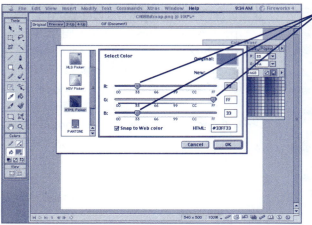

4. On a Mac, click and drag each slider to adjust the red, green, or blue level of the new color you want to use. If you're using Windows, choose a basic color by clicking on a color square, or click on a Custom color square and then click on a color in the right pane. Click to the right of the bar to select the brightness of the color. Then, click on the Add to Custom Colors button. The selected color will appear in the selected Custom Color square.

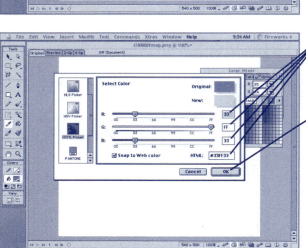

5. View the hexadecimal value for each color in the text boxes in the color picker window.

6. Select the color you want to use from the color picker window. Then, click on the OK button to save your changes.

Picking a Contrasting Color

Three primary colors define all other colors in the color spectrum: red, blue, and yellow. If you've seen the color bar in the Color Mixer panel, you've seen the primary colors and their relationship to other colors that result from blending the primary colors together. For example, mixing red with blue creates purple, and mixing yellow and blue creates green. Colors also vary in contrast from light to dark.

If you were to put red, blue, and yellow on a color wheel and then show their blended colors, such as green (mixing yellow and blue) and purple (red and blue), you might notice that green is on the opposite side of the color wheel from purple, just as black and white are opposite colors. You can use color relationships to select contrasting colors for your Web graphics. The following steps show you how to use the Color Mixer panel to choose a contrasting color for a vector object.

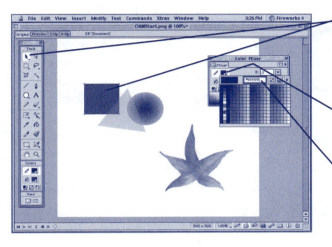

1. Open a document containing several bitmap and vector objects. Click on the Pointer Tool (V) and select a vector or bitmap object.

2. Click on the Stroke or Fill color well in the toolbox or Color Mixer panel.

3. Click in the text box located at the top of the Color pop-up menu. You can type a contrasting hexadecimal number into the text box, or drag the mouse over a contrasting color square.

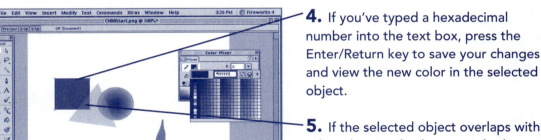

4. If you've typed a hexadecimal number into the text box, press the Enter/Return key to save your changes and view the new color in the selected object.

5. If the selected object overlaps with other objects, check to see whether the color of the overlapping objects is complimentary to other objects on the page.

Matching Colors

You can use the Color Mixer panel to match colors in bitmap objects with colors in vector objects. The following steps show you how to use the Eyedropper Tool to view the RGB value of a color in a bitmap object and then apply that color to a vector object. These steps show you how to change the stroke color of a vector object to the same color in a bitmap object, using the Eyedropper tool.

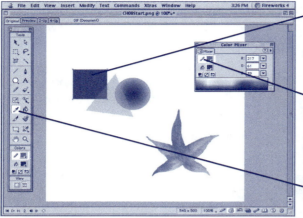

1. Open a document containing several bitmap and vector objects. Click on the Pointer Tool (V) and select a vector object in the document window.

2. Click on the Stroke color well in the Color Mixer panel or in the toolbox. The stroke color for the vector object will change to the selected color.

3. With the vector object selected, click on the Eyedropper Tool (I) in the toolbox.

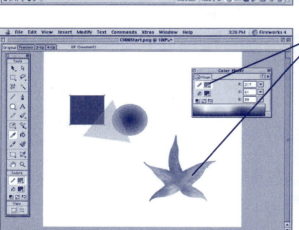

4. Now choose a color in the bitmap object that you want to use as the stroke color in the vector object. Use the Eyedroper Tool to click on a color in a bitmap image object. The selected color in the bitmap image will appear in the Stroke color well, and the vector object's stroke color will change to the selected stroke color.

TIP

You can use the Eyedropper Tool to select a color in another document. First, open a browser window or document in another application that contains several colors. Adjust the Fireworks document windows so that they do not cover the browser or application document window. Click on the Stroke or Fill color well and drag the cursor over the colors in the browser or application window. You will see the Stroke or Fill color change as you move the cursor over each color.

Defining Alpha Channel Masks

Each bitmap image is a 32-bit image. The RGB channels define 24 bits of data; the remaining 8 bits of information is an alpha channel. You can set a mask to display its image with a grayscale appearance, which usually displays both objects in a mask based on the brightness of each object's pixels. This type of mask enables light pixels to display the mask object (the top object) and darker pixels to show the image behind the mask.

Alternatively, with a bitmap mask you can choose to display its alpha channel instead of its pixels. This results in a masked image that retains the shape of the object in the top layer of the mask, but the color of the object in the bottom layer. The following steps show you how to change a bitmap mask from a grayscale appearance to an alpha channel mask.

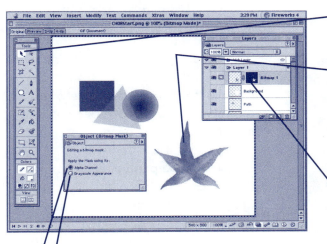

1. Click on the Pointer Tool (V) in the toolbox.

2. Select a bitmap-masked image in the document window. To create a mask, position two image objects so that they overlap each other. Then choose Group as Mask from the Modify, Masks menu.

3. Click on the mask icon for the object in the Layers panel.

4. Choose Object from the Window menu or press Alt/Option + F2 on the keyboard to open the Object panel. View the mask settings for the bitmap mask. The default value for a bitmap mask is Grayscale Appearance.

5. Click on the Alpha Channel radio button in the Object panel. The grouped mask image will change into an alpha channel. The object on the bottom level of the mask will appear as a solid color. For example, if the top image contains a gradient, the gradient will not appear in the alpha channel mask.

> **TIP**
>
> Another way to create a bitmap mask is to copy a bitmap object. Select a vector or bitmap object, then choose Paste as Mask from the Edit menu. The pasted bitmap becomes the mask for the selected object.

Adjusting Opacity

An object's opacity, or transparency setting, is located in the top-left corner of the Layers panel. You can adjust the transparency, or opacity, of an object by increasing or decreasing the percentage value in the Transparency text box in the Layers panel. A lower value increases an object's opacity, while a higher value decreases the transparency of the selected object. The following steps show you how to change an object's opacity.

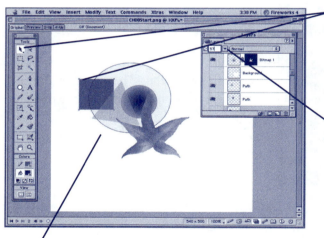

1. Click on the Pointer Tool (V) in the toolbox. Select a bitmap object in the document window. Alternatively, you can select an object by clicking on that object in the Layers panel.

2. Click on the pop-up menu beside the Opacity text box in the Layers panel. Drag and release the mouse to select a new opacity setting. Alternatively, you can type a number between 0 and 100 to set the opacity level for the selected object.

3. View the selected object in the document window. If it overlaps another object, you should be able to see any objects located directly below it.

Feathering an Object's Edges

You can apply the Feather command to a bitmap object. The Feather command blends the edges of the object's color with the color directly behind it. Depending on the object and colors, this command may or may not change an object's appearance. The following steps show you how to apply the Feather command to a bitmap object.

1. Select a bitmap object from the Layers panel or from the document window. The document will change to Bitmap Mode.

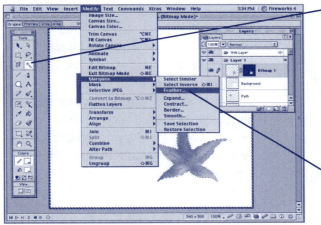

2. Choose the Magic Wand Tool (W) from the toolbox. You can also choose the Marquee (M) or Lasso (L) tools to select a group of pixels. Then, click on a color in the bitmap object, or select all colors in the bitmap object. The selected color(s) will be surrounded by a marquee boundary.

3. Choose the Feather command from the Modify, Marquee menu.

4. The Feather Selection window will appear. Type a number into the Radius text box to set the number of pixels that you want to apply with the Feather command.

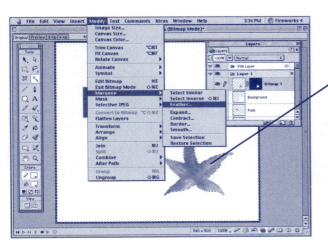

The default value is 10. Click on the OK button to save your changes and apply the command to the selected pixels.

The Feather command will be applied to the selected object or color. View the results in the document window. In this example, there is no background object and the canvas color is white. However, you will see the shape of the marquee change after the Feather command is applied to the selected object.

Adjusting Levels

If you have to work with a dark or overexposed image, try choosing the Levels filter in the Xtras, Adjust Color menu, or from the Effect, Adjust Color pop-up menu located in the Effect panel. You might be able to increase details in a bitmap image that is too bright or too dark, while ensuring that it remains viewable. Adjust high, mid or low tonal range settings from the Levels window. The following steps show you how to work with the Levels filter, located in the Effect panel.

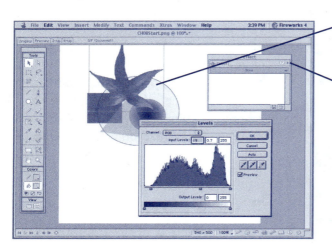

1. Select a bitmap object in the document window.

2. Choose Levels from the Effect, Adjust Color pop-up menu. The Levels dialog box will open. If you want to automatically adjust the tonal ranges in the selected object, click on the Auto button. Alternatively, you can choose the Auto Levels command from the Effect, Adjust Color pop-menu if you want Fireworks to adjust the levels for you.

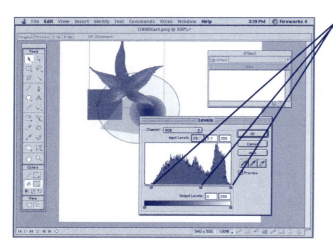

3. Click and drag a slider control to adjust the high, mid, or low tonal ranges in the selected image object. The left slider control adjusts the low tonal range values in the image object. The slider control on the right adjusts the high tonal range values, and the middle control enables you to change the mid-range tonal values. If you check the Preview check box, you can view your changes in the document window.

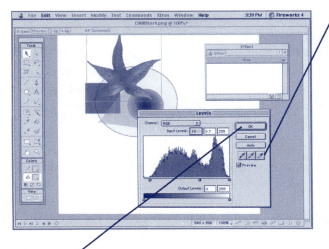

4. Three eyedropper icons are located on the right side of the Levels dialog box. The highlight eyedropper (the white eyedropper) enables you to click on a tonal range in the histogram, or in the image object located in the document window, to reset the highlight value for the image. Similarly, the shadow (black eyedropper) and midtone (gray) eyedropper tools can be used to reset the shadow and midtone levels for the selected image. Preview the changes in the document window.

5. Click on the OK button to save your changes and exit the Levels dialog box.

Choosing a Color Palette

You can load a previously saved color palette into a document, or choose from one of five built-in color palettes. The following steps show you how to change the color palette from the Swatches panel.

1. Select a bitmap object in the document window.

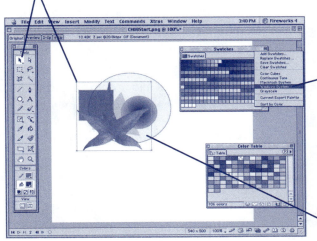

2. Choose Swatches from the Window menu. The Swatches panel will open.

3. Click on the pop-up menu in the Swatches panel and choose a new color palette. The color palettes are listed in the middle of the menu list. Choose from Color Cubes, Continuous Tone, Macintosh System, Windows System, or Grayscale color palettes.

4. View the adjusted colors in the selected image.

Adding Colors to the Swatches Panel

As you work with the stroke and fill colors available in Fireworks, you might want to add a few custom colors to extend a small color palette or experiment with new colors. You can select a custom color from the color picker window or from the Stroke or Fill color wells. Then, add that color as a new swatch in the Swatches panel. Here's how:

1. Open a document in Fireworks.

2. Choose Swatches from the Window menu or press Ctrl/Command + F9 to open the Swatches panel.

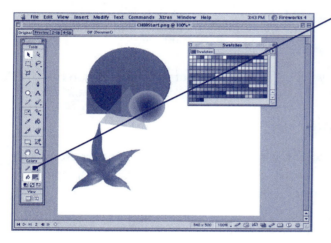

3. Click on the Fill color well in the toolbox, then choose the color wheel from the color pop-up menu. If you have a Windows PC, select a custom color square in the lower-left corner of the color picker window and then drag the slider on the right side of the color picker window. Click on a color in the large square located on the right side of the color picker window. The color will appear in the rectangle above the Add to Custom Colors button. After you've selected the color you want to add to the Swatches panel, click on the Add a Custom Color button. If you're using a Macintosh computer, click on the HLS Picker icon in the color picker window. Then, adjust the slider control and click in the color wheel to select a new color.

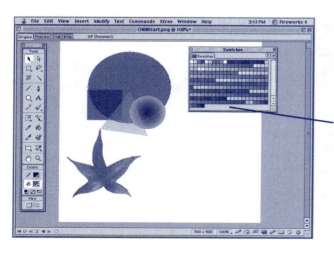

4. Move the cursor over the bottom portion of the Swatches panel, in the gray area below the color squares. The cursor will change to a paint bucket icon. Click once to add the selected color to the Swatches panel. To save the swatch, choose the Save Swatches command from the Swatches pop-up menu.

Working with Masks and Color

Don't be surprised if you can't figure out all the different ways you can create and edit a mask in Fireworks. After you start exploring all the different ways you can create a mask, it might be difficult to make yourself stop experimenting. But what's the big deal about masks? What is a mask?

A mask, in general, consists of two objects. The object in the top layer acts as a mask for the object below it. That means that two objects must overlap and be grouped or pasted together to create a mask. Fireworks enables you to create a mask from two separate objects or by pasting a single object mask into a second object. If you're grouping two objects together to create a mask, the top object acts as the mask for the object it overlaps. When you apply the Group as Mask command to two objects, the color of the background object usually appears blended with the masked area of the foreground object.

After you create a mask, you can always reselect it and edit any part of it. However, you can permanently apply a mask to another object, but then that masked object permanently changes into a newly-reshaped vector or bitmap graphic object.

You can create masks out of two vector objects, two bitmap objects, or a combination of vector and bitmap objects. Vector or bitmap objects can be paths, shapes, bitmap images, or text. You can create a bitmap or vector mask, depending on whether a vector or bitmap object is the top layer of the mask. You can also create a mask with a single object. Simply select the object and click on the mask icon in the Layers panel to change the selected object into a mask.

When you create a mask with a single object, white shows the masked object, and black hides the masked objects and enables the object below the mask to be seen. Fireworks enables you to paste an object as a mask, paste an object inside a mask, group two objects together to create a mask, create a mask out of an individual object, or create an empty mask. An empty mask is either a white or black object that can be used to show or hide another object.

The following sections show you how to create and edit different kinds of masked objects.

Changing Colors with Masks

How does a mask affect the color of the mask objects? The Stroke, Fill, Effect, or transparency settings you've added to each object can all affect the final color of the two objects used to create a mask. For example, you can add a texture combined with a blending mode to an object and then use it to mask a solid-colored object. The resulting color will look different than if you masked two solid objects together without any texture or blending mode applied to either object.

Similarly, if you apply a gradient or transparency setting to an image object, its colors will interact differently with the object below. I wish there were an easy way to predict how all these different mask and color combinations would turn out, but there isn't. I suggest experimenting with different objects, masks, and colors to create a unique design or effect. The following list shows you how to identify different elements that define a mask.

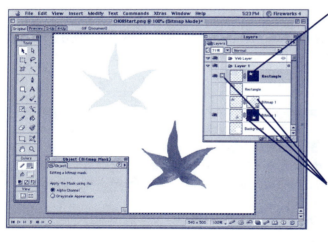

- **Mask objects**. Choose Layers from the Window menu or press F2 to view the Layers panel. The fastest way to find out whether there's a mask in a document is to look at the objects in the Layers panel. A masked object will consist of at least two linked thumbnail images. The mask thumbnail will only contain black or white (no colors).

- **Mask-related icons**. After the Layers panel is open, you can see the object thumbnail on the left and the mask thumbnail on the right. A mask icon also appears to the left the object thumbnail in the Layers panel.

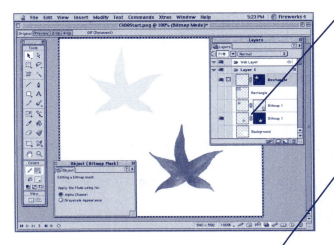

- **Applying a mask to an object**. The link icon between these objects indicates that the mask is currently applied to the object to which it's linked. If you click on the mask thumbnail, the canvas area will be surrounded by a black and yellow candy-striped line.

- **Layers and masks**. Look for the mask icon beside an object in the Layers panel. The mask icon is located between the eye icon and the object's thumbnail image. If the mask icon appears in this middle column of the Layers panel, that object contains a mask.

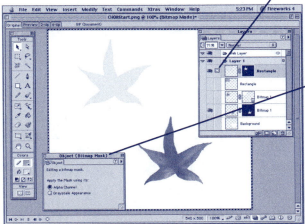

- **Masks and the Object panel**. Press Alt/Option + F2 to open the Object panel. Select a masked object and view its mask options in the Object panel.

Adjusting Mask and Color Settings

Any mask can be modified in Fireworks. First, click on the link icon located between the object and its mask. This will unlink the mask from the object in the Layers panel. Then, click and drag either the top or bottom object in the document window to change the position of each of the objects. You can also apply effects, or change the stroke, fill, and optimization settings. You can also change each object's color, opacity setting, and so on. The following sections show you how to edit a mask, change its blending mode, and then apply the Feather command.

Editing the Color of a Masked Object

The following steps show you how to change the tonal range of colors for the bitmap image, which is a mask for the rectangle vector object below it.

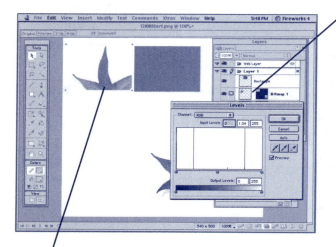

1. Click on the link icon between the mask and object thumbnail images of a mask object in the Layers panel. The objects will become unlinked, and the link icon will disappear. The outlines for the two objects will appear in the document window.

2. Choose Effect from the Window menu or press Alt/Option + F7 to open the Effect panel.

3. Click on the bitmap image object for the mask and then choose the Levels command from the Effect, Adjust Color pop-up menu. The Levels dialog box will open.

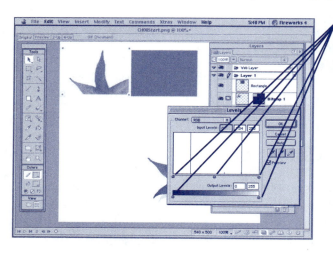

4. Click and drag the slider controls to adjust the tonal range of the bitmap image.

5. Click on the OK button to save your changes and close the Levels dialog box.

Adjusting the Blending Mode of a Masked Object

With the two objects unmasked, you can select both objects and apply a blending mode to them. Like masks, blending modes require two overlapping objects. A blending mode creates a resulting color based on the type of blending mode you choose combined with the colors of the overlapping objects. The following steps show you how to apply a blending mode to two objects.

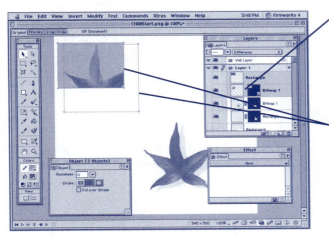

1. Click on the link icon between the mask and object thumbnail images of a mask object in the Layers panel. The outlines for the two objects will appear in the document window.

2. If the mask objects are not highlighted, select both mask objects using the Pointer Tool (V). You will be able to see the outlines of both objects highlighted in the document window.

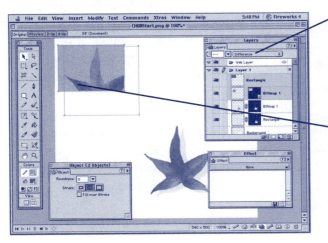

3. Click on the pop-up menu located at the top of the Layers panel. The default setting in this pop-up menu is Normal. Select a blending mode. In this example, I chose the Difference blending mode.

4. The overlapping areas of the mask objects will display the resulting blending mode. If you don't like the new color, press Ctrl/Command + Z or choose the Undo command from the Edit menu.

Applying the Feather Command

Because a mask is essentially a cutout image, you might want to smooth the mask's edges to help it blend in with the colors from the object below it. You can do this by selecting the object and applying the Feather command. Here's how:

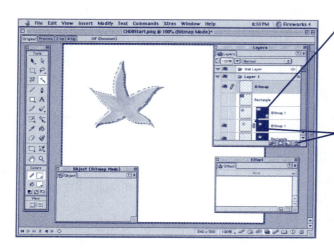

1. Click on the link icon between the mask and object thumbnail images of a mask object in the Layers panel. The outlines for the two objects will appear in the document window.

2. As an alternative, you can apply the mask to the object by removing the mask from the document. To do this, select the mask object in the Layers panel and then click on the Trash button located in the lower right corner of the Layers panel. Click on the Apply button to convert the mask into a bitmap image.

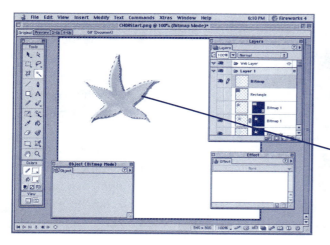

3. Choose Feather from the Modify, Marquee menu. The Feather window will open. Type the number of pixels you want to apply with the Feather command into the text box. Then, click on the OK button.

The marquee surrounding the selected object will change its shape, indicating that the Feather command has been applied to the selected object.

Creating an Alpha Channel Mask

Before you explore the deeper meaning of what an alpha channel mask is, let me try to avoid a little feature confusion. If you open the Effect panel (press Alt/Option + F7), you'll notice a Convert to Alpha command in the Effect, Other pop-up menu. This effect converts a selected object into a gradient transparency using the transparency information for the object. This effect is an entirely different feature than the one I'm about to discuss in the following sections.

You can only create an alpha channel mask with a bitmap image in Fireworks. If you're not sure whether a mask is a bitmap or vector, click on the mask and view its object name in the Layers panel. Fireworks will label a bitmap mask with a name that includes the word *bitmap*. You can also select the mask thumbnail in the Layers panel and open the Object panel (press Alt/Option + F2) to find out whether a mask is a bitmap or vector mask. The type of mask will appear in the Object panel's title bar. For example, *Object (Bitmap Mask)*.

An alpha channel mask applies the alpha channel of the bitmap mask (the bottom object, which can be a vector object) to the bitmap mask object above it. The following sections show you how to create a text mask using the alpha channel feature and then adjust several mask settings to change different color elements in that mask.

Creating Mask Objects

As I mentioned before, you can create a mask with text, vector objects, or bitmap objects. In this example, the group mask consists of a bitmap text object as the mask, or the top object, and a bitmap image of tree leaves as the bottom object. You can move or copy this masked object just like you would copy a vector or bitmap object. If you edit this mask (by clicking on the link icon), you will only be able to move the bitmap image (or bottom object). The following steps show you how to create a mask with a vector text object combined with a bitmap image object.

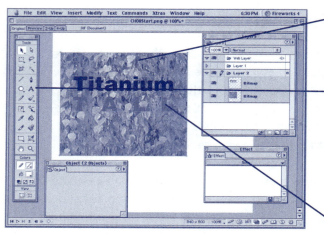

1. Copy and paste a bitmap image into a new document window, or import an image into a document.

2. Select the Text Tool (T) from the toolbox. Type some text into the Text Editor window. Select the text and apply any formatting to it. Then, click on the OK button. The text object will appear in the document window.

3. Select the text object and then choose Convert to Bitmap from the Modify menu.

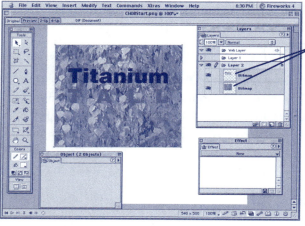

4. Hold down the Shift key and click on the bitmap and text objects in the document window. Both objects will be highlighted in the Layers panel, indicating that both objects are currently selected.

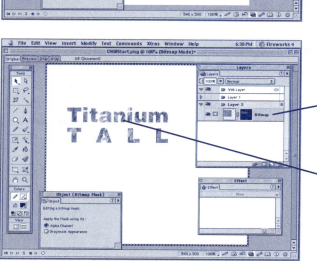

5. Choose Group as Mask from the Modify, Masks menu.

Both objects in the Layers panel will become a single object. The object name for the mask will be Bitmap.

6. View the bitmap image showing through the text mask in the document window.

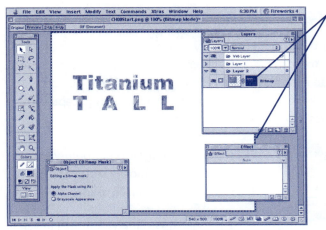

7. Click on the mask thumbnail in the Layers panel. A black and yellow candy-striped line will appear around the canvas area in the document window, indicating that a mask object is selected.

NOTE

To see a different mask effect, place the text object below the bitmap image object. For example, click and drag the text object and move it below the image object in the Layers panel.

Then, select both objects and apply the Group as Mask command from the Modify, Masks menu. In this example, the blue color from the text will show through the bitmap mask image.

Creating an Alpha Channel Mask

Now that the mask has been created, see what happens if you select the Alpha Channel setting in the Object panel. The following steps show you how.

1. Select the mask object in the Layers panel.

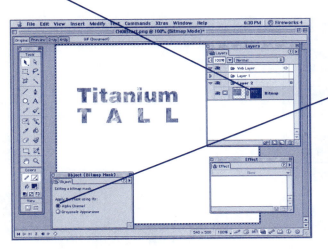

2. Choose Object from the Window menu or press Alt/Option + F2 to open the Object panel.

3. Click on the Alpha Channel radio button in the Object panel. Fireworks uses the alpha channel from the bottom object to define the mask. Because the background image is already showing through the text object, there is no visible difference between the Alpha Channel and Grayscale Appearance options in the Object panel.

Adjusting Mask Colors

Another way to adjust the color of a mask is to apply an effect from the Adjust Color menu in the Effect panel. You can have the flexibility of modifying the mask with an effect without actually altering the image. Simply click on the eye icon beside the effect to hide that effect for the mask object. The following steps show you how to adjust the hue and saturation levels of a mask.

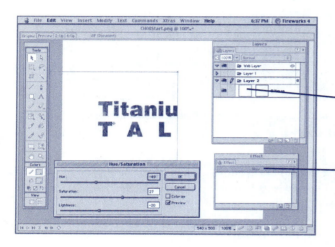

1. Place the image object below the text object and choose Group as Mask from the Modify, Masks menu.

2. Click on the image thumbnail in the Layers panel. The mask objects will be selected with Fireworks in Vector Mode.

3. Choose Hue/Saturation from the Effect/Adjust Color pop-up menu. The Hue/Saturation dialog box will open.

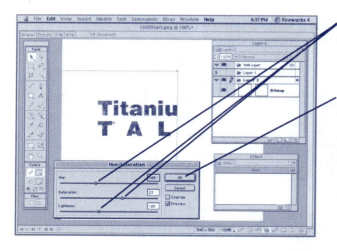

4. Click and drag the Hue, Saturation, and Lightness slider controls to adjust the color values in the mask.

5. Click on the OK button to save your changes and close the Hue/Saturation dialog box.

Editing Masks

You can move each object in a mask. If you're combining different object shapes to create a custom shape, you might need to adjust the placement of either object in addition to tweaking the color of the mask. The following steps show you how to move each object in a group mask.

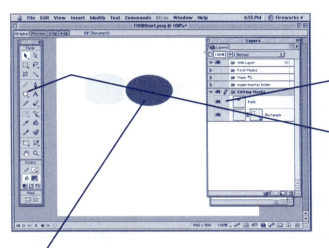

1. Open a document that contains a mask object or create a new document.

2. If you created a new document window, select a tool from the toolbox and create an object. In this example, I selected the Rectangle Tool (R) from the toolbox and created a square with a blue fill color.

3. Add a second object to the document window. Place it over the first object. In this example, this object is a purple ellipse.

4. Choose Group as Mask from the Modify, Masks menu.

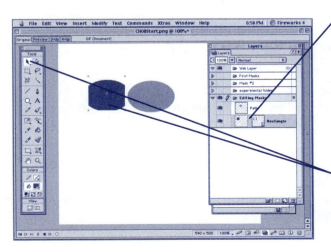

5. Click on the link icon between the object and mask thumbnail images for the mask object in the Layers panel. The link icon will disappear from the Layers panel. The mask will be separated from the object below it.

6. Both objects are now editable. Choose the Pointer Tool (V) and click and drag the mouse over the mask object to move the bottom object. Click on the Alt/Option key with the Pointer Tool (V) selected and then click and drag the top object in the mask.

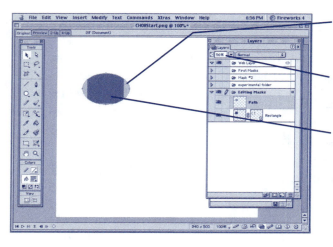

7. Move another object so that it covers the mask object.

8. Type a new value into the Opacity text box in the Layers panel.

The color of the mask object will change because it is being filtered through the transparent gray color.

Reveal and Hide All Masks

Another way to create a mask is to select a vector object and apply the Reveal All or Hide All commands from the Modify, Mask menu. The Reveal All command creates an empty white mask for the selected object. As you might have already guessed, the Hide All command creates an empty black mask for the selected objects. The following steps show you how to apply the Reveal All command to a vector object.

1. Open a new or existing document. Create a few objects in the document window.

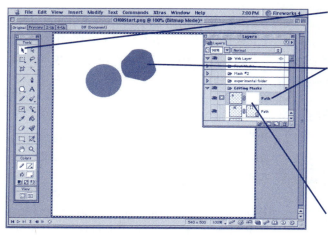

2. Select the Pointer Tool (V) from the toolbox.

3. Click on an object to select it. You can select a bitmap or vector object to use with either command. In this example, I've selected a vector object.

4. Choose Reveal All from the Modify, Masks menu.

A white matte will appear beside the object in the Layers panel.

NOTE

The Reveal/Hide Selection commands can be applied to a bitmap object. To create a mask with these commands, select the Marquee or Lasso tool from the toolbox. Then, click and drag the mouse over part of the bitmap object. Choose the Reveal Selection command from the Modify, Masks menu to change the selected area into a mask. Conversely, choose the Hide Selection command to hide the selected area but show the rest of the object as the mask.

Object Opacity and Masks

You can change the opacity (transparency) setting for a mask object just as you would for a vector or bitmap object, including text. You can select multiple objects all at once and assign the same opacity value to them all, or you can select a single object and adjust its opacity value. The following steps show you how to adjust the transparency level for several objects at one time.

1. Open a document containing more than one image object.

2. Select the Pointer Tool (V) from the toolbox.

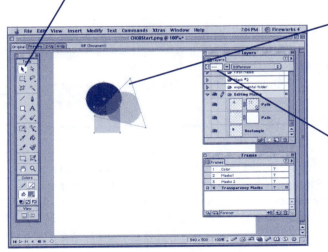

3. Click on the first object.

4. Hold down the Shift key and select a few more image objects. Try to select objects that overlap each other.

5. Type a new value into the Opacity text box in the Layers panel, or click and drag the slider in the Opacity pop-up menu. If a lower number (for example, 50) is input into the Opacity text box, you will be able to see through the selected overlapping objects in the document window.

Adjusting Matte Colors

The matte color fills in transparent colors in a document with the selected matte color. If the document does not contain any transparent colors, the matte color is ignored. The following steps show you how to set the matte color for an image object.

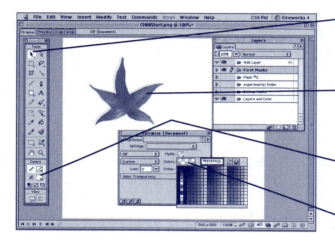

1. Open a document containing more than one image object. Select the Pointer Tool (V) from the toolbox.

2. Click on the object you want to mask and place it over another object in the document window.

3. Click on the Fill color well in the toolbox and view the object's fill color.

4. Click on the Matte box in the Optimize panel. Type the hexadecimal value of the fill color for the selected object in the color pop-up menu for the Matte field.

5. Click on the Preview tab in the document window to see how the selected matte color affects the other objects in the document. In this example, the canvas color is white, and I typed CCFF00 in the color pop-up menu for the Matte field. If you preview the document, the canvas will change to the yellow color of the leaf mask.

TIP

Background matting can be applied to JPEG or GIF images. If you want to apply a matte color to a JPEG image, the background color of the Web page must be a solid color. If the matte color matches the background color of the Web page, the matte color will replace any transparent pixels in the Fireworks document.

Adjusting Colors with Layers

You can create interesting combinations of colors by choosing a blending mode for two or more objects, or by simply overlapping an object over one or more other objects. Fortunately, all these layer-related controls are located in the Layers panel. The following sections show you how to blend, group, and apply effects and gradients to change the overlapping colors of objects.

Changing an Object's Color

Give two or more objects a new set of colors by applying a blending mode to them. Blending modes combine the foreground and background objects in an image to create a new result color in the overlapping areas of those objects. The following sections show you how to change the blending mode for selected objects and adjust the color of certain objects by changing their layer order in the Layers panel.

Adjusting the Blending Mode

You might have already figured this out if you've been doing some ad hoc experimentation. Changing the blending mode between two or more objects is as simple as selecting those objects and then picking a new blending mode from the Layers panel. The following steps show you how.

1. Open a document containing several image objects.

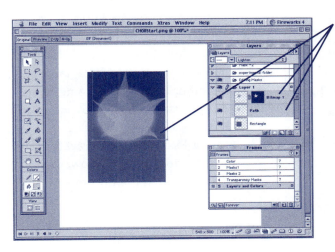

2. Select the Pointer Tool (V) and select two or more overlapping objects. In this example, I've selected two objects from the Layers panel.

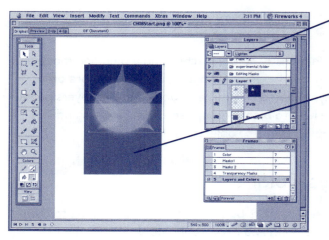

3. Click on the pop-up menu located at the top of the Layers panel. Choose a blending mode from the menu.

4. View the changes in the document window.

> ### NOTE
>
> To find out more information about blending modes, see Chapter 8, "Modifying Vector and Bitmap Graphics."

Layer Placement and Overlapping Objects

Another way to change an object's color is to overlap it with different objects in the document window. You can arrange an object's position in the document window by moving its position within a layer or moving it to a different layer in the Layers panel. The following steps show you how to change the color of an object by changing the order of objects in the Layers panel.

1. Open a document containing several image objects.

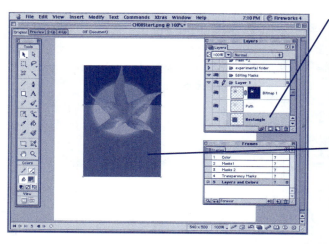

2. Select the Pointer Tool (V) and click and drag an object in a lower layer to a higher layer in the Layers panel. You can also move an object in a higher layer to below another object in the same layer, or to a completely different layer.

3. Wait for Fireworks to redraw the object in the document window, then view the changes in the document window.

Adjusting Opacity to Create New Colors

Adjust the transparency values for background and foreground objects to soften a color, add a new color to the foreground object, or create interesting image and color combinations. You can adjust the opacity of any object from the Opacity controls located at the top of the Layers panel. The following sections use a combination of bitmap images and vector shapes to change colors by modifying object opacity settings and creating an index transparency.

Mixing Colors by Changing Opacity Settings

Opacity is another word for transparency. The lower the number you type into the Opacity text box in the Layers panel, the more transparent the selected object becomes. If an object has a dark fill color, you can lighten the entire object and blend it into the color of the object behind it by lowering the transparency value in the text box. The following steps show you how to mix the color of the background object by changing the opacity value for the foreground object in the Layers panel.

1. Place a bitmap object over a solid color object in a new or existing document window.

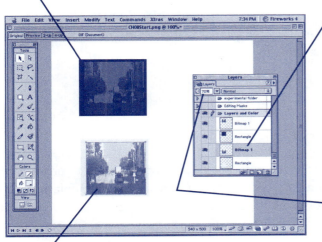

2. Choose the Pointer Tool (V) and then select the bitmap object or click on the bitmap object in the Layers panel.

3. Type a lower value into the Opacity text box.

The color of the solid object behind the bitmap image will blend in with the bitmap object. That is, the bitmap object located in the foreground becomes more transparent after you enter a lower transparency value, revealing the color of the background object.

Creating an Index Transparency

Earlier in this chapter, I discussed a little color theory and how the primary colors are red, blue, and yellow. If you mix some combination of them together, you create new colors. You can overlap objects with varying levels of transparency to suggest new colors where those objects overlap. Here's how:

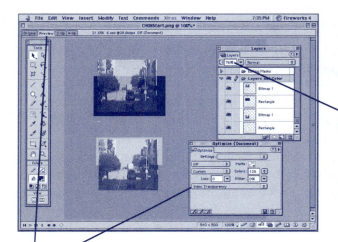

1. Open a document containing bitmap and vector objects. Place the bitmap objects so that they overlap the solid-colored vector objects.

2. Deselect any objects by selecting a layer from the Layers panel. Then, type a lower opacity value in the Opacity text box. In this example, I typed 76 into the text box. The blue color of the solid object behind the bitmap will be visible behind the bitmap image.

3. Choose Index Transparency from the bottom pop-up menu in the Optimize panel.

4. Click on the Preview tab to view the transparency changes to the selected image objects, as well as to the canvas.

Grouped Objects and Color

Another way to suggest color is to place different-colored objects next to or over each other, with or without any transparency setting. For example, if you place a red square over a blue square, some might see the color purple because red and blue mixed together create purple. The following steps show you how to group objects together across layers.

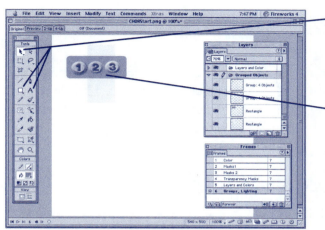

1. Open a new or existing document. Create several bitmap or vector objects and choose different colors for each selected object.

2. Place the objects so that they overlap each other in the document window. Select a background object and choose a fill color that is lighter than the foreground objects.

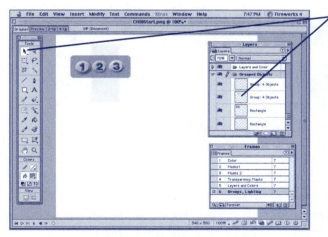

3. Select the Pointer Tool (V) from the toolbox. Select two or more objects in the document window, then choose Group from the Modify menu. The selected objects will become grouped as a single object in the document window and in the Layers panel.

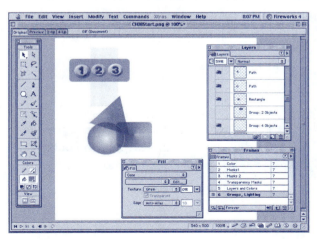

Adjusting Color with Overlapping Gradients

You can combine opacity settings with objects containing gradient fill colors to create new colors where those objects overlap. Here's how:

1. Open a new or existing document. Create several graphic objects and place them so that they overlap each other.

2. Select an object and then press Shift + F7 to open the Fill panel. Pick a gradient for the object.

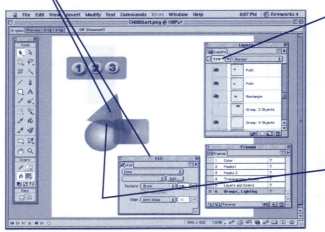

3. Type a low transparency value in the Transparency/Opacity text box in the Layers panel. You will see the objects below the top object appear.

4. View the colors of the overlapping objects. Increase the transparency of the objects to adjust the colors created by the overlapping areas of the objects.

Color and Interactive Web Elements

This last section is a little ahead of its time. All these Web elements are described in full detail in Part III, "Designing Interactive Web Graphics." However, most of these Web design elements should seem familiar to you if you've surfed the Web recently. If the concept of a simple button baffles you, return to this section after you've read Chapter 10 "Introduction to Slices, Hotspots, and Image Maps," and Chapter 12, "Making Buttons with the Button Editor." The following sections show you how to adjust color settings for buttons, text, and their counterpart graphics.

Creating a Simple Button

One of the most basic graphics you'll find in computer software, including Web pages, is a simple button. A simple button has two states: up and down. Up means the button has not been pressed, while the down state indicates that the button has been clicked on, or is currently selected. The following steps show you how to create the initial button graphic.

1. Open a new or existing document window.

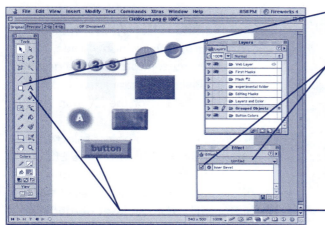

2. Select a shape tool, such as the Rectangle Tool (R), and create a shape.

3. Choose the Effect command from the Window menu or press Option + F7 to open the Effect panel. With the shape object selected, choose Inner Bevel from the Effect, Bevel and Emboss pop-up menu. The rectangle object will become a more three dimensional button.

4. Select the Text Tool (T) and add some text to the button object. Apply the Inset Emboss effect to the text to blend it into the rectangle object behind it.

Blending Buttons with a Nav Bar

Usually you won't find just one button on a Web page. You're more likely to find a navigation bar, or nav bar. *Nav bar* is the term used to describe a common set of buttons organized in a navigational bar so that someone visiting your Web site can quickly skip from one area of your site to another without having to constantly click on the Back button. The following steps show you how to blend a button into the base nav bar graphic object.

1. Open a new or existing document window.

2. Select a shape tool, such as the Rectangle Tool (R), and create a shape. Open the Effect panel by choosing Effect from the Window menu. Select the Inner Bevel menu item from the Effect, Bevel and Emboss pop-up menu in the Effect panel. The rectangle shape should look like a button graphic.

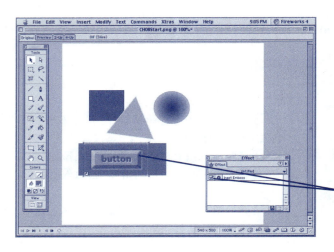

3. Choose the Convert to Symbol command from the Modify menu. Click on the Graphic radio button and type a name for the button symbol in the Symbol Properties window. Then, click on the OK button to create the graphic symbol. Place the graphic symbol over the base graphic for the nav bar.

4. With the button object selected, choose Inset Emboss from the Effect, Bevel and Emboss pop-up menu in the Effect panel. The outer edges of the button will create an inset border into the nav bar graphic behind it.

Choosing Colors for Button States

Although up and down are the two most commonly used button states, you can create additional button states, which in turn will require variations on colors for the button object. Fireworks enables you to create custom graphics for up to four different button states: Up, Over, Down, and Over While Down. However, if you're a JavaScript expert, you can also create your own custom routines to create new button states. The following steps show you how to create a button and add the Over While Down state for that button in the Button Editor.

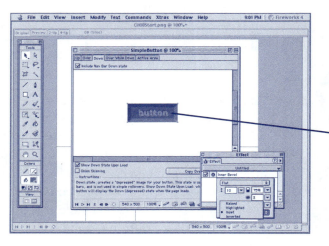

1. First, create a button. Create a vector object, and apply the Inner Bevel effect to that object. See the "Creating a Simple Button" section of this chapter for more detailed steps.

2. Select an image object in the document window and then choose the Copy command from the Edit menu. Choose New Button from the Insert menu. Paste the copied object from the document window into the Button Editor window.

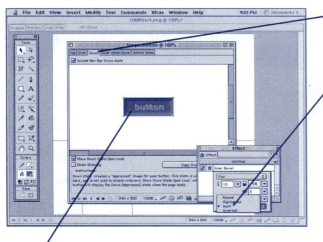

3. Click on the Down tab and paste the image object into the Button Editor window.

4. Now create the image for the Down button state. Choose Effect from the Window menu. Click on the I icon beside the Inner Bevel effect in the Effect panel. Select the Inset menu item from the lower pop-up menu.

The button graphic's shape will change, and the button graphic will look like the button has been selected.

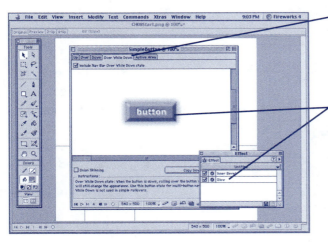

5. Now create a third button state. Click on the Over While Down tab and paste the button graphic into the Button Editor window.

6. Choose the Glow effect from the Effect, Shadow and Glow menu in the Effect pop-up menu. By changing the effect for this button state, you can visibly identify the Over While Down state of the button when you preview the button states in a browser window.

Choosing a Text Color for Buttons and Menus

Each button state will also probably include a text object. You can modify text color for a button in the same way that you'd edit the color of a text object in the document window. The following steps show you how. These steps are a continuation of the steps from the previous section.

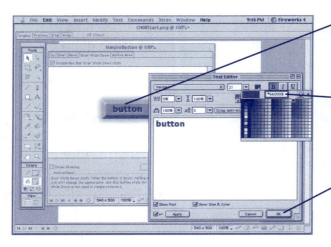

1. Double-click on the text object in the Over While Down tab. The Text Editor window will open.

2. Click and drag the mouse over the text in the Text Editor window. Then, click on the color well and select a new color for the text object.

3. Click on the OK button in the Text Editor window to save your changes.

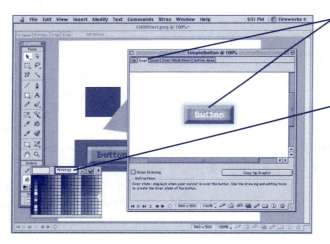

4. Repeat the steps in the preceding section and add an Over button state to your document.

5. Click on the text object in the button window, then click on the Stroke color well in the toolbox. Select a new color for the text. Press the Enter/Return key to save your changes. The text color will change to the color you selected in the Stroke color well.

8

Modifying Vector and Bitmap Graphics

A computer graphic can be a bitmap image or a vector drawing. A vector graphic is created with a mathematic algorithm, calculated by the application. Designers use them to create precise, scalable graphics. On the other hand, bitmap graphics are pixel-based images that are not as easily scalable as vector graphics. A good example of a bitmap image is a picture taken with a digital camera.

Graphic applications usually enable you to create, view, and edit either bitmap or vector graphics. Macromedia FreeHand, for example, is a great application for creating vector graphics. On the other hand, Adobe Photoshop is an excellent application for creating and editing bitmap images. Fireworks' ability to create and edit vector and bitmap graphics is one of the main reasons why it's so attractive for designing Web pages. In this chapter you'll learn how to:

- ● Edit bitmap and vector objects
- ● Transform objects
- ● Change stroke and fill settings
- ● Add transparency to an object or document

Changing Bitmap Objects

A *pixel* is a tiny square of color information created in software and displayed on your computer monitor. The larger the desktop you choose, the smaller each pixel becomes. Setting your operating system to display a higher number of colors increases the color accuracy of bitmap graphics.

Generally, higher quality bitmap images, such as a 2-megapixel image from a digital camera, consist of thousands of pixels, each capable of displaying millions of colors. You can magnify or shrink part of a 2-megapixel image and not notice a big difference in image quality. However, if you were to increase the size of an icon, a 16 pixel by 16 pixel image, you would be able to identify the pixels in the icon as the image grows larger.

If you want to edit a pixel, you'll probably want to change its color. But it's not that easy. Because each bitmap is comprised of so many pixels with such a wide range of colors, you might need to apply an effect, such as a Sharpen Tool to adjust the color of a group of pixels, or the Levels Tool to adjust the image's tonal range of colors. The following sections give you a brief tour of some of the most commonly used bitmap editing tools in Fireworks.

Aligning Objects

You can apply the Align commands to bitmap or vector objects. Fireworks enables you to align objects eight different ways: Left, Center Vertical, Right, Top, Center Horizontal, Bottom, Distribute Widths, and Distribute Heights. The following steps show you how to use the Center Horizontal and Distribute Heights Align commands.

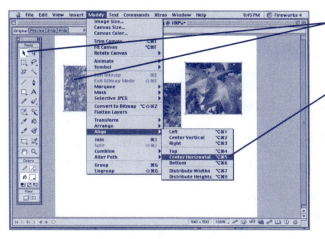

1. Choose the Pointer Tool (V) and then click on two or more objects in the document window.

2. Select Center Horizontal from the Modify, Align menu. The selected objects will line up horizontally in the document window.

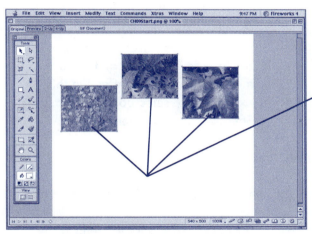

3. Select three or more objects, and then choose Distribute Heights from the Modify, Align menu.

Fireworks will align each image in the document window, distributing its location based on each object's height.

NOTE

The Align commands can help you quickly lay out button graphics or a cartoon strip of images for a Web page layout. Experiment with different combinations of Align commands and then select the ones you might use most frequently and save them as a command.

Commands enable you to automate a task in Fireworks and can help you prototype Web graphic designs faster than if you had to choose each menu command manually. To find out more about how to work with commands, see Chapter 16, "Exploring Automation and Updating Projects."

Applying Effects to Bitmaps

You can combine effects to change a bitmap object into a three-dimensional graphic, such as a button. Fireworks enables you to apply an Xtra as a more permanent effect, or apply an editable, or Live Effect, from the Effect panel. The following steps give you a brief tour of the effects installed with Fireworks.

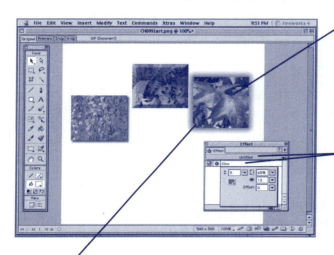

1. Press V or select the Pointer Tool from the toolbox. Select an object in the document window. Hold down the Shift key and select more than one object if you want to apply the same effect to each one.

2. Choose Effect from the Window menu, or press Alt/Option + F7 to open the Effect panel. Click on the pop-up menu and choose an effect. In this example, I've selected Glow from the Shadow and Glow menu.

The effect will be applied to the selected object.

3. With the Pointer Tool (V) selected, click on another object in the document window.

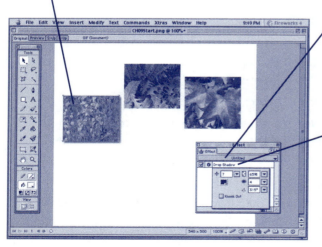

4. Click on the pop-up menu in the Effect panel and chose an effect for the object. In this example, I chose the Drop Shadow effect from the Shadow and Glow menu.

The effect will be added to the object, and will appear in the window list in the Effect panel. You can check or uncheck the check box to turn an effect on or off for the selected object. This check box feature is what Macromedia refers to as a Live Effect.

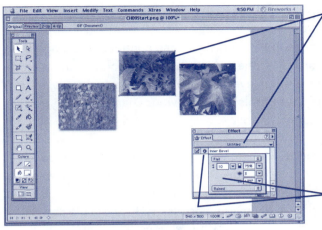

5. Choose another object in the document window and select an effect from the pop-up menu of the Effect panel. In this example, I chose the Inner Bevel command from the Bevel and Emboss menu.

6. View the effect applied to the selected object.

7. Click on the i icon in the Effect panel to view or edit the settings for a particular effect.

8. Reselect an object and apply another effect to it. In this example, I chose the Gaussian Blur effect from the Blur menu.

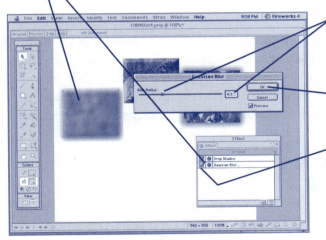

9. Click and drag the slider control or type a number into the text box to adjust the blur area for the effect.

10. Click on the OK button to save your changes and apply the effect.

11. To view an effect, select the check box for that effect in the Effect panel. You can uncheck it to hide an effect.

TIP

To find out more about Xtras and Effects, see Chapter 9, "Applying Effects."

Adjusting Bitmap Image Settings

After you've opened a bitmap image in Fireworks, you can continue to change the way it looks. For example, you can adjust the image's brightness and contrast, add a fill color, change the hue and saturation levels, or tweak the tonal range levels of the image. You explored some of these tools in the previous chapter when you worked with color and bitmap images.

In addition to the filter tools, if you're working with a JPEG image, you can adjust the Selective JPEG settings for a bitmap image. Selective JPEG settings enable you to optimize some pixels in a bitmap and not others. You can retain some of the high-resolution image quality in part of an image, and also reduce the file size by applying a selective JPEG to a bitmap. The following sections show you how to work with the controls in the Levels dialog box and Selective JPEG Settings dialog box to customize a bitmap image.

Applying the Levels Tool

If you've opened a photo in Fireworks, you can adjust the tonal range of light and dark colors with the Levels Tool. Each bitmap image contains a red, green, and blue channel. Each color channel contains a unique set of pixels. Together, they create the image you see in the document window. The Levels Tool displays the tonal range of information as a histogram in the Levels dialog box. The following steps show you how to adjust the controls in the Levels dialog box.

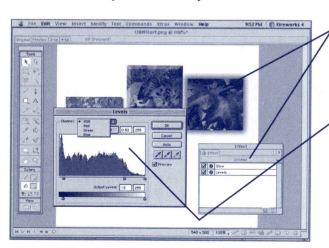

1. Use the Pointer Tool (V) to select an image in the document window. Choose Levels from the Effect, Adjust Color pop-up menu in the Effect panel.

The Levels dialog box will open. The histogram representing the red, green, and blue tonal ranges of the image will appear in the Levels dialog box. More pixels in a particular tonal range are respresented by a taller, or higher, bar.

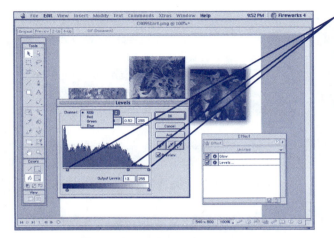

The histogram represents tonal values ranging from zero to 255. The slider on the left represents the darker colors in the image, the middle slider represents midrange tones, and the right slider represents highlight tones. The slider controls located on the bottom of the Levels dialog box enable you to adjust the output levels of the image.

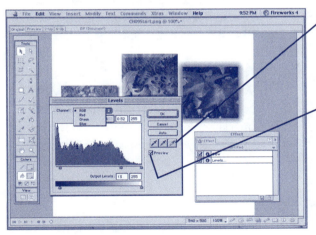

2. Click on the shadow, midtone, or highlight color eyedropper to select a particular range of values in the selected image object.

3. Check the Preview check box to view your changes in the document window.

NOTE

The Levels Tool and the controls in the Levels dialog box in Fireworks work similarly to the Levels Tool in Photoshop.

Applying the JPEG Selection Tool

The JPEG Selection Tool enables you to assign different levels of compression to selected areas in a JPEG file. You can choose the level of quality at which a JPEG image compresses its image information, and you can define whether text quality is preserved, or, if the image contains a button, you can define the quality of a button image in the JPEG file. The following steps will familiarize you with the Selective JPEG settings.

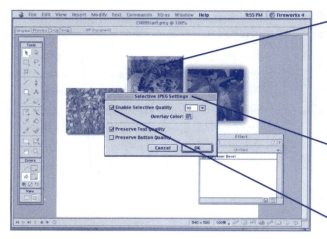

1. Press V or choose the Pointer Tool from the toolbox. Select an object in the document window. Hold down the Shift key and select more than one object if you want to apply the same effect to each one.

2. Choose Settings from the Modify, Selective JPEG menu. The Selective JPEG Settings dialog box will open.

3. Check the Enable Selective Quality check box to activate the compression setting in the text box on the right side of the Selective JPEG Settings dialog box.

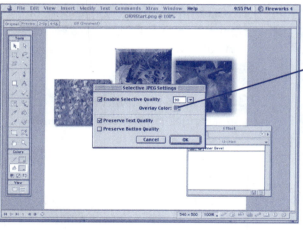

4. Click on the Overlay Color well if you want to choose a different overlay color for the selected image object. An overlay color enables you to view where the selective compression will affect the image.

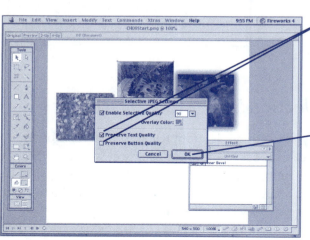

5. Check the Preserve Text Quality or Preserve Button Quality check boxes if you want to retain as much of the image quality as possible for these image elements.

6. Click on the OK button to save your changes and apply them to the selected object.

Cropping a Bitmap

Cropping tools enable you to clip part of an image from a document. These tools work best on a single image. However, you can crop a group of bitmap images, too. I got mixed results trying to apply this tool to the sample file shown in the following steps. Sometimes the image would crop; other times it would not. If you experience this same behavior, be patient and try again. The following steps show you how to crop a bitmap from a document window.

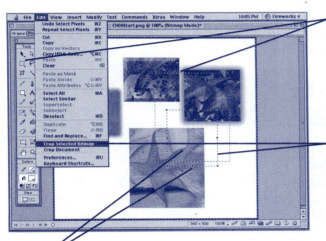

1. Use a selection tool, such as the Rectangle Marquee Tool (M), to highlight a selected area in the document window. Alternatively, you can also choose the Crop Tool (C) from the toolbox and select part of the document you want to crop.

2. Choose Crop Selected Bitmap from the Edit menu. The selected area will become highlighted, and the Crop Tool boundary box will surround the selected area.

3. Click and drag the handles of the boundary box to resize the cropped area. Click inside the boundary box and drag the cursor to move the selected crop area.

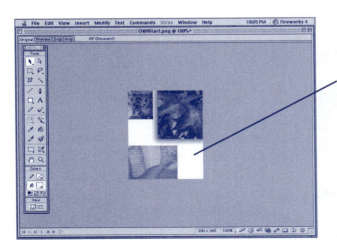

4. Choose Crop Document from the Edit menu.

Fireworks will discard the image information outside the cropped area and adjust the canvas size to match the cropped area of the image.

Resizing Bitmaps

Digital pictures are usually too large to use for a Web graphic. Most digital cameras create 640 × 480 or more pixels per image. You will probably have to resize a digital image if you want to use one with your Web graphics.

There are a couple different ways you can resize a digital picture. You can crop of a digital picture or resize the entire image. When you resize an image, Fireworks applies an interpolation algorithm to resample the pixels in an image. You can set the interpolation method in the General Preferences window. Bicubic interpolation (which is the default setting) enables Fireworks to preserve the image quality when you reduce the size of an image. The following steps show you how to resize an entire image using the Image Size command. However, you can also resize a bitmap or vector image using the Scale Tool in the toolbox or in the Modify, Transform menu.

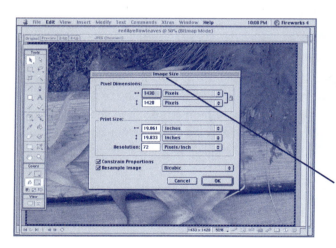

1. Select the Open command from the File menu. Navigate the hard drive and open the image file you want to resize.

2. Choose Image Size from the Modify menu. The Image Size dialog box will open.

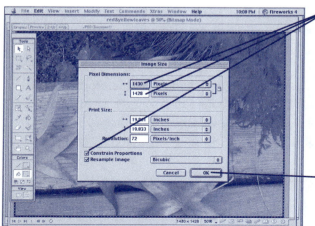

3. Type a number in the Width or Height text box to change the size of the document. If the Constrain Proportions check box is selected, the corresponding Width or Height value will automatically be calculated after you type a new value for either setting into the Image Size dialog box.

4. Click on the OK button to save your changes and resize the image.

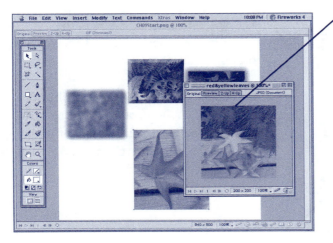

The resized image will appear in the Fireworks workspace. I resized the image in this example to 200 × 200 pixels.

Distorting, Skewing, and Rotating Bitmaps

You can customize the shape of a bitmap by applying one of the Transform commands: Free Transform, Scale, Skew, Distort, Numeric Transform, Rotate, and Flip. You can access one of three Transform tools from the toolbox. Press Q to select the Transform Tool, and press Q again to cycle through the Scale, Distort, and Skew tools. If you want to combine Transform commands, choose Free Transform from the Modify, Transform menu. The following steps show you how to apply the Distort Tool to a bitmap.

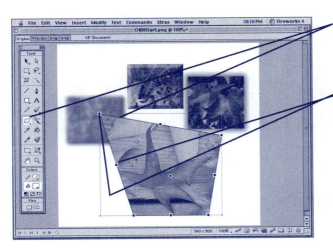

1. Select an object in the document window, then click on the Distort Tool (Q) in the toolbox.

2. Click and drag the corner handle to grow a corner of the image. Click and drag one of the middle handles to stretch the side of the image object.

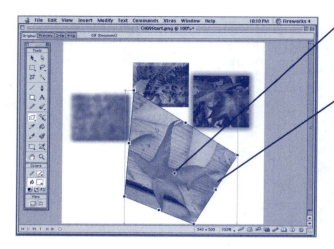

3. Click and drag the circle in the center of the object to adjust the rotation point of the object.

4. Adjust as many sides of the object as you want. When you're ready to save the distorted image, click on a different tool in the toolbox, or choose a different layer in the Layers panel.

Editing a Bitmap Mask

To create a bitmap mask, you can group or paste a bitmap object with a second vector or bitmap object. When you create a mask, the pixels of the top object act as a mask for the selected object below it. Both objects retain their fill, stroke, and effect settings after being formed into a mask. You can edit the mask object as you would edit any bitmap object. The following steps show you how to modify a bitmap image.

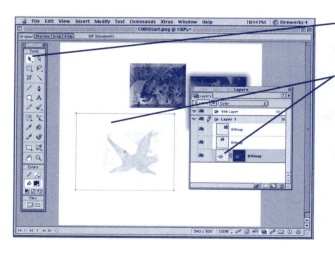

1. Select two or more objects in the document window.

2. Choose Group as Mask from the Modify, Mask menu. The two objects will be reselected as an image mask object in the document window.

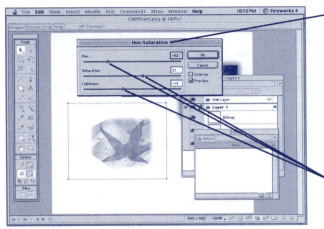

3. There are several ways to modify a bitmap image. You can use the Rubber Stamp Tool (S); you can add a fill color; or you can tweak the brightness, contrast, hue, or saturation. In this example, I chose the Hue/Saturation Effect from the Adjust Color pop-up menu in the Effect panel.

4. Click and drag the slider controls to adjust the Hue, Saturation, or Lightness in the selected object.

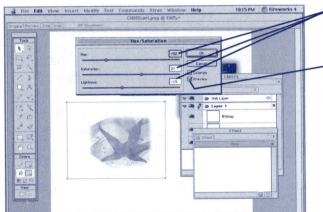

5. Alternatively, you can type a value for each setting.

6. Check the Preview check box to view your changes in the document window as you adjust settings in the Hue/Saturation dialog box.

7. Click on the OK button to save your changes, or click on the Cancel button if you do not want to change any settings.

Erasing Pixels in a Bitmap

Don't be fooled by the knife icon in the toolbox. It's called the Eraser Tool, even though the eraser icon won't appear until you actually start erasing pixels from a bitmap. However, if you apply this same tool to a vector object, it acts as a knife and splits a path into two. The following steps show you how to remove pixels from a bitmap image.

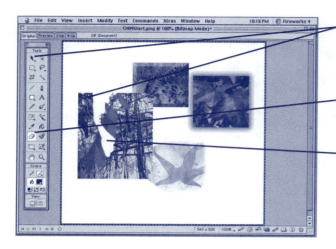

1. Choose the Pointer Tool (V) from the toolbox, then select an image in the document window.

2. Click on the Knife/Eraser Tool (E) in the toolbox.

3. Click and drag the tool in the selected bitmap. The document will switch to Bitmap Mode while you are using the Eraser Tool. Release the mouse button to complete the erasure.

Copying Bitmaps with the Rubber Stamp Tool

If you're working with a vector object that contains a solid fill color, you can convert it to a bitmap object using the Convert to Bitmap command in the Modify menu. You can copy or edit a bitmap image using the selection, drawing, and Paint Bucket tools. If you're working with a more sophisticated image, such as a picture from a digital camera, you can use the Rubber Stamp Tool to copy or edit it. The following steps show you how to copy a bitmap using the Rubber Stamp Tool.

1. Double-click a bitmap image or select a bitmap object and then choose Edit Bitmap from the Modify menu.

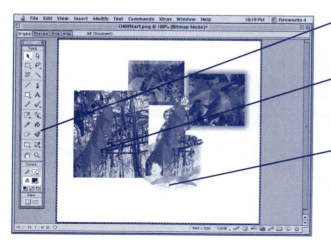

2. Select the Rubber Stamp Tool (S) from the toolbox.

3. Hold down the Alt/Option key and click and drag the Rubber Stamp tool in the document window.

4. Pick another location in the document window. Click and drag the mouse in the new location. The area that you Alt/Option-clicked and dragged the mouse over will appear in the new location.

NOTE

The Rubber Stamp Tool (S) in Fireworks works similarly to the Clone Stamp Tool in Photoshop.

Modifying Vector Graphics

A bitmap image is a collection of pixels that form an image. As a bitmap is enlarged, the clarity of the image degrades. Vector graphics, unlike bitmaps, are easily scalable, enabling a wider range of design possibilities. Any objects drawn with the Pen, Pencil, Brush, or Shape tools from the toolbox are vector graphics. Vector objects whose ends do not meet are called open path objects. You might have already guessed that objects whose end paths meet are called closed path objects. The following sections show you how to edit different kinds of vector objects.

Editing Paths

Vector drawings are comprised of points and paths. Use the drawing tools in Fireworks to create and modify vector graphics. You can edit line art imported from Illustrator or FreeHand, or create it all in Fireworks. The following sections show you how to extend a path, grow a curve, cut a path, and automatically join two similar paths into one.

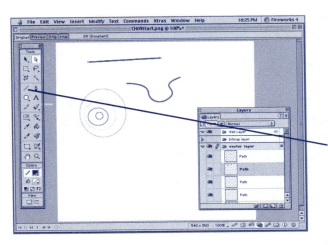

Extending a Line with the Pen Tool

You can shrink or grow any path object in Fireworks. Choose the Subselection Tool to both select and edit a path. Here's how:

1. Create a line with the Line Tool (N).

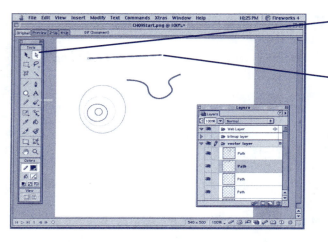

2. Click on the Subselection Tool (A) in the toolbox.

3. Click on the end point of a path and drag it to adjust its size. Release the mouse button to complete the change to the path.

NOTE

You can create a dotted or dashed line with the Line Tool by changing the Stroke settings in the Stroke panel. Use the Line Tool to create a line in a document window. Select the line object, and then choose Random and Dots from the pop-up menus in the Stroke panel. Select the Edit Stroke command from the Stroke pop-up menu and choose the Options tab in the Edit Stroke window. Type 1 in the Tips text box, and adjust the thickness of each dot by increasing the value in the Spacing text box. Select the Sensitivity tab, and change all of the Scatter and Size settings to zero. Click on the OK button to save your changes. Choose the Save Stroke As menu command from the pop-up menu in the Stroke panel to save the stroke settings.

Changing the Arc of a Curve

In addition to modifying a straight line, you can also edit a curved path with the Subselection Tool. The Subselection Tool can be used to both select and modify a vector object. Once this tool is selected, you can click on an object, or click and drag one of its points to change the shape of that object. The following steps show you how to modify a vector object with the Subselection Tool.

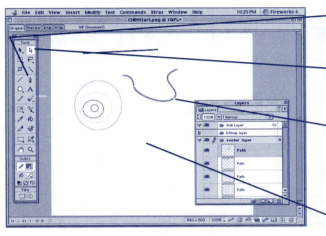

1. Create a curved path using the Pen Tool (P).

2. Choose the Subselection Tool (A) from the toolbox.

3. Click on a point on the curve and drag it to resize the shape of that curve. Click and drag the end points of a curve's handles to adjust the angle of a curve.

4. Click outside the curve's path to deselect the path.

TIP

You can create a unique path using the Subselection Tool, by combining different vector paths as you design a path. For example, you can create a path with the Line Tool (N). Then, choose the Subselection Tool (A) from the toolbox and select the Pen Tool (P) to add a curve to the end of the line path.

NOTE

You cannot modify a grouped object with the Subselection Tool. You must first select the grouped objects and then choose the Ungroup command (Shift + Ctrl/Command + G) from the Modify menu. Once the objects are ungrouped, you can edit each individual object as you like.

Cutting a Path with the Knife Tool

The Knife Tool enables you to remove part of a path or split a path to create a new path object. Click and drag the Knife Tool over a path to split a path. Select one of the split paths and press the Backspace/Delete key to remove that path from the document. The following steps show you how to use the Knife Tool with a vector object.

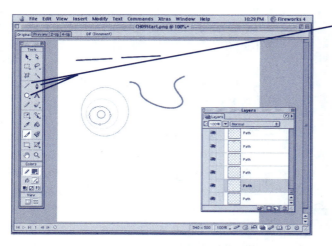

1. Create a path with the Rectangle/ Shape (R), Line (L), or Pen (P) Tool.

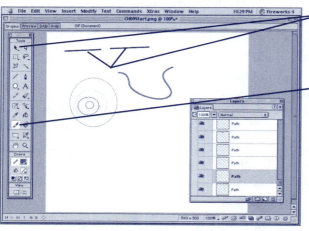

2. Choose the Pointer Tool (V) from the toolbox and select the path you want to split.

3. Select the Knife Tool (E) from the toolbox.

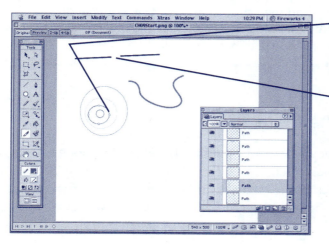

4. Click and drag the Knife Tool over the object's path. A point will appear on the path.

5. Click and drag the Knife Tool over the point you created in Step 4. The path to the right of the knife cut will be separated from the rest of the path.

TIP

If you drag the Knife Tool over an existing point in a closed path, the Knife Tool will turn that point into two separate end points. You can use the Subselection Tool to separate these points and create a new shape, or convert a closed path into an open path. To find out more about cutting an object, see the "Cutting a Closed Path" section later in this chapter.

NOTE

If you click on a vector object, you can select the Knife Tool from the toolbox. However, if you click on a bitmap object, the Knife Tool changes to the Eraser Tool. Both tools share the same shortcut key (E).

Auto-Joining Similar Paths

Bring two paths together by choosing the Subselection Tool and rejoining them. The two paths must share the same stroke settings for the auto-joining feature to function. The following steps show you how to automatically reconnect two similar paths.

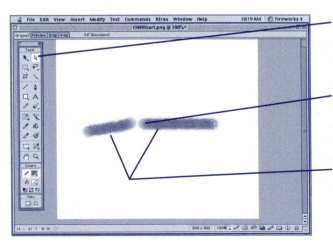

1. Click on the Subselection Tool in the toolbox. Select one of the two path objects in the document window.

2. Click on the end point of the path. Then, click and drag it near the end point of the other path.

The two paths will join. If you click on one end of the path, the other end will also become selected.

Pushing a Path

Another way to change the shape of a path is to apply the Reshape Area Tool. Three additional tools are located in the same location as the Reshape Area Tool in the toolbox. Each tool can be used to customize the shape of a path object. Perform the following steps to push a path.

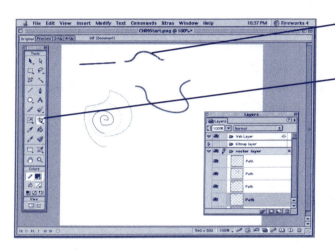

1. Create a vector path in the document window, then select that path.

2. Choose the Reshape Area Tool (F) from the toolbox.

3. Click and drag the tool near the path in the document window. The path will be pushed as you drag the cursor against it.

Pulling a Path

The Freeform Tool shares the same space as the Reshape Area Tool and the Path Scrubber tools in the toolbox. Press the F key as a shortcut to cycle through the four tools that are located with the Freeform Tool. The following steps show you how to apply the Freeform Tool to pull a path.

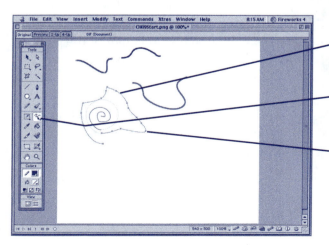

1. Create a path object in the document window. Select the path.

2. Click on the Freeform Tool in the toolbox.

3. Click and drag the tool near the path to pull it.

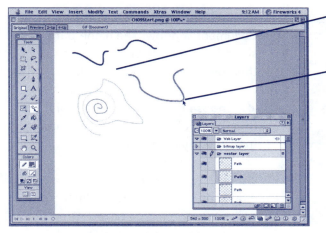

4. Click outside the object to deselect the path.

5. Select another path object. Click and drag the tool near the path to create the pull effect. You can drag the tool in any direction to modify a path.

NOTE

The Path Scrubber tools share the same tool location as the Freeform Tool (F) in the toolbox. Choose the additive or subtractive Path Scrubber Tool (F) to beef up or thin down a path's stroke size and color. Select the path you want to modify, then choose one of the Path Scrubber tools to edit that path.

Redrawing Paths

Hidden alongside the Brush Tool is the Redraw Path Tool. After you've created an open or closed path, you can redraw it using this tool. The path's stroke, fill, and effect settings are preserved when you redraw the path. The Stroke color of the object is used to display the redrawn path in the document window. If the selected object does not have a stroke color assigned to it, you should choose one, and also consider choosing a wider stroke so that you can preview the redrawn path as you create it. The following steps show you how.

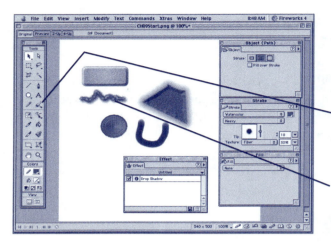

1. Create a path object in the document window. The name *path* should appear beside the object's thumbnail in the Layers panel.

2. Choose the Redraw Path Tool (B) from the toolbox. Select the path object from the Layers panel.

3. Click on the path and hold the mouse button down. The selected path will change from blue to red. Drag the tool to create a new path. Drag the cursor over part of the original path line to complete the redrawn path. Release the mouse button to view the new path.

4. Select another shape in the document window.

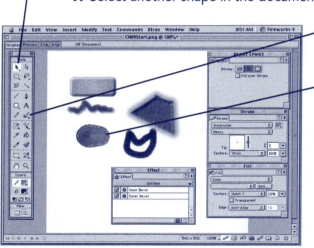

5. Choose the Redraw Path Tool or press B to switch to this tool.

6. Click and hold the mouse button on the light-blue line defining the path object. The light blue line will turn red, indicating the location of your cursor on the path and the area of the path that will be redrawn. Drag the mouse to create a new path, then end the path by dragging the mouse over part of the original path. The redrawn area of the original path will be colored red. Release the mouse button to create the redrawn path.

If you click on the end point of a selected path, the cursor will change into a Brush icon with a Plus symbol. Hold the mouse button down and drag the brush cursor to extend the end point of the path.

Cutting a Closed Path

Create custom shapes by removing part of a shape using the Knife Tool. In the first part of this section, I showed you how to edit an open path. The following steps show you how to remove part of a closed path object.

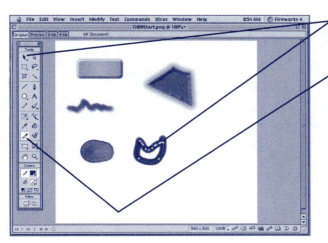

1. Select one or more objects in the document window.

2. Click on the Knife Tool (E) and drag it across two points on a path. When the Knife Tool is selected, the points on each selected vector object will change from solid color to white. After you drag the knife over a closed path object, an additional white box, or point, will appear on the path, indicating the path has been cut.

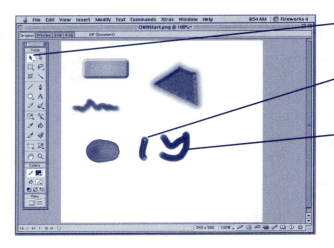

3. Choose the Pointer Tool (V) from the toolbox.

4. Click and drag the separated path away from the object.

The closed path object will now be an open path object.

> **NOTE**
>
> Select more than one object and apply the Knife Tool across layers. You can modify a group of objects with the Knife Tool, or edit each object one by one.

Cropping Paths

You can use the Crop command to combine two objects into a new one. The following steps show you how to apply the Crop command to create a new kind of path.

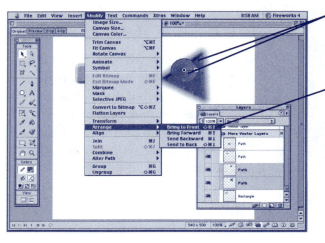

1. Click on an object in the document window. Hold down the Shift key and select another object.

2. Press Ctrl/Command + Shift + Up Arrow to bring the objects to the top layer in the document. Alternatively, choose the Bring to Front command from the Modify, Arrange menu.

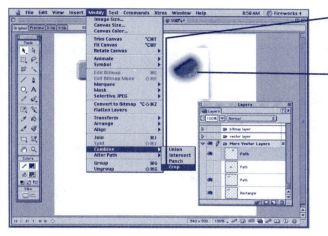

3. Choose the Crop command from the Modify, Combine menu.

Fireworks will crop and combine the objects to create a new, single path from the overlapping areas.

Changing a Path into a Mask

Any file opened in Fireworks becomes a PNG graphic file. The PNG file format enables you to edit complex line art using vector drawing tools. You can also edit pixels in image files, using tools like filters and effects.

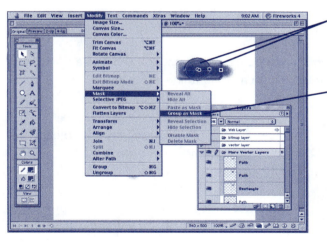

1. Click on the Pointer Tool (V) and select two objects in the document window.

2. Choose the Group as Mask command from the Modify, Mask menu.

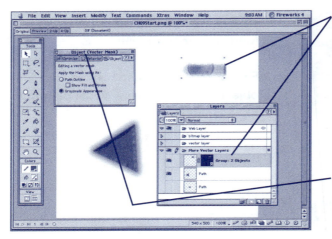

The object layers will be grouped together in the Layers panel, and the two paths will become a single masked object in the document window.

3. Choose Object from the Window menu to view additional mask settings in the Object panel.

TIP

To find out more information about how to create masks, see Chapter 5, "Creating and Designing Graphics." For more information about editing Photoshop masks, see Chapter 6, "Opening and Editing Files."

Adding a Point

You can use the Subselection Tool to add points to a path. You can add a point to change the direction of a path or to change a straight line into a curve. The following steps show you how.

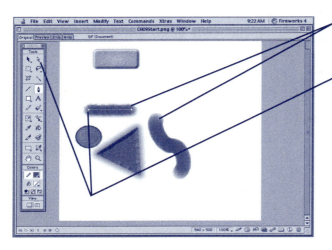

1. Create one or more path objects in the document window.

2. Choose the Subselection Tool (A) and click on a path object. The points on the path will appear and will be highlighted.

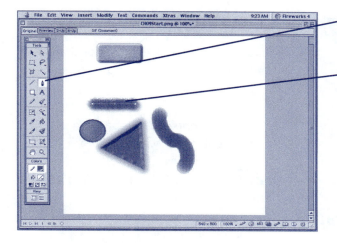

3. Select the Pen Tool (P) from the toolbox.

4. Click on the path of the selected object. A point will appear on the path.

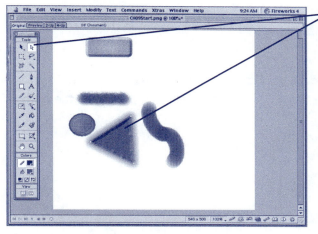

5. Add a point to another path. Choose a different path object with the Subselection Tool (A). The path and its point will be highlighted.

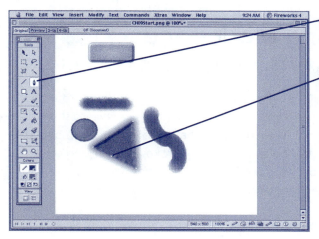

6. Select the Pen Tool (P) from the toolbox.

7. Click on the path of the selected object. A point will appear on the path.

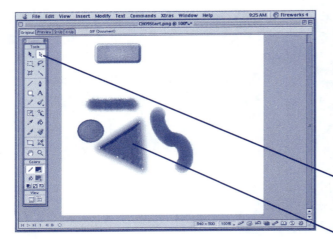

Deleting a Point

Deleting a point is even easier than adding one. The following steps show you how.

1. Create one or more paths in a document window.

2. Choose the Subselection Tool (A) from the toolbox.

3. Click on an object.

4. Click on a point in the selected object.

5. Press the Backspace/Delete key. The point will disappear from the path.

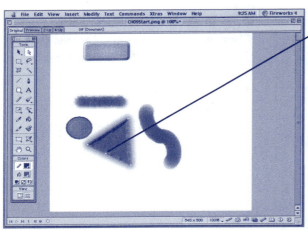

Adjusting Blending Modes and Styles and Transforming Objects

Each vector and bitmap object resides in its own layer in the Layers panel. You can modify objects by selecting them and applying a blending mode or style to them. Fireworks contains thirteen different blending modes that enable you to combine the colors between two or more objects. You can also apply stroke, pattern, and effect styles from the Styles panel. The following sections show you how to apply the Transform commands, in addition to blending modes and styles, to image objects.

Distorting Objects

To distort an object, select an it and choose the Distort Tool from the toolbox. You can make a subtle adjustment to the shape of an object, or drag each end of the object to dramatically alter its appearance. The following steps show you how to apply the Distort Tool to a closed vector path.

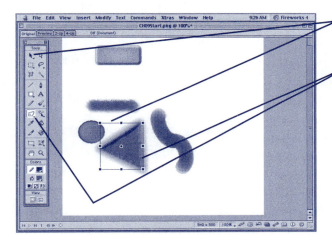

1. Select an object in the document window.

2. Click on the Distort Tool (Q). The bounding box for the selected object will change from a light blue line to a black line.

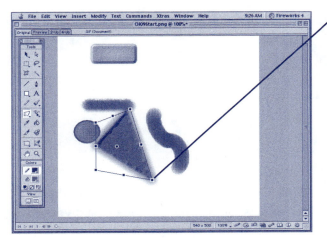

3. Click and drag a corner handle of an object to distort it. The bounding box will change its size as you resize the selected object.

4. Click outside the bounding box to save the changes made to the object. Choose Undo from the Edit menu to reverse your changes, or press Ctrl/Command + Z.

Rotating Objects

You can rotate an object three different ways, or flip it horizontally or vertically. The Rotate and Flip commands are located in the Modify, Transform menu. The following steps show you how to rotate an object 90 degrees clockwise.

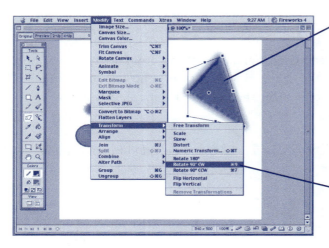

1. Create an object in the document window. Select it with the Pointer Tool (V). If you've already begun editing an object with one of the Transform tools, move ahead to the next step. You can apply a number of different Transform commands to the same object without having to deselect and reselect it.

2. Choose Rotate 90° CW from the Modify, Transform menu.

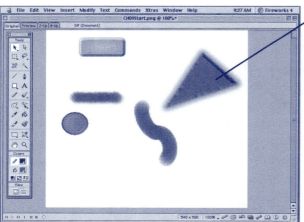

The selected object will be rotated in the document window.

Scaling Objects

Shrink or grow an object to create dynamic or precise graphic designs. Although you can scale both vector and bitmap objects, bitmap objects look best if you shrink them and less than great if you try to make them larger. Vector graphics generally scale well. However, your mileage might vary depending on the stroke, fill, and effect that is assigned to the object you want to resize. The following steps show you how to scale an object.

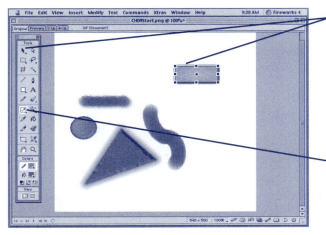

1. Create a vector object in the document window. Then, select it with the Pointer Tool (V). In this example, I've created a rectangle shape and applied fill and stroke settings, along with effects and fill textures, to create a rectangle that looks like a button.

2. Click on the Scale Tool (Q) in the toolbox. A bounding box will appear around the object.

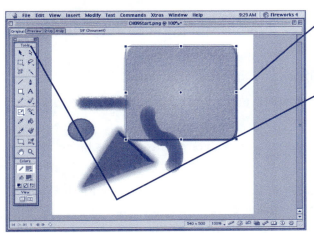

3. Click and drag the middle handles on the top, bottom, or sides of the object to resize it to a larger or smaller object.

4. Select another tool in the toolbox or click outside the object to deselect it. View the object in the document window.

NOTE

The Scale Tool enables you to resize an object. If you want to resize the entire document, choose the Image Size command from the Modify menu. For more information about how to use the Image Size command, see the "Resizing Bitmaps" section earlier in this chapter.

Applying Blend Modes

To apply a blending mode, you must select at least two image objects. You can select two vector or bitmap objects, or combine vector and bitmap objects. For best results, select the objects you want to work with and move them to the front, or top, layers of the document.

You should become familiar with a few terms before experimenting with blending modes. The base color is the color of the bottom object. The blend color is the color of the top object. The resulting color appears wherever the two objects overlap. Adjusting the opacity of an object determines how much of the blending mode is applied to the overlapping objects. The following list provides a brief explanation of how each blending mode works.

- **Normal**. The Normal setting does not apply a blending mode to the selected object.

- **Multiply**. The base color is multiplied by the blend color to create darker colors.

- **Screen**. The inverse of the blend color is multiplied by the base color to create a bleaching effect.

- **Darken**. The darker blend color and the base color are used in this blend mode, replacing pixels that are lighter than the blend color.

- **Lighten**. The lightened blend color and base color are used to create the final color, replacing only pixels that are darker than the blend color.

- **Difference**. This setting subtracts the color with less brightness from the color with greater brightness.

- **Hue**. The hue value of the blend color is combined with the luminance and saturation values of the base color.

- **Saturation**. The saturation of the blend color is combined with the luminance and hue of the base color.

- **Color**. The hue and saturation of the blend color is combined with the luminance of the base color to create the final color. Gray levels for monochrome and tinting color images are preserved.

- **Luminosity**. The luminance of the blend color is combined with the hue and saturation of the base color.

- **Invert**. The base color value is inverted.

- **Tint**. Gray is added to the base color to create the final color.

- **Erase**. Base color pixels, including background image base colors, are removed.

The following steps show you how to apply a blending mode to two overlapping objects.

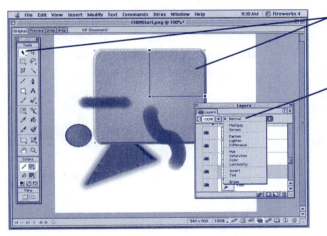

1. Select an object in the document window. Place it above or below another object.

2. Click on the pop-up menu in the Layers panel and choose a blending mode.

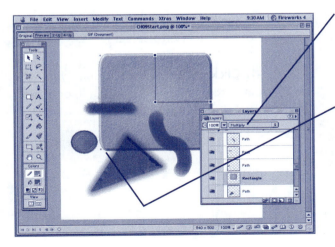

The color of the selected object might change. The blending mode will appear in the Layers panel if the layer object is highlighted.

One of the hidden objects below the selected objects will now be visible as a result of changing the blending mode.

Applying a Style

Select a bitmap or vector object and then click on a style in the Styles panel. A style can consist of a combination of stroke, fill, and effect settings. Since bitmap objects do not have stroke or fill settings, applying a style to a bitmap image will only add an effect to that object. For best results, apply styles to vector objects. The following steps show you how to apply a style to a vector object.

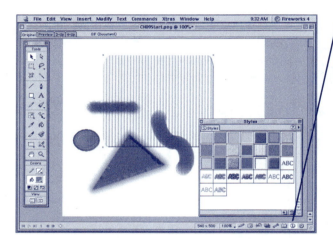

1. Create a vector object in the document window. Choose Styles from the Window menu, or click on the Styles shortcut located in the mini-launcher area of the document window.

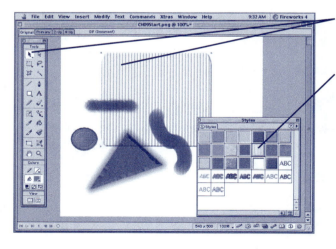

2. Click on the vector object with the Pointer Tool (V) to select it.

3. Click on a style icon in the Styles panel to change the stroke, fill, or effect settings for that object.

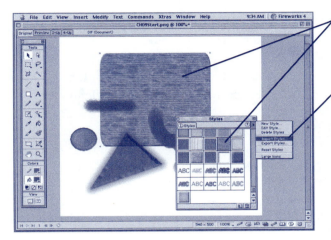

4. Click on a different style in the Styles panel. The object style will change in the document window.

5. Choose Import Styles from the Styles panel pop-up menu to access additional object styles from the Styles panel. You can download PNG, GIF, or JPEG files from the Internet or create your own.

Creating a Custom Style

You can customize an object by choosing a custom set of stroke and fill settings. If you want to use that special combination of settings with other objects, you can save them as a style. Here's how:

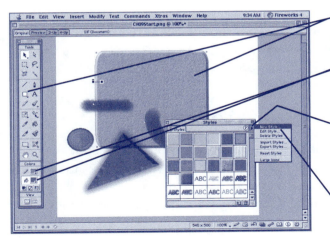

1. Create a vector object with shape or drawing tools.

2. Apply the stroke, fill, patterns, textures, and effects as you want.

3. Click on the triangle icon in the Styles panel to view the pop-up menu commands for the panel.

4. Select the New Style command. The New Style dialog box will open.

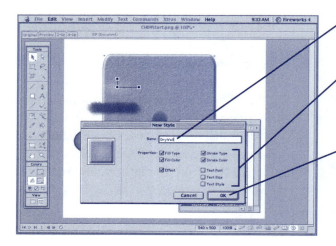

5. Type the name of the new style in the Name text box.

6. Check or uncheck any of the Properties check boxes to define the style.

7. Click on the OK button to save the new style.

Adding Stroke and Fill Settings

A vector object's stroke and fill settings can be modified at any time. You can change the color, transparency, texture, pattern, or gradient from the Fill panel. You can also adjust the thickness of a stroke and the stroke's color, opacity, and texture from the Stroke panel. Stroke and Fill settings overlap, depending on which stroke and fill patterns are selected. You can change the way they overlap with each other from the Objects panel. The following sections show you how to view and edit Stroke and Fill settings from their respective panels. These sections assume that you already have the Stroke and Fill panels open.

Changing an Object's Stroke Settings

Each vector object can display one of twelve possible strokes: None, Basic, Air Brush, Calligraphy, Charcoal, Crayon, Felt Tip, Oil, Pencil, Watercolor, Random, and Unnatural. Each stroke has a unique group of settings and interacts differently with other objects, including the canvas. The following steps give you a brief tour of the settings in the Stroke panel.

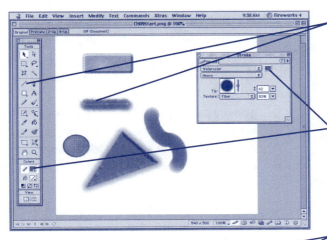

1. An object's stroke appears around the border of the object. Select a drawing tool from the toolbox and create an object. In this example, I've created a path with the Line Tool (L).

2. Adjust the stroke color from the toolbox or from the Stroke panel. The path will be drawn with the current stroke and fill settings from the Stroke and Fill panels.

3. Use the Pointer Tool (V) to select an object if you want to edit it.

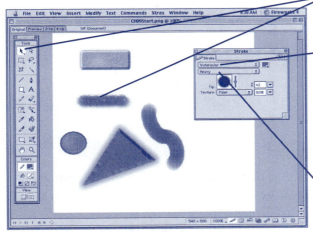

4. Change the object's stroke. Click on the top pop-up menu in the Stroke panel to choose a different stroke. Choose from None (no stroke), Basic, Air Brush, Calligraphy, Charcoal, Crayon, Felt Tip, Oil, Pencil, Watercolor, Random, and Unnatural strokes.

5. After you've selected a stroke, you can customize that stroke. The pop-up menu directly below the stroke pop-up menu enables you to choose additional settings that affect the selected stroke. Heavy, Thick, and Thin are the menu options for the Watercolor stroke.

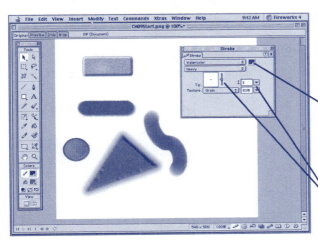

6. The stroke color can be changed as often as you want. Click on the color well to change the stroke color. The stroke color also appears in the toolbox.

7. Adjust the tip size and thickness by selecting and dragging the slider controls, or by typing a new value in the text box.

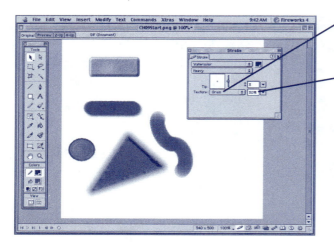

8. Click on the Texture pop-up menu and choose a texture for the stroke.

9. To view the texture of the stroke, you need to choose a non-zero value for the opacity setting. The higher the opacity setting, the more transparent the texture will appear in the stroke. Depending on the selected stroke, you might not even be able to see the stroke.

Changing Stroke Settings

If you're not sure how you want a button or graphic to look, experiment with its appearance by choosing and viewing different strokes for that object. Here's how:

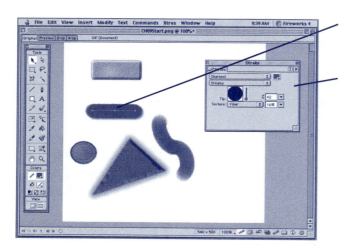

1. Select an object in the document window.

2. Choose different stroke settings to experiment with the appearance of the object.

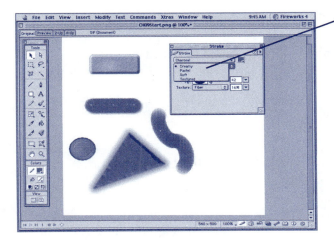

3. Adjust the stroke by choosing a stroke option from the pop-up menu.

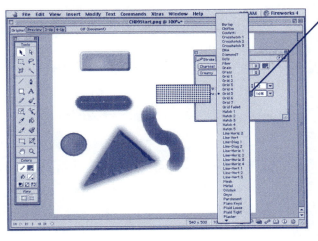

4. Click on the Texture pop-up menu to apply a texture to the stroke.

NOTE

Select a vector object in the document window and then choose Object from the Window menu. Click on a Stroke button to adjust how the stroke settings sit on the object path. The stroke settings can be located inside, on, or outside the object's path.

TIP

Customize additional stroke settings by choosing the Edit Stroke command from the Stroke panel's pop-up menu.

Applying a Stroke's Texture

You can choose from a long list of textures to use for an object's stroke. The following steps show you how to choose different textures for the selected stroke.

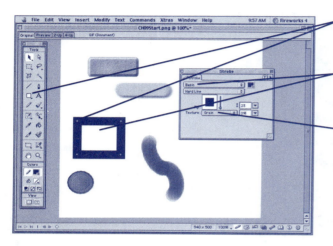

1. Create a path object in the document window.

2. Select the object and choose a stroke from the pop-up menu.

3. Pick a texture from the Texture pop-up menu. Some strokes are unable to be combined with a texture. In this example, I've chosen the Basic stroke, which doesn't change its appearance no matter which texture is selected.

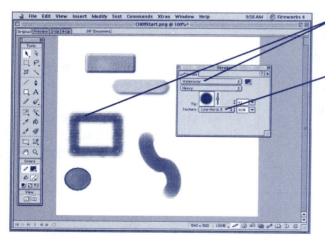

4. Choose a different stroke from the Stroke panel.

5. Pick different textures and change the object's stroke as you like.

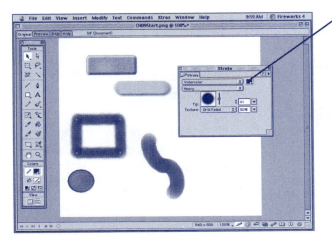

6. Select a different color and compare the object's color and texture with other Web design images.

NOTE

As you adjust the amount of the texture applied to the stroke size, you might notice that some strokes look better with some textures, whereas other combinations don't work together as well. Try different strokes and textures together until you find combinations that you like.

Adjusting a Stroke's Texture Level

Each object can have a unique set of stroke settings. The texture setting enables you to adjust how much of the selected texture appears in the object's stroke. The following steps show you how to use this feature.

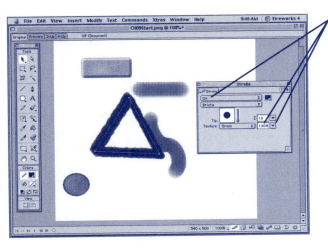

1. Create a closed path object and then select it to view its stroke settings in the Stroke panel. Each stroke has its own unique settings. Some strokes have a higher level of texture visibility as a default setting, such as Watercolor. Others, such as Basic, cannot be made transparent.

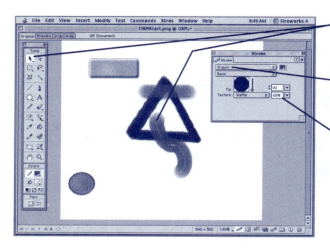

2. Create and select an open path object.

3. Choose a different stroke for the selected object.

4. Adjust the texture level for the stroke by typing a value into the text box, or choose a value using the slider control.

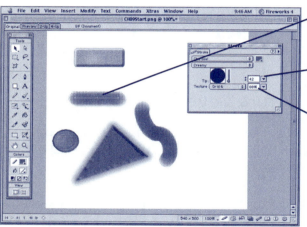

5. Create and select an open path object in the document window.

6. Choose a larger tip size to thicken the stroke.

7. Increase the stroke's texture level to view the texture in the open path object.

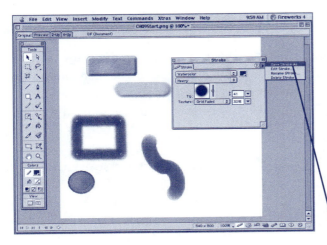

Creating Custom Strokes

Save a magic combination of stroke settings by choosing the Save Stroke command from the Stroke panel options pop-up menu. Here's how:

1. Apply the stroke settings you want to use with an object. Modify the tip size, texture, or amount of texture in the Stroke panel.

2. Choose Save Stroke As from the pop-up menu in the Stroke panel. The Save Stroke dialog box will open.

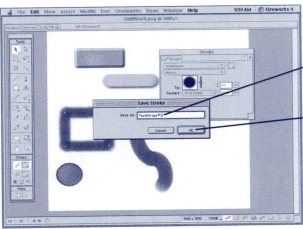

3. Type a name for the stroke in the Save As text box.

4. Click on the OK button.

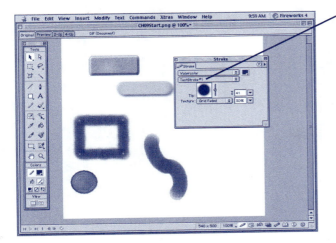

The new stroke setting will appear in the Stroke panel.

Adding Solid Fills

You can create new objects without a fill area. The icon containing the diagonal red line will appear in the fill color box in the toolbox if a selected object contains no fill area. You will be able to see through an empty fill area of an object and view any objects located directly below it. The following steps show you how to fill in an empty object.

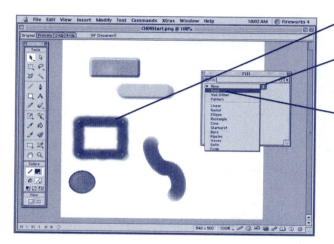

1. Create an object and select it.

2. Click on the pop-up menu in the Fill panel.

3. Choose a fill for the selected object. In this example, I've chosen the Solid fill.

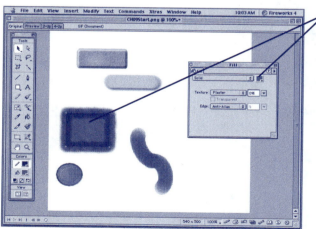

The fill color will appear in the selected object, and in the Fill panel and the Colors section of the toolbox.

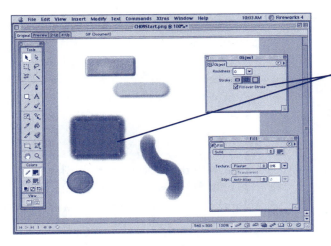

4. Choose Object from the Window menu.

5. Check the Fill over Stroke check box if you want the fill area to overlap the object's stroke.

Combining Patterns and Textures

The Fill panel contains four kinds of fill options. Choose from None, Solid, Pattern, or Web Dither. Each setting interacts differently with the list of gradients located at the bottom of the pop-up menu in the Fill panel. You can choose a pattern and then combine it with a texture to create realistic-looking image objects. Here's how:

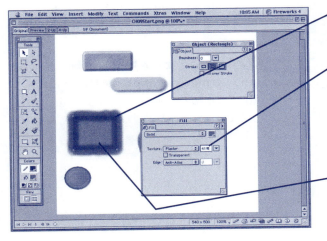

1. Create an object in the document window. Select the object.

2. Type a value in the Texture text box. A higher value shows more texture. If you type zero into the text box, no texture will appear in the fill area of the object.

3. View the fill texture in the selected object.

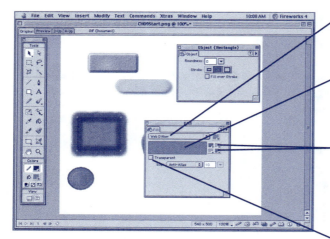

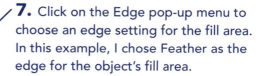

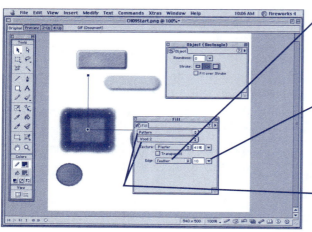

4. Choose Web Dither from the Fill pop-up menu.

A preview window along with four color picker windows will appear in the Fill panel.

5. Click in a color well to choose a color to use with the Web Dither fill. The top two color wells share the opposite colors of the bottom two color wells.

6. Check the Transparent check box to apply a transparent dither to the fill area.

7. Click on the Edge pop-up menu to choose an edge setting for the fill area. In this example, I chose Feather as the edge for the object's fill area.

8. If you selected Feather from the Edge pop-up menu, type the number of pixels for the Edge setting in the text box.

9. Choose Pattern from the Fill pop-up menu to apply a pattern from the secondary pop-up menu to the selected fill area.

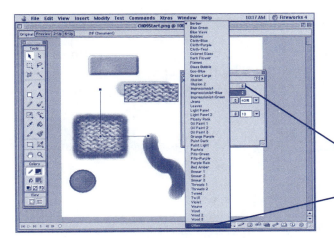

Creating Custom Patterns

You can create your own fill pattern by opening an existing GIF, PNG, or JPEG file on your hard drive. The following steps show you how.

1. Choose Pattern in the top Fill pop-up menu.

2. Click on the second pop-up menu and choose Other.

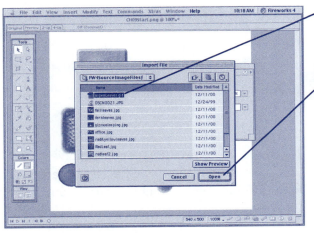

3. Navigate your hard drive and locate an image file you want to use as a fill pattern.

4. Select the file in the Locate File/ Import File dialog box. Then, click on the Open button.

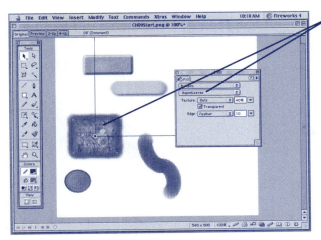

The new pattern will appear in the fill area of the selected object, and the file name for the new pattern will appear in the secondary pattern pop-up menu.

Working with Gradient Fills

The bottom half of the Fill pop-up menu contains built-in gradient fill patterns. Choose one of them to enhance the existing fill settings for an object. The colors for each gradient can be edited, and the direction of the gradient can also be adjusted. The following steps show you how.

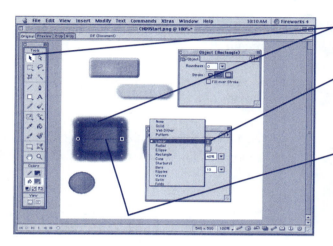

1. Create an object in the document window, then select it.

2. Choose a gradient fill from the Fill panel. In this example, I've chosen the Linear gradient.

A horizontal line will appear across the middle of the selected object, indicating the starting point and direction of the gradient.

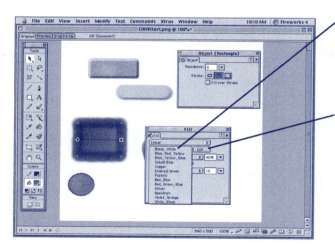

3. Click on the secondary gradient pop-up menu to view a list of preconfigured color combinations for any gradient.

4. Select one of the existing gradient color combinations, or click on the Edit button to edit the currently selected gradient colors.

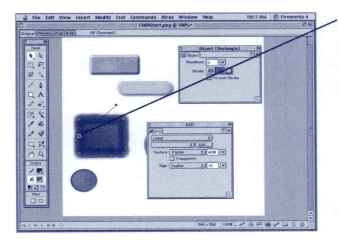

5. Click and drag the gradient fill line in the object to change the direction of the gradient.

Working with Transparency Settings

There isn't one central location for all the transparency settings available in Fireworks. However, Macromedia placed each one in a convenient, almost logical location. The following sections show you how to adjust several different kinds of transparency settings located in a number of different menus, check boxes, and panels in Fireworks.

Changing an Object's Opacity

You can soften the appearance of a vector or bitmap image by increasing its level of transparency. Most objects are created or opened with no transparency. If you select an object in the Layers panel, the text box in the upper-left corner of the Layers panel will probably show 100%. A value of 100 indicates that the selected object does not contain any opacity. A value of zero will make that object completely opaque; you won't be able to see the selected object in the document window. Type a value between 0 and 100 to set the opacity or transparency of an object and view any objects that might be positioned below it.

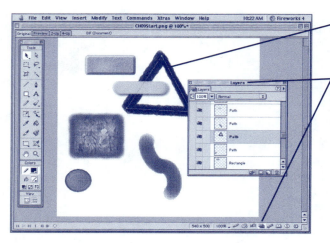

1. Select an object in the document window.

2. Click on the Layers shortcut in the document window to open the Layers panel.

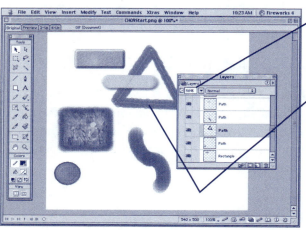

3. Type an opacity level to set the transparency level of the selected object.

The object will appear lighter in the document window.

Setting Alpha Transparency

The Alpha Transparency setting is located in the Optimize panel. It affects how all objects interact with the color of the canvas. If you select Alpha Transparency, the image objects will be exported against a transparent background. The following steps show you how to set and view a document using alpha transparency.

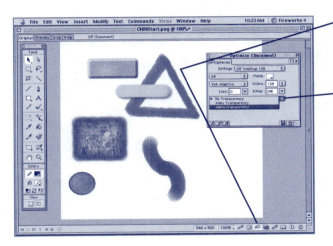

1. Choose Optimize from the Window menu or click on the Optimize shortcut in the document window.

2. Choose Alpha Transparency from the pop-up menu in the Optimize Panel.

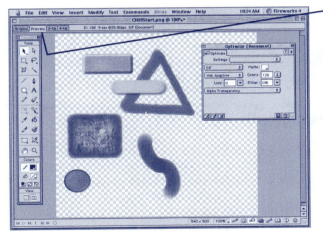

3. Click on the Preview tab in the document window. The canvas color will appear transparent, and all objects will remain as-is in the document window.

Applying an Index Transparency

If a Web page uses a specific solid color for its background color, you can apply an index transparency to blend in objects with the background color of the Web page. The following steps show you how to set and view a document with index transparency.

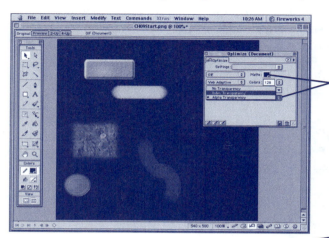

1. Open the Optimize panel and choose Index Transparency from the pop-up menu. The canvas color will appear in the Matte color box in the Optimize panel.

2. Click on the Preview tab in the document window.

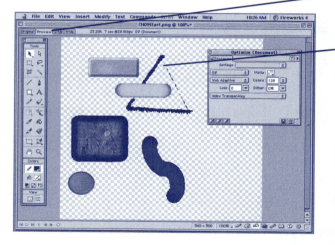

3. View the objects with the index transparency setting. Objects that share the canvas colors will also become transparent if the object or document is exported from Fireworks.

CAUTION

Using opacity and transparency settings on path or image objects from the Optimize panel can affect which file formats you can use when you want to optimize images for the Web. For example, if you want to use an index or alpha transparency setting with an image, you must choose a GIF or PNG file format. The JPEG file format does not support these transparency settings. However, you can change an object's transparency (or opacity) setting from the Layers panel, and export the resulting opaque image with the rest of the document as a JPEG file.

Adding Transparency to Gradient Fills

You guessed it. You can modify a gradient fill by setting one or more of its colors as transparent in the Table panel. When a color in an object is transparent, the color behind it shows through. On a Web page, this enables you to display the background color of the Web page through a transparent color in an object. The following steps show you how to do this.

1. Select an object containing a fill area.

2. In the pop-up menu in the Fill panel, change the fill area to Solid.

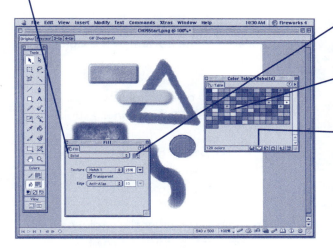

3. Click on the Color pop-up menu and view the value of the fill color.

4. Select the same color from the Color Table panel.

5. Click on the Transparent icon in the Color Table panel.

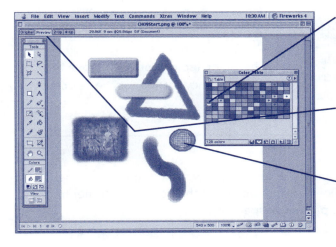

The selected color will become transparent. Notice the gray-and-white checkerboard pattern where the original color used to be in the color table.

6. Click on the Preview tab.

The colors in the gradient matching the color selected in Step 4 have become transparent.

Modifying a Path's Transparency Settings

You can also adjust how well you can see through an object or across objects. There are several different panels you can use to set object opacity. Opacity settings also work with the blending and transparency modes assigned to Fireworks objects.

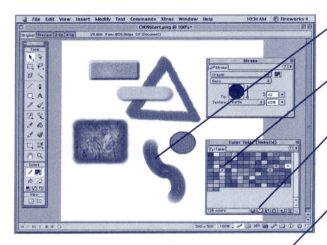

1. Select an object in the document window.

2. Click on the stroke color of the object in the Color Table panel.

3. Click on the Transparent button located at the bottom of the Color Table panel.

Depending on the stroke settings, you might not see a change in the stroke color.

4. Click on the Preview tab in the document window and view the transparency of the object.

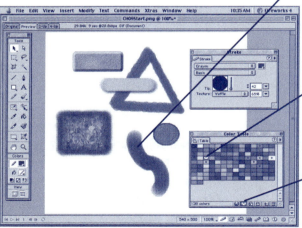

You can tell whether the stroke color is transparent, because its color will appear as a gray-and-white checkerboard in the Color Table panel.

5. Click on the Transparent icon in the Color Table panel to remove the transparency setting for the selected color.

TIP

You can also adjust a path's opacity, or transparency, from the Layers panel. Click and drag the opacity slider control located in the upper-left corner of the Layers panel to change a path's transparency.

Editing Animation

As you change the layout of a Web page or add new elements, such as text, to an animation, you will probably need to tweak something selected in one frame or in all frames of the animation. The following sections show you how to make several different kinds of changes to an animation.

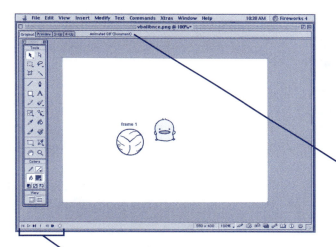

Viewing an Animation File

Many elements are at work when you create and play back an animation in Fireworks. The following list points out the visible and invisible components required to put an animation together.

- **Type of file**. The type of file appears at the top of the document window. If the file is an animated GIF, it probably contains animation.

- **Frame controls**. Step forward or backward through the file frame by frame, or click on the Play/Stop button to view the animation.

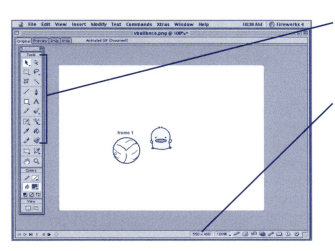

- **Editing tools**. You can edit the image objects in an animated GIF file just as you would edit any other image objects in Fireworks.

- **Image size**. The canvas size appears at the bottom of the document window.

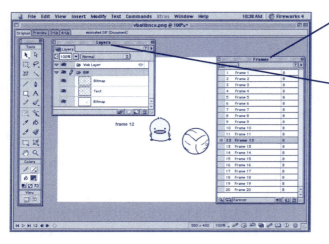

• **Frames panel**. View, select, and modify any frame in a document from the Frames panel.

• **Layers panel**. View, select, or modify any Web object, graphic object, or layer in a document from the Layers panel.

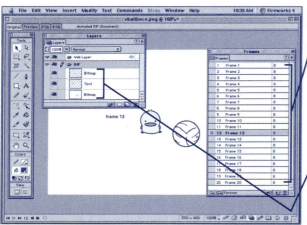

• **Each frame of the animation**. Step through each frame of animation, or play back the animation in real time. The currently selected frame appears in the document window. All frames for the animation are located in the Frames panel.

• **Each object in the animation**. Use the Pointer Tool (V) to select any vector or bitmap object in the document window. Click and drag an object in the document window to modify a frame of animation.

Converting an Image to an Animation Symbol

Create a more efficient animation by using symbols instead of vector or bitmap graphics. You can view all symbols in a document from the Library panel. The following steps show you how to convert a vector graphic to an animation symbol.

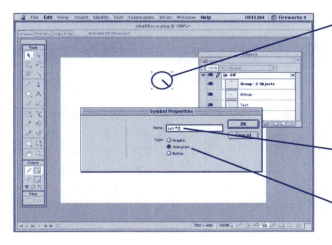

1. Create an object in the document window.

2. Select the object, then choose Convert to Symbol from the Insert menu. The Symbol Properties dialog box will open.

3. Type a name for the symbol in the Name text box.

4. Click on the Animation radio button.

5. Click on OK to save your changes and create the symbol. The Animate window will open. To find out more about the Animate window, see Chapter 5, "Creating and Designing Graphics."

Adjusting Animation Settings

Each frame of an animation contains a couple of settings: Frame Delay and Include when Exporting. These settings are stored in the Frame Properties window. Double-click on the delay time for a frame to open the Frame Properties window. The following steps show you how to adjust animation settings in the Frame Properties window.

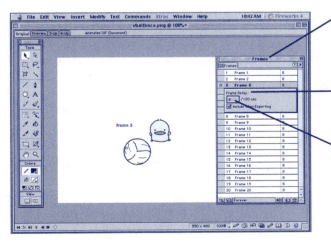

1. Select Frames from the Window menu, or press Shift + F2 to open the Frames panel.

2. Click on the number of a frame to view the frame's properties.

3. Type a number in the text box to increase or decrease the delay time for that frame. A larger value displays that frame for a longer period of time, while a smaller value shortens the frame's display time.

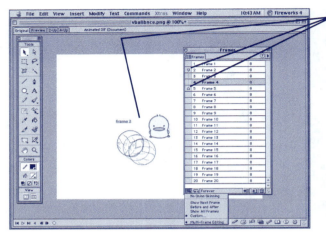

4. Click in the left column above or below the selected frame in the Frames panel. The onion skinning icon (a down arrow overlapping an up arrow icon) will split into two icons. A vertical line will appear beside the frames affected by the onion skinning feature, and the objects in the selected frame will appear in the document window. Objects in the previous or next frame (or frames) will appear as opaque objects in the document window. If you click on a different frame in the Frames panel, the previous or next frame marked by the onion skinning icon will change accordingly.

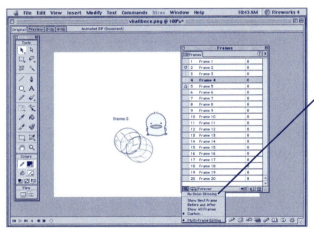

5. Double-click on a frame to turn off onion skinning. Alternatively, click on the pop-up menu located at the bottom of the Frames panel and choose No Onion Skinning.

Previewing Animation

As you add objects, create layers, and reorganize the frames of an animation, you should preview some or all of them in the document window. The key to previewing animation is to pretend that you are the target audience, perhaps someone with a browser, viewing the animation after you've posted it to your Web site. The following steps show you how to preview your animation from the Export Preview window.

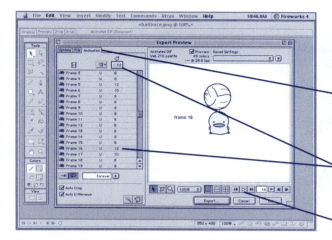

1. Open an animation containing two or more frames. Choose Export Preview from the File menu.

2. Click on the Animation tab and view the frames and file settings for the animated GIF.

3. Click on a frame in the Animation list and type a new delay time in the text box.

4. Select the Play/Stop button to view the animation in the Export Preview window.

5. Click on the OK button if you want to save your changes.

6. Choose one of the Frame Controls in the document window to view a file frame by frame, or play it straight through.

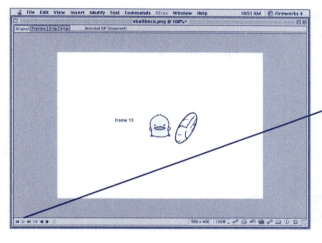

Optimizing Animation

After you've locked the last objects down in a layer or frame, you can start to optimize the animation. The goal of optimizing an animation is to reduce the file size and retain its image quality. The following steps show you how to use the settings in the Optimize panel to optimize an animated GIF file.

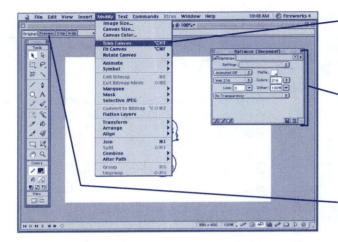
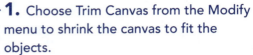
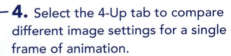
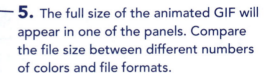

1. Choose Trim Canvas from the Modify menu to shrink the canvas to fit the objects.

2. Choose different optimization settings from the Optimize panel. For example, you can choose a different color palette for the animation or experiment with different transparency settings.

3. Click on the Preview, 2-Up, or 4-Up tabs to view the optimized image.

4. Select the 4-Up tab to compare different image settings for a single frame of animation.

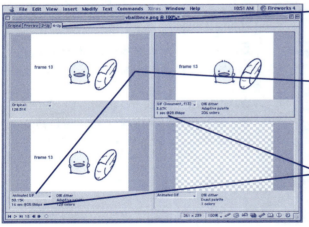

5. The full size of the animated GIF will appear in one of the panels. Compare the file size between different numbers of colors and file formats.

6. Compare the download time between individual files.

Exporting Animation

After you've fine-tuned your animation, you're ready to share it with the world. Before you export the animated GIF or SWF file, you should preview it in the Export Preview window. You can preview each frame of animation, or check the settings for the file before you export it from Fireworks. The following steps show you how to export the edited file as an animated GIF.

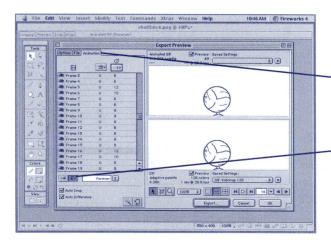

1. Choose Export Preview from the File menu.

2. Click on the Animation tab to view the settings for the animated GIF or SWF file.

3. Set the number of times you want the animation to play back in the browser window.

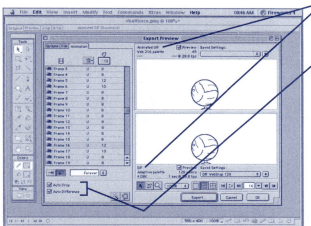

4. Compare image settings in the right side of the Export Preview window.

5. Check the Auto Crop and Auto Difference features in the Export Preview window. If the Auto Crop check box is checked, Fireworks will reduce the file size of the animation by comparing each frame with the previous frame, and cropping each frame to the pixel area of the previous frame. If the Auto Crop feature is checked, you can also select the Auto Difference check box. The Auto Difference check box enables Fireworks to further reduce the file size by converting any pixels that don't change between frames into transparent pixels within the auto-cropped area of the animation. Both settings can optimize the file size of an animation by about 50 percent.

6. Click on the Export button when you're ready to save the file to your hard drive and post it to a Web server. The Export dialog box will open.

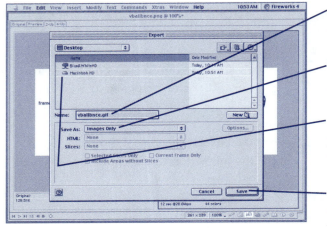

7. Type a name for the animated GIF in the Name text box.

8. Choose Images Only from the Save As pop-up menu.

9. Navigate your hard drive and choose the folder where you want to save your file.

10. Click on the Save button to save the animated GIF to your hard drive.

NOTE

If you plan to use the animation with Macromedia Director, uncheck the Auto Crop and Auto Difference features in the Export Preview window. If these check boxes are checked, the animation might not play back properly in Director.

Editing Text

If a picture is worth a thousand words, why would Fireworks need a text tool? Okay enough silliness. You already know that you can add a text object to a document. It's probably no surprise that you can edit text too, as long as you don't convert it to a bitmap object after you've created it using the Text Tool. The following sections introduce you to a few different ways that you can modify text objects.

Working with Text Styles

Apply a style from the Styles panel to a text object in the same way that you would apply a style to an image object. Text styles appear as alphabet characters (ABC) in the Styles panel. The following steps show you how to apply a style to a text object.

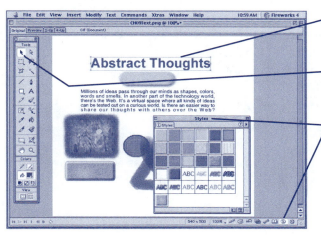

1. Create a text object in the document window.

2. Select the text object using the Pointer Tool (V).

3. Choose Styles from the Window menu, or click on the Styles shortcut from the mini-launcher located at the bottom of the document window.

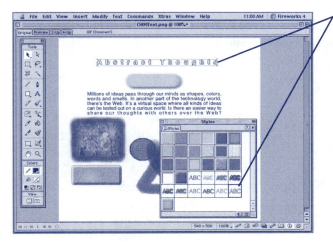

4. Click on a style icon in the Styles panel. The selected text will change to match the style you chose from the Styles panel.

Creating a Text Mask

If you want to liven up some text, you can use the Paste into Mask or Paste Inside commands on a text object. A text mask enables you to view a bitmap (such as a photo) inside one or several characters of a text object. The result can really make your Web page look interesting. The following steps show you how to create a text mask using the Group as Mask command.

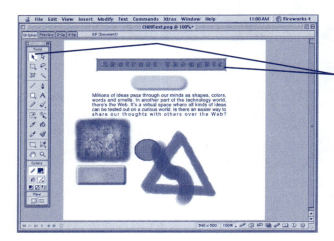

1. Add a vector object to the document window.

2. Select the vector object, plus the text object.

3. Choose Group as Mask from the Modify, Mask menu.

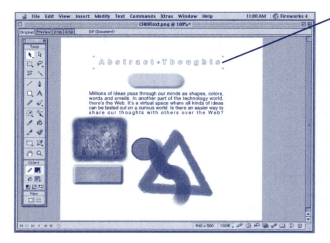

The two objects will be grouped into a single mask object.

NOTE

Try copying a text object, and then selecting a bitmap object and choosing the Paste as Mask command from the Modify, Mask menu. The text becomes a mask for the image object. You might need to select a larger font to view the image object within each text character of the text object.

Grouping Text with Objects

Keep text objects organized by proximity by applying the Group command to two or more selected objects. Here's how:

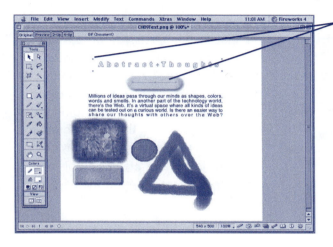

1. Hold down the Shift key and use the Pointer Tool (V) to select two objects in the document window.

2. Click on the Modify menu and choose the Group menu command or press Ctrl/Command + G.

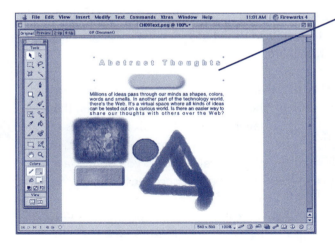

The text and vector object will be grouped in a single, selectable object.

TIP

If you need to edit any object that has been grouped with another object, select the grouped object, and then choose the Ungroup command from the Modify menu, or press Shift + Ctrl/Command + G.

Animating Text

Make text jump, rotate, flip, and disappear into thin air by animating text with frames. Animating text is almost exactly the same as animating vector, bitmap, or symbol objects. The following steps show you how to make text move in Fireworks.

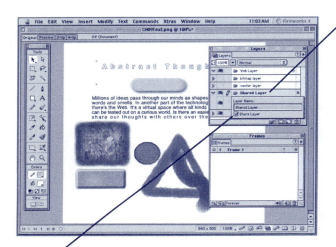

1. Place any objects you want to use in each frame of the animation into the same layer in the Layers panel. In this example, some objects are shared and others are not. You will need to ungroup the text object from the vector graphic (the yellow rounded rectangle). Move the text object and the circle object into a new, non-shared layer in the Layers panel.

2. If you want to include a static (non-moving) graphic object in all frames of the animation, move these objects into one layer in the Layers panel. Double-click on the name of the layer and check the Share Layer check box.

3. Click outside the Layers panel to exit the Layer Properties window. A dialog box will appear, indicating that any objects in other frames will be deleted from that layer. Click on the OK button to save the shared layer across frames. Or, click on the Cancel button if you don't want to share the layer contents across frames.

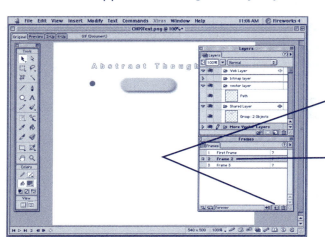

4. Click on the Add/Duplicate Frame icon in the Frames panel.

A new frame will appear in the Frames panel.

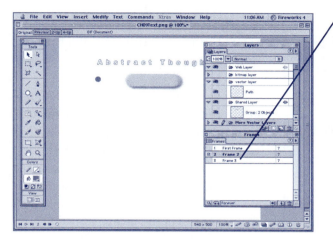

5. Repeat Step 3 and add a third frame to the document. Then, copy and paste the text and vector objects from First Frame into each of the three frames in the document window.

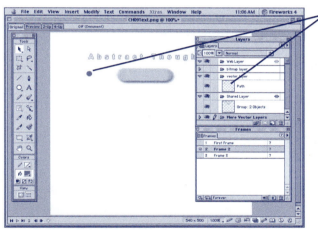

6. Click on the first frame of the animation. In this example, I've renamed Frame 1 to First Frame. Then, use the Pointer Tool (V) and click on the vector object you want to animate from the document window. Move the selected object to the starting position of the animation. In this example, I've moved the small circle to the left of the text object.

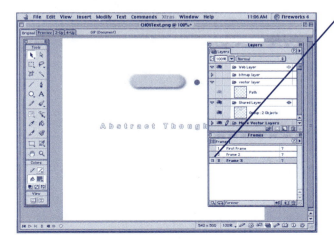

7. Click on another frame in the animation. In this example, I chose the last frame of the animation.

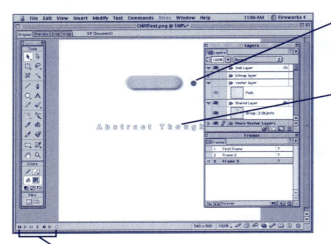

8. Choose the Pointer Tool (V) and select the same vector object in the document window.

9. Move the object to another location in the document window. In this example, I moved the circle to the right side of the text object. I also moved the text object below the circle object. This will create a text animation that moves the text from the top of the first frame to the middle of the last frame of the animation.

10. Click on the Frame Controls to play the animation. View the animation in the document window.

9

Applying Effects

Image effects enable you to modify the appearance of an image object. Macromedia uses the term Live Effects to describe effects applied from the Effect panel. You can turn each of these effects on or off in the Effect panel. In contrast, if you choose an effect from the Xtras menu, it is applied to the image but will not appear in the Effect panel. You must click on a previous document state to remove the effect from the selected object in the document window.

In this chapter you'll learn how to:

- Apply an effect
- Access Photoshop effects in Fireworks
- Work with Live Effects

In Fireworks, you can apply any of the preinstalled effects, as well as most Photoshop filters, to one or more selected image objects. For example, you can add an effect such as a drop shadow or bevel to a shape object or a photographic image. A complete list of effects is available in the Effect panel. A smaller group of Xtra effects and any Photoshop plug-ins are accessible from the Xtras menu.

You can add an effect located in the Effect panel to any vector or bitmap image selected in the document window. Effects located in the Xtras menu, including Photoshop plug-ins, can only be applied to bitmap images. There's no limit, memory and disk space permitting, to the number of effects you can add to an object. After an effect is added, you can turn any one of them on or off from the Effect panel.

Adding Effects to Image Objects

Effects are used to enhance the appearance of an image or object. You can add effects to an image object to improve its brightness, contrast, color levels, or tonal range, or to add an inner or outer shadow, bevel, glow, and so on. Macromedia installs a set of effects with the Fireworks application. They can be accessed from the Xtras menu. However, you can also add any Photoshop plug-ins and use them with a Fireworks document.

Applying an Effect

Applying an effect is as simple as selecting an object and then choosing an effect from the Effect pop-up menu. Because you can add or remove an effect at any time from the Effect panel, Macromedia calls them Live Effects. All the examples in this chapter apply Live Effects to paths and bitmap images.

You can also apply effects that appear in the Xtras menu. However, when you apply an effect from the Xtras menu, you cannot toggle that effect on or off as you continue to work with a document. Effects from the Xtras menu also require you to convert an object to a bitmap. I recommend adding effects from the pop-up menu in the Effect panel.

You can test an effect by selecting an object and then applying the effect. If you like the effect, you might want to save a copy of the image. If you don't like it, choose Undo from the Edit menu, or open the History panel and drag the slider back to a previous document state. The following sections show you how to apply effects that can be found in both the Xtras menu and the Effect panel.

Viewing Effects

All the effects in Fireworks are located in the Xtras menu or in the Effect panel. Click on the Xtras menu to view the main menu of available effects for bitmap objects. Click on the pop-up menu in the Effect panel to view a complete list of effects installed with Fireworks. The following set of steps shows you how to view the list of installed effects from the Xtras menu or the Effect panel.

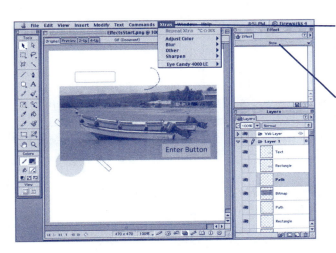

1a. Open the Xtras menu to view the list of plug-ins currently installed with Fireworks.

1b. Click the Effect pop-up menu to view any plug-ins, filters, or effects installed with Fireworks.

Sharpening Effects

Don't be surprised if you don't notice much of change after applying a sharpen effect to an object. Sharpen effects are designed to increase the contrast of adjacent pixels in an object. However, depending on what colors are in the image object, you may or may not see any change after applying this particular effect. The following steps show you how to apply a sharpen effect to an image object.

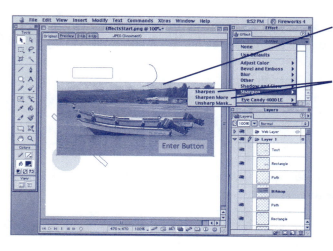

1. Select an image object in the document window.

2. Choose Sharpen or Sharpen More from the Effect pop-up menu.

NOTE

The Sharpen More effect has the approximate effect of applying the Sharpen effect three times.

Unsharp Mask

You can also sharpen an image by adjusting the contrast of the image edges. The Unsharp Mask effect contains three sliders: Sharpen Amount (ranging from 0 to 500), Pixel Radius (ranging from .l to 250), and Threshhold (ranging from 0 to 255). A threshhold of 0 sets all pixels to their sharpest setting. The following steps show you how to apply the Unsharp Mask effect to a bitmap image.

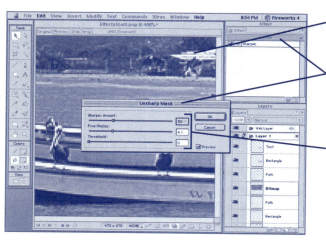

1. Select an image object in the document window.

2. Choose Unsharp Mask from the Effect pop-up menu. The Unsharp Mask dialog box will open.

3. Adjust the slider controls to the amount of sharpness you want to apply to edges in the image.

NOTE

If an object is selected with this effect, the object path will be converted to a floating image in the document window.

CAUTION

One combination of settings you might not want to use is high Sharpen Amount with low Threshhold settings. These settings can create a halo or glow effect around objects on a Web page.

Beveling Effects

You can add an inner or outer bevel edge to an image or an object such as button. The Emboss effects appear different, but can be applied in the same way that Bevel effects are applied to an image. You can also combine effects to help an object blend in with a background or foreground object. The following steps show you how to apply a Bevel effect to an object.

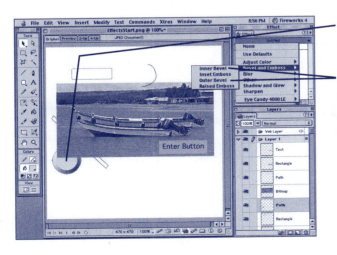

1. Select an image object in the document window.

2. Choose Inner Bevel or Outer Bevel from the Effect pop-up menu. In this example, I've applied an inner bevel to the ellipse object.

Blurring Effects

Decrease the contrast of adjacent pixels by using the Blur filters. Use the slider control to adjust settings for the Gaussian blur. Here's how:

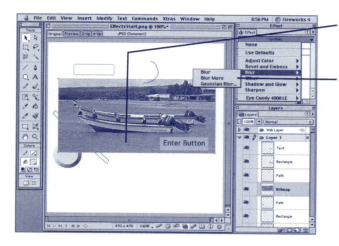

1. Select an image object in the document window.

2. Choose Blur, Blur More, or Gaussian Blur from the Effect pop-up menu.

> **NOTE**
>
> You might need to increase the amount of memory for Fireworks 4 if you plan to use the Gaussian Blur effect with a high Blur Radius value. The Blur Radius value can range from .1 to 250. The higher the number, the more blur applied to the selected object.

Converting to Alpha

You can apply the Convert to Alpha filter to convert image objects or text into a gradient transparency based on the transparency of the image. Here's how:

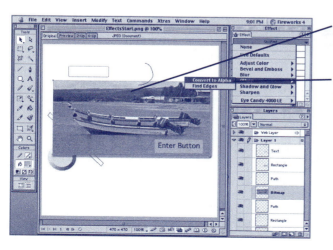

1. Select an image object in the document window.

2. Choose Convert to Alpha from the Effect pop-up menu.

Shadowing Effects

Add a Shadow effect to an image or behind an object, such as a button. I use this effect quite a bit on my Web site with text and button graphics. The following steps show you how to apply the Drop Shadow effect to an image object.

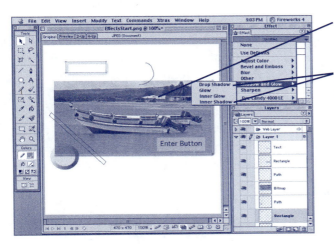

1. Select an image object in the document window.

2. Choose Inner Shadow or Drop Shadow from the Effect pop-up menu.

Glowing Effects

Add a glow or inner glow to an image or object, such as button. The following steps show you how to apply the Glow effect to an image object.

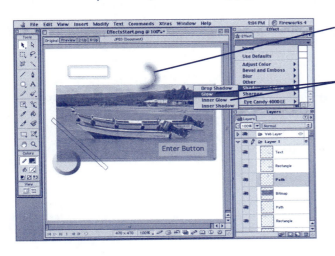

1. Select an image object in the document window.

2. Choose Inner Glow or Glow from the Effect pop-up menu.

Adding Motion Trail Effects

Attach a Motion Trail to an object or image. The following steps show you how to apply this effect to a vector object.

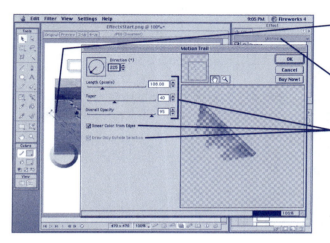

1. Select an object in the document window.

2. Choose Motion Trail from the Effect, Eye Candy 4000 LE pop-up menu.

3. Adjust settings for the Motion Trail effect. Click and drag the cursor in the Direction graphic located in the upper-left corner of the Motion Trail dialog box. This setting changes the direction of the motion trail, which you can preview in the right pane of the dialog box. Adjust the Length, Taper, and Overall Opacity settings by clicking and dragging the triangle icon for each setting, or type a new value in one of the three text boxes. Check the Smear Color from Edges check box if you want to create a slightly different effect in the motion trail. If the Smear Color from Edges check box is not selected, you can choose the Draw Only Outside Selection check box to prevent the motion trail from affecting the vector or bitmap object.

4. Click on the OK button to save your changes.

Applying Bevel Boss Effects

You can create a custom-shaped bevel in the fill area of a selected object with the Bevel Boss Eye Candy effect. The Bevel Boss effect opens a dialog box containing three tabs: Basic, Lighting, and Bevel Profile. You can adjust the width, height, and smoothness of a beveled image, in addition to several other dynamic features. The following steps give you a brief tour of the Bevel Boss dialog box.

1. Select an image object in the document window.

2. Choose Bevel Boss from the Effect, Eye Candy 4000 LE pop-up menu.

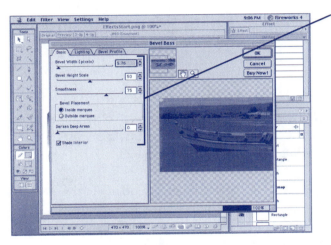

3. Adjust settings for the Bevel Boss effect. Click on a tab to access Basic, Lighting, or Bevel Profile settings. The Basic settings consist of Bevel Width, Bevel Height Scale, Smoothness, and Darken Deep Areas settings. Adjust these settings by typing a value in a text box, or by clicking and dragging the triangle control buttons. Select either the Inside Marquee or Outside Marquee radio button to select a Bevel Placement for the selected object, which you can preview in the right pane of the dialog box. Check the Shade Interior check box if you want to add a shade gradient to the top area of the button object.

4. Select the Lighting tab in the Bevel Boss window if you want to view or adjust the direction or inclination of the light source for the selected object. Or, change the Highlight Brightness or Highlight Size values. Choose the Bevel Profile tab to view or select a custom profile for the object. Choose from Carve, Cutaround, Flat, Grooved, Hump, Mesa, Subtle Button, or Subtle Hump profiles. Click and drag the cursor in the left pane to customize a profile. Add, rename, or delete a profile if you want. Click on the OK button to save your changes.

Working with Live Effects

Although there is one set of effects that you can apply to any object, there are two different ways that you can apply effects to an object. If you choose an effect from the Xtras menu, it won't appear in the Effect panel. Choosing an effect from the Xtras menu will also require you to convert a vector object into a bitmap.

On the other hand, if you choose that same effect from the pop-up menu in the Effect panel, you can show or hide it by checking or unchecking that effect in the Effect panel window list. You can apply an effect to a vector or bitmap object without having to convert it. Applying a Live Effect enables you to experiment with different combinations of effects without having to permanently change an image object. This can be a real timesaver when you're experimenting with different combinations of graphics.

Hiding an Effect

You can add or remove a Live Effect to or from each bitmap image object in a document window. The list of Live Effects can be found in the Effect panel. The following steps show you how to hide an effect in the Effect panel.

1. Select an image object in the document window.

2. Clear the check box for an effect in the Effect panel to turn off the effect. Select the check box to turn the effect on again.

Editing Live Effects

After you've added a Live Effect to an image object, you can continue to change the settings for the effect. The following steps show you how to edit Live Effects that have been applied to an object.

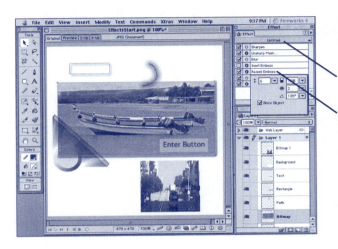

1. Select a bitmap object in the document window.

2. Select an effect in the Effect panel.

3. Double-click on the effect to view its settings. Make any adjustments to the effect.

Changing Lighting Effects

When you add an effect to an object, such as the Inner Bevel effect, you can also adjust the angle of lighting for that effect on the selected object. Here's how:

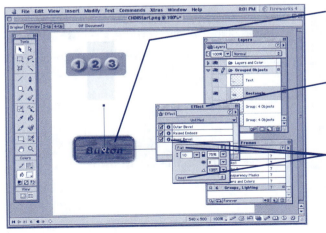

1. Open a new or existing document. Create a rectangle shape. Then, add some text to the graphic object.

2. Choose Effect from the Window menu, or press Alt/Option + F2 to open the Effect panel.

3. Select the Inner Bevel effect from the pop-up menu. Click on the i icon to view the settings for the effect. In this example, I chose Flat from the top pop-up menu and Inset from the bottom pop-up menu to define the attributes for this button.

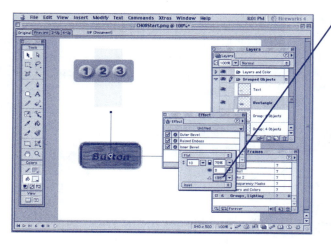

4. Click in the angle text box and type a new angle for the effect. Alternatively, you can click on the pop-up menu beside the text box and pick an angle using the graphic in the pop-up menu. The lighting effect in the selected object will change each time you adjust the angle for that effect.

Adjusting Eye Candy Effects

You can edit an Eye Candy effect in the same way that you can edit any other Live Effect in Fireworks. Simply click on the i icon of an effect to view its settings. Eye Candy effects have several options that open into a full-screen dialog box. The following steps show you how to adjust Eye Candy effect settings.

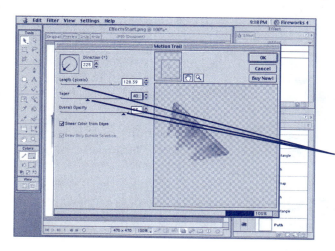

1. Select an image object in the document window.

2. Double-click on the effect to view its settings. In this example, I've chosen the Motion Trail Eye Candy effect.

3. Drag slider controls to edit the effect.

4. Click on the OK button to save your changes.

Customizing Effects

Fireworks contains many customizable effects. Save any custom effects by choosing Save Effect As from the Effect pop-up menu. The following sections show you how to combine, remove, and add filter effects.

Adding Effects to Grouped Objects

Combine object paths by using the Group command in the Modify menu. You can then apply effects to groups of objects. Here's how:

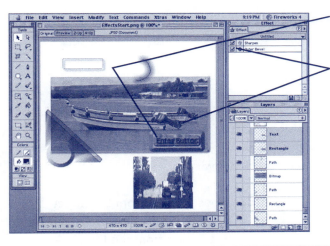

1. Select a bitmap object in the document window.

2. Choose an effect from the Effect panel. View the applied effect.

CAUTION

Keep in mind that not all effects, such as Convert to Alpha, can be applied to a group of objects without affecting other effects applied to an object in that group. For example, if an object already has effects applied to it, selecting a second object and applying Convert to Alpha removes any previously applied filters to both objects.

Removing Effects

If you decide you don't like a particular effect, you can permanently remove it from the Effect panel. This task is different from simply hiding the effect by unchecking it in the Effect panel's window list. The following steps show you how to remove an effect from the Effect panel.

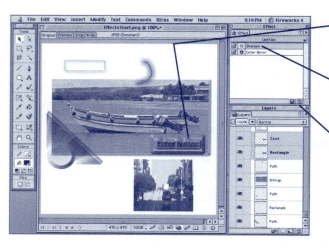

1. Select an image object in the document window.

2. Select an effect from the window list in the Effect panel.

3. Click on the Trash icon in the Effect panel. The selected effect will disappear from the Effect panel.

Applying Filters as Effects

You can choose a filter and apply it to an image. Filters are also added to the list of Live Effects in the Effect panel. Here's how:

1. Select an image object in the document window.

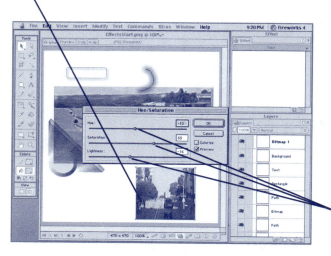

2. Choose a filter from the Effect pop-up menu. In this example, I chose Hue/Saturation from the Effect, Adjust Color pop-up menu. The filter effects are located in the Adjust Color menu in either the Xtras or Effect pop-up menu. Choose from Auto Levels, Brightness/Contrast, Color Fill, Curves, Hue/Saturation, Invert, or Levels.

3. Click and drag the slider controls in the Hue/Saturation dialog box to adjust the settings for this effect.

4. Click on the OK button to save your changes.

Using Photoshop Plug-Ins and Effects

You can create your own effects or add effects from other applications, such as Adobe Photoshop. These examples include plug-in files added from Adobe Photoshop 5.5. At press time, Photoshop 6.0 plug-in files did not work with Fireworks 4. If you select a Photoshop 6.0 plug-in from the Xtras menu or Effect panel, you will see a message saying that there was an internal error and the effect could not be processed. This message appears because all Photoshop 6.0 plug-ins look for a code that's present in Photoshop but currently is not available in Fireworks 4.

Installing a Photoshop Plug-In

Although some Photoshop plug-ins will not work as Live Effects in Fireworks, you can install them onto your computer. Most plug-in installers place Photoshop plug-in files into Photoshop's Plug-ins folder. If you have Photoshop, that's okay. You can simply add that folder location to your Fireworks folder preferences so that Fireworks can access all your Photoshop plug-in files. If you do not have Photoshop installed on your computer, you can manually move the plug-in file to the Fireworks Xtras folder after the plug-in is installed on your computer. Be sure to exit Fireworks before adding plug-in files to Fireworks.

Locating the Plug-Ins Folder

There are three different ways that you can get Fireworks to recognize a Plug-ins folder. Fireworks loads plug-in files configured from the Plug-in settings in the Preferences window, files chosen from the Locate Plug-ins pop-up menu command, or files installed in the Fireworks Xtras folder. The following steps show you how to choose a plug-ins folder from the Effect panel.

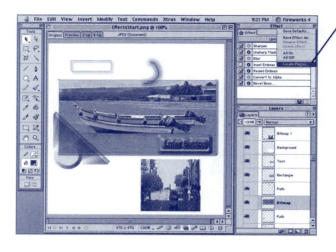

1. Click on the pop-up menu in the Effect panel and choose the Locate Plugins menu command if you want to choose a single effect.

2. Select the Adobe Photoshop Plug-Ins folder. Click on the Choose button located at the bottom of the Open File dialog box.

3. Click on the OK button in the message window. Quit Fireworks 4 and then start the application to load the new plug-in files.

TIP

Photoshop plug-ins are identified by icons having a three-pronged shape. The Eye Candy effects use icons that look like snowflakes.

NOTE

For best results, choose the Photoshop Plug-in folder from the Fireworks Preferences window (select Preferences from the Edit menu). Then, you won't have to manually copy or delete a plug-in file that you want to use with both Photoshop and Fireworks.

You can also move or create a copy of the Photoshop plug-in files directly into the Fireworks Xtras folder, which is located inside the Configuration folder in the Fireworks 4 folder.

Using the Xtras Menu

After you've installed plug-ins on your computer, you can start the Fireworks application to access the new plug-in files. Open any Fireworks documents you want to use with these plug-ins. The following steps show you how the Photoshop plug-ins appear in the Xtras menu.

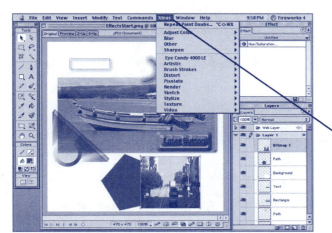

1. Select an object in the document window.

2. Click on the Xtras menu and select an effect from one of its submenus.

Adding a Photoshop Effect

You can apply a Photoshop plug-in to a bitmap object in the same way that you would apply a native Live Effect to a bitmap object in Fireworks. Plug-ins are also accessible from the Effect panel, in addition to the Xtras menu. The following steps show you how to apply an effect to a bitmap image by accessing a plug-in from the Xtras menu.

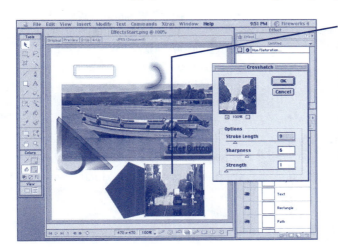

1. Select an object in the document window.

2. Choose an effect from either the Effect panel pop-up menu or the Xtras menu. In this example, I chose the Cross Hatch effect from the Xtras, Brush Strokes menu.

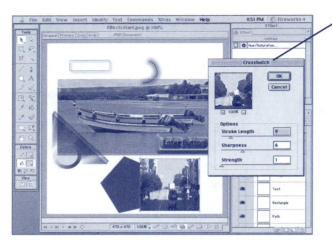

3. Adjust the settings for the effect. Selecting some effects will result in a dialog box of effect options opening. When you are finished adjusting the settings, click on the OK button in the effect dialog box to save your changes.

4. View the effect in the document window.

NOTE

If you've configured Fireworks to recognize the location of the Photoshop plug-in files on your hard drive, Photoshop plug-ins will appear as Live Effects in the Effect panel pop-up menu. Add a Photoshop effect to an image object. Then, turn any Photoshop effect on or off after applying the effect to an image object.

Adding a Photoshop Effect as a Live Effect

You can activate several effects from the Effects panel to modify an image or object. You can also combine Photoshop effects with other Live Effects in Fireworks. Experiment with different combinations of effects to give a bitmap image a unique look, or to create a whole new look for a Web page or Web site. The following steps show you how to apply Photoshop effects as Live Effects in Fireworks.

1. Select an image object from the Layers panel, or from the document window.

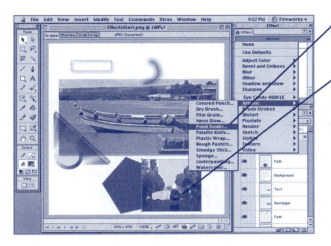

2. Click on the Effect pop-up menu and select an effect.

3. View the applied effect. Most effects should create a noticeable change in the object selected in the document window.

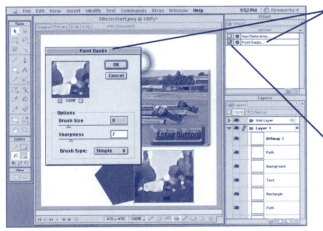

4. Double-click on the effect in the Effect panel to change any of its settings. Click on OK when you're finished changing any settings, or click on Cancel if you don't wish to save any of the changes you made to the effect.

5. Clear the check box to deactivate the effect.

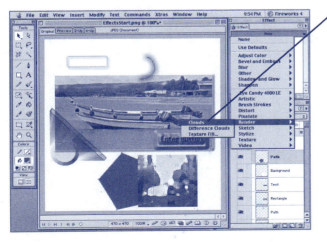

6. Select a different image object in the document window. Choose another effect from the Effect panel pop-up menu.

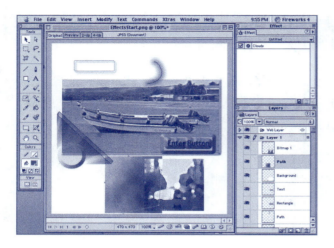

7. View the effect, which is now added to the previous effect.

NOTE

Not all Photoshop 5 or Photoshop 6 plug-in files work with Fireworks 4. For example, none of the Photoshop 6 plug-ins work with Fireworks 4.

PART III

Designing Interactive Web Graphics

After you've drawn, imported, or edited your graphics in Fireworks, you can add Web Layer objects and behaviors to define exactly how someone will interact with your Web graphics. If you've already laid out your Web graphics, you might want to revisit the layout and consider making a few minor adjustments. Depending on how you want users to interact with those graphics, you might need to add a little more space between or around objects in the layout, so that you can fit the different interactive elements on one page. Interactive Web graphics can be a simple rollover, swap image, or an onMouseOver (pop-up menu) behavior assigned to a Web object, which Fireworks creates by generating JavaScript code.

Several tools, panels, and menu commands enable you to work with both graphic objects and Web Layer objects in a Fireworks document. Web Layer objects appear in the Layers panel. Hotspots and slices created with their respective tools in the toolbox are each created as a separate object under the Web Layer folder in the Layers panel. The chapters in this part of the book show you how to work with the Slice and Hotspot tools, and how to create buttons, rollovers, and pop-up menus in Fireworks.

10

Introduction to Slices, Hotspots, and Image Maps

You can use two primary tools to create Web layer objects in Fireworks: the Slice and Hotspot tools. Both tools have similar features; however, when you apply the Slice Tool to an image, the image will be divided into separate files when you export the document. When you apply the Hotspot Tool, Fireworks creates an image map in JavaScript code for each of the behaviors you want to add to that particular area of the image, without splitting that file up when the document is exported. You can work with the Hotspot or Slice tools to add a rollover behavior such as an up or down button state. You can view or assign settings to a slice in the Object panel, or view or change behavior information in the Behaviors panel. This chapter shows you how to create Web layer objects with the Hotspot and Slice tools. In this chapter you'll learn how to:

- Create an image map with hotspots
- Assign behaviors to hotspots
- Add a URL to a hotspot
- Slice an image
- Assign behaviors to slices

Image Maps and the Hotspot Tool

The words "image map" might conjure images of a table of contents for a photo album or a map of images on a Web site. An actual HTML image map isn't too far from what you might imagine. When you add a hotspot or a slice to an image file, Fireworks keeps track of the coordinates of the image, as well as the coordinates of the hotspot or slice. When you export the image, that image map information is converted into JavaScript and HTML code. When someone visits your Web page, the browser application interprets the JavaScript and HTML code. When the cursor clicks within the coordinates of the image map the corresponding JavaScript code is executed, showing you a new button image or taking you to a new page. Before you can create an image map you'll need to know how to use the Hotspot and Slice tools. The following sections show you how to create, edit, and hide a rectangular, elliptical, or polygonal hotspot.

Creating an Image Map with the Hotspot Tool

The steps in this section show you how to create a rectangle-shaped hotspot with the Rectangle Hotspot Tool. The Rectangle Hotspot Tool is the default hotspot shape available in the toolbox. However, you can also create hotspots with the Elliptical or Polygonal Hotspot tools. Each hotspot you create can have a unique shape, color, URL, or rollover assigned to it.

You can add a hotspot to a document in three different ways. One way is to select an object and then choose Insert Hotspot from the Insert menu. Another way is

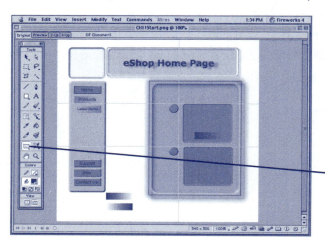

to select an object and then select a behavior in the Behaviors panel. The following steps show you a third way to create a hotspot with the Rectangle Hotspot Tool.

1. Open a document containing several image objects.

2. Click on the Hotspot Tool (U) in the toolbox.

3. Click in the document window and drag the mouse up or down. The outline of the hotspot will appear as you drag the Hotspot Tool in the document window. Release the mouse button to create a hotspot in the document window. Its default color will be light blue.

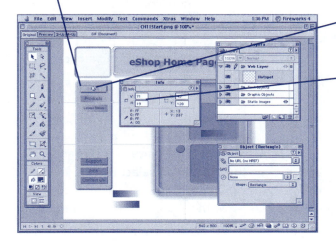

4. Click on the hotspot, and the drag-and-drop handle button will appear.

If the Info panel is open, the dimensions of the hotspot will appear in the W and H text boxes.

> **NOTE**
>
> For more information about how to use the drawing tools, see Chapter 5, "Creating and Designing Graphics."

Creating an Elliptical Hotspot

Now that you've created a rectangular hotspot, try making an elliptical one. The following steps show you how to create a circle-shaped hotspot and then assign a URL and a custom color to it.

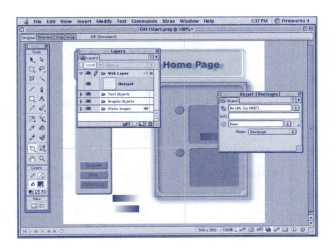

1. Create a new document and add at least one elliptical object to it. You can select the Elliptical Shape Tool (R) from the toolbox, or press R to cycle through each tool that lives with the Rectangle Tool. Alternatively, you can open an existing document that contains graphic objects.

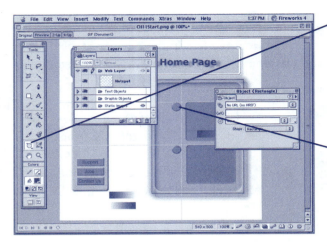

2. Select the Elliptical Hotspot Tool (U) from the toolbox. You might need to click and hold the mouse on the Rectangle Hotspot icon to select the elliptical (round) icon. Its icon will appear selected in the toolbox.

3. Click and drag the mouse over a circular-shaped object.

4. Choose the Pointer Tool (V) and click on the hotspot to select it.

5. View the Web object in the Layers panel. Click on the hotspot object to select it.

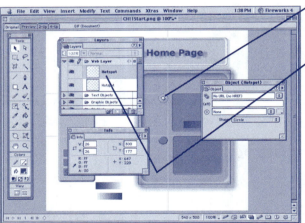

NOTE

To change a hotspot's name, double-click on the hotspot in the Layers panel.

6. Choose Object from the Window menu or press Alt/Option + F2 to open the Object panel.

7. Click in the top text box in the Object panel. This is the URL or link text box. Type a URL or select an existing one from the pop-up menu located to the right of the text box.

8. View the shape of the hotspot in the Shape pop-up menu.

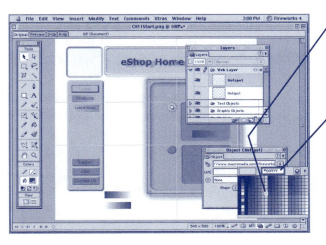

9. Assign a custom color to the ellipse. Click in the color well to view a menu of squares from which you can choose a color.

10. Drag the mouse over a color square and then press the Enter/Return key to select the new color. Alternatively, type a hexadecimal value in the text box.

Designing a Polygonal Hotspot

The Polygonal Hotspot Tool (U) works a little differently than the other Hotspot tools. Instead of drawing a simple shape to create the hotspot, you must click to create each corner (or side) of the polygon shape. As you click, Fireworks redraws the shape of the hotspot to fit its new dimensions. The following steps show you how to create a polygon-shaped hotspot.

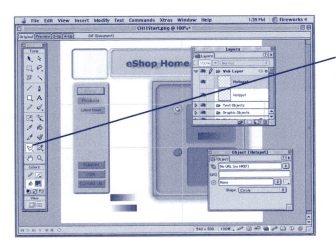

1. Open a new or existing document.

2. Select the Polygon Hotspot Tool (U) from the toolbox.

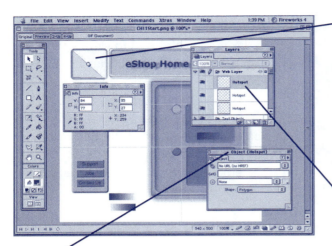

3. Click once in the document window to create the first point of the polygon. Click a second time in a different location. Add points or corners to the polygon by clicking in the document window. As you click in the document window, Fireworks will redraw the hotspot to show you its new shape.

4. Choose Layers from the Window menu or press F2. The new polygon hotspot will appear in the Layers panel.

5. Select Object from the Window menu or press Alt/Option + F2. The Object panel will open. If the polygon hotspot is selected, its object information will appear in the Object panel.

TIP

If you want to create a hotspot for a map, you can scan an image into Fireworks and place it in one layer. Create a second layer in the Layers panel, then use the Pen Tool to create closed path vector objects from the scanned map image. Select a vector object, and then choose Hotspot from the Insert menu. A hotspot Web object will be created, matching the shape of the vector object.

Customizing Spacer Settings

When you create a hotspot in Fireworks, you're creating an image map for one or more images that will be placed in a table on a Web page. A table is a commonly used feature of the HTML language and works similarly to a spreadsheet application on a computer. A table can consist of one or more columns and rows. A table cell can span a single column or row, or be spread across several columns or rows. Although you'll never see this table information in Fireworks, you will see it after you export images and HTML from Fireworks and open them in Dreamweaver or an HTML editor application. The following steps show you how to adjust the HTML setup preferences for exporting tables from any Fireworks document.

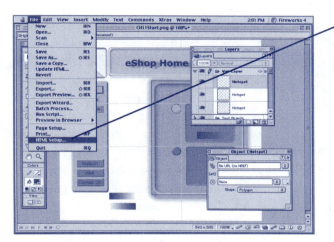

1. Choose HTML Setup from the File menu. The HTML Setup dialog box will open.

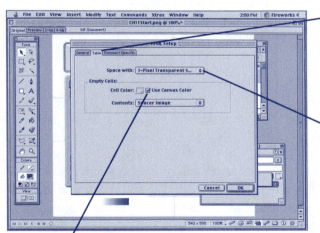

2. Click on the Table tab to view the export settings for tables. The settings in this window affect the HTML code generated for the slice objects in a document.

3. Click on the Space With pop-up menu to choose one of three options: Nested Tables–No Spacers, Single Table–No Spacers, or 1-Pixel Transparent Spacer. Each option adjusts what will be used to fill the empty areas of an image map. The Nested Table option creates a table within a table for each slice object. The 1-Pixel Transparent option uses a spacer file in addition to the slice to place the slice in each table cell. The No Spacers setting creates a single table, places each slice in a cell, and disregards any settings in the Contents pop-up menu in the HTML Setup dialog box.

4. Check the Use Canvas Color check box if you want to use the document's canvas color for the cell color of the table.

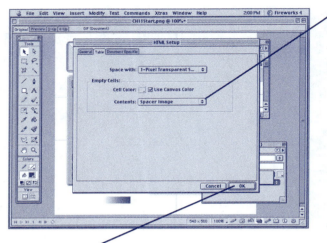

5. Click on the Contents pop-up menu to choose from one of three options for defining empty cells in a table: None, Spacer Image, or Non-breaking Space. The options in the Contents menu enable you to determine how spaces for empty cells will appear in the generated table. The Spacer Image is simply a file containing no image contents that can fill a particular size table cell. If you choose not to fill empty cells, Fireworks can generate HTML table cell coordinates only for the images being exported.

6. Click on the OK button to save your changes.

Editing a Hotspot

Unlike other image objects, Web objects only have a single state, so you don't have to worry about Vector or Bitmap modes when you're working with hotspots or slices. Resizing and moving Web objects is done much like the way you'd apply these same changes to a vector or bitmap object. The following steps show you how to assign a behavior, and view hotspot information in the Behaviors panel and the Object panel.

1. Select the Pointer Tool (V) from the toolbox.

2. Click and drag the corner of a hotspot to resize it.

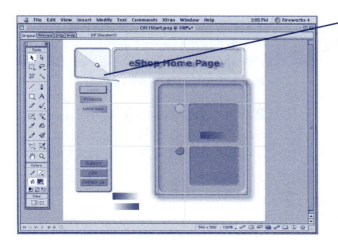

The newly shaped hotspot will appear in the document window.

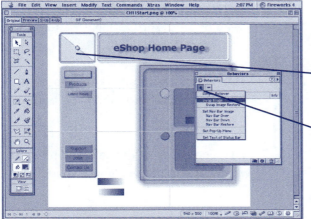

3. Choose Behaviors from the Window menu or press Shift + F3 to open the Behaviors panel.

4. Select a hotspot in the document window.

5. Click on the Plus button to view a list of behaviors. Choose the Swap Image behavior from the menu list. The Swap Image dialog box will open. This dialog box contains a couple window lists, a section where you can select the image with which you want to swap, and a couple check boxes that affect the way the images are loaded and restored whenever the behavior is selected.

6. Click on the Frame No. pop-up menu to select a frame in the current document that you'd like to swap into the selected hotspot.

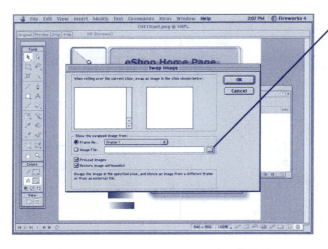

7. Alternatively, you can click on the Image File folder icon and choose a file on your hard drive as the image that will be swapped into the hotspot.

8. Click on the OK button to save your changes.

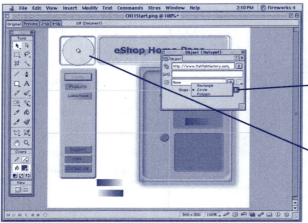

9. Choose Object from the Window menu or press Alt/Option + F2 to open the Object panel.

10. Select a hotspot. Then, choose a different shape from the Shape pop-up menu.

11. The shape of the selected hotspot will change in the document window.

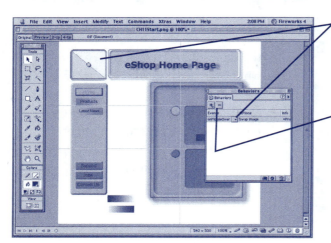

12. If you've added a behavior to a hotspot, you can edit the behavior at any time. Select a hotspot and then select a behavior in the Behaviors panel.

13. Click on the Minus button if you want to remove a behavior from a hotspot.

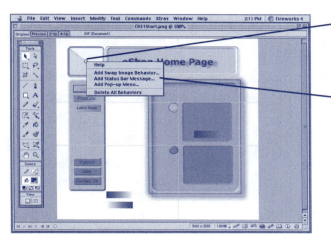

14. Click and hold the mouse button on the drag-and-drop handle in the center of a hotspot.

15. View the list of menu commands for the hotspot. Select one to modify the hotspot.

NOTE

Although Fireworks doesn't prevent you from overlapping hotspots or slices, try to avoid overlapping them because each Web object's location eventually affects the way the user will interact with these graphics and also how the document will be exported.

Hiding Hotspots

As you add hotspots to a document, you might want to edit the image objects below them. Fireworks provides two handy buttons that enable you to quickly hide and show the Web Layer for a document. The following steps show you how to hide the Web Layer in a document.

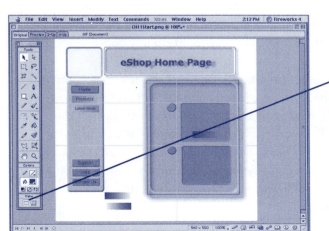

1. Press 2 or choose the Hide Slices button in the toolbox. The objects in the Web Layer of the document will no longer appear in the document window.

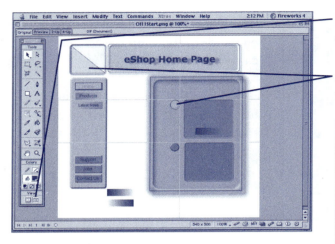

2. Click on the Show Slices button in the toolbox or press 2 a second time.

All hotspots and slices for the document will appear in the document window.

TIP

Need to a little more room but don't want to constantly open and close each panel? Press the Tab key to hide the panel windows in the Fireworks workspace. Press Tab again when you want the panels to be visible.

Assigning Behaviors to Hotspots

When you assign a behavior to a hotspot, Fireworks adds an additional element to your document as well as your Web page. The behavior itself is created with JavaScript code. JavaScript is a scripting language originally designed by Netscape. It has evolved when companies such as Microsoft have released new browsers. If you're familiar with programming or scripting languages, you can customize the Fireworks JavaScript routines or add additional routines to check a browser's version number or count visitors to your Web site. If you're new to JavaScript and HTML, Fireworks allows you to export the HTML and JavaScript code as a Dreamweaver Library, enabling you to create interactivity without touching any code.

Depending on the options you select for a behavior, you can make a hotspot link to a new page or show a new image. The JavaScript code can contain routines to locate an image map on your Web page or a list of files to preload when the browser loads your Web page. Fireworks can also generate HTML code that enables your Web page to look for a file to swap in the hotspot area on your hard drive (or on a Web site), or to load a URL (*Universal Resource Locator*) if you want to link to another Web page. The following sections show you how to create, edit, and preview a hotspot behavior.

Choosing a Behavior

To give your hotspot some action, you need to assign a URL or at least one behavior to it. Hotspots and slices can have any of the behaviors that appear in the Behaviors panel assigned to them. As you add behaviors, keep track of what each one does. Try not to add different behaviors that perform the same task. The following steps show you how to assign a behavior to a hotspot.

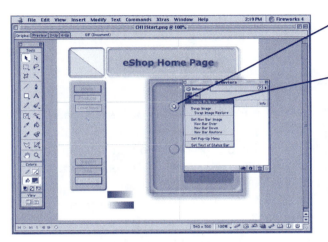

1. Select a hotspot in the document window.

2. Click on the Plus button in the Behaviors panel and select Simple Rollover from the menu. The selected behavior will appear in the window list in the Behaviors panel. Whenever you select that hotspot, you'll see any of its behaviors appear in the Behaviors panel.

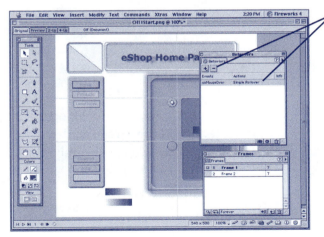

3. Select the Simple Rollover behavior and click on the Minus button to remove the behavior.

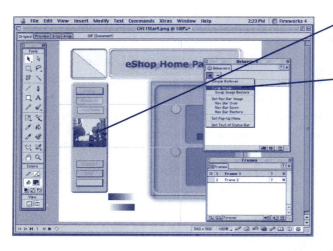

4. Select an image object (not a hotspot) in the document window.

5. Click on the Plus button and choose the Swap Image command from the pop-up menu.

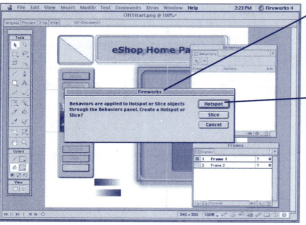

A Fireworks dialog box will appear, asking whether you want to create a hotspot or a slice so that you can add a behavior to the selected object.

6. Click on the Hotspot button to add a hotspot to the selected object. The Swap Image dialog box will open.

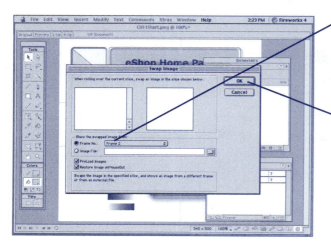

7. Click on the Frame No. pop-up menu and select the second frame in the document as the swap image behavior for the hotspot.

8. Click on the OK button to save your changes.

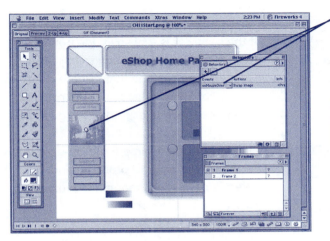

A hotspot object will be created over the image object. The hotspot behavior will appear in the Behaviors panel whenever that hotspot is selected.

Changing a Behavior

Experiment with a hotspot by trying out different behaviors. You can assign a behavior and then modify it by choosing a different swap image or by assigning a different event to it. You can also add multiple behaviors to a hotspot to experiment with different interactive states. The following steps show you how to change different settings for a behavior.

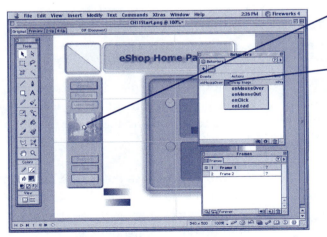

1. Select a hotspot in the document window.

2. Click on the pop-up menu immediately to the right of the behavior event in the Behaviors panel. Select a different event for an existing behavior from this menu.

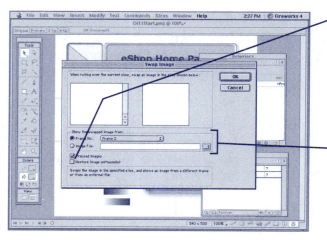

3. Double-click on a behavior to edit it. If the behavior is a swap image behavior, the Swap Image dialog box will open. Check or uncheck the appropriate check box to configure the behavior to preload or restore the images for the image swap.

4. Click on the Frame No. pop-up menu or the Image File radio button and select a path to an image file you want to swap into the hotspot.

5. Click on the OK button to save your changes and return to the document window.

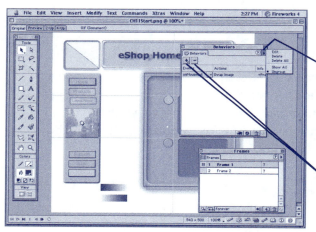

6. Click on the pop-up menu for the Behaviors panel to view a list of menu commands. You can edit, delete, or ungroup behaviors for a selected Web object.

7. Add or remove behaviors by clicking on the Plus or Minus buttons in the Behaviors panel.

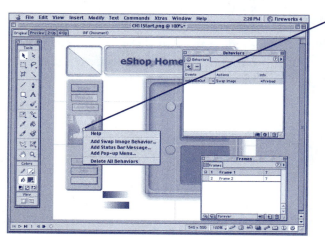

8. Click on the drag-and-drop behavior handle on a hotspot. The cursor will change to a hand and then a fist as you click.

9. When you release the mouse button a pop-up menu will appear, showing a list of menu commands for the drag-and-drop behavior handle. Click on a menu command to select it.

Previewing Hotspot Behaviors

After you've added a behavior to a hotspot, try it out in a browser window. You won't be able to experience the interactive elements in Fireworks, though. The following steps show you how to configure the primary browser for Fireworks and then preview a hotspot in Internet Explorer.

NOTE

If the swap image behavior is not visible in the browser window, it may because Fireworks did not create any JavaScript code for the behavior. Fireworks also may not recognize any of the frames assigned to the swap image behavior for the hotspot. If you're not code-shy, you can create the JavaScript and HTML code for the hotspot's swap image behavior and preview your hand-made HTML code in the browser window.

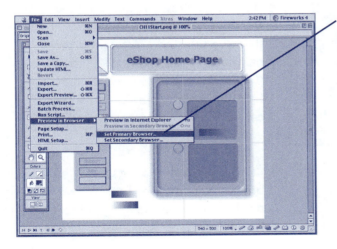

1. Choose Set Primary Browser from the File, Preview in Browser menu. The Locate Primary Browser dialog box, which contains a list of files and folders on your hard drive, will open.

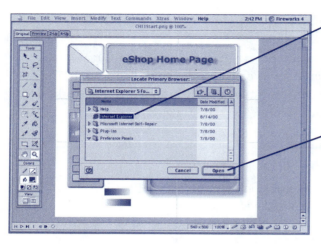

2. Navigate to the folder containing Internet Explorer or Netscape Navigator. After you've located the browser's application icon, select it in the window list.

3. Click on Open. The selected browser will be defined as the primary browser for Fireworks.

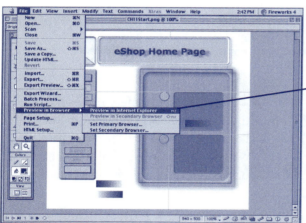

4. Open a document containing vector or bitmap objects and at least one hotspot with at least one behavior assigned to it.

5. Choose Preview in Internet Explorer from the File, Preview in Browser menu. If you've selected a different browser, its name will appear in the File, Preview in Browser menu. Fireworks will start the Internet Explorer application and will create a new window to display your Web page.

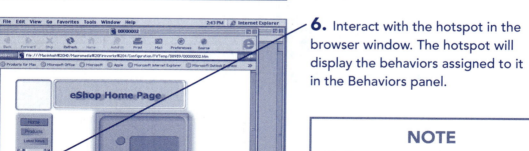

6. Interact with the hotspot in the browser window. The hotspot will display the behaviors assigned to it in the Behaviors panel.

NOTE

To find out more about how to create buttons, see Chapter 12, "Making Buttons with the Button Editor."

Adding a URL to a Hotspot or Slice

A hotspot or slice can have the same behavior as a link. You can assign a URL to a hotspot, in addition to a behavior, so that when someone clicks on the hotspot, a new Web page will load in the browser window. Fireworks provides a full-featured URL panel to enable you to assign, store, and view plenty of URLs at a moment's notice.

Working with the URL Panel

The URL panel actually shares much of its information with the Object panel. You can select a hotspot and type a URL into either panel. However, the URL panel has a Plus button that enables you to quickly add a new URL to a list of URLs available to any document in Fireworks. The following steps give you a brief tour of the URL panel.

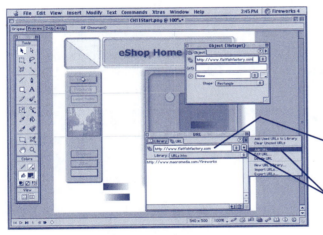

1. Choose URL from the Window menu or press Alt/Option + Shift + F10 to open the URL panel.

2. Type a URL in the text box if you want to add it to the URL list in Fireworks.

3. Click on the Plus button to add a URL to the URLs.htm file. Or, click on the pop-up menu in the URL panel and choose the Add URL command.

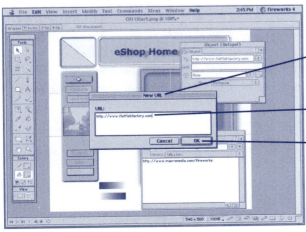

4. If you chose the Add URL command, the New URL dialog box will open.

5. Type a URL in the text box.

6. Click on the OK button to save your changes.

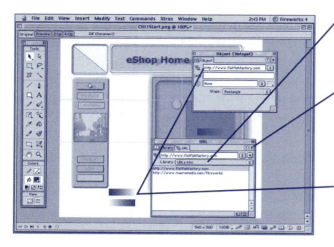

The URL will be stored in a file titled URLs.htm. This file name will appear in the Library pop-up menu in the URL panel.

7. Choose New URL Library from the pop-up menu if you want to store different sets of Web addresses in separate HTML files.

The URL selected in the URL panel will also appear in the Object panel whenever the associated hotspot is selected.

NOTE

The URLs.htm file is located in the URL Libraries folder in the Configuration subfolder of the Fireworks folder on your hard drive. You can modify the URL list with an HTML editor.

TIP

If you're not sure what the exact URL is, try it out in a browser window before adding it to a hotspot.

Assigning a URL to a Hotspot

When you're ready to add a Web address to a hotspot, open the Behaviors panel and assign a simple rollover behavior to the hotspot. The following steps show you how to assign a URL to a hotspot.

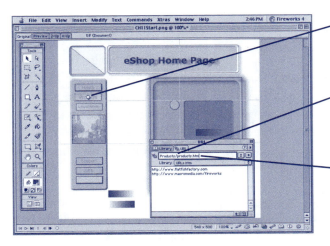

1. Choose the Pointer Tool (V) and then click on a hotspot in the document window.

2. Type a URL in the text box located at the top of the URL panel, or choose a URL from the pop-up menu.

If you know where the particular file will be located on your Web server, you can type a path relative to the Web page. Alternatively, you can type the full URL, beginning with http://, into the text box.

TIP

If you want to navigate to a different folder located in a directory above your Web page, type ../ to move up one level in the directory path on your hard drive. A directory is another name for a folder.

NOTE

You can also assign a URL to a hotspot or slice from the Object panel. The Object panel enables you to assign an alternate name for the URL, as well as a target. If you're working with a Web page that contains frames, you can type the name of the frame in which you want the URL to appear. The pop-up menu located to the right of the Target text box enables you to open the URL in a new browser window (_blank), a parent frameset (_parent), the current frame (_self), or all frames (_top).

Slicing an Image

The Slice Tool enables you to break up a document into separate smaller files. Fireworks provides three different ways to apply the Slice Tool to an image: as a tool from the toolbox, as a menu command, or as a dialog box option when you assign a behavior to an object. When you create a slice, the entire canvas area of the document becomes divided along the red slice guidelines that appear in the document window. The red lines mark the borders of each image file, resulting from creating the first slice.

A green shaded area represents the slice itself. This slice can be assigned behaviors and URLs, much like you'd assign these elements to a hotspot. Other image files resulting from the sliced image cannot be assigned behaviors unless you create a slice. In addition to these behaviors, you can also use slices to create more sophisticated, interactive Web behaviors, such as a disjointed rollover. You can also replace individual slices or create empty slices that contain text instead of an image. The following sections show you how to create a slice using the different Slice tools and commands.

Applying the Slice Tool

You can apply the Slice Tool using the same techniques you would use to create a rectangle or polygon hotspot. You can also add a slice to a document in two other ways. To create a slice that matches a specific object, you can select that object and then choose the Slice command from the Insert menu. You can also select an object and then choose a behavior from the Behaviors panel. If you do this, a Fireworks dialog box will open. Click on the Slice button to create a slice for the selected object. However, the easiest way to create a slice object is to click on the Slice Tool in the toolbox. The following steps show you how to create a slice with the Slice Tool.

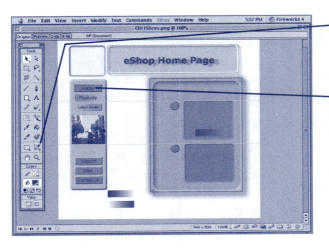

1. Open a document containing several graphic objects. Then, click on the Slice Tool (G) in the toolbox.

2. Click and hold the mouse button in the document window, then drag the cursor to create a rectangle-shaped slice. A light blue border will appear as you drag the mouse.

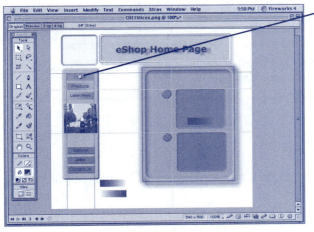

3. Release the mouse button to create the slice object. The slice will have a light green fill area. A light blue line will border the slice object, and red guide lines will extend across the canvas. A white button with target marks will be located at the center of the selected slice.

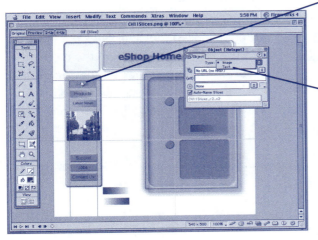

4. Choose Object from the Window menu to open the Object panel. Then use the Pointer Tool (V) to select the slice object.

5. Image is the default setting in the Type pop-up menu in the Object panel. This setting indicates that the image below the slice will be exported along with the HTML information for the Web page. If you do not want the image to appear with the rest of the slices, choose Text from the Type pop-up menu.

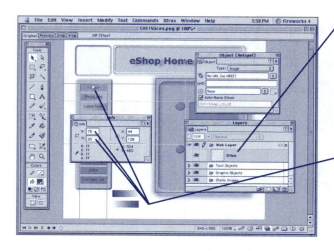

6. When you create a slice, a Web object is created in the Layers panel. Each slice object is given a generic name. Double-click on the slice name in the Layers panel to change it.

7. Choose Info from the Window menu to open the Info panel. Select a slice object. You can view the slice object's width and height information (in pixels) in the Info panel.

TIP

You can convert a hotspot to a slice. Select the hotspot and then choose Insert Slice from the Insert menu. The light blue hotspot will change to a green slice with accompanying slice guides.

Creating a Polygonal Slice

Click to create each corner or point of the polygon shaped slice. This tool can be helpful if you plan to update an odd-shaped area in a sliced image. The following steps show you how to create an odd-shaped four-corner slice.

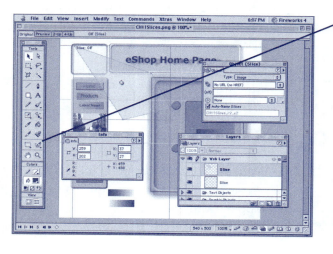

1. Click on the Slice Tool (G). If the Polygon Slice tool icon does not appear in the toolbox, hold down the mouse button when you click on the Slice Tool. A submenu will appear with two icons. Select the Polygon Slice Tool from the submenu.

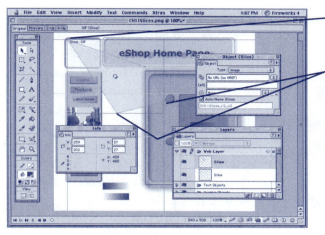

2. Click once in the document window to create the first point of the slice.

3. Click in another location in the document window to add another point to the slice. Continue to click, surrounding an object or adding points as you like. Click on the first point of the slice to complete the polygon slice shape.

CAUTION

After you create a slice or a hotspot, you can resize the object area. However, you cannot add or remove points in a hotspot or a slice. If you want to delete a slice or hotspot object, select it and then press the Backspace/Delete key. Then, use a Slice or Hotspot Tool to create a new one.

Viewing Multiple Slices in a Document

Fireworks allows you to create multiple slices that overlap each other. When you export the document, Fireworks will not generate extra files for any overlapping

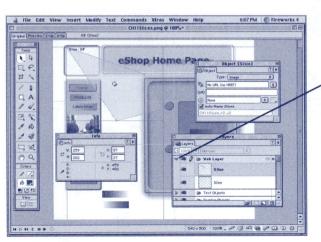

areas between sliced objects. The following steps show you how to work with multiple slices.

1. View all the slice objects in the Layers panel. Click on the triangle icon to expand the Web Layer. There are two basic types of layers: the Web Layer (only one can exist per document) and objects layers (or, as Macromedia calls them, layers).

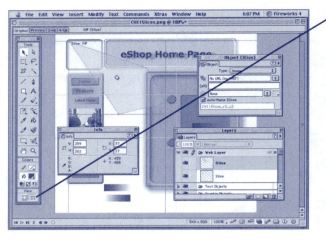

2. In the View area of the toolbox, you can show and hide the Web Layer by pressing the Hide button on the left, or the Show button on the right. For this example, click on the Show Slices button to view the Web Layer in the document window. When you select the Show Slices button, hotspots and slices will appear in the document window. It's okay to overlap a hotspot and a slice, but you might want to avoid overlapping two slices, if possible.

Resizing Slices

As you organize the layout of a Web page, the location or size of an object might change. You can adjust the size of a slice using the same steps you would use to resize a hotspot or other vector object. The following steps show you how.

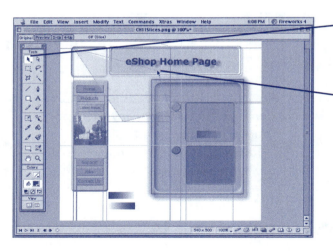

1. Open a document that contains slice objects. Select the Pointer Tool (V) from the toolbox.

2. Click on the slice you want to resize. Click and drag a point on the slice to adjust the shape of the slice.

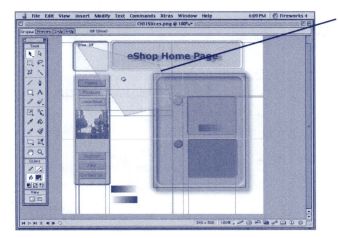

3. View the new slice shape in the document window.

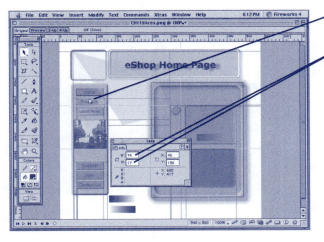

4. Click on a different slice object.

The width and height of the slice will appear in the Info panel. You can use the width and height information to determine precise measurements of slices in a document.

Changing Slice Settings

When you add a slice to a document, that document can turn into several image files instead of just one file. Each slice is given a unique name based on the original file name, so Fireworks can generate JavaScript code that can place each slice in the image map. The following steps show you how to access and change the naming settings for slices.

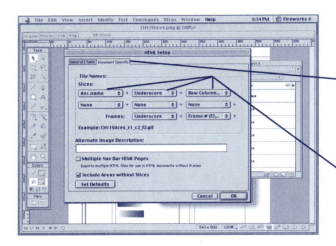

1. Choose HTML Setup from the File menu.

2. Click on the Document Specific tab in the HTML Setup dialog box. This dialog box contains file name settings for slices.

3. Click on a pop-up menu to choose how you want each slice file to be named when the slices are exported from Fireworks.

4. View an example of the file name at the bottom of the File Names section of the dialog box.

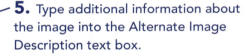

5. Type additional information about the image into the Alternate Image Description text box.

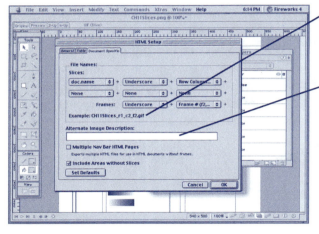

6. Click on a pop-up menu to view the naming options for a slice file. Choose from doc.name, slice, slice plus a number or alphabet character, row column, underscore, period, space, or hyphen.

7. Click on the OK button to save your changes. Or, click on Cancel to exit the window without saving new information.

NOTE

Fireworks converts the slice information into HTML. In HTML code, the slice becomes a table or a table cell, which you can edit in Dreamweaver.

TIP

You can export the full document along with slices by choosing the Include Areas without Slices check box. If you deselect this check box, only slice objects will be exported from the document.

Assigning Behaviors to Slices

Most of the interactive Web elements you can create in Fireworks involve slices. Because a slice divides an image into smaller sections (or files), you can place a slice over an image or an animated GIF. Then, assign a swap image behavior to the slice to display a different animation when the slice is selected. The following sections show you how to work with slices and slice behaviors.

Choosing a Behavior

When you assign a behavior to a slice, you are adding an effect to the image or image object located below that slice. Each slice has its own custom set of behaviors, although any slice or hotspot has access to the same menu list of behaviors. The following steps show you how to add a behavior to a slice.

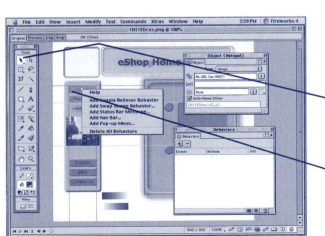

1. Open a document that contains image objects and slice objects. Then, click on the Pointer Tool (V) in the toolbox.

2. Select a slice object in the document window.

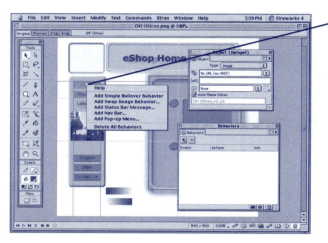

3. Click on the drag-and-drop handle located in the center of the slice. A pop-up menu will appear with a list of menu commands. Choose a behavior from the menu list. In this example, I chose the Swap Image behavior.

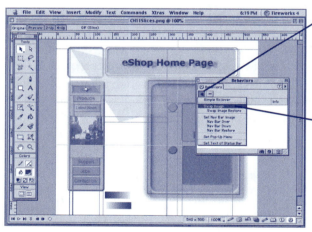

4. Alternatively, you can choose Behaviors from the Window panel or press Shift + F3 to open the Behaviors panel. Click on the Plus button to view a list of behaviors.

5. Click on a behavior from the list in the Behaviors panel.

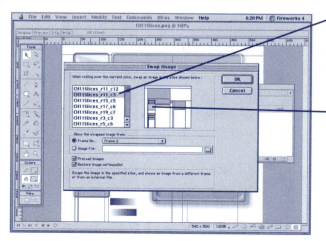

6. If you've selected the Swap Image behavior from the Behaviors panel, the Swap Image dialog box will open. Select the current slice from the left window list.

7. Click on the target slice in the right pane.

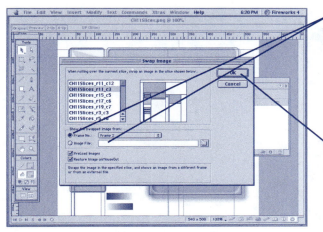

8. Choose the Frame No. radio button if you want to swap an image with another frame in the current document. Otherwise, click on the Image File radio button and choose a file located on your hard drive.

9. Click on the OK button to save your changes.

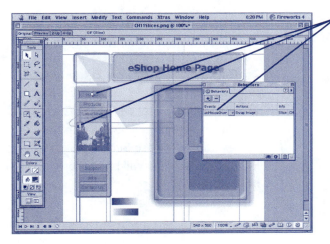

10. View the newly added behavior in the Behaviors panel.

Selecting Multiple Slices

Another way to add behaviors to slices is to select more than one slice and then assign a behavior to them. The first time you try the following steps, the window list might not update in the Behaviors panel. But have no fear; these steps produce behaviors.

1. Open a new or existing document and add several image and Web objects to it. Click on the Pointer Tool (V) in the toolbox.

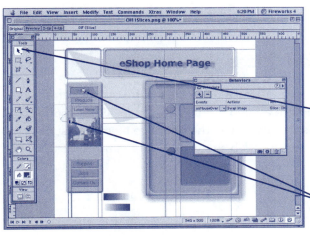

2. Click on a slice in the document window.

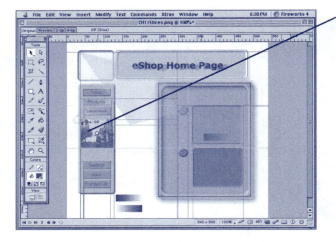

3. Hold down the Shift key and click on another slice in the same document window.

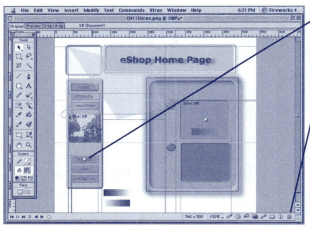

4. Repeat step 3 as many times as you want, to select more slices.

5. Click on the gear icon in the lower-right corner of the document window. The Behaviors panel will open. Click on the Plus button and select a behavior. For example, choose Simple Rollover. Each selected slice will have that behavior assigned to it.

Working with Exported Slices

Because buttons can have so many states, it's a good idea to test them before you add them to a bigger project or before adding more HTML or JavaScript code to complete your Web site. When testing, try to use the interface elements, such as buttons, in the same way a visitor to your Web site would use them.

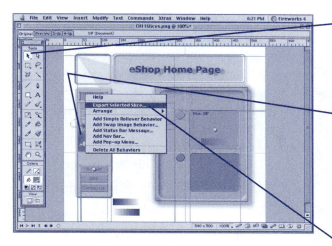

1. Open a document containing several image and slice objects. Click on the Pointer Tool (V) and then select a Web object in the document window.

2. If you are using a Mac, hold down the Ctrl key and then click on the drag-and-drop handle located in the center of the slice. If you are using Windows, right-click on the drag-and-drop handle. A pop-up menu will appear.

3. Choose the Export Selected Slice command from the pop-up menu.

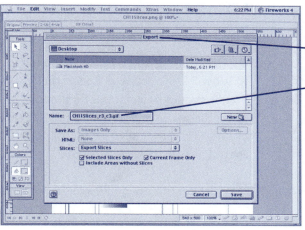

4. The Export dialog box will open.

5. The name of the slice will appear in the Name text box.

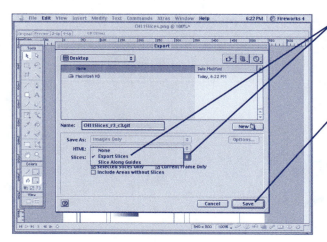

6. Click on the Slices pop-up menu to view the export options for the file. Choose Export Slices from the pop-up menu, if it's not already selected.

7. Click on Save to export the slice file.

Assigning an External File to a Swap Image Behavior

If you've assigned a swap image behavior to a slice, you'll probably want to swap an image in another frame from the same document. That way, when you export the sliced images for that document, you won't have to worry about skipping any files that might be located in a different folder on your hard drive. The problem with assigning a file as a swap image behavior is that if you move it or delete it, you'll need to remember to select a replacement image for that behavior. Otherwise, when you export the document, the behavior will no longer work. However, you can select an external file to work with the swap image behavior assigned to a slice. Here's how:

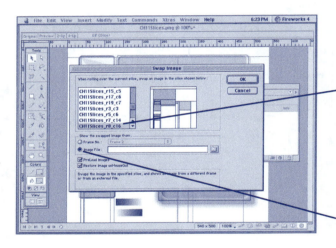

1. Double-click on a swap image behavior for a slice in the Behaviors panel.

2. Click on the source slice in the left window list of the Swap Image dialog box. It should be selected by default when the Swap Image dialog box first opens. The target slice in the right pane should also already be selected.

3. Click on the Image File radio button.

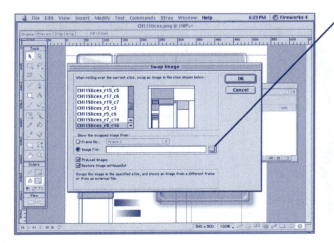

4. Click on the folder icon button located on the right side of the Image File text box. You can also type the path to the file in the text box, if you want.

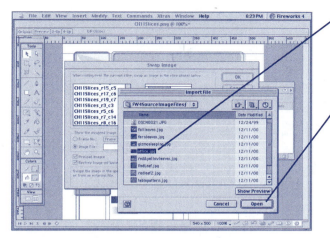

5. Navigate your hard drive and select the image file you want to use as the swapped image for the selected slice object.

6. Click on Open to select the file and add its path to the Image File text box, then click on the OK button to save your changes.

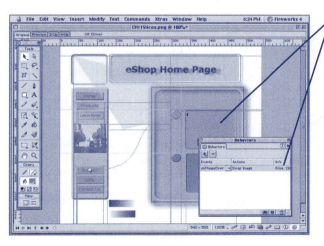

Fireworks will update the document window. The drag-and-drop handle will contain a line that extends to the target slice. The file name for the swap image will appear in the Info column of the Behaviors panel, beside the Swap Image behavior. You might have to grow the size of the Behavior panel to view the file name.

Creating a Text Slice

A text slice is an HTML-based slice that does not contain an image. Macromedia uses the term *empty slice* to refer to a text slice. A text slice retains the shape of the slice object but only displays text, or no text at all, instead of displaying an image. If you add text to an image map, you can update text-based messages on a Web page or Web site without having to create an image slice. If you create an empty slice containing no text, the text slice acts a placeholder and can help reduce the overall size of the exported document. The following steps show you how to change an image slice into a text slice.

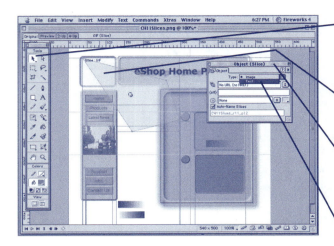

1. Open a document containing several image and Web objects. Click on the Pointer Tool (V) in the toolbox.

2. Click on a slice object in the document window.

3. Choose Object from the Window menu, or press Alt/Option + F2 to open the Object panel.

4. Click and hold the mouse button on the Type pop-up menu, and select Text from the menu.

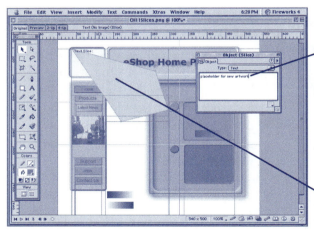

5. Type some text into the text box in the Object panel. This text will appear as HTML text when you export the slice. If you do not type text into the text box, you will create an empty slice, which will help reduce the overall size of the exported document.

Fireworks will re-label the Web object from a GIF to a text object in the document window.

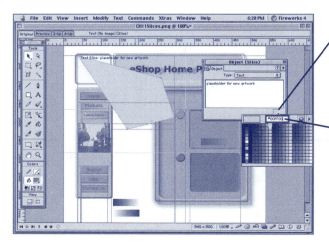

6. Now, assign a color to the slice object. Click on the color well in the Object panel to assign a custom color to the text slice.

7. Drag the mouse over a color or type a hexadecimal value in the text box in the color pop-up menu. Then, press the Enter/Return key to select the color and apply it to the selected slice.

Working with Layers of Slices

Although Fireworks can process overlapping slices, try to avoid overlapping slices if you can. The following steps show you how to resize a text slice that overlaps an image slice.

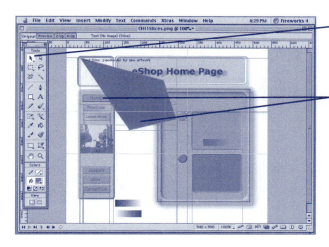

1. Continuing from the previous set of steps, select the Pointer Tool (V) from the toolbox.

2. Click on a corner of the slice nearest to the overlapping area. Try to resize the overlapping slice so that it no longer covers the other slice.

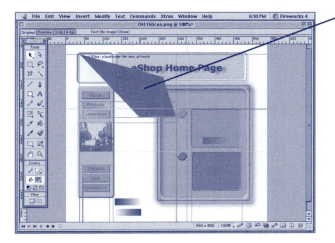

3. View the resized slice in the document window.

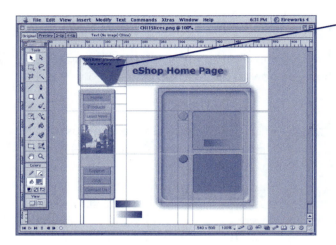

4. If the document contains several slices, try to shrink the size of the slice down to the smallest possible size.

TIP

If you want to avoid overlapping slices, consider adding guides to your document and activating the Snap to Guides command located in the View, Guides menu.

11

Creating Navigation Bars

If you're familiar with Web pages, you've seen a navigation bar. A navigation bar enables you to navigate a Web site. As you move from one Web page to another, the navigation bar can show you other Web pages available on a Web site, and let you know which section you're currently visiting. Typically, a navigation bar, also called a nav bar, contains a common set of buttons that appear across all, or at least most, pages of a Web site. Creating a navigation bar involves designing text and graphics, adding buttons and rollover behaviors to those buttons, and then exporting and integrating the nav bar components with each page of your Web site, using HTML and JavaScript code. This chapter shows you how to create some simple navigation bars. In this chapter you'll learn how to:

- ● Create buttons and design a navigation bar
- ● Add rollover states to navigation bar buttons
- ● Assign behaviors to buttons
- ● Preview the navigation bar in a browser

Designing a Navigation Bar

Because the navigation bar is a basic element for your Web pages, try to make it as easy to use as possible. Remember that people will be using this particular graphic to navigate your Web site. If it's not easy to use, visitors probably won't get to see much of your Web site. You might want to design your nav bar based on some key pages on your Web site. If you have some favorite Web sites that you think are easy to navigate, try deconstructing the nav bars for those sites to find out what you like or don't like about them. Then, apply the things you like to the nav bar for your Web site. The following sections show how to create different components of a nav bar.

Creating a Button Symbol for the Nav Bar

A nav bar design can use the same vector or bitmap objects you would use to create any other kind of graphic in Fireworks. I've created a simple nav bar for this example. The nav bar contains three buttons: News, Events, and Search. I've initially created vector and text objects for each button. The following steps show you how to convert a text and graphic object into a button.

1. Choose the Pointer Tool (V) and click on the text and graphic objects you want to change into a button. In this example, I've select a vector rectangle shape and a text object. Press Ctrl/Command + C to copy the selected objects, or select the objects and then choose the Copy command from the Edit menu.

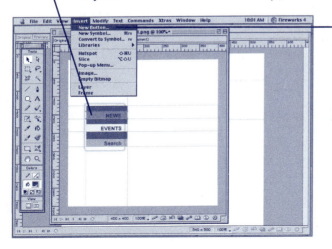

2. Choose New Button from the Insert menu. The Button Editor window will appear.

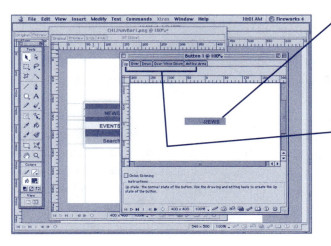

3. Click in the Button Editor window, then press Ctrl/Command + V or choose Paste from the Edit menu. The text and graphic will appear in the Button Editor window.

4. Click on a tab in the Button Editor window to create a different button state.

NOTE

For more information about how to create buttons, see Chapter 12, "Making Buttons with the Button Editor."

Converting an Object to a Button Symbol

Another way to create a button is to choose the Convert to Symbol command from the Insert menu. A symbol can become one of three things: a graphic, an animation, or a button. The following steps show you how to create a button by selecting the Convert to Symbol menu command.

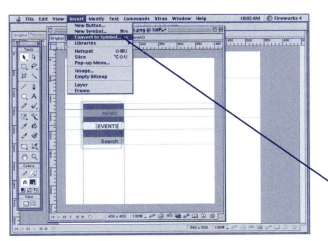

1. Choose the Pointer Tool (V) and click on a text or graphic object. Hold down the Shift key and click on another object if you want to convert more than one object into a button symbol. After the objects are selected, press Ctrl/Command + Copy, or select the Copy command from the Edit menu.

2. Click on the Insert menu and select the Convert to Symbol command. The Symbol Properties dialog box will open.

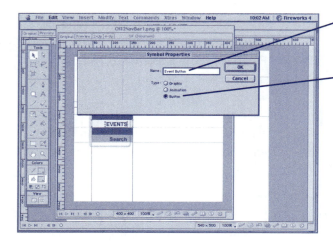

3. Type a name for the button in the Name text box.

4. Click on the Button radio button to create a button symbol.

5. Click on the OK button in the Symbol Properties dialog box. The Button Editor window will appear. Paste the button text and graphic in the Button Editor window. Then, click on the Close box to exit the Button Editor window.

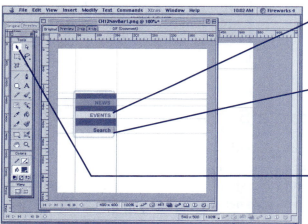

When the symbol is not selected, it will look just like any other graphic object in the document window.

6. View the layout of the nav bar. Make sure that each button has enough space above and below it so that it can be clearly seen.

7. Click on the Pointer Tool (V) in the toolbox.

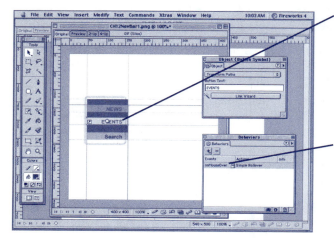

8. Click on the button you just created. A drag-and-drop handle icon will appear in the center of the button. A small arrow icon, indicating that the graphic is an instance of a symbol, will appear in the lower-left corner of the button graphic.

9. Choose Behaviors from the Window menu or press Shift + F3 to open the Behaviors panel. When a button symbol is created, a simple rollover behavior will be assigned to it.

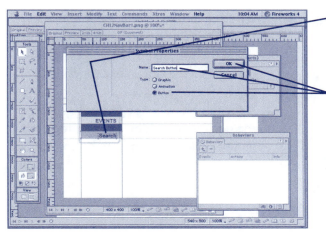

10. Select another graphic object in the document window and choose Convert to Symbol from the Insert menu.

11. Type a unique name for the symbol, select the Button radio button, and then click on the OK button to change the selected objects into a button symbol for the nav bar.

Laying out the Navigation Bar

Now take a slightly different approach to nav bar design. The next sections show you how to create a few different nav bar objects. But first, take a look at some tools that might help you create a nice, clean layout for your nav bar. Back in Chapter 3, "Getting Familiar with Tools, Objects, and Panels," the rulers, guides, and grids features were explained. You can use the rulers and guides to help nav bar graphics snap into place as you experiment with different layouts. The following steps show you how to add guides to a new document.

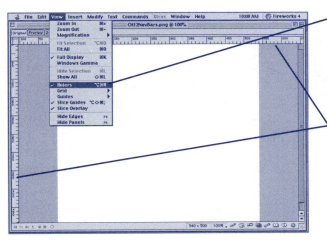

1. Open a new document window. Choose Rulers (Alt/Option + Ctrl/Command + R) from the View menu. You must activate rulers before you can add guides to a document.

2. Rulers will appear at the top and left side of the document window.

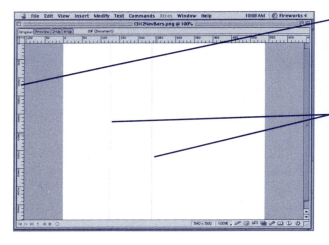

3. Click on the ruler area on the left side of the document window. Hold down the mouse button and drag the cursor into the document window.

A green vertical guide line will appear in the document window as you drag your mouse. Release the mouse button to place the guide in the document window.

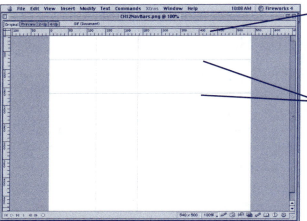

4. Click in the ruler area at the top of the document window. Hold down the mouse button and drag the cursor into the document window.

The cursor will change to an icon containing two horizontal lines and an up and a down arrow. A green horizontal line will appear in the document window. Release the mouse button to place the guide in the document window. You can move any guide by simply clicking and dragging it with the Pointer Tool (V).

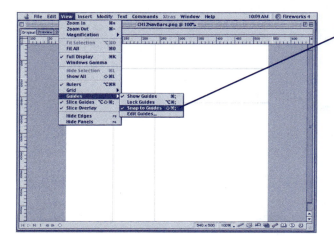

5. If you would like image objects to snap to the guide lines, choose Snap to Guides (Shift + Ctrl/Command + ;) from the View, Guides menu to activate this feature.

TIP

Choose Lock Guides (Alt/Option + Ctrl/Command + ;) from the View, Guides menu if you don't want to accidentally move a guide while you're moving image objects around in the document window.

NOTE

To remove a guide, click and drag it out of the canvas area of the document window. When you release the mouse button outside the canvas area, the selected guide will be removed from the document window.

Designing Nav Bar Graphics

You can design a nav bar with or without guides. Guides can help you align buttons or other graphic objects on the nav bar. If you add horizontal or vertical guides to a document, you can use the Snap to Guides command to lay out your nav bar.

Graphic objects can be imported into Fireworks, or you can use the drawing and shape tools combined with one or two effects to design the base and button graphics for a nav bar. Try to design a nav bar that matches the rest of the Web site design and is easy to use. The following steps show you how to create the base graphic and button objects for a nav bar.

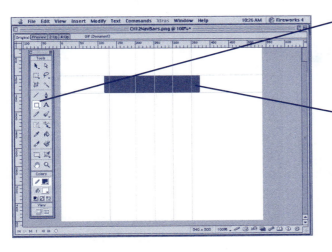

1. Click on a tool in the toolbar and create an object in the document window. In this example, I've selected the Rectangle Tool (R).

2. Click and drag the mouse in the document window to create a shape. Assign a fill color to it if you want. In this example, the rectangle is the base graphic for the nav bar. I will add button graphic objects on top of the rectangle.

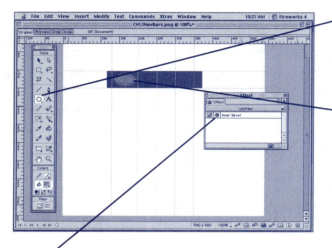

3. Select a drawing tool or a shape tool to create a graphic for a nav bar button. In this example, I've selected the Ellipse Tool (R).

4. Apply the tool to the document window to create an oval shaped object. Place the shape on the rectangle object.

5. Choose Effect from the Window menu or press Alt/Option + F7 to open the Effect panel.

6. Select the oval shape and then choose an effect from the pop-up menu in the Effect panel. In this example, I chose the Inner Bevel effect.

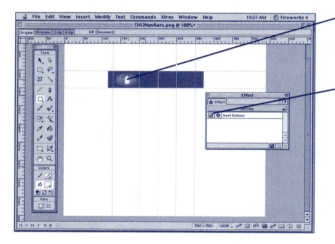

7. Create a graphic object and place it in the center of the oval shape created in the previous steps.

8. If you've closed the Effect panel, reopen it. Select the object and then choose an effect. I chose the Inset Emboss effect to help blend the top object with the object below it.

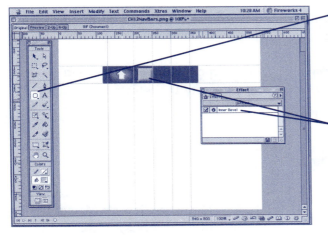

9. Create another button for the nav bar. Choose a drawing or shape tool and then apply it to the document window to create another button object. I've selected the Rounded Rectangle Tool (R).

10. Place the button object on the nav bar graphic and then apply an effect to it if you want.

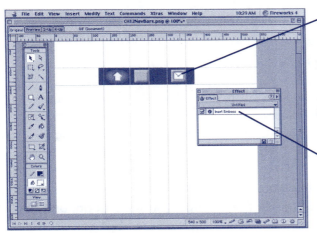

11. Create a graphic object for the button. I've created a copy of the rounded rectangle. Then, I created a simple graphic using the shape and line tools. I grouped the objects together and placed the graphic over the button object.

12. If you've closed the Effect panel, reopen it. Select the graphic object and apply an effect to it. I've chosen Inset Emboss.

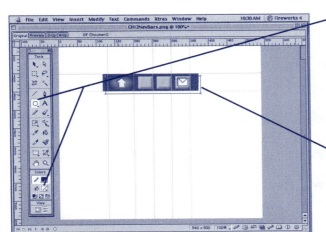

13. These next two steps are optional. I wanted to experiment with adding a line graphic around the main nav bar graphic. I selected the Rounded Rectangle Tool (R) and turned off the fill color.

14. Create a shape or drawing in the document window.

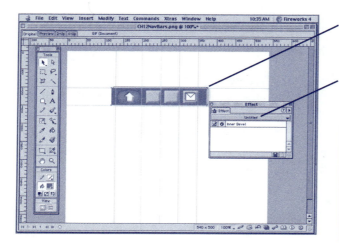

15. Select the shape in the document window.

16. Open the Effect panel and choose an effect for the selected object.

NOTE

Nav bars can also contain pop-up menu buttons. To find out more about pop-up menus, see Chapter 14, "Designing Pop-Up Menus."

Adding Text to a Button

The previous steps showed you how to add a graphic object to a nav bar button. You can also add text to a button object and apply many of the same effects to a text button as you would to a graphic button. The following steps show you how to add text to a button.

1. Click on the Text Tool (T) in the toolbox. Then, click once in the canvas area of the document window. The Text Editor window will open. All the font options, text formatting tools, and text color options are located in this window. You can use this window to both create and edit any vector text in Fireworks.

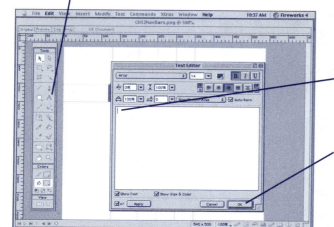

2. Click in the large text box area in the center of the Text Editor window. Type some text.

3. Click on the OK button to save the text changes to your document.

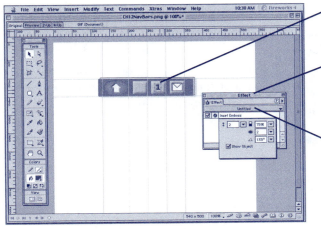

4. Place the text object over a button object.

5. Press Alt/Option + F7 or choose Effect from the Window menu to open the Effect panel.

6. Click on the Effect pop-up menu and choose an effect for the selected text object. I chose the Inset Emboss effect.

Editing Text Settings

Text is created as a vector object in Fireworks. You can convert a text object into a path or bitmap. However, you can only edit text if it is a vector object. I usually don't convert text objects into paths or bitmaps for this very reason. The following steps show you how to invoke the Text Editor and tweak a variety of text settings.

1. Select a text object in the document window.

2. Choose the Editor menu command from the Text menu. Alternatively, you can double-click on a text object to access the Text Editor window. The Text Editor window will open.

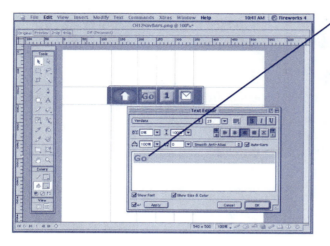

3. Click and drag the mouse over the text in the Text Editor window to select it. You can give each text character a unique font, font style, font size, or other formatting characteristics in the Text Editor window.

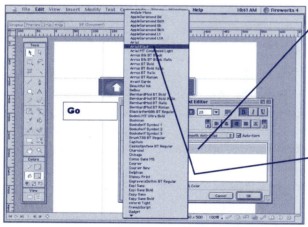

4. You can assign a new font to some text. First, select some text in the Text Editor window.

5. Click on the Font pop-up menu located in the upper-left corner of the Text Editor window. View the list of fonts installed with your computer's operating system.

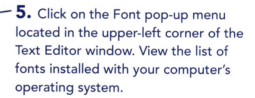

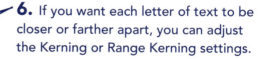

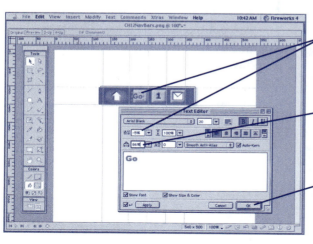

6. If you want each letter of text to be closer or farther apart, you can adjust the Kerning or Range Kerning settings.

7. You can also adjust the horizontal scale of the text in the Text Editor window.

8. Click on the OK button to save your changes.

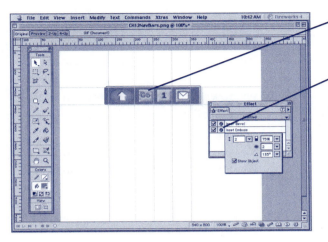

9. View the new changes to the text object in the document window.

10. Add an effect to the text from the Effect panel. First select a text object, then click on the Effect pop-up menu and choose an effect.

TIP

Convert text to a path if you want a text object to take the shape of a path, such as a line or circle. To convert text to a path, first choose a text object and then choosing Convert to Path from the Text menu, or by pressing Ctrl/Command + Shift + P.

TIP

If you want to customize a particular text character by adding or removing its pixels, you can convert the vector text object into a bitmap text object. Convert text to a bitmap object by first selecting a text object and then choosing Convert to Bitmap from the Modify menu, or by pressing Ctrl/Command + Alt/Option + Shift + Z.

Creating a Text Button

You can create a text button out of a text object. One way this particular type of object might backfire is if you place a text button over a graphic button instance that has another set of different behaviors. In short, if you create a text button, use it as a button and don't combine it with other buttons with different behaviors. The following steps show you how to create a button out of a text object.

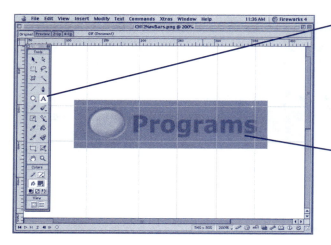

1. Click on the Text Tool (T) in the toolbox. Then, click in the document window. The Text Editor window will open. Type some text into the Text Editor window and then click on the OK button to add text to the document window.

2. Select the text object in the document window. Then, choose Copy from the Edit menu or press Ctrl/Command + C to copy the selected text object.

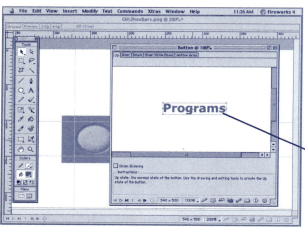

3. Convert the text object into a button by selecting Convert to Symbol from the Insert menu. Click on the Button radio button, type a name for the button, and then click on the OK button in the Symbol Properties dialog box. The Button Editor window will appear.

4. Paste the previously selected object into the Up tab of the Button Editor window. Congratulations, you've just created an Up button state for your nav bar!

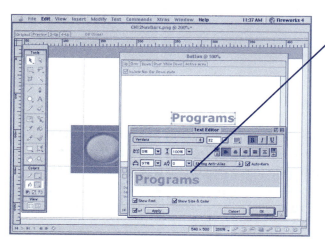

5. Choose a different button state in the Button Editor window by clicking on a tab. In this example, I selected the Down button state. To create the down state of the button, the text object will be changed from the settings used in the Up button state. Double-click on the text object in the Button Editor window. Highlight the text you want to modify in the Text Editor window.

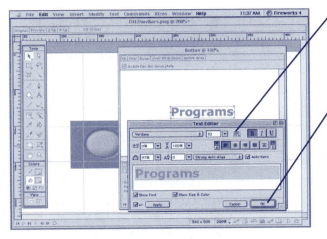

6. Select a different color for the text. Click on the color well in the Text Editor window to view and choose a new color for the selected text.

7. Click on the OK button to save your changes and return to the Button Editor window. Click on the Close box to exit the Button Editor window.

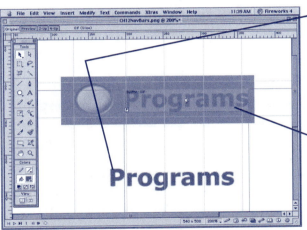

8. A new button symbol will appear in the document window. Click and drag the previous graphic object away from the nav bar graphic. Click on the eye icon in the Layers panel to hide this text object.

9. Move the button symbol onto the nav bar graphic.

NOTE

You can copy the graphic from the previous button state by choosing the Copy Graphic button in the Button Editor window. Each button state is saved in a separate frame. In order to copy the button graphic across button states, there must be an object in the previous button state, or frame. For example, if you try to click the Copy Over Graphic button in Step 5, no new image object will appear in the Button Editor window because you did not create a graphic for the Open button state. To successfully use the Copy Graphic button, you must create each consecutive button state moving from the Up tab to the Over, Down, and Over While Down tabs in the Button Editor window.

Adding Rollover States to Each Button

Fireworks provides each button with up to four different rollover states: Up, Down, Over, or Over While Down. A rollover state can also be referred to as a button state. Button states on a Web page work similarly to button states in a Windows or Macintosh application. The basic function of a button is to trigger a new event when it is clicked. The button graphic might change if the mouse hovers over the button, or if the button is clicked.

You can create each button state manually, using the drawing or shape tools from the toolbox. Or, you can copy a graphic as you create different button states. The graphics are just one of two main elements that define a button state. When you export the document, you can view the JavaScript code that Fireworks creates to enable a browser to swap images for each button state. The following sections show you how to add button states to the buttons on a nav bar.

Designing Button States

Each panel in the Button Editor consists of a canvas, similar to the canvas in the document window. You can access any of the tools in the toolbox and apply them to the Button Editor window to create a particular button state. The following steps show you how to create the Up and Down button states.

1. Double-click on a button instance in the document window. The Button Editor window will appear.

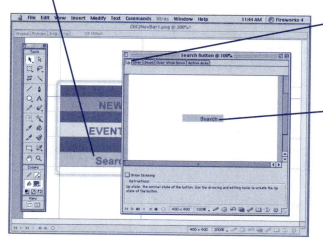

The Up tab is the default tab selected in the Button Editor window. The Up state represents the button in its default, unselected state.

2. One way to create the Up state is to copy the text and graphic objects from the document window into the Button Editor window. However, you can also create new text and graphic objects using the toolbox tools.

3. Click on the Down tab, then paste an image into the Button Editor window to create the Down button state. Use the Pointer tool (V) to select the text object in the Button Editor window.

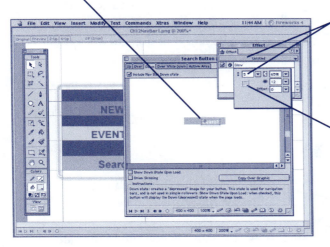

4. Press Alt/Option + F7 to open the Effect panel, or choose Effect from the Window menu. Choose an effect from the Effect pop-up menu. I chose the Glow effect.

5. After the effect is applied to the text, click on the i icon to edit the effect's settings. For example, choose a different color for the text to create a custom graphic for the Down state. Click on the Close box to exit the Button Editor window.

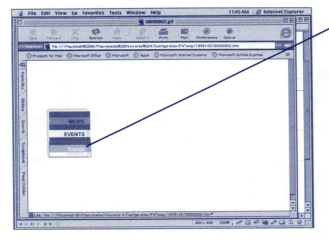

6. Choose the Preview in Internet Explorer (or other browser application name) command from the File, Preview in Browser menu. The nav bar will appear in the browser window. The Up state for each button will also appear. Click on a button to view its Down state.

Adding Interactive Text

There are many different ways you can change the way a button looks to suggest a particular button state. One way is to change the way the text or button name appears for each button state. The following steps show you how to change the color of a text object and add an effect to enhance a button state.

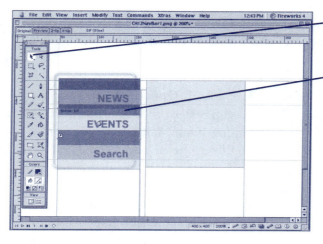

1. Select the Pointer Tool (V) from the toolbox.

2. Double-click on a button instance to open the Button Editor window. The graphic and text objects will appear in the Button Editor window.

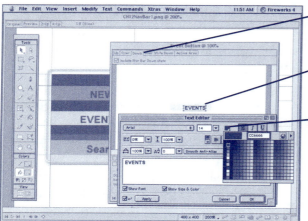

3. Select the Down tab in the Button Editor window.

4. Double-click on the text object to open the Text Editor window.

5. Click on the color well in the Text Editor window and assign a darker color for the text object. Or, you can type a hexadecimal color value into the text box. Then, press the Enter/Return key to exit the Color pop-up menu. Click on the OK button to save your changes and exit the Text Editor window.

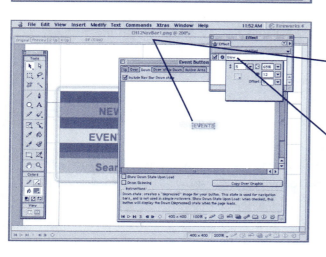

6. Click on the text object. Then, press Alt/Option + F7 to open the Effect panel.

7. Choose an effect from the pop-up menu in the Effect panel. In this example, I chose the Glow effect. Click on the Close box to exit the Button Editor window.

Assigning Behaviors

You can combine button states with behaviors to create sophisticated nav bar interactions. JavaScript is used to define both behaviors and button states. However, some behaviors, such as the Swap Image behavior, consist of several additional options, compared to the simple rollover behavior used to create different button states. The following sections show you how to add different behaviors to a button object.

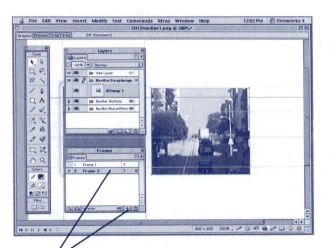

Adding a Swap Image Behavior

One of my favorite behaviors to add to a button is the Swap Image behavior. I've used this behavior to add pop-up menus and create a simple animation with text and graphic objects imported or created in Fireworks. The following steps show you how to add a Swap Image behavior to a button instance.

1. Open a document that contains at least one button instance, preferably a nav bar containing button instances. Click and drag the first frame of the document onto the New/Duplicate Frame icon in the Frames panel. A second frame will appear in the Frames panel.

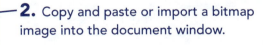

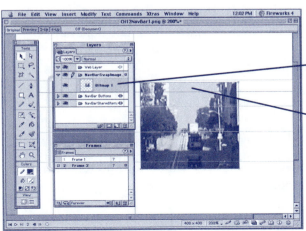

2. Copy and paste or import a bitmap image into the document window.

3. Place the image beside the nav bar.

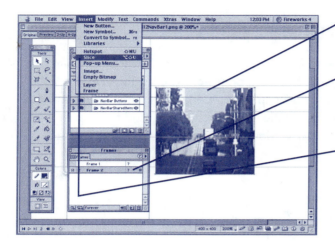

4. Choose the Pointer Tool (V) and select the bitmap image.

5. Check the Frames panel to make sure that you're modifying the second frame of the document.

6. Choose the Slice menu command from the Insert menu. A slice object will appear over the selected image.

7. Select the first frame of the document. Then, click on the Plus button in the Behaviors panel. Choose the Swap Image behavior. The Swap Image dialog box will open. Select the slice in the nav bar from the left window list.

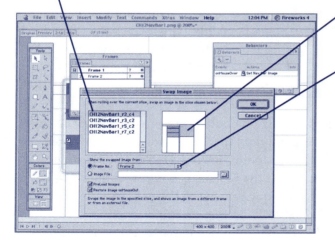

8. Click on the target slice from the right pane.

9. Choose the Frame No. radio button and then select Frame 2 from the pop-up menu. The image in frame 2 will appear when the button instance is selected in frame 1.

10. Click on the OK button to save your changes. The new behavior will appear in the Behaviors panel.

Linking a Button to a URL

Because buttons are expected to behave like links, most buttons go to a new Web page when clicked. The following steps show you how to add a URL to a button instance.

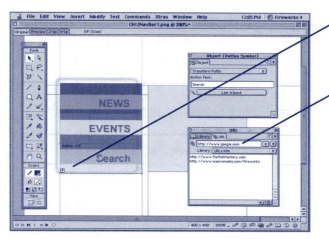

1. Use the Pointer Tool (V) to select a slice that overlaps a button instance in the document window.

2. Choose URL from the Window menu, or press Alt/Option + Shift + F10 to open the URL panel. Type a URL in the Link text box.

TIP

You can also assign a URL to a hotspot or slice from the Object panel. The Object panel enables you to assign an alternate name for the URL, as well as a target. If you're working with a Web page that contains frames, you can type the name of the frame in which you want the URL to appear. The pop-up menu to the right of the Target text box enables you to open the URL in a new browser window (_blank), a parent frameset (_parent), the current frame (_self), or all frames (_top).

Modifying Behaviors

Fireworks documents are designed for repeated use. For instance, you can create a simple Web page to get your Web site going. Save the Web graphics as a PNG or native Fireworks file. Then, add more sophisticated behaviors to enhance the page. The following steps show you how to change the Swap Image behavior for a button instance.

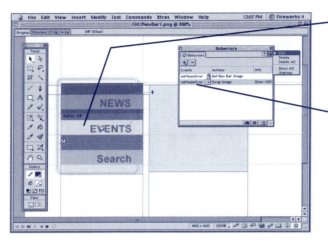
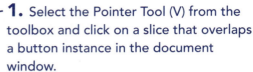

1. Select the Pointer Tool (V) from the toolbox and click on a slice that overlaps a button instance in the document window.

2. Click on a behavior in the Behaviors panel. In this example, I chose the Swap Image behavior.

3. Choose the Edit command from the pop-up menu in the Behaviors panel.

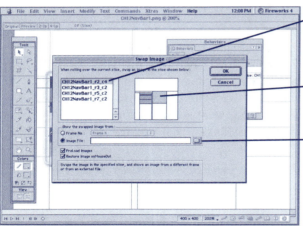

The Swap Image dialog box will open, and the current slice will be selected in the left window list.

4. Click on the target slice in the right pane.

5. Choose the Image File radio button. Type a path to the image file you want to use, or click on the folder button to select an image file that will be swapped with the slice object.

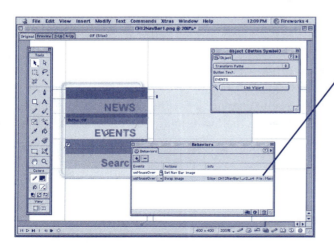

6. Click on the OK button to save your changes.

The changes you made will appear in the Info column for the Swap Image behavior.

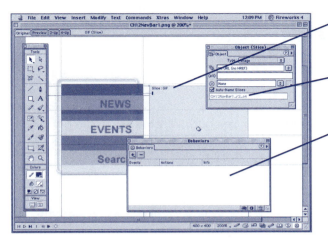

7. Click on the slice object in the first frame of the document.

8. View the name of the slice in the Object panel.

Notice that this object doesn't have any behaviors assigned to it, even though it is a target object for the Events button's Swap Image behavior.

Behaviors and the Slice Tool

Add a behavior to a slice object by simply dragging and dropping the drag-and-drop handle over a target object in the document window. Access the same options as you would if you were using the Behaviors panel. The following steps show you how to modify a slice object by adding a drag-and-drop behavior.

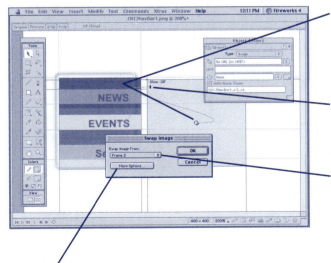

1. Click on the drag-and-drop handle of a slice object. Hold down the mouse button and drag it over the target object. Then, release the mouse button.

A small, black rectangle will appear in the target object if a behavior has already been added to it.

2. The Swap Image dialog box will appear. Click on the Swap Image From pop-up menu to select the frame containing the target image for the target slice.

3. Click on the More Options button to access the full-featured Swap Image window.

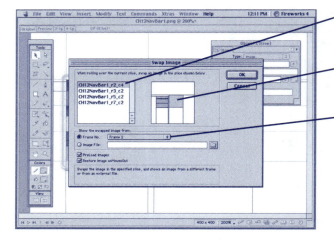

The current slice will appear in the left window list.

4. Click on the target slice in the right pane.

5. Select the Frame No. radio button. Then, choose the frame containing the image for the target slice.

6. Click on the OK button to save your changes and return to the document window.

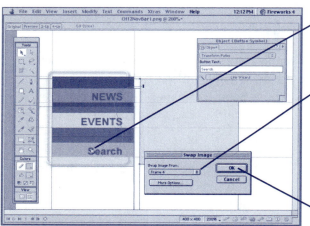

7. Wasn't that easy? Let's try it again! Select a slice and then click and drag the drag-and-drop handle over a target slice.

8. Choose a frame in the Swap Image From pop-up menu. This frame will contain the image (which needs to be located below the target slice in that frame) that will be swapped into the target slice frame.

9. Click on the OK button to create the new behavior for the selected button instance.

Previewing Button Interaction

Wondering what your nav bar really looks like in a browser window? The fastest way to preview your work is to use the Preview in Browser command, located in the File menu in Fireworks. If your computer has enough free memory available, Fireworks will be able to open the primary browser and display the Web graphics combined with the HTML and JavaScript code needed to make your Web page go. The following sections show you how to set up your Fireworks file and then preview it in a browser window.

Checking Behaviors with Frames

It's okay to choose the Preview in Browser command whenever you want. If you've never used this command, be forewarned that it will take Fireworks a few minutes to take all the information from your Fireworks file and send it out to your local browser. The following steps show you how to check a few settings in your Fireworks file so you don't have to sit and wonder why things don't look quite right in the browser when you're previewing your work.

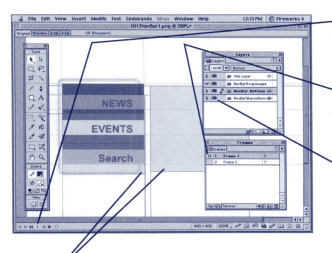

1. Check the current frame number for the document in the lower-left corner of the document window.

2. If the Frames panel is open, you will see the same frame number selected there.

3. If the Layers panel is open, check to make sure that any graphic layers you want to use are visible. Hidden layers will not appear if you preview the document in a browser.

4. View the graphic and Web objects in the document window. Make sure that these are the correct objects that should appear in the first frame of the file.

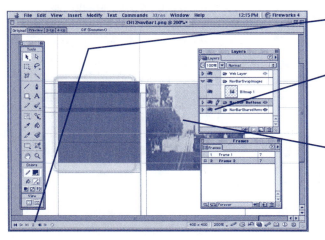

5. Select the second frame of the document.

6. Verify that the layers you want to view are marked as visible in the Layers panel.

7. Look in the document window and make sure that the correct image objects appear in the correct location.

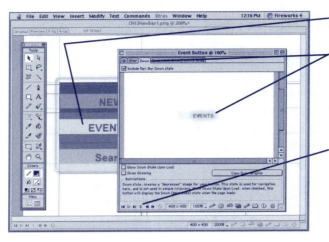

8. Double-click on a button instance.

9. Select one or two button states. Make sure that the correct graphics appear for each button state you want to preview.

10. View the frame number for each button state in the Button Editor window.

Locking Layers

As you finalize the layout for different nav bar elements, you can move them to one layer in the Layers panel. Then lock that layer, so that those objects won't accidentally move or change while you're adding or modifying other nav bar objects or behaviors. When a layer is locked, you won't be able to select its objects with the Pointer Tool, and you won't see any of the object's outlines in the document window. The following steps show you how to lock a layer and an object.

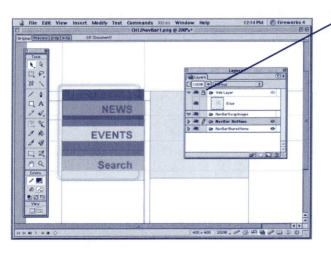

1. Click in the middle column of the Layers panel. A lock icon will appear beside the layer icon if the layer is locked. In this example, I've locked the Web Layer, preventing hotspots and slices from being moved or edited. However, I can add a new slice or hotspot while the Web Layer is locked.

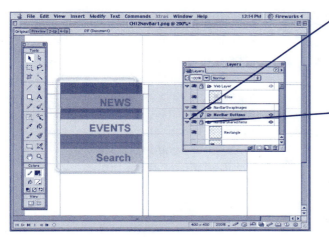

2. Expand a layer to view its objects or object layers. Click in the middle column beside a layer to lock all objects in that layer.

A lock icon will appear beside the layer in the Layers panel. When an object is locked it cannot be moved, selected, or edited in the document window. If a layer is locked, none of the objects in that layer can be moved, selected, or edited.

Previewing the Nav Bar in a Browser

As you design your nav bar, you should preview different button behaviors in at least one browser application. Internet Explorer is currently the most widely used browser application. Netscape Communicator 4.75 or 6.0 is another browser you might want to use to test button states and behaviors. The following steps show you how to preview nav bar behaviors in Internet Explorer 5.

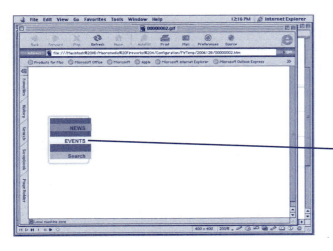

1. Add images and graphics, and create buttons and rollover states in a Fireworks document. Choose Preview in Browser from the File menu. Then, view the graphic objects in the browser window.

2. Move the cursor over a button with a rollover event assigned to it.

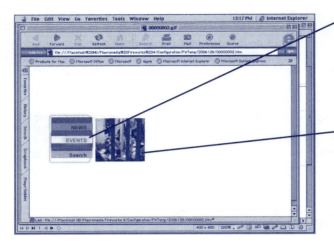

3. View the layout and button appearance in the browser window. If the button contains a Down state, make sure that the correct graphic appears in the browser.

4. If the button has a Swap Image behavior assigned to it, view the swapped image in the browser.

12

Making Buttons with the Button Editor

Buttons are similar to links. Both can point to another Web page, and both can change state or color when selected in a browser. What makes a button different than a link is that a button can be made of one or several graphic images and can be associated with one or more links.

In this chapter, you'll learn how to:

- Design a button
- Create a button symbol
- Add button states using the Button Editor window

Assembling Buttons

Any button you create with the Button Editor can have up to four possible states: Up, Over, Down, or Over While Down. These button states are named to describe how the button interacts with the mouse cursor and the button graphic in a browser window. A button can be created with a single vector or bitmap object, or a combination of image objects and text objects grouped together.

You can also create a button by inserting a slice or hotspot over a vector or bitmap object. The JavaScript code for slice or hotspot buttons is very similar. The main difference between the two is that a slice can break up a document and a hotspot can't.

In addition to adding a slice or hotspot to an image object, you'll also need to create a frame for each button state. You can copy and paste the button graphic from frame to frame to create any button states you want. Then, assign a Swap Image behavior for each rollover you want to add to the slice or hotspot. For more information about how to create buttons and rollovers with slices and hotspots, see Chapter 10, "Introduction to Slices, Hotspots, and Image Maps."

Designing Button Graphics

You can create button graphics with any of the tools in the toolbox, such as the Rectangle Tool. You can also import graphics from other applications and turn them into buttons. Alternatively, you can select a button from the built-in library. The following steps show you how to create a button using the Rectangle Tool and the Inner Bevel effect.

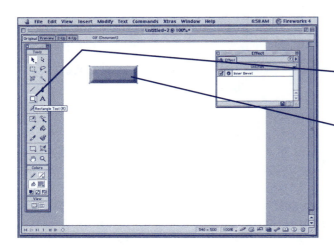

1. Select the Rectangle Tool (R) from the toolbox.

2. Click and hold the mouse button in the document window. Then, drag the mouse to create the rectangle shape. Light blue lines will appear as you drag the mouse. These lines indicate the edges of the rectangle. Release the mouse button to create the rectangle, and apply a fill color to the shape.

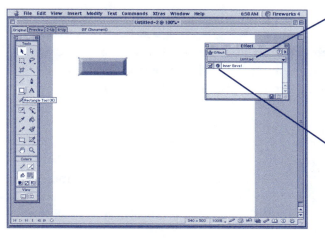

3. Choose Effect from the Window menu or press Alt/Option + F7 to open the Effect panel. Select the rectangle shape, then click on the Effect pop-up menu and choose Inner Bevel from the Bevel and Emboss pop-up menu.

4. Select the default settings for the effect, or click on the i icon and customize the Inner Bevel effect for the rectangle.

5. Click on the Insert menu and choose the Convert to Symbol menu command. Select the Button radio button and type a name for the button. Then, click on the OK button.

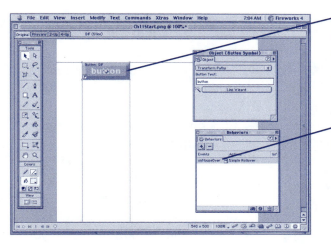

A slice object will appear over the button graphic. The button graphic will be changed into an instance of a symbol, which will be stored in the Library panel (F11).

Fireworks will create a simple rollover behavior for the newly created button.

NOTE

For more information about how to use the graphics tools, see Chapter 5, "Creating and Designing Graphics."

Symbols, Instances, and Buttons

To use the Button Editor to create a button, you must convert a graphic into a button symbol. You can use one symbol to create different instances that have unique characteristics, even if they're on the same page. Here's how:

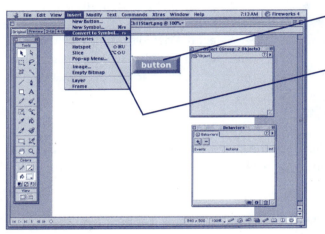

1. Select a vector graphic in the document window.

2. Choose the Convert to Symbol command from the Insert menu. The Symbol Properties dialog box will open.

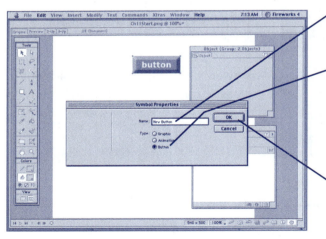

3. Type a name for the button symbol in the Name text box.

4. Click on the Button radio button to create a button symbol. If you click on the other radio buttons, you won't be able to use the Button Editor window to add button states to a symbol.

5. Click on the OK button to save your changes.

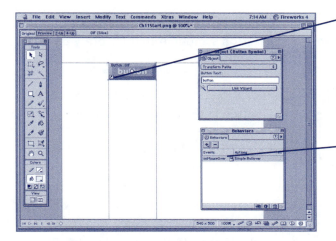

It's not easy to tell an instance from any other object. However, an instance can be detected by selecting an object. The appearance of a small arrow in the lower-left corner of the object indicates that it is an instance.

A locked simple rollover behavior will automatically be created for a new button symbol.

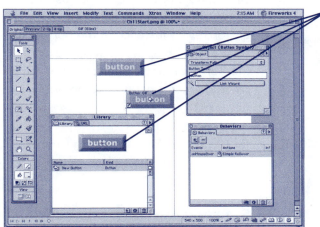

6. Drag a symbol from the Library panel to the document window as many times as you want. Each instance can have its own unique settings.

TIP

Choose Select All from the Edit menu. Any instances in the document window will appear with the small arrow in the lower-left corner of the object.

Using the Link Wizard

You can assign link, target, file name, and export settings for a button symbol by accessing the Link Wizard. The Link Wizard is only available for button symbols. You must select a button symbol before you can access the Link Wizard button in the Object panel. Click on the Link Wizard button to assign export, URL, and other settings to the selected button symbol. You can use the Link Wizard to view and configure a full range of link settings for any button instance.

1. Create a button using the tools from the toolbox and then convert that button to a symbol. Alternatively, click and drag a button symbol from the Library panel to the document window.

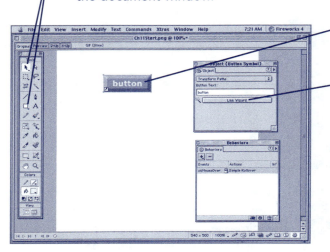

2. Select a button or an instance of a button in the document window.

3. Click on the Link Wizard button in the Object panel. If there is more than one instance of the same button in the document window a dialog box will appear, asking you if you want to edit all instances of this button or just the current button. If you select the All button, every instance of the button symbol will be updated. If you click on the Current button, a new symbol will be created for the instance being edited.

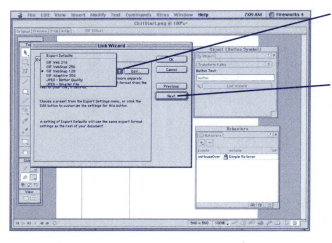

4. Choose an Export Setting from the pop-up menu in the Link Wizard dialog box.

5. Click on Next to continue to the next tab in the dialog box.

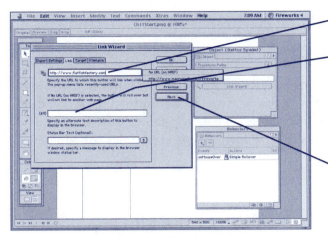

6. Type a URL in the link text field.

7. Type an alternate description for the button. The alternate name will appear at the bottom of the browser window when the mouse is placed over the button symbol.

8. Click on Next.

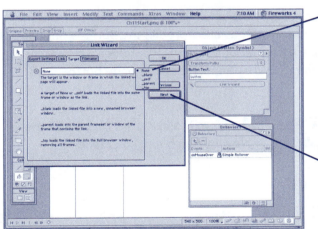

9. Type a target or select a target from the pop-up menu. The Target pop-up menu located to the right of the Target text box enables you to open the URL in a new browser window (_blank), a parent frameset (_parent), the current frame (_self), or all frames (_top).

10. Click on Next.

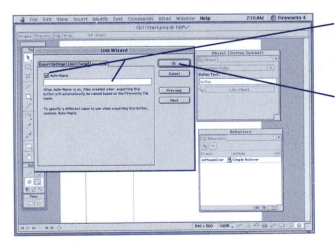

11. Select the Auto-Name check box or clear the box and type a name in the file name text box.

12. Click on OK to save your changes and exit the Link Wizard.

Working with Buttons and the Button Library

You've already learned how to create several different types of buttons in previous chapters. Although the Library panel is the doorway to the Button Editor, you can also use the Button Editor to automate button creation in the sense that you do not have to write any HTML or JavaScript; Fireworks can export this code for you.

Importing a Button from the Buttons Library

You can also access the Button Editor window when you import a button from the Fireworks Buttons library. These button images are stored in the Buttons.png file located in the Configuration: Libraries folder of the Fireworks folder. This section shows you how to create a button graphic by importing a premade button from the Buttons library.

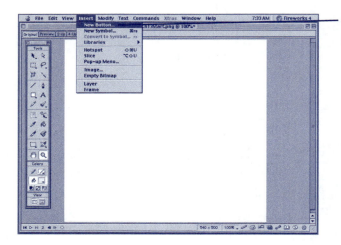

1. From the Insert menu, choose the New Button menu command.

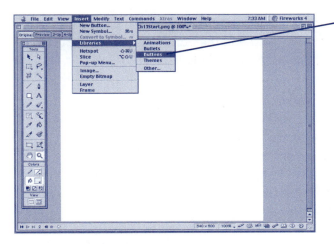

2. Alternatively, from the Insert menu, choose Libraries, Buttons to open the Button Editor window.

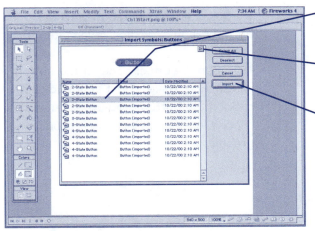

3. Select a button object from the list of items in the Import Symbols: Buttons list.

4. Click on the Play button to view each button's state or states.

5. Click on Import.

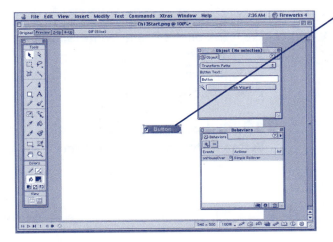

An instance of the selected button will appear in the document window.

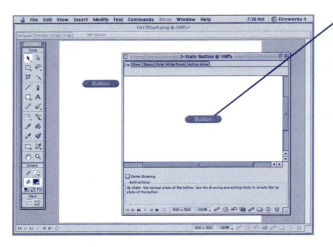

6. Double-click on the button instance to edit the button states in the Button Editor window.

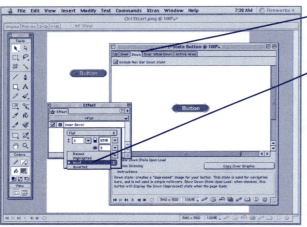

7. Select the Down tab to view the button graphic for the Down state.

8. Open the Effect panel. If the button has an Inner Bevel effect assigned to it, click on the bottom pop-up menu and choose Inset to change the button graphic.

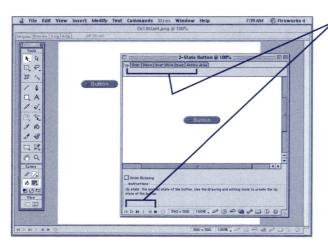

9. View or add buttons states as you like. Click on the Frame Controls located at the bottom of the window to cycle through each state, or click on a tab to view a specific button state.

10. Click on the close box of the Button Editor window to save your changes.

> **NOTE**
>
> The Buttons library contains several button images installed with Fireworks 4. This is a completely different set of images than the buttons you create in the Library panel.

Editing a Button

As long as the file is saved as a Fireworks (PNG) file, you can edit a button at any time. The following steps show you how to add the Over button state to the button created in the previous section.

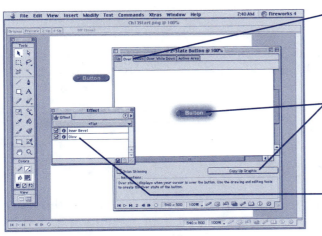

1. Double-click on the button instance created in the previous section. Then, click on the Over tab in the Button Editor window.

2. Click on the Copy Up Graphic button to add the button image object to the Button Editor window. Select the button graphic using the Pointer Tool (V).

3. Choose Effect from the Window menu (Alt/Option + F7). Select Glow from the Shadow and Glow pop-up menu in the Effect panel. The effect will appear in the Effect panel's window list.

4. Click on the Behaviors shortcut (the gear icon) in the document window.

5. Select the button instance. Then, click on the Plus button in the Behaviors panel to add a new behavior to the button.

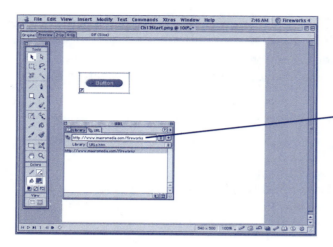

6. Choose URL from the Window menu or press Alt/Option + Shift + F10 to open the URL panel.

7. Select the button graphic. Then, type a URL in the link text box in the URL panel or double-click on an existing URL.

NOTE

Whenever you attempt to edit an instance of a symbol, Fireworks 4 will ask whether you want to change all instances of that symbol or only the current one. If you choose the Current button, a new symbol is created, whereas if you choose the All button, the original symbol is edited.

Assigning Button Behaviors

Although a button can have up to four states, you can assign one, two, or three states to any button from the Behaviors panel. The following steps show you how to assign a Swap Image behavior to a button instance.

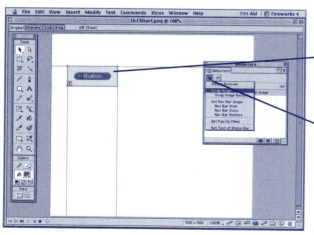

1. Create a button from the Library panel and then add rollover states using the Button Editor.

2. Click on the Plus button in the Behaviors panel and choose Swap Image from the Plus pop-up menu.

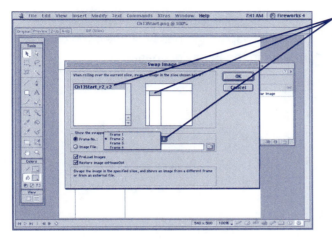

3. Double-click on a Swap Image behavior in the Behaviors panel. The Swap Image dialog box will open. Define the swap image rollover in the Swap Image dialog box.

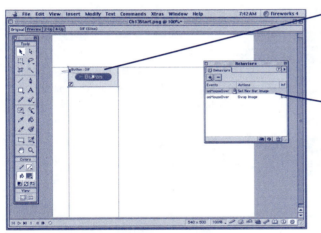

Fireworks will update the button instance with a graphic, indicating that a Swap Image behavior has been added to it.

4. View the rollover events and behaviors in the Behaviors panel. Events with a lock icon cannot be edited.

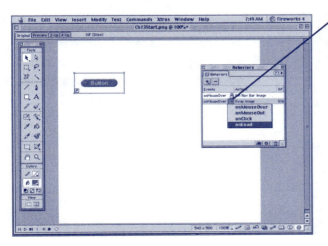

5. You can modify the event for a behavior. Click on the pop-up menu beside the event name to view a menu list.

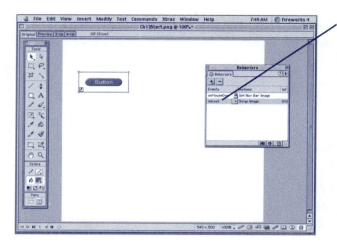

6. Select the onLoad event from the Swap Image behavior. View the change in the Behaviors panel.

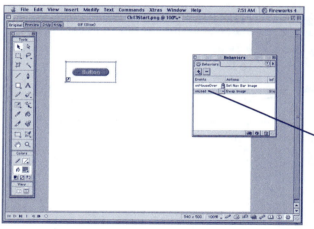

Changing Rollover States

You can change, add, or remove a button's rollover states any time you want. Add a URL in the Object or URL panel. Here's how:

1. Double-click on a rollover state that you want to edit.

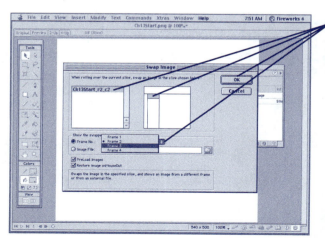

2. If you're swapping an image with a button, choose a specific frame in the Frame No. pop-up menu. Verify the slice or button to which you want to add this rollover state, then click on OK.

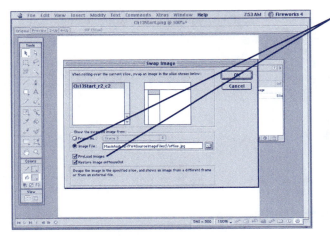

3. Alternatively, you can choose a file to use with the selected behavior. Click on the PreLoad Images check box if you want the button images to all load before the viewer clicks or drags the mouse over a button.

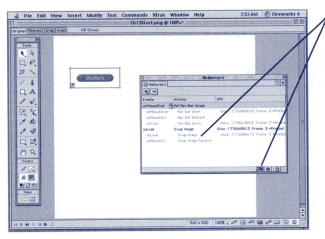

4. In addition to the four previously mentioned button states, a fifth state, such as the Swap Image Restore event, can occur when the button is clicked. Select the eye icon in the Behaviors panel to view grouped behaviors with each rollover event.

Importing an Animation Instance from the Animations Library

You can import an animation using almost the same set of steps you used to import a button instance into a document. Import an animation from the Animations.png file, located in the Configurations: Libraries folder of the Fireworks application folder. The Animations library consists of seven animations files: Clock, Countdown – Red, Countdown – Yellow, Planet, Recycle, Spider, and Steaming Cup. When you import an animation from the Import Symbols dialog box, the animation symbol is automatically added to the Library panel in addition to the document window. The following steps show you how to add an animation instance from the Animations Library to a document window.

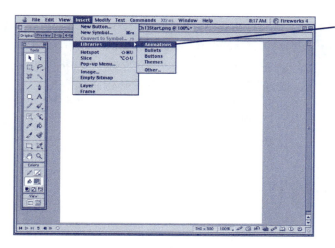

1. Choose Libraries, Animations from the Insert menu.

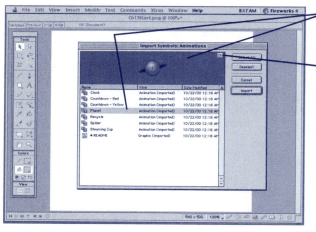

2. Click on an animation from the Import Symbols: Animations list.

3. View each animation by clicking on the Play button located in the upper-right corner of the window.

4. Select an animation you want to add to your document, then click on the Import button.

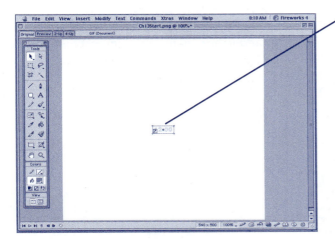

An instance of the animation will be added to the document window.

Building a Nav Bar with the Themes Library

Although many people cannot explain what makes a Web site easy to navigate, the navigation bar is one tool that's easy to understand. Macromedia uses the abbreviated term *nav bar* to refer to a navigation bar. The following sections show you how to create and edit a navigation bar.

Creating a Navigation Bar

Fireworks includes several built-in navigation bars, selected from the Nav Bars window. Creating a nav bar is similar to creating a button that uses more than one instance in the same window. The following steps show you how to create a simple nav bar using the Themes components built into Fireworks.

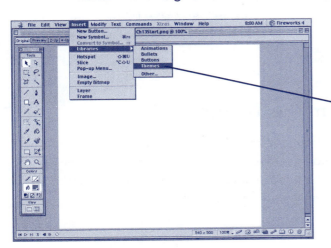

1. Select Themes from the Insert, Libraries menu.

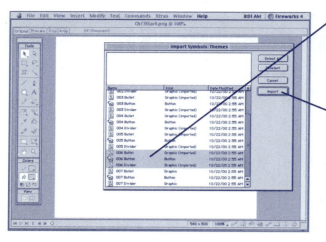

2. Review the list of nav bar buttons and image maps in the Import Symbols: Themes dialog box. Select a bullet, button, and divider graphic.

3. Click on Import.

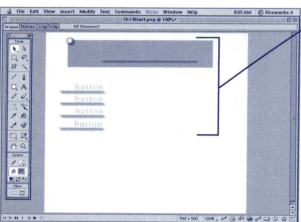

4. Resize the instances in the document window and create a simple nav bar layout.

TIP

Hold down the Shift key and click on all the theme elements in the Import Symbols: Themes window. The theme elements will appear in the Library panel. Select and drag any theme element to the document window to put together a Web page.

Editing a Button from the Themes Library

A navigation bar can be created from any image map, using any graphic you want for buttons and rollovers. Depending on the image map you choose, you might need to do more or less editing in the document window. The following steps show you how to take the initial theme elements and lay out the navigation bar.

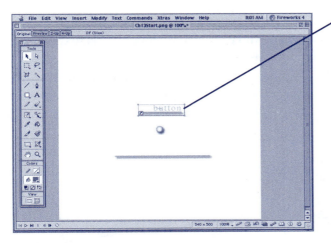

1. Choose a selection tool from the toolbox, then double-click on a nav bar or image map to be edited. A nav bar is actually comprised of other symbols in the Library panel and multiple instances in the document window. Double-click on any image in a nav bar to edit it.

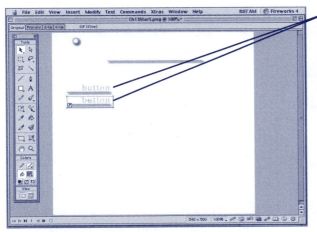

2. You can copy and paste an instance to create additional buttons for the nav bar. Or, you can click on a symbol in the Library panel and drag it to the document window to create a new button instance.

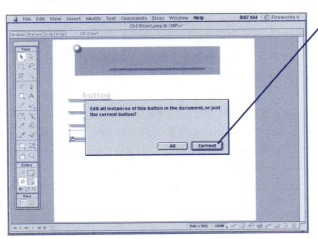

3. Double-click on an instance if you want to edit it. The Button Editor window will open. If you've select one of several instances in the same document, Fireworks will ask whether you want to edit all instances or only the selected one. In this example I chose Current.

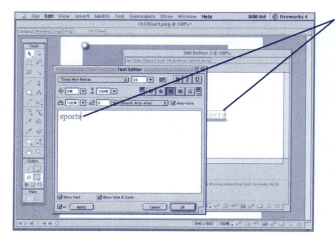

4. View any settings for the object in the panels or, if the object is text, view the settings in the Text Editor window. A dialog box will appear, asking whether you want to update the other buttons. I chose No for this example.

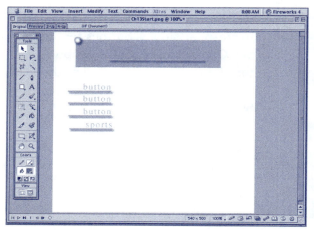

5. Close the Symbol window to save the changes to the nav bar. Choose File, Save to save the changes to the Fireworks file.

Converting and Removing Instances

You can convert rollovers created in previous versions of Fireworks into buttons. Change rollover behavior, add a theme to a Web page, or remove rollovers from a Web page. The following sections show you how to modify objects that contain rollover behaviors.

Converting a Graphic Instance to a Button Instance

A graphic symbol can be used to create a new button symbol. If the instance for the graphic already appears in the document window, you can convert the graphic instance into a button instance by performing the following steps, and a new button will appear in the Library panel. However, hotspots and slices are not converted with the rollover to the new button.

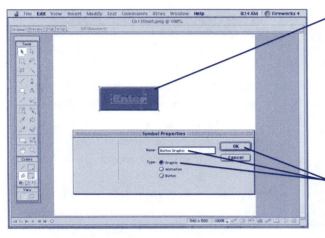

1. Create a graphic symbol in a new or existing document window. First, select a shape or drawing tool to create a simple graphic.

2. Select the graphic object and then choose Convert to Symbol from the Insert menu.

3. Click on the Graphic radio button and type a button name in the Name text box. Click on the OK button to create the graphic symbol. Its instance will appear in the document window.

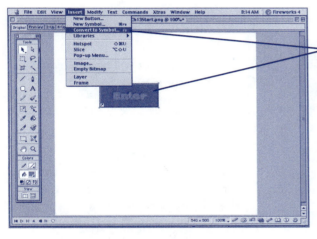

4. Select the graphic instance and then choose Convert to Symbol from the Insert menu.

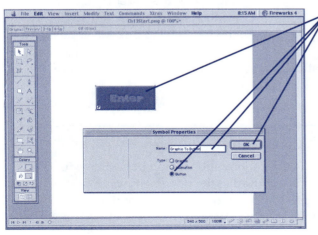

5. This time, click on the Button radio button. Then, type a new name in the Name text box. Click on the OK button to create the new button symbol and its instance.

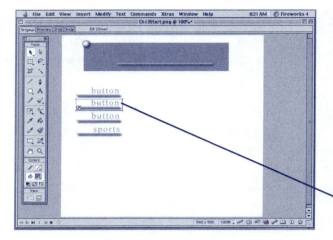

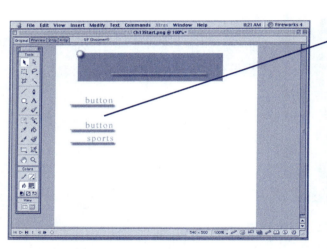

Removing a Button

You can also select any vector, bitmap, or instance object in the document window and delete it. If the object is an instance, its original symbol will remain in the Library panel. The following steps show you how to remove button instance from a document.

1. Select an object instance you want to remove from the document window. In this example, I've selected a button instance. Then, press the Delete/Backspace key.

The selected object will be removed from the document window.

TIP

You can also delete a symbol from the Library panel. Select the symbol you want to remove from the Library panel window list. Then, click on the Trash button located in the lower-right corner of the Library panel. If a symbol is in use, a dialog box will appear. Click on the Delete button in the dialog box to confirm the deletion, or click on the Cancel button if you do not want to delete the selected symbol.

CAUTION

Fireworks 4 does not display a delete confirmation dialog box when you delete a symbol or instance that is not used in the document window. The dialog box only appears if you try to delete a symbol that has an instance in the document window.

13

Working with Rollovers

Graphic objects, text, and behaviors are the main components that make a button work like a button. In the previous chapters, you've seen how slices and hotspots work and how to create buttons and navigation bars. Now take a closer look at object behaviors.

Behaviors enable you to assign a specific rollover action to a button object. A simple rollover works similarly to a link. If you click on the button, a simple rollover will take you to a new Web page and possibly show the Down state of a button. As you add button states and behaviors to a button or to other graphic objects in Fireworks, you can design some pretty sophisticated rollovers. This chapter shows you how to create both simple and not-so-simple rollovers. In this chapter you'll learn how to:

- Add rollover states to objects
- Create rollovers with symbols
- Assign multiple behaviors to an object
- Design a disjointed rollover
- Test a rollover

Designing Rollovers

A button can have up to four possible states: Up, Over, Down, or Over While Down. These button states are named to describe how the button interacts with the cursor in the browser window. The button can be made up of one graphic or a combination of graphics and text grouped together.

Designing Up and Down States

The simple rollover might seem familiar to you. If you've already created a button symbol, you've probably seen the simple rollover behavior listed in the Behaviors panel. A simple rollover in the Behaviors panel uses the first two frames of the document to create the Up and Over button states for the object located below a slice or hotspot.

Creating Up and Over states is one way of designing a simple rollover. Another way is to create Up and Down states for a button. This kind of button works well if the button is in a nav bar and you want to keep the Down state of the button to let your Web visitors know which part of the Web site they're surfing. The following steps show you how to create a simple rollover by creating Up and Down button states.

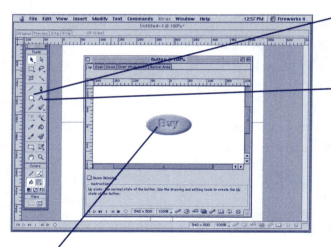

1. Click on a tool in the toolbox and create a button graphic object in the document window.

2. Select the Text Tool (T) if you want to add text to the button graphic.

3. Select the graphic and text objects and then choose Convert to Symbol from the Insert menu. Give the button a name and don't forget to select the Button radio button. Then, click on the OK button.

4. Double-click on a button instance in the document window. The Button Editor window will open. View the Up state for the button in the Button Editor window. Select the graphic for the button and select the Copy command from the Edit menu, or press Ctrl/Command + C.

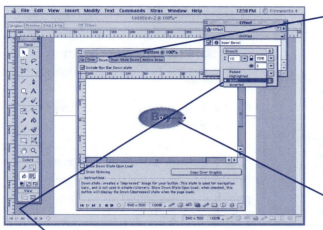

5. Click on the Down tab in the Button Editor window. If rulers are activated (Alt/Option + Ctrl/Command + R), you can click and drag horizontal or vertical guides into the Button Editor window. Select the Paste command from the Edit menu or press Ctrl/Command + V to add the button graphic for the Down state in the Button Editor window.

6. Select the graphic object in the Button Editor window.

7. Press Alt/Option + F7 to open the Effect panel. If the object already has an effect, click on the i icon in the Effect panel. Choose Inset from the bottom pop-up menu to change the state of the button.

Rollover States

Now that you've seen how the Up and Down button states look, take a quick tour of each of the four built-in button states in the Button Editor window. By default, each window in the Button Editor window is completely empty. You'll need to either click on the Copy button, or copy and paste a button or text object into the Button Editor window to create each button state. The Copy button is located in the Over, Down, Over While Down, and Active Area tabs in the Button Editor window. The following steps aren't actually steps, but they'll walk you through each button state in the Button Editor window.

1. Click in the Up tab in the Button Editor window.

2. View the Up state of the button. If you want to use this graphic for other button states, select it with the Pointer Tool (V) and then choose the Copy command from the Edit menu, or press Ctrl/Command + C.

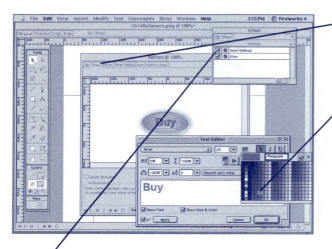

3. Select the Over tab in the Button Editor window. Click on the Copy Up Graphic button to add the button graphic to the Button Editor window.

4. Double-click the text object in the Button Editor window. The Text Editor window will open. Select a different color from the Color pop-up menu in the Text Editor window. Open the Effect panel and select the Glow effect from the Effect panel.

5. With the text object selected, choose the Inset Emboss effect from the Effect panel to push the text into the vector graphic behind it.

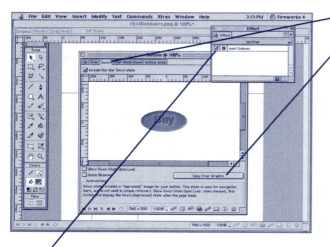

6. Click on the Down tab.

7. Click on the Copy Over Graphic button, or paste a button graphic into the Button Editor window. Select the vector object (not the text object), then choose the Inner Bevel effect from the Effect, Bevel and Emboss pop-up menu in the Effect panel. Click on the i icon for the Inner Bevel effect. Then, choose the Inset command from the pop-up menu located at the bottom of the Effect Properties pop-up menu.

8. Click on the text object. Select the Inset Emboss effect from the Effect, Bevel and Emboss pop-up menu in the Effect panel.

TIP

If you're creating a button for a nav bar, you might want it to appear in the Down state when the Web page first loads. The Down state of the button can let the person visiting your Web page know which area of your Web site they're currently viewing. Click on the Show Down State upon Load check box in the Down state of the Button Editor window to enable this feature.

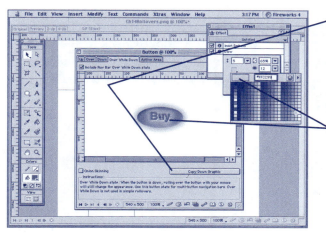

9. Choose the Over While Down tab in the Button Editor window. Then, click on the Copy Down Graphic button. A button object will appear in the Button Editor window.

10. Select the text object, then open the Effect panel. Click on the i icon and select a different color for the Glow effect.

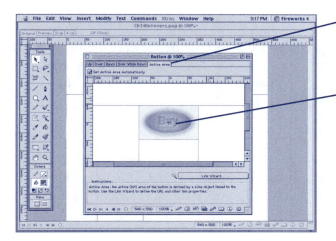

11. Click on the Active Area tab. This window displays the slice object for the button.

12. Select the slice object. You can click and drag it to move it around in the Button Editor window. The slice object should be placed so that it covers the entire button graphic object for each button state. If other button states extend beyond the Up state, these objects will appear in this window. However, you will not be able to move or edit them from the Active Area view in the Button Editor window.

Drag-and-Drop Rollovers

If you like working with the Button Editor window, you'll probably also like working with the drag-and-drop handle in slice and hotspot objects. This magic handle enables you to create a behavior simply by clicking and dragging it onto a target slice or hotspot. It's not exactly the same as assigning behaviors to an object from the Behaviors panel, though. For one, the Behaviors panel contains a longer list of behaviors than the drag-and-drop handle button. The following steps show you how to add a Swap Image behavior to a slice object using the drag-and-drop handle.

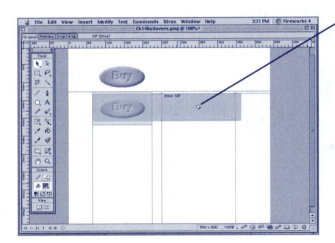

1. Click on the target slice in the document window. Check to see whether any overlapping slices exist below it by looking in the Layers panel.

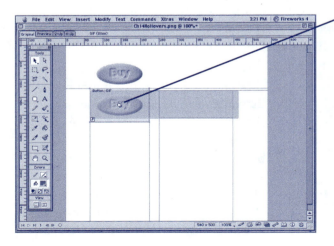

2. Select the button slice in the document window. Click on the drag-and-drop handle and drag it to the target slice.

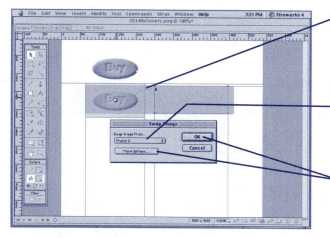

The Swap Image dialog box will open. Notice that Fireworks has added a line connecting the button object with its target.

3. Select the frame containing the image object for the target graphic from the Swap Image From pop-up menu.

4. Click on the OK button to save your changes. If you want to view more options, click on More Options.

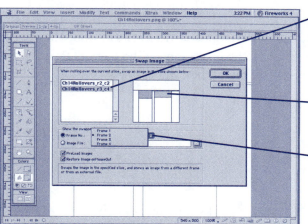

If you clicked on the More Options button, a larger Swap Image window will open. The slice object will be selected in the left window list.

5. Click on the target slice in the right pane.

6. Choose the target frame from the Frame No. pop-up menu. Then, click on the OK button to complete the Swap Image behavior.

Creating Rollovers with Symbols

One way you can create a rollover is to first design a vector or bitmap object and then assign a behavior to a Web object placed on it. To find out more about how to create this kind of rollover, see Chapter 10, "Introduction to Slices, Hotspots, and Image Maps." Another way to create a rollover is to convert the vector or bitmap object into a button symbol. The following sections take a closer look at creating rollovers for button symbols or, rather, instances of button symbols. If you've used another Macromedia application already, such as Flash 4 or Flash 5, you might already be familiar with the concepts for the Library and symbols and instances. One of the biggest advantages to designing a button symbol and instance is that it can help shrink the file size of your Web graphics. The following sections show you three different ways to create a button with one or more rollover states.

Creating a Button Symbol

If you've already created button symbols in Chapter 12, "Making Buttons with the Button Editor," you might want to skip this section. You can create a button symbol in Fireworks in three ways. The following steps show you how.

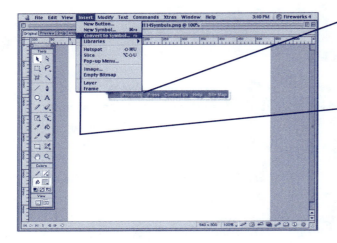

1. Create a graphic object and combine it with a text object to create a button.

2. Use the Pointer Tool (V) to select it.

3. Choose Convert to Symbol from the Insert menu. The Symbol Properties dialog box will open.

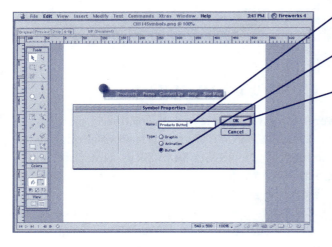

4. Type a name in the Name text box.

5. Click on the Button radio button.

6. Click on the OK button to create the button symbol.

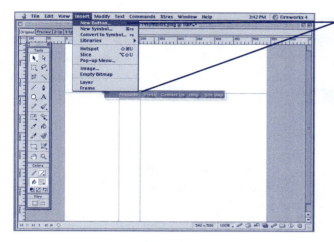

7. Another way to create a button is to select and copy a graphic object and then choose the New Button menu command from the Insert menu. The Button Editor window will open.

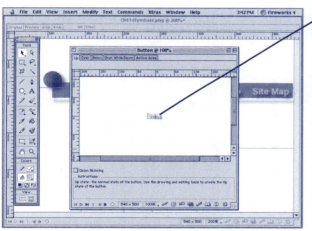

8. Copy and paste an object into the Button Editor window, or create a new button using the tools in the toolbox. Use the Pointer Tool (V) to select an object in the Button Editor window. Click on the Close box to exit the Button Editor window.

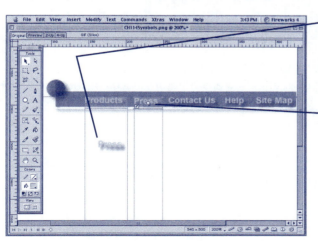

9. After you've created a button symbol, you can click and drag a regular graphic object away from the other Web graphics.

10. Move the button symbol on the nav bar, or position it in the layout with other Web graphics.

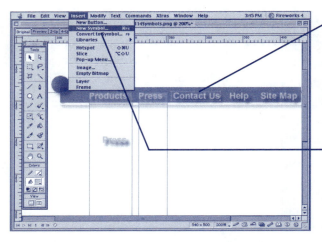

11. The third way to create a button symbol is to use the New Symbol command. If you've already created a button graphic, you can select it and then choose the Copy command from the Edit menu.

12. Choose the New Symbol menu command from the Insert menu. The Symbol Properties dialog box will open.

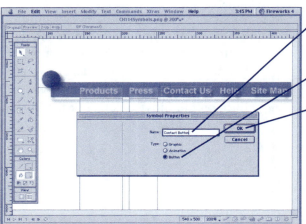

13. Type a name for the button in the Name text box.

14. Click on the Button radio button.

15. Click on the OK button. The Button Editor window will appear. Create the button symbol as you did in the previous steps.

TIP

Choose the Break Apart command from the Modify, Symbol menu if you want to modify an instance without affecting any other instances or the original symbol.

Assigning Button Behaviors

Behaviors are assigned to a hotspot or slice that is placed directly over a button graphic. You can hand-draw a slice or hotspot, or create a Web object that matches the exact shape of a text box, vector, or bitmap object. If you assign different behaviors to slices that overlap each other, you might need to manually edit the JavaScript code. If you assign different interactive behaviors to what appears as a single object, someone visiting that Web page might get a little confused when he mouses over or clicks on that Web graphic. The following steps show you how simple it is to assign a behavior to a button.

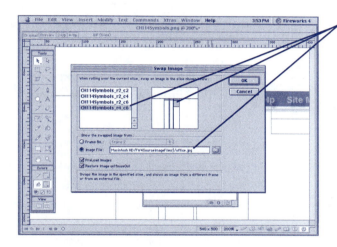

1. You can assign the target and swap image for a Swap Image behavior. Double-click on the Swap Image behavior in the Behaviors panel to open the Swap Image dialog box and view or edit the settings for the Swap Image behavior.

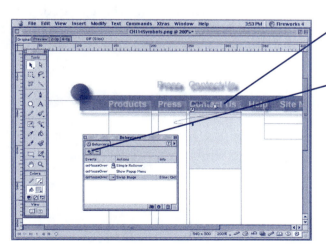

2. Click on a slice or hotspot to view any behaviors already assigned to it.

3. Add or assign new behaviors to the selected slice or hotspot by clicking on the Plus button and then choosing a behavior from the menu list.

Previewing Each Rollover State

You can preview your Fireworks document in a browser window to check and see whether each behavior is working correctly. Keep in mind that when you are

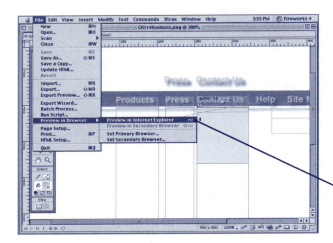

previewing your Fireworks file, all the files are stored locally on your hard drive. If you post these graphics and Web objects to a Web server, interacting with the different rollovers and buttons might be slightly slower, depending on the speed of your Internet connection. The following steps show you how to preview your Fireworks file in Internet Explorer.

1. Choose Preview in Internet Explorer from the File, Preview in Browser menu.

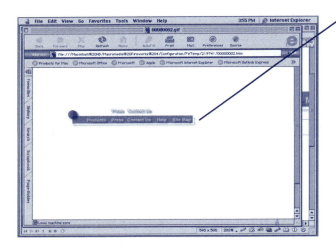

Fireworks will create a temporary HTML file and open a new window in Internet Explorer. It might take a minute or two for all the objects you created in Fireworks to appear in the browser window. When the files have loaded, the first frame of the Fireworks document will appear in the browser window.

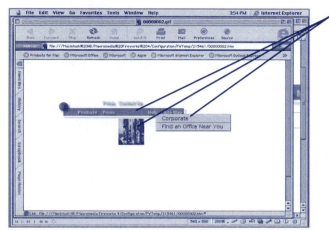

2. Move the cursor over a button object to view its behaviors. In this example, I forgot to add the Over state to the Contact Us button. However, the pop-up menu and the Swap Image behaviors work as expected. If you're familiar with viewing the HTML and JavaScript generated by Fireworks, you can choose the Source command (Ctrl/Command + E) from the View menu to take a look at the code behind the rollover in the browser window.

NOTE

A rollover's appearance can vary from browser to browser. Most JavaScript generated by Fireworks 4 will work with Internet Explorer 5 browsers. However, you may or may not find additional problems using Netscape 4.7 or 6.0. Previous versions of the browsers do not support some of the more sophisticated JavaScript code generated by Fireworks 4. For example, pop-up menus probably will not work with earlier versions of Internet Explorer or Netscape.

Creating a Rollover with Multiple States

Assigning a rollover behavior to an object is straightforward. However, creating more advanced Web designs might involve creating buttons with some similar and different behaviors. Because you can edit a behavior at any time, one of the more cumbersome tasks you might find yourself doing is making sure that each button has all the correct behavior settings. The following sections show you how to work with multiple buttons, slices, hotspots, and behaviors.

Designing Rollover Graphics

Keep the layout of the Web page in mind when you create the graphic, text, and button objects. As you add the different graphic elements, decide which behaviors each one might have. The following steps show you how to put together a simple Web page.

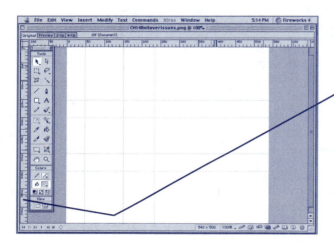

1. Open a new document window. Choose Rulers (Alt/Option + Ctrl/ Command + R) from the View menu.

2. Click in the top or side ruler to add horizontal or vertical guides to the document window.

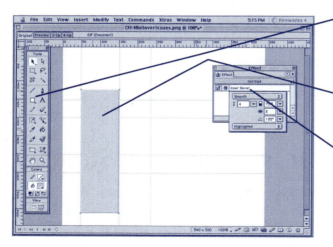

3. Select a shape tool to create the base of a nav bar. In this example, I chose the Rectangle Tool (R).

4. Add a shape to the document window.

5. Open the Effect panel and apply an effect to the vector graphic. In this example, I chose the Inner Bevel effect.

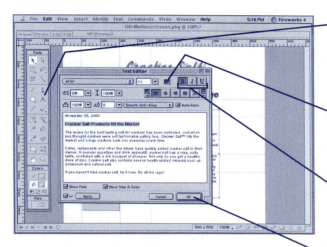

6. Choose the Text Tool (T) and then click in the document window. The Text Editor window will open. Type some text in the Text Editor window.

7. Click on the color well and choose a color for the text selected in the Text Editor window.

8. Click on the Bold, Italic, or Underline button to apply a font style to the selected text.

9. Click on the OK button to add the text to the document window.

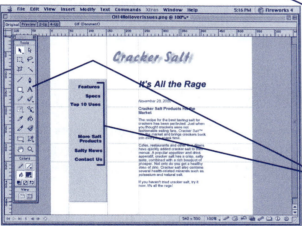

10. If you're swapping an image with a button, choose a specific frame in the Frame No. pop-up menu. Verify the slice or button to which you want to add this rollover state. Then, click on OK.

11. Add text objects for any menus or buttons you want to add to the Web page layout.

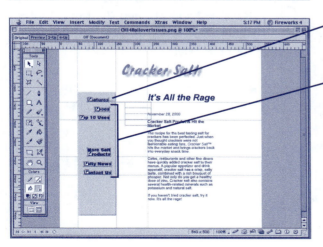

12. Convert each text object into a button symbol.

13. Hold down the Shift key and click on another button symbol. Repeat this step if you want to select several symbols and assign the same behavior to each of them.

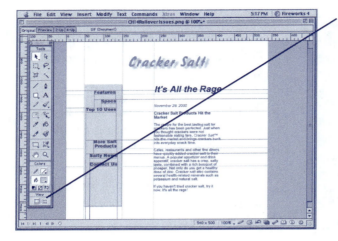

14. Click on the Show Slices button to see all the visible Web objects in the document.

> **NOTE**
>
> The Show and Hide Slices buttons in the toolbox only enable you to view any slices or hotspots that have the eye icon in the Layers panel. If you hide a particular Web object in the Layers panel, the only way to show that item is to open the Layers panel and click in the Show/Hide box.

Slicing an Image Containing a Rollover

Overlap a slice with a hotspot if you want to create two different behaviors for a single object. No, this isn't something standard that you should put on every Web page; consider it an experiment. The following steps show you how to create a dual-behavior Web graphic.

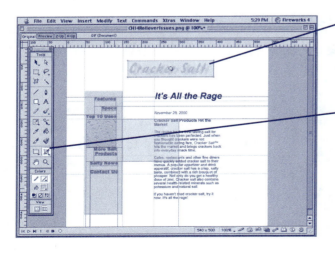

1. Click on a graphic object in the document window and then select Insert Hotspot (Shift + Ctrl/Command + U) from the Insert menu.

2. Select the Slice Tool (G) from the toolbox.

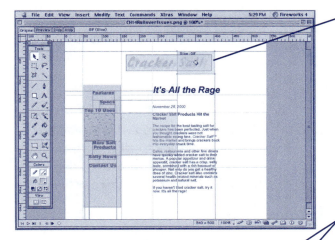

3. Add a slice object that overlaps the hotspot object you just created.

4. Open the Behaviors panel. Click on the Plus button and choose Swap Image from the menu list. Click on the target slice from Step 3 in the right pane of the Swap Image dialog box. Then, select a target file in the Image File section of the Swap Image dialog box.

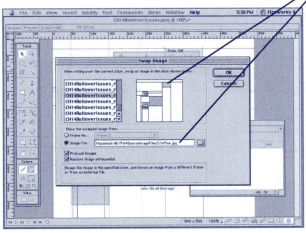

5. Click on the OK button to save your changes. In this example, if you preview the document in a browser window, you'll see the hotspot behavior on the left side of the text, and the Swap Image behavior for the slice will occur when the mouse hovers over the Salt text located on the right side of the text object.

Assigning Similar and Different Behaviors

You can add multiple instances of the same symbol to a document window. You can open the Library panel and click and drag a button as many times as you want to add a button to the document window. The tricky part is trying to decide whether every single button will have the same behaviors. You see, after you click on the Current button, Fireworks saves a new symbol to the Library for the selected instance. So plan your behaviors carefully (which isn't the same as be careful and behave). The following steps show you how to create similar and unique behaviors for button symbols and instances.

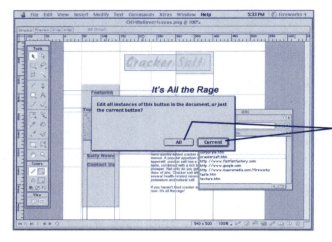

1. Add several instances of the same button to a document window. Select one of those instances, then choose a behavior from the Behaviors panel. A dialog box will open.

2. Click on All if you want to add the selected behavior to all instances of that button. Choose Current if you only want to edit the selected instance with the selected behavior.

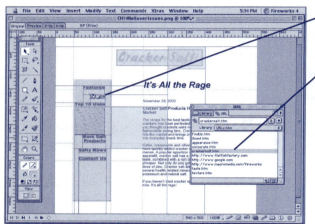

3. Select an instance in the document window.

4. Click on a URL in the URL panel to assign a link to the selected instance.

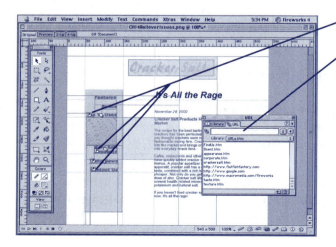

5. Shift-click to select several instances.

6. Type a URL in the text box or select a URL you want to assign to every selected instance.

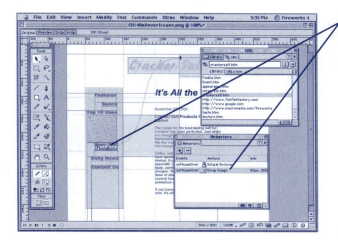

7. Select an instance to view its assigned behaviors. Double-click on a behavior to edit it.

Changing a Behavior

You can edit any behavior assigned to an object. Now, if you stop and think, you might recall that double-clicking on the Simple Rollover behavior only brought up a dialog box telling you the Up and Over states and frames 1 and 2 were used for this behavior. Even though you can't edit a simple rollover from the Behaviors panel, you can edit the Up and Over button graphics for a button symbol, right? The following steps show you how to modify the Set Nav Bar Image behavior, view behavior information in the Behaviors panel, and change the event for a behavior.

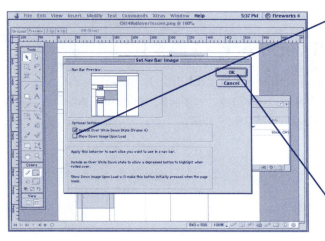

1. Select a button instance in the document window. Open the Behaviors panel and double-click on a behavior you want to edit. In this example, the Set Nav Bar Image dialog box opened. You can check or uncheck two different check boxes in the window for this behavior. I chose to uncheck the Show Down Image Upon Load check box.

2. Click on the OK button to save your changes.

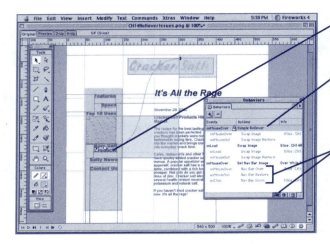

3. Select a button instance in the document window.

4. Click on a behavior in the Behaviors panel. A lock icon indicates that the behavior is not editable.

5. Click on the eye icon to view a detailed list of behaviors for the selected object.

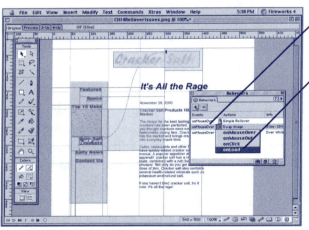

6. Click on the Event pop-up menu in the Behaviors panel.

7. Choose an event from the menu list. In this example, I changed the event from onMouseOver to onLoad.

Choosing Different Swap Image Files

You can also edit behaviors created with the drag-and-drop handle. Even if the behavior wasn't originally created using the drag-and-drop technique, you can still modify or remove it. The following steps show you how:

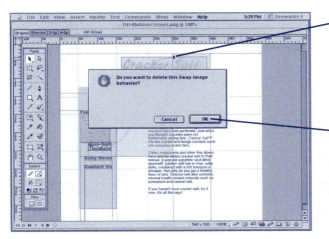

1. Click on the black rectangle button that marks the end point of the drag-and-drop handle path. The black button is located on the left side of the target slice for a Swap Image behavior.

2. A dialog box will appear, asking whether you want to delete the current Swap Image behavior. Click on the OK button. Then, create a new Swap Image behavior for the selected slice or hotspot.

Designing a Disjointed Rollover

Another type of rollover you might have seen on a Web page is the disjointed rollover. A disjointed rollover refers to a Swap Image behavior where the target slice is not the same as the source or selected slice or hotspot. For example, a disjointed rollover can display different images in one square of a Web page as the person visiting that page moves her cursor over different buttons or links on a menu list. The following sections show you how to create a disjointed rollover.

Laying out the Objects

For the following sections, a simple restaurant Web page will be used to illustrate a disjointed rollover. Obviously, layout plays a big role in any Web page design. Designing a disjointed rollover is no exception. This example employs a basic design with some common and some different graphic elements spread across five frames. The following steps show you how to create a simple layout for a disjointed rollover.

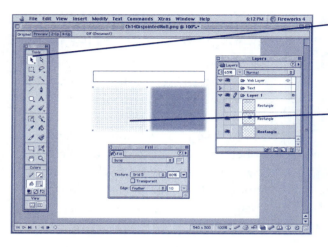

1. Create several image objects and combine fill colors and textures for each one. Then, choose the Pointer Tool (V) from the toolbox.

2. Place each object on the first frame of the document.

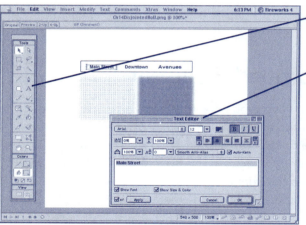

3. Use the Text Tool (T) to add text objects to the document.

4. Format the text in the Text Editor window.

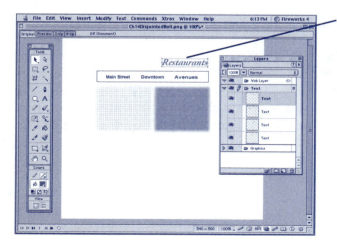

5. Create a theme graphic or text object and place that object in the layout.

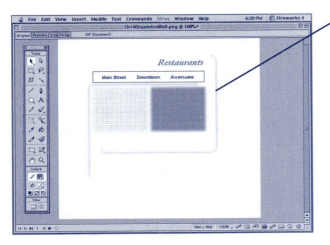

6. Add additional colors, shapes, or paths to the document to complete the Web page layout.

Importing Graphics

You can add colorful images to your Web page. You can copy and paste an image from another document or from another application into the Fireworks document. Or, you can use the Import command. The following steps show you how to import a GIF image into a Fireworks document.

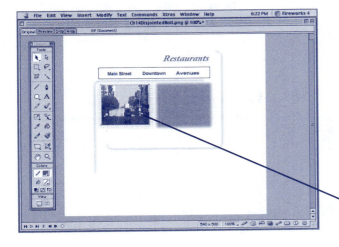

1. Choose the Import menu command from the File menu. Navigate your hard drive and select an image you want to import to the Fireworks document. An angle icon will appear.

2. Place the angle icon over the canvas area of the document window. Click to import the image into the document.

The selected image will appear in the document window.

Assigning Behaviors

Now for the moment you've been waiting for…assigning behaviors. Designing a Web page that contains a disjointed rollover isn't that much different than designing any other kind of Web page. You need to remember which frames contain the images you want to use with the Swap Image behavior so that the correct image matches up with its corresponding slice or hotspot. The following steps show you how to assign a Swap Image behavior to the first text object you created in the "Laying out the Objects" section.

1. Create a slice object for each behavior you want to add to the document.

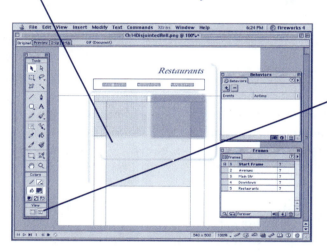

2. Duplicate the first frame or create a new frame to contain the swap image for each slice or hotspot.

3. Click on the Show Slices button to view all the Web objects for the document. Choose the Swap Image behavior from the Plus button's menu list in the Behaviors panel. The source object will appear in the left window list in the Swap Image dialog box, and the target slice will be selected in the right pane.

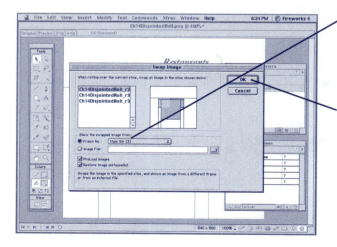

4. Choose the frame you want to use with this Swap Image behavior. The image in the frame will create the disjointed effect.

5. Click on the OK button to save your changes.

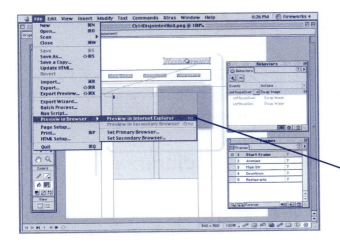

Previewing a Disjointed Rollover

Add several disjointed rollovers to your Fireworks document. After you've assigned all the behaviors, preview them in a browser. Here's how:

1. Choose Preview in Internet Explorer from the File, Preview in Browser menu.

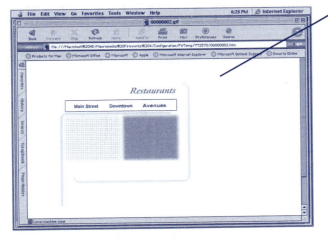

2. View the first frame of the document in the browser window.

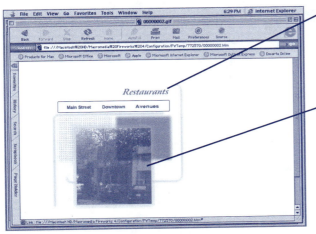

3. Move the cursor over a graphic or text object that contains a disjointed rollover. In this example, I moved my cursor over the Restaurants text.

The swapped images will appear in the lower area of the browser window.

Testing Rollovers

There's a time to be creative and a time to do some rote testing. Testing isn't the most exciting aspect of Web page design, but it's essential if you want your Web page visitors to have a fun and bug-free experience. The following sections explain some simple things to keep in mind when you're testing rollovers.

Testing a Rollover with Internet Explorer

Having the original file is the best way to know exactly how a behavior is supposed to work. Without it, it will be difficult to fix a problem if you find one. The following steps show you how to view a button state in the Fireworks file and check its behavior in a browser.

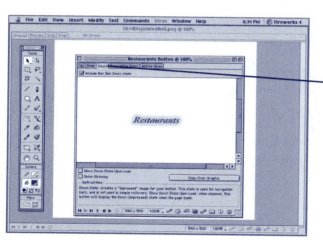

1. View a button state in the Fireworks document. In this example, I'm viewing the Down button state for the Restaurants button text in the Button Editor window.

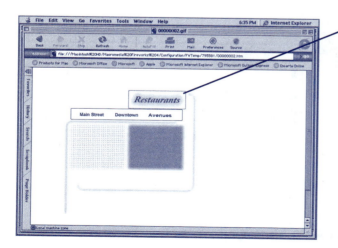

2. Preview the document in a browser. Click on the text object. The same graphic selected in the Fireworks document will appear in the browser window.

Viewing the HTML for a Rollover

If you don't have the original Fireworks file to check a rollover behavior, never fear; you can view the source code in the browser application. The following steps introduce you to the JavaScript routines and HTML code that make a rollover, well, roll over.

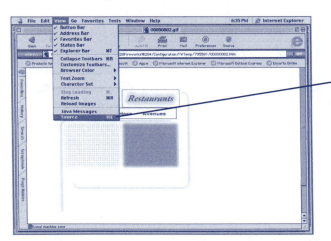

1. Preview your document in a browser window. Then, choose Source from the View menu in Internet Explorer. There's a similar Source menu command in Netscape Communicator.

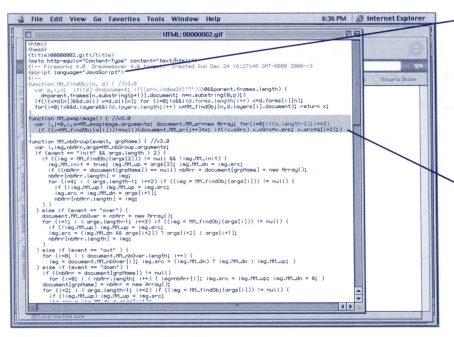

2. The JavaScript language tag will appear near the beginning of the HTML document. Several JavaScript functions will be located below it.

3. The Swap Image function tells the browser how to swap one image with another.

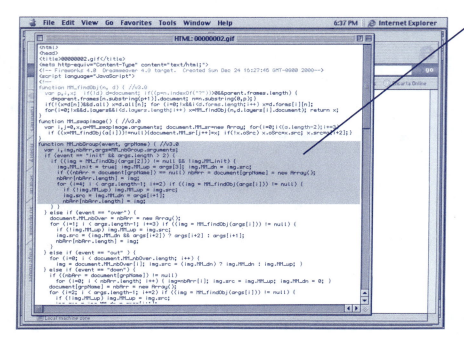

4. The MM_nbGroup function is one of the larger JavaScript functions included with this example. It contains several else statements. This routine handles different button states created by button instances.

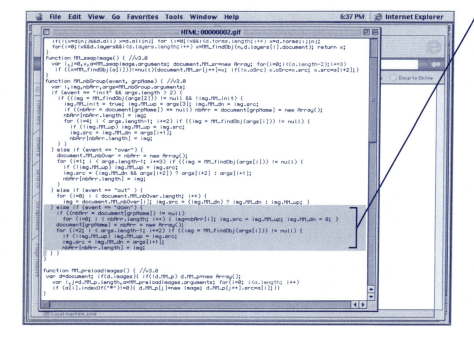

5. This else if statement handles the Down button state.

6. The document-specific code follows all the JavaScript functions.

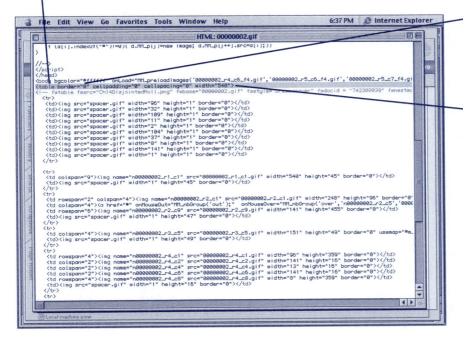

7. The table border tag setting should always be set to zero.

8. The width and height of the table can also be defined along with the table tag. If the dimensions of the table don't match the corresponding image, the table won't appear correctly in the browser window.

14

Designing Pop-Up Menus

Although you could create pop-up menus in previous versions of Fireworks, the Pop-up Menu Wizard in Fireworks 4 enables you to create a particular kind of pop-up menu very easily. A *pop-up menu* is a menu list that appears when you hover over an image map or click on an image map on a Web page. The pop-up menus created by Fireworks work similarly to the ones that appear in each of the panel windows, except that you can customize a pop-up menu's colors, font, and highlight colors.

In this chapter you'll learn how to:

- Design a pop-up menu with the Pop-up Menu Wizard
- Create primary and secondary pop-up menus
- Create a disjointed pop-up menu
- Customize pop-up menu settings

Pop-Up Menus and Web Pages

Pop-up menus for Web pages can have a broader range of functionality than their counterparts on traditional applications and operating systems. For example, on a Web page, you can have a pop-up menu appear just below the hotspot or slice. Menu commands can appear vertically or horizontally, although the Pop-up Menu Wizard only generates vertical pop-up menus. You can also created disjointed pop-up menus, where each menu list appears in one centralized location on the Web page, or in another location on the Web page that's not immediately nearby the main menu command. This chapter shows you how to create regular and disjointed pop-up menus using the Pop-up Menu Wizard.

Pop-up menus are probably one of the most complex interactive Web graphics to design. They are most commonly used as sophisticated navigation bars. However, you can also create pop-up menus that mimic command execution, as if you were using an application on a Web page.

Before you create pop-up menus, you'll need to assess how many menus will be on a Web page and what menu commands will appear in each menu list. After you've figured out how much data you want to show in each menu, you'll need to figure out how big or small to make all the menu elements compared to the rest of the content on each Web page on your site. The following sections show you how to create a pop-up menu containing primary and secondary menus.

Designing a Pop-Up Menu

You can use the built-in tools in Fireworks to create the graphics and text for the pop-up menu. Pop-up menus can drop down from a menu bar located at the top of a Web page or open up from the left or right side of a page. The pop-up menus generated by Fireworks only highlight the currently selected menu item. You can add additional behaviors if you want the menu name to highlight whenever its menu is open. The following steps show you how I put the graphics together for this pop-up menu exercise.

1. Choose a shape or drawing tool from the toolbox.

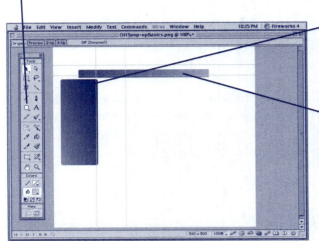

2. Click and drag the mouse in the document window to create a shape. Add a fill pattern, such as a gradient, if you want.

3. Create other Web graphic objects that you want to use as base graphics for your pop-up menus.

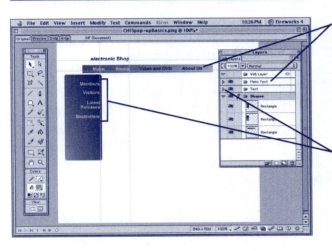

4. Select the Text Tool (T) from the toolbox and add text to the document window. In this example, I will create pop-up menus for both vector objects. Each text object will appear in the Layers panel.

5. Organize each group of menu text objects into the same layer in the Layers panel.

Creating the Primary Menus

When you first click on a menu button, the initial menu list you see is the primary menu. These menu commands should have some sort of relevance to the selected menu button. Each menu item that appears in the pop-up menu can have a link assigned to it. The following steps show you how to create a pop-up menu.

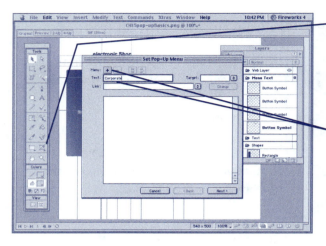

1. Insert a slice object into one of the text objects in the document window. Choose Pop-up Menu from the Insert menu. The Set Pop-Up Menu dialog box will appear.

2. Type a menu name into the Text text box. Then, click on the Plus button to create a menu item in the window list.

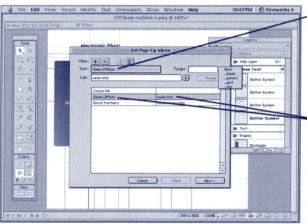

3. Type another menu item name into the Text text box. Then, type a URL into the Link text box. When this menu item is selected, the corresponding URL will load in the browser window.

4. View the menu item in the window list. The URL or relative Web page will appear beside its corresponding menu item. Click on an item in the window list to edit its settings in the text boxes at the top of the window.

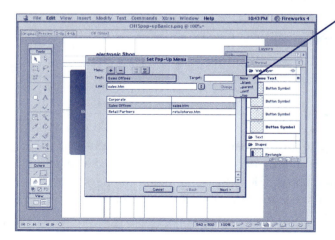

5. Click on the pop-up menu beside the Target text box to view a list of targets for the selected pop-up menu item. The Target text box enables you to open the URL in a new browser window (_blank), a parent frameset (_parent), the current frame (_self), or all frames (_top). If the Target text box is empty, or if None is selected, the URL will open in the current browser window. When you've finished adding your menus, click on Next.

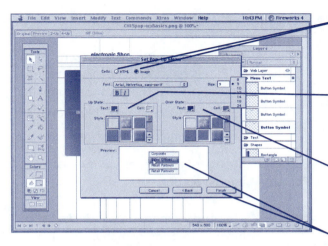

6. Choose between the HTML or Image radio buttons to determine how the pop-up menu list will be generated.

7. Pick a text or cell color for the Up state of the pop-up menus. Click on a style from the Style list.

8. Select a text or cell color for the Over state of the pop-up menus. Click on a style from the Style list.

9. Preview the pop-up menu in the Preview section of the window. When you've selected your pop-up menu settings, click on the Finish button.

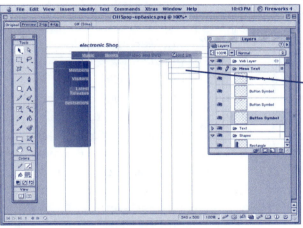

10. If you use the Pointer Tool (V) to select the pop-up menu slice. An outline of the pop-up menu will appear in the document window. You can click and drag the outline to set the location of the pop-up menu.

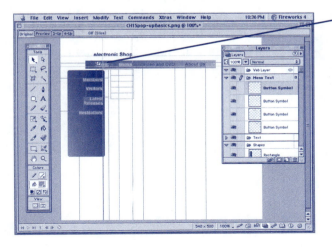

11. Create another pop-up menu for another button symbol. If there isn't enough space for the menu to drop directly below the menu button, try to place the pop-up menu nearby.

Defining Secondary Menus

Secondary menus, also known as submenus, appear when a primary menu is selected. Each submenu command can have a URL assigned to it, just like a primary link. However, you can't assign a tertiary menu (submenu for the secondary menu) with the Pop-up Menu Wizard. The following steps show you how to add secondary menus to the previous list of menu items.

1. Double-click on an existing pop-up menu, or create a new pop-up menu and add several menu items in the Set Pop-Up Menu dialog box.

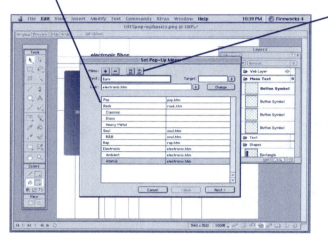

2. Secondary menus are indented, compared to primary menus, which are aligned flush left. You can select any existing menu item and click on the Indent/Create Menu button located at the top of the window. You can create third-level menus by clicking on the Indent/Create Menu button a second time. Each space added to the left of a menu name can be used to create an additional level of pop-up menus. Conversely, you can click on the Outdent/Promote button to bump a pop-up menu up a level.

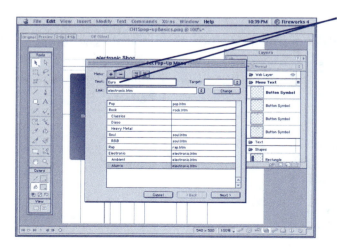

3. If you want to add a secondary menu to the window list, type some text into the Text field. Then, click on the Plus button.

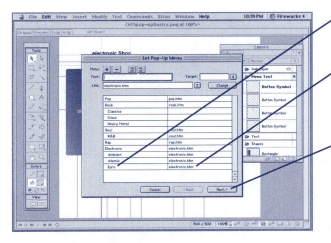

Each submenu item will appear in the window list.

If a URL is assigned to the secondary menu, it will appear in the window list too.

4. Click on Next to preview the pop-up menu's appearance settings. Secondary menus will appear with the same font, font size, font style, and Up and Over states as all the other menu items in the pop-up menu.

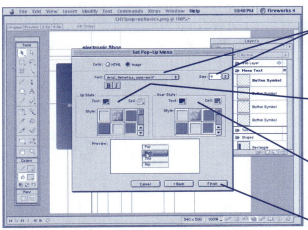

5. Click on the Font pop-up menu to select a font for the pop-up menu. Type a font size into the Size text box.

6. Adjust the text and cell colors and choose the style for the Up state of the pop-up menu.

7. Repeat Step 6 for the Over state of the menu. Preview the menu.

8. Click on Finish to create or modify the pop-up menu.

TIP

You can customize pop-up menu styles by modifying the Styles.sti file located in the Configurations, Nav Menu folder in the Fireworks folder.

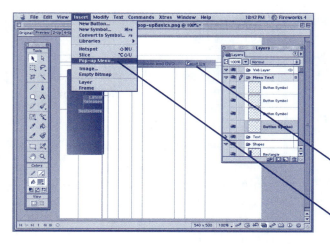

Previewing Pop-up Menus

Although you can adjust the way a pop-up menu will look in the Set Pop-Up Menu dialog box, you should also preview a pop-up menu in a browser window. The following steps show you how:

1. Create a button symbol, then select it with the Pointer Tool (V).

2. Choose Pop-up Menu from the Insert menu. The Set Pop-Up Menu dialog box will open. Add menu names and links for the pop-up menu. Click on the Next button and then choose a font, font size, menu style, and menu colors. Click on the Finish button to create the pop-up menu for the button symbol.

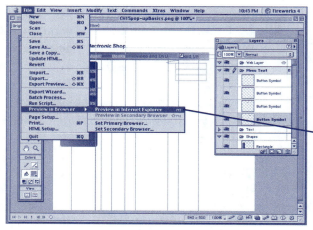

3. Choose the Preview in Internet Explorer command from the File, Preview in Browser menu.

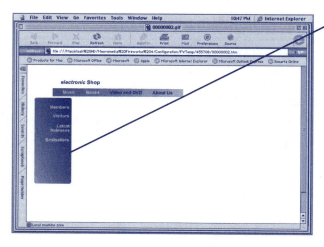

4. Wait for Fireworks to process the command. Then, view the first frame of your Web page in the browser window.

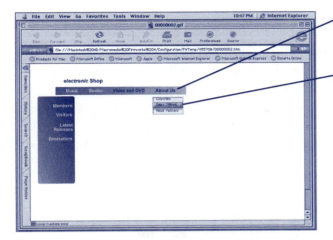

5. Click on a menu button to view the pop-up menu.

6. Drag the mouse over each menu item to view the Up and Down button states in the pop-up menu.

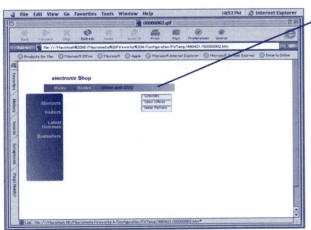

7. Click on the menu button to view each button state. In this example, I forgot to add a button state. That's why no text appears in the menu bar, even though the pop-up menu is visible.

Creating a Simple Pop-Up Menu

The title of this section might be a little misleading. The previous section already showed you how to create a pretty complicated pop-up menu containing menus and submenus. What else could there be?

I have a sincere belief that a pop-up menu can't really exist all by itself on a Web page. The base graphics, text, and button states all enhance the experience of interacting with a pop-up menu. The following sections show you how to design and lay out the base graphics to create a basic pop-up menu.

Designing the Graphic Objects

Don't wince; this isn't another lesson about rulers and guides. Actually it is, just a little different. You can place guides in the document window to mark where you want your pop-up menus to appear. Anything outside those guides is free reign across frames for other Web page layout elements. The following steps show you how to create some of the base graphics for the pop-up menu. The steps don't follow a specific order for creating these graphics. Instead, they show you how the graphic objects are combined and laid out.

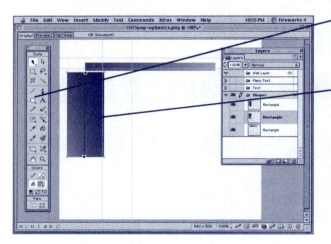

1. Add a shape to the document window, or design a closed path object. Assign a gradient to it.

2. Select the graphic in the document window. You can adjust the direction of the gradient by clicking and dragging the square in the selected object. Move the circle to change the starting point of the gradient.

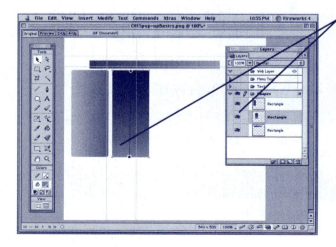

3. You can also combine two gradient objects to create a unique gradient effect. In this example, I've placed a vertically applied linear gradient rectangle over a copy of the same rectangle that has a horizontal linear gradient.

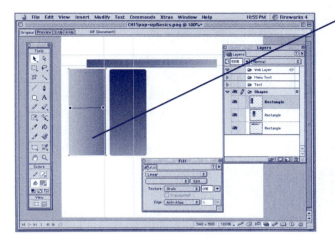

4. Select an object to view its gradient settings. Open the Fill panel to view or edit the gradient or the gradient colors.

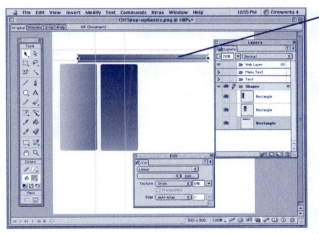

5. Apply the Rectangle Tool (R) to the document window to create a horizontal menu bar shape. In this example, I applied a horizontal linear gradient to the vector object.

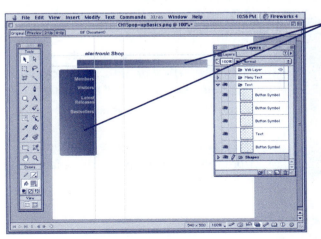

6. Place each menu bar object in the document window to create a simple layout. Select one or more text objects and convert them into button symbol objects. Then, click on a button symbol and add a pop-up menu to it.

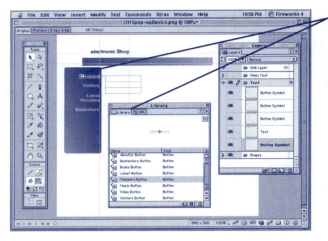

7. Open the Library panel to view a list of symbols available to the document. Click on a button instance to view an outline of the pop-up menu. In this example, I've selected a button instance that contains a pop-up menu.

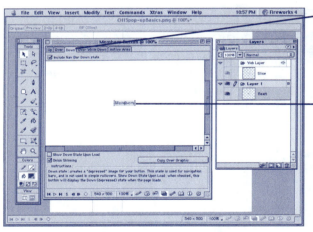

8. Double-click on a button instance to edit each button state. Click on a tab in the Button Editor window to view or edit a button state.

9. Double-click on a text object to open the Text Editor window if you want to customize a text setting.

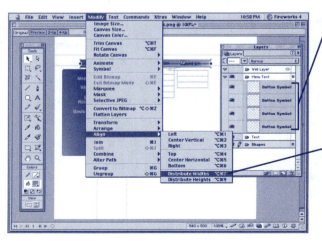

10. After you've created several button instances and their pop-up menus, select each instance sharing a common vertical or horizontal location. Each selected object will be highlighted in the Layers panel, if it is open.

11. Select an alignment command from the Modify menu. In this example, I've selected Distribute Widths.

Inserting a Pop-Up Menu

Inserting a pop-up menu isn't quite as easy as inserting a slice or converting a symbol. For example, if you select a text or graphic object and then try to insert a pop-up menu, Fireworks will tell you that you must select a hotspot or slice first. The following steps show you how to insert a pop-up menu by selecting a pop-up menu command from the drag-and-drop handle button.

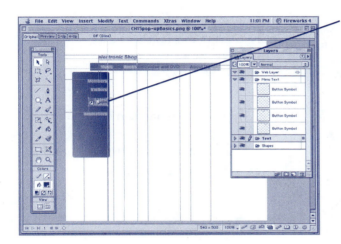

1. Select a button symbol from the document window. Button symbols are created with a slice object. Click and hold the mouse on the drag-and-drop handle button.

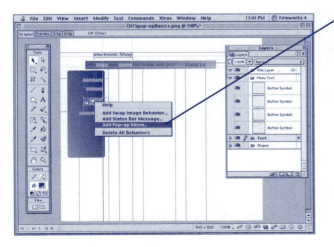

2. Choose the Add Pop-up Menu command from the menu. The Set Pop-Up Menu dialog box will open.

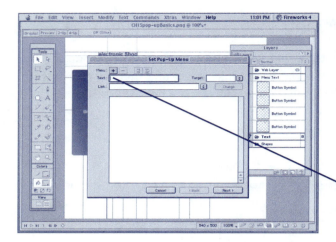

Defining Menu Names

If you're already too familiar with creating and editing menu items in the Set Pop-Up Menu window, skip ahead to the next section. The following steps show you how to add items to a pop-up menu.

1. Click in the Text text box.

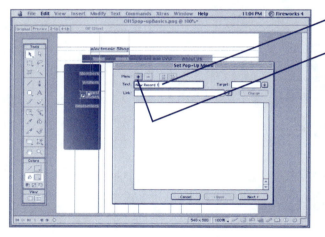

2. Type a menu name in it.

3. Click on the Plus button to turn that text into a pop-up menu item.

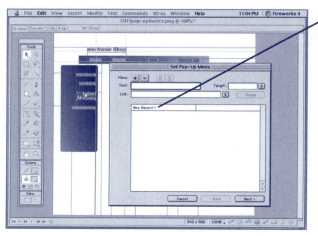

The menu name will appear in the window list.

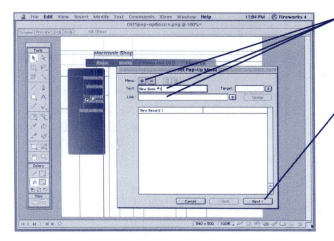

4. Add another menu name in the Text field. Type a URL in the Link text box. Then, click on the Plus button to add another menu item to the pop-up menu.

5. Click on Next.

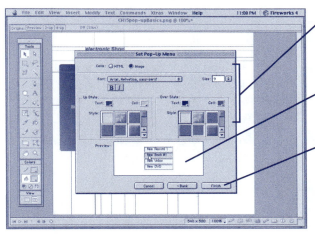

6. Adjust the appearance of the pop-up menu in the second screen of the Set Pop-Up Menu dialog box.

7. Preview the pop-up menu as you make changes.

8. Click on the Finish button to create the pop-up menu.

The JavaScript code used to create the pop-up menus in Fireworks is stored in a file called fw_menu.js in the Configurations, HTML Code folder of the Fireworks folder. You can modify this file in an HTML editor. After you export the pop-up menu from Fireworks, you can use Dreamweaver to modify the JavaScript code used to lay out the pop-up menu elements. For example, if you want to modify the way a pop-up menu appears, you can customize the FW_showMenu routine and change the X and Y coordinates for a pop-up menu. Or, you can remove the borders on a pop-up menu, changing the values for the following variables to zero:

this.menuBorder = 0;this.menuItemBorder = 0;.

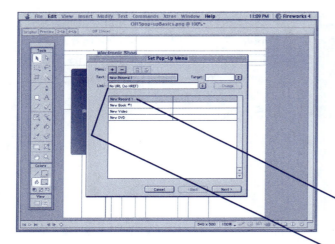

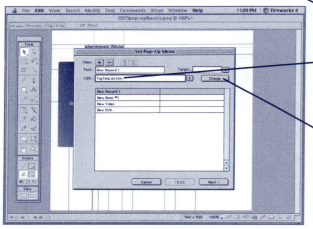

Assigning Rollover Targets

Don't set your expectations too high. When you're working with a pop-up menu, you won't be able to swap bitmap images or do all the fancy behaviors you can with the other Web objects. But you can assign a URL to every item in a pop-up menu. Here's how:

1. Click on a menu item in the window list.

2. View the empty link in the Link text box.

3. Type a relative path to a local HTML file, or type a full URL in the Link text box.

4. Click on Change to add the link to the selected menu item.

Viewing the Web Layout

After you've created all the Web objects and twiddled with the Web page layout, view the Web Layer in the document window. If the document contains more than one frame of content, view each frame and make sure that the slices, hotspots, and pop-up menus don't overlap. The following steps show you how to view the Web Layer and its Web objects.

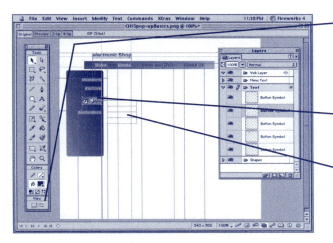

1. Select the Show Slices button in the toolbox. All the hotspots and slices (at least the visible ones in the Layers panel) will appear in the document window.

2. Choose the Pointer Tool (V) and select a slice or button symbol.

3. View the pop-up menu location for each button symbol. Adjust the pop-up menu location if you want.

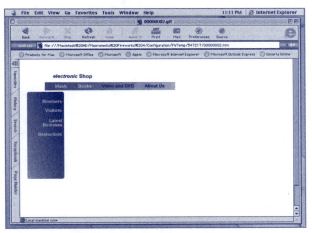

Testing the Menu

How did this happen? Here we are again in the test zone. Now that you've created a pop-up menu, take a look at how you can test it in a browser window. The following steps show you how.

1. Choose Preview in Internet Explorer from the File, Preview in Browser menu. Wait for the browser window to open and then view your Web page.

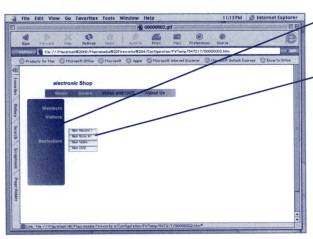

2. Move the cursor over a button symbol.

3. If you're expecting a pop-up menu to appear, make sure that it does.

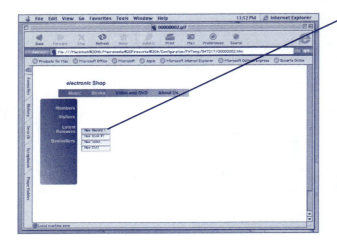

4. Move the cursor over each pop-up menu item. Make sure that the Down state appears with the correct colors, style, and font.

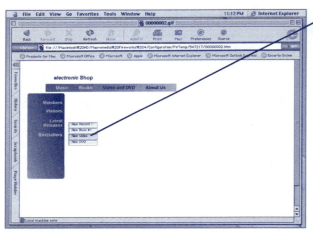

5. Select each item in the pop-up menu.

Creating Disjointed Pop-Up Menus

In the previous chapter, we created disjointed rollovers. Disjointed pop-up menus are similar, except that the menus appear in a disjointed location. The following sections show you how to assemble a disjointed pop-up menu.

Defining the Layout

You can create a central location for each pop-up menu to appear in, or you can randomly create a slice to define the disjointed location for the pop-up menu.

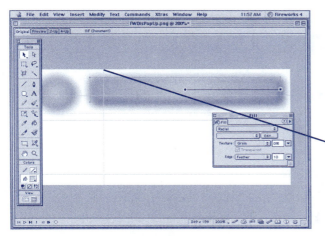

In this example, I'm going to create three different kinds of disjointed pop-up menus, so that you can see some of the design issues inherent to each one. The following steps show you how to lay out the base graphics for the menu bar.

1. Add vertical guides in the document window to help you lay out the menu buttons. Each menu button, or text object in the nav bar, will contain a pop-up menu.

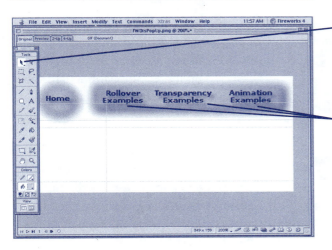

2. Adjust the horizontal and vertical guides so that you can plan your Web page layout.

3. Select a base graphic object and assign a gradient or adjust its fill colors. If you haven't selected the final colors for the text and graphics for the nav bar or pop-up menus, you can create the base graphics in a shared layer in the Layers panel. When you change the color in one frame, all the frames will be updated.

4. Use the Text Tool (T) to add each menu bar item to the base graphic. Use the Pointer Tool (V) to lay out each text object.

5. Place each text object along the horizontal guide. You can use the alignment tools to evenly space each object along the base graphic.

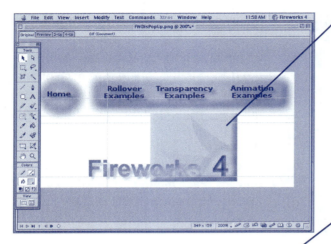

6. Add any additional background graphics to the document window.

7. Create additional frames in the Frames panel to represent the pop-up menu for each menu name added to the base graphic. For example, select Frame 2 to add one of the disjointed pop-up menus.

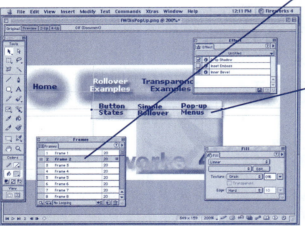

8. Use the shape and text tools to design a horizontal pop-up menu base graphic. Place the text objects over the base graphic for the pop-up menu. Apply an opacity setting from the Layers panel to the pop-up menu base graphic if you want to see through the pop-up menu graphic in the browser window.

9. If you want to create another level of interactivity, you can create an additional frame for each text object in each pop-up menu. Apply effects to the pop-up menu graphic and change the color of the menu name to indicate that the menu is open.

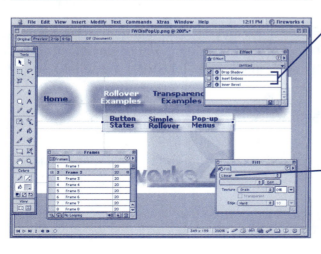

10. Select the graphic object for the pop-up menu and customize the fill pattern, texture, or gradient as you like. Create disjointed pop-up menus for the other two menu buttons.

Adding Slices to the Layout

The secret to getting a disjointed rollover to work is knowing which slice to create and where. If you've already created each pop-up menu graphic, use the Slice Tool to insert a slice over each menu object. If you want the text to highlight, you can also add hotspots combined with Swap Image behaviors to create the interactive text effect. The following steps show you how to add slices to the disjointed pop-up menu layout.

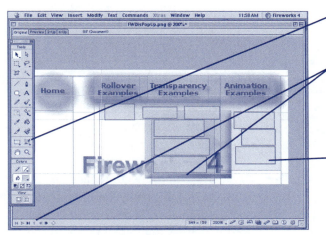

1. Select the Slice Tool (G) from the toolbox.

2. Use the Frame Controls to choose a frame containing a disjointed pop-up menu. Create a slice over the pop-up menu graphic.

3. View the Web layout. Try to avoid overlapping slices if you can.

Assigning Behaviors

You'll need to create each frame for each disjointed rollover state in the document before you can add the corresponding Swap Image behaviors. It might be easier to track each group of menus if you click and drag similar frames near each other in the Frames panel. The following steps show you how to add a Nav Bar Down behavior to create a disjointed rollover.

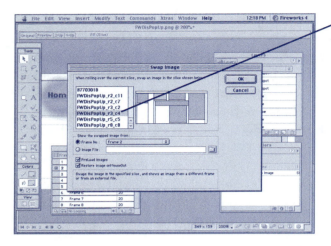

1. First, set up the menu swapping behavior for the main menu. When the visitor clicks on the menu name in the browser window, you want the menu name to become highlighted in addition to making the pop-up menu appear. Select the first frame of the document, then click on the menu button to which you want to assign the rollover behavior. Choose Nav Bar Down from the Behaviors panel. The selected slice will appear in the left window list in the Nav Bar Down dialog box.

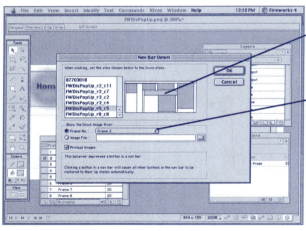

2. Choose the target slice in the right pane. In this example, I chose the slice object that covers the menu text.

3. Select the frame containing the pop-up menu graphic from the Frame No. pop-up menu list. The frame you select should contain the image that you want to appear in the selected slice area. In this example, I chose Frame 2 from the pop-up menu. Frame 2 contains the highlighted text object that will appear when the user clicks on the menu name.

4. Click on the OK button to create the behavior.

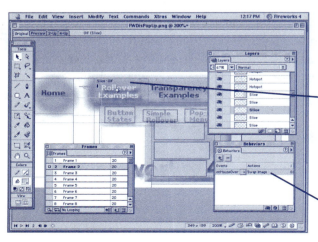

5. Select the slice in the document window to view its behaviors in the Behaviors panel. You should see the behavior you just created highlighted in the Behaviors panel window list.

6. Double-click on a behavior to view more detailed information.

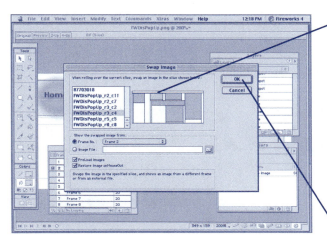

7. Next, make the pop-up menu appear when the menu name is selected. Add a Swap Image behavior to the slice covering the menu name. This time, select the slice containing the pop-up menu name as the target slice. In this example, the target slice is the slice object covering the pop-up menu area. The target frame is Frame 2, which contains the pop-up menu image objects.

8. Click on the OK button to save the Swap Image behavior to the slice object.

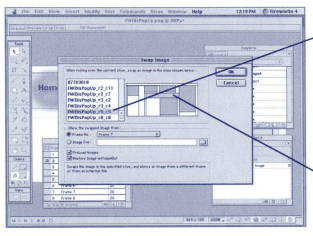

9. Next, highlight the text if the mouse hovers over menu item in the pop-up menu. Click on a hotspot covering one of the pop-up menu text objects. You might need to move the slice object if it is covering the hotspot object. Assign a Swap Image behavior to that hotspot.

10. Select a target slice from the right pane in the Swap Image dialog box. Because the hotspot overlaps the slice, the slice name will appear in the left window list.

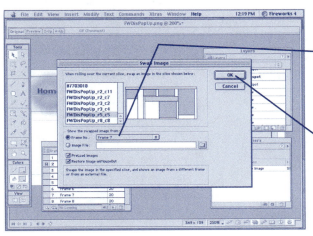

11. Choose a target frame for the image swap. In this example, I chose Frame 7, which contains the highlighted text for that particular text object.

12. Click on the OK button to save your changes.

Viewing Results in a Browser

Now that you've added a disjointed pop-up menu, test-drive it in a browser window. The following steps show you how.

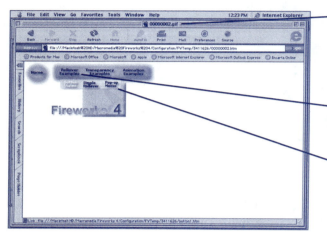

1. Choose Preview in Internet Explorer from the File, Preview in Browser menu. Wait for the files to load in the browser window.

2. Move the cursor over the menu button.

3. View the disjointed rollover in the browser window. Select a menu item to see how the highlighted text appears in the browser.

Customizing HTML Output

If you're happy with the way your pop-up menus look in a browser, you're done. Next, you'll want to export those slices and HTML files out of Fireworks so that you can put them on a Web server. The following steps show you how to customize the naming settings for the HTML file that will be exported along with all the slice files.

1. Choose HTML Setup from the File menu. The HTML Setup dialog box will open.

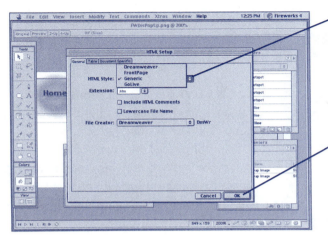

2. Click on the HTML Style pop-up menu. If you're using Dreamweaver to create your Web pages, choose Dreamweaver from the menu list. If you're using an HTML editor such as BBEdit, choose Generic.

3. Click on the OK button to save your changes.

Customizing the Pop-up Menu

Because Fireworks supports plug-ins, extensions, and other ways of adding effects, textures, and patterns, you can customize a pop-up menu in many ways, especially if you're creating one from scratch. The following sections show you how to add interactive text, adjust gradient colors, and change behaviors to customize a pop-up menu.

Adding Interactive Menu Objects

You can combine effects and colors to create unique interactive elements in pop-up menus. Apply a glow effect to a text object to design a text object in a pop-up menu that appears to be selected. Or, change the color of the text object to create a visual cue when the mouse hovers over or clicks on the text object. In the example pop-up menu, I created different effects with highlighted text in each disjointed pop-up menu. The following steps show you how to apply some effects to text objects.

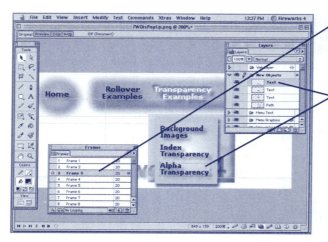

1. Select a frame containing a generic pop-up menu, where no menu items are selected.

2. Click on a text object representing one of the menu items in the pop-up menu. View or add any effects, text, or fill settings for that text object. You might want to copy and paste this object to another frame if you want to use the same font and font size for that menu item across frames.

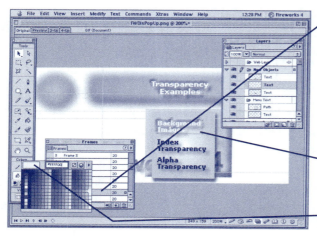

3. Create a second frame containing the same menu and text objects. The number of frames you'll create will depend on the number of menu items in the pop-up menu. Select a frame you can to use to create a highlighted text object.

4. Click on the text object you want to modify.

5. Choose a different color for the text object from the Fill color well in the toolbox.

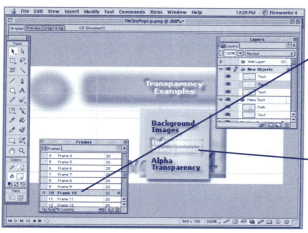

6. Click on another frame containing another text object for the same pop-up menu. In this example, I've grouped the text objects for a pop-up menu in the Frames panel.

7. Select the text object you want to edit.

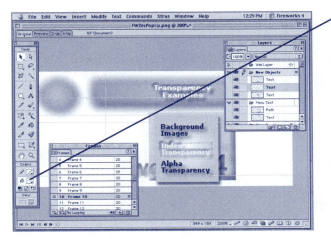

8. Choose a color for the selected text object from the Fill color well. In this example, I also applied the Inset Emboss effect to make the selected text appear pushed into the menu.

Changing Gradient Colors

After you've added the disjointed pop-up menus, you might want to adjust some or all of the original colors in the base graphics. The following steps show you how to change a gradient color in a rectangle shape.

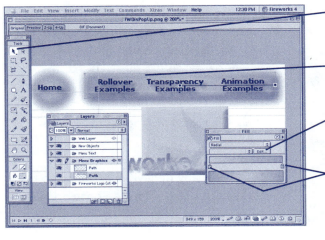

1. Select the Pointer Tool (V) from the toolbox.

2. Click on a graphic object containing a gradient fill.

3. Open the Fill panel and click on the Edit button.

4. Click on one of the color boxes in the Color pop-up menu.

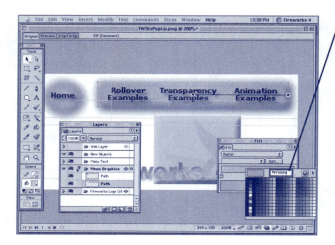

5. Select a different color for the gradient. Press the Enter/Return key to exit the Color pop-up menu.

Adjusting Behaviors

As you put together the behaviors for a pop-up menu, you'll notice that it's easy to leave a Swap Image behavior out of one menu or choose the wrong slice for another. The following steps show you how to edit behaviors for pop-up menus.

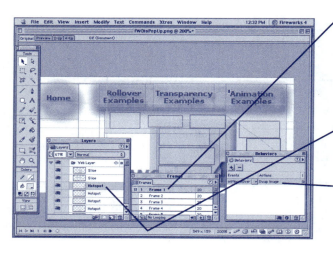

1. Select the first frame of the document. This is how the Web graphics will appear in the browser window, although slices appear the same across all frames.

2. Click on a hotspot in the Layers panel.

3. View any behaviors assigned to the selected hotspot in the Behaviors panel.

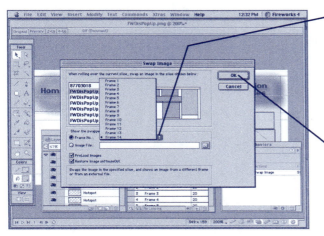

4. Double-click on a behavior to edit it. In this example, I selected a Swap Image behavior, so the Swap Image dialog box appeared. Select the frame for the Swap Image behavior in the Frame No. pop-up menu.

5. Review the source and target settings. Then, click on the OK button to save your changes.

6. If you need to add a Swap Image behavior, click and drag the drag-and-drop handle onto the target slice.

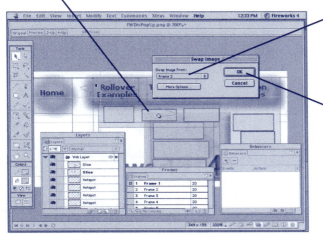

7. In the resulting dialog box, select the frame number containing the target image from the Swap Image From pop-up menu.

8. Click on the OK button to save your changes and update the behavior settings.

15

Optimizing Web Graphics

The term *optimize* has several different meanings or, depending on how you look at it, no clear definition. In the software world, optimizing involves removing redundancies and streamlining processes so that, theoretically, you remove code without affecting the quality or functionality of the software, while making it perform faster.

Optimizing an image file in Fireworks is similar to optimizing software. When creating graphics for Web pages, the key is to create impressive graphics that load quickly for people who visit your Web site. The process of improving the quality and reducing the size of an image is called *optimization*. In this chapter you'll learn how to:

- Optimize vector and bitmap objects
- Selectively optimize and export slices
- Optimize the file size of a document
- Optimize the image quality of a document

Optimizing Image Maps

One way to help a large image load quickly in a Web browser is to break the image into smaller pieces. The inherent problem with this concept is that you then need to create JavaScript or HTML code to reassemble the pieces in their proper location. Otherwise, the image might never make it to a browser window, or it might display with missing pieces. Creating a sliced image is easy to do in Fireworks because Fireworks generates the HTML and JavaScript code for each sliced image. The following sections discuss all the issues related to creating, optimizing, and exporting slices. Each set of steps assumes that you have already created a document that contains image objects and slices.

Slicing Graphics for Optimization

Slices can be rectangles or custom shapes. This example uses the Polygon Slice Tool. However, you can also select the Rectangle Slice Tool from the toolbox. The following steps show you how to add a slice to an image.

1. Select the Rectangle or Polygon Slice Tool (G).

2. In the document window, drag the mouse to create a rectangle.

The slice guides will indicate how the rest of the document will be sliced.

3. Choose the Pointer Tool (V) and select a slice object in the document window. You can click and drag the slice object to move its location. Click and drag a corner point to resize its shape.

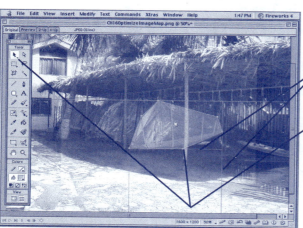

Comparing Slices to Hotspots

Hotspots and slices can share the same behaviors and URLs. However, each one is fundamentally different than the other. After you slice an image, all other frames associated with the document will be sliced in the same way. Choose the Slice Tool and outline a rectangle to define the slice areas. If you're working with a fairly small image and you only want to add behaviors or a link to it, you can create a hotspot over the image. The following list highlights some features of slices and hotspots.

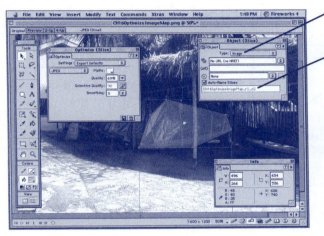

- **Image or text slices**. A slice can either contain an image or text.

- **Divide an image**. Each slice is a separate image file. Fireworks creates a table from the coordinates of the full image and then creates table cells or a nested table for each slice. You can also give each slice a custom file name.

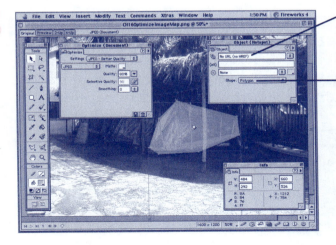

- **URLs and behaviors**. You can assign a URL to a hotspot or a slice using the Object or URL panel.

- **Shapes**. Select a different shape for a hotspot from the Object panel.

Optimizing Slices with the Object Panel

The Object panel is one of the few panels that changes content dynamically. Click on an object, such as a vector object, and then select a mask or slice to see the settings in the Object panel change. The following steps introduce you to the Object settings for slice objects.

1. Select a slice object in the document window. If you're working with an image slice, you can optimize the quality or file size of that slice by choosing a different file format in the Optimize panel.

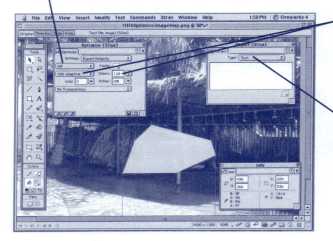

2. Choose a different color palette or reduce the number of colors available to a palette to see whether this affects the image quality or file size of the slice.

3. Choose Text from the Type pop-up menu in the Object panel if you want to create a slice that contains text instead of an image.

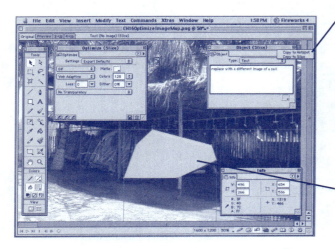

4. Choose Copy to Hotspot or Copy to Slice from the Object panel pop-up menu if you want to duplicate the current slice or hotspot. For example, if you've created a text slice that you want to place in another location in the document, choose Copy to Slice to copy the object settings along with the slice object.

The duplicate slice or hotspot will appear in the same location as the previously selected slice or hotspot.

Choosing Optimization Settings

Fireworks contains several built-in optimization settings for JPEG and GIF files. However, you can also save a file as a standard BMP (for Windows computers) or PICT (if you're using a Mac) file. The following steps give you a brief tour of some of the settings in the Optimize panel.

1. Open a document that contains several image and Web objects. Choose Optimize from the Window menu or click on the Optimize shortcut in the document window (it's the red clamp tool icon). Click on the Settings pop-up menu and choose either GIF Web 216, GIF Websnap 256, GIF Websnap 128, GIF Adaptive 256, JPEG – Better Quality, or JPEG – Lower Quality. Each pop-up menu item will change all the other settings that appear in the Optimize panel.

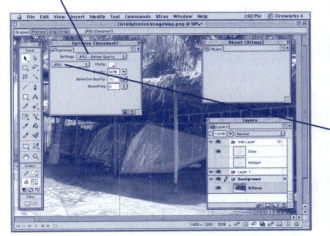

2. Choose a file format for the document from the pop-up menu on the left. Select one of 14 different file formats: GIF, Animated GIF, JPEG, PNG 8, PNG 24, PNG 32, WBMP, TIFF 8, TIFF 24, TIFF 32, PICT 8, PICT 24, BMP 8, and BMP 24.

3. Click on slice to view its file format and optimization settings.

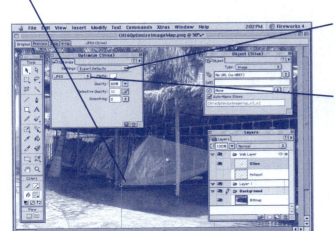

Export Defaults will appear in the Settings pop-up menu of the Optimize panel when a slice object is selected.

4. Choose a different file format for the selected slice from the left pop-up menu.

TIP

Although Fireworks enables you to optimize the file size or quality of an image, you can also try to design objects that optimize more easily than others. For example, an object with a hard edge is more difficult to compress than an object with blurred edges. If you select JPEG from the Optimize panel, you can adjust the blur level of the edges of the objects by increasing the number value in the Smoothing text box, which is also located in the Optimize panel.

Exporting Spacers

A *spacer* is an image used to space cells in a table on a Web page. When you slice an image in Fireworks, all the slices become table tag elements in HTML. You can export a sliced page with or without spacers. The following steps show you how to access the different spacer settings.

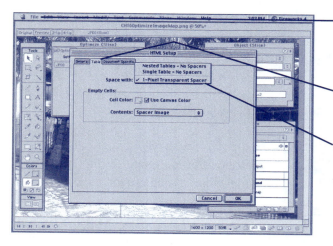

1. Choose HTML Setup from the File menu. The HTML Setup dialog box will open.

2. Click on the Table tab to view the Spacer settings for the document.

3. Choose either 1-Pixel Transparent Spacer or Single Table – No Spacers from the Space With pop-up menu.

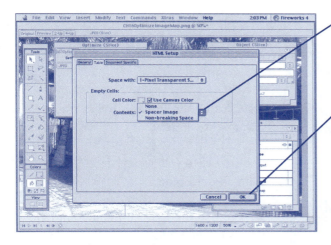

4. Click on the Contents pop-up menu. Choose from one of three options: None, Spacer Image, or Non-breaking Space.

5. Click on the OK button to save your changes.

Exporting Nested Tables

A *nested table* is a table located within a table. Nested tables do not use spacers and can include additional HTML code, which might affect the loading time of a Web page. The following steps show you how to select the Nested Table option from the HTML Setup dialog box.

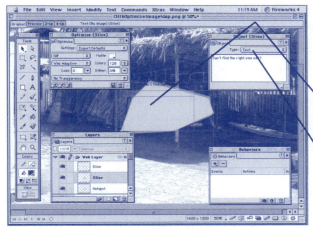

1. Click on a slice in the document window.

2. Open the Object panel. Select the Text menu item from the Type pop-up menu.

3. Choose the HTML Setup command from the File menu. The HTML Setup dialog box will open.

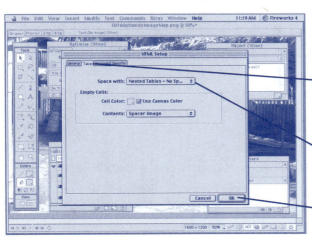

4. Click on the Table tab to view the Nested Table export settings for the document.

5. Choose Nested Tables – No Spacers from the Space With pop-up menu.

6. Click on the OK button.

Exporting Text Slices

Use text slices to update messages on a Web page without creating new graphics. The following steps show you how.

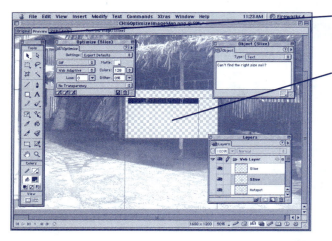

1. Click on the Preview tab in the document window.

The text slice will appear as a transparent object.

2. Choose the Export menu command from the File menu.

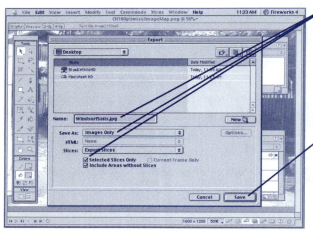

3. Type a new name for the exported slice in the Name text box. If you only want to export the image file, choose Images Only from the Save As pop-up menu. Check the Selected Slices Only check box to export the selected slice.

4. Click on Save.

Replacing Slices

One advantage to slicing an image is that you can update one or two slices without having to wait for the image to upload to the Web server or download to a browser. The following steps show you how to replace a slice using the Swap Image dialog box.

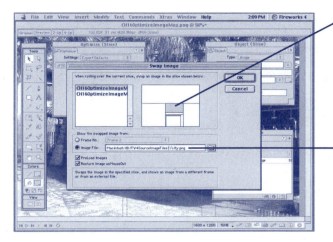

1. Double-click on the Swap Image behavior in the Behaviors panel. The Swap Image dialog box will open. Click on the target image slice in the right pane. This is the slice that will be replaced in the document.

2. Type a directory path in the Image File text box, or click on the folder icon and choose an image file to be swapped into the target slice. Then, click on the OK button to save your changes.

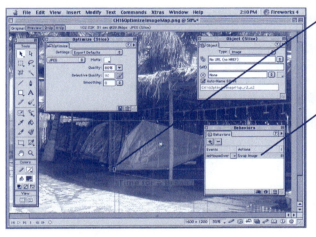

3. The new Swap Image behavior will be reflected in the drag-and-drop handle graphic when the slice object is selected in the document window.

4. Double-click on the behavior if you want to choose a different image to appear in the slice object area.

Optimizing a Slice with the Optimize Panel

Preview a slice or the full document in one of three different preview panels in the document window. In the 2-Up and 4-Up preview panels, the left pane remains the active document window. To view and change the optimization settings for a slice, simply click on the slice object with the Pointer Tool. Then, select and compare different settings in the 2-Up or 4-Up preview panes.

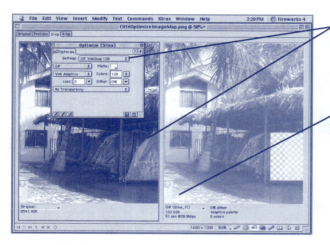

1. Select a slice object in the left preview pane. Then, choose an image file format from the Settings pop-up menu in the Optimize panel.

2. Preview the image in the right pane of the document window. In this example, I selected the 2-Up tab.

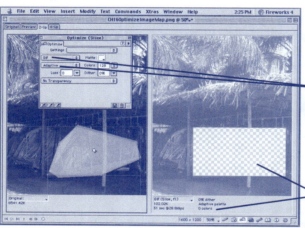

3. Select the slice in the left pane. The name of the slice will appear in the lower-left corner of the right pane.

4. Select a file format from the top-left pop-up menu in the Optimize panel. Choose a color palette from the pop-up menu immediately below the file format pop-up menu.

5. View the file size, download time, and color information in the right pane.

Optimizing Overlapping Slices

Hotspots and image slices are a great way to add interactivity to a Web page. For most graphics, hotspots are used to jump to another Web page or URL. Hotspots and buttons have two basic states: Selected and Unselected. However, you can add additional states such as Mouse Over, Mouse Out, On Click, and On Load from the Behaviors panel. These steps show you how to add more than one behavior to a hotspot.

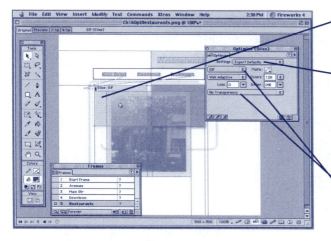

1. Select a slice that overlaps a second slice.

2. Open the Optimize panel. Export Defaults will appear in the top pop-up menu. This is the default setting that appears in the Optimize panel when a slice is selected in the document window.

3. View the file format in the top-left pop-up menu. Also, view the transparency setting. For this particular slice, I've selected No Transparency.

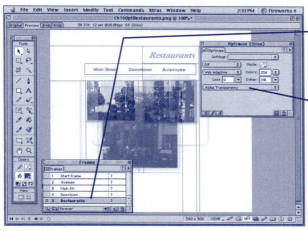

4. Click on the frame containing the second sliced object. Select the slice object for the overlapping image.

5. You can choose a different file format and other optimization settings. In this example, I've chosen the Alpha Transparency setting.

6. Click on the Preview tab and view the slice image areas as they will appear when you export the file.

Previewing Slice File Formats

Don't feel obligated to save all the slices in a document as a GIF, JPEG, or PNG file. You can select a unique file format for any slice. This feature can help you create a smaller overall picture without affecting the image quality of the slice that contains the most visible or important image for a Web page. The following steps show you how to preview different file formats for a selected slice.

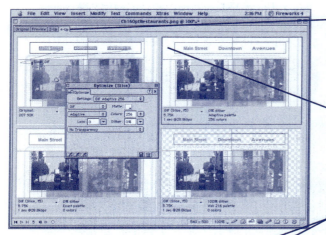

1. Open an image file that contains slice objects. Click on the 4-Up tab and navigate to the frame that contains the slice images.

2. Click on one of three panels in the 4-Up view. The two lower panes and the right pane enable you to view whatever settings you choose from the Optimize panel.

3. Open the Optimize panel. You can optimize the full document, or choose the Pointer Tool (V) and select a slice to optimize. In this example, I've selected the slice in the upper-left corner of the document.

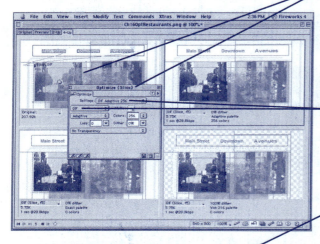

4. Choose a setting from the Settings pop-up menu or from the left pop-up menu.

5. Select a different file format for the slice object.

6. View the image in the selected preview pane. The file size, quality, and download times for the slice will appear in the left corner of each preview pane.

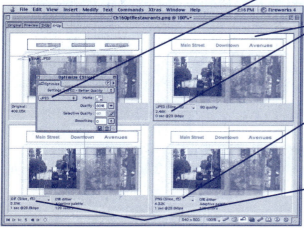

7. Choose a different preview pane and then select a different file format. In this example, I chose PNG 8.

8. Repeat Step 7 for the third preview pane in the 4-Up window. In this example, I chose the GIF file format.

Optimizing a Document

Before you export a slice from a document, you might want to compare the file sizes of different file formats for the entire image. Although the full document is rarely smaller than a single slice, you might want to compare download times and file sizes between the document and its slices. If slices only shave one or two seconds off a 28.8 kbps download time, you might not need to break up that file into slices after all. The following steps show you how to optimize two different documents in the 2-Up preview window.

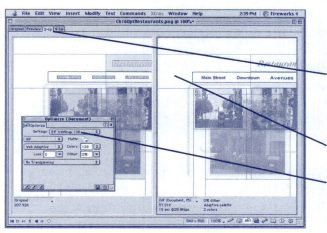

1. Open a document containing several image objects and slice objects. Click on the 2-Up tab in the document window.

2. Click on the right pane.

3. Choose a file format from the top pop-up menu in the Optimize panel. Preview the results in the right window.

4. Open a second document that contains several image objects and slices. Select the 2-Up tab and then click on the right pane.

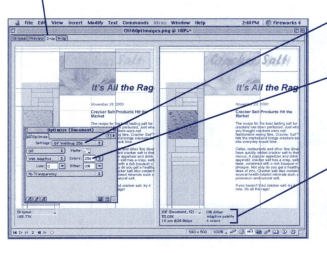

5. Select a file format from the Settings pop-up menu in the Optimize panel.

6. Adjust the number of colors you want to use in the color palette for the document. Then, preview the image in the right pane.

7. View the file size, download time, color palette, and number of colors in the lower-left corner of the preview window.

Optimizing Images with Transparency Settings

The term *transparency*, like the term *optimize*, has several meanings in Fireworks. Actually, Fireworks has several different transparency settings. First, you can create an object that uses a transparent fill. Choose Web Dither from the Fill pop-up menu and then check the Transparency check box.

Then, there's the Index Transparency and Alpha Transparency settings in the Optimize panel. The Index Transparency setting sets the canvas color as the index color for the document. This color will appear transparent if you export the document and view it in a browser window. You can select a custom color as the transparency if you choose Alpha Transparency in the Optimize panel. However, you can only use either the Index Transparency or Alpha Transparency setting in a document, not both at the same time.

You can also add a transparent setting to specific colors in the Color Table panel. In the Layers panel, you can select any image object and adjust its opacity, or transparency value. Then, you can preview those transparency settings in the Preview, 2-Up, or 4-Up views in the document window.

Except for the absence of color, transparency settings don't really impact the optimization of a slice or the document. Try experimenting with colors in the Color Table panel and choose different file formats (except JPEG, which is a file format that does not support transparency) in the Optimize panel to see whether the file size is affected by different transparency settings. In most cases, you won't see a much smaller or larger file size with or without transparency settings. The following sections show you how to apply transparency settings in the Optimize panel and the Export Preview window.

Working with the Optimize Panel

In addition to being able to preview different file formats, color settings, image quality, and other related settings, you can also set the Index or Alpha Transparency for a document from the Optimize panel. Transparency is represented by a gray-and-white checkerboard pattern that appears in the canvas area of the document window. If a color or if the canvas is transparent, you'll see this checkerboard pattern. The following steps show you how to apply an index transparency to a document.

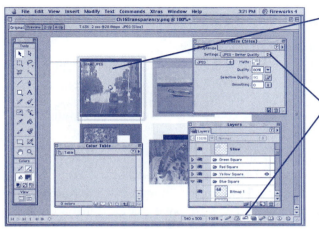

1. Open a document that contains several image and slice objects. Then, select a slice object in the document window.

2. Choose Optimize from the Window menu, or click on the red clamp icon located in the lower-right corner of the document window. Choose a file format setting from the Settings pop-up menu.

In this example, a JPEG file format is selected. This particular file format does not support transparency settings.

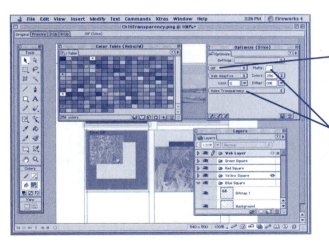

3. Choose GIF from the left pop-up menu. The settings for the GIF file format will appear.

4. Select Index Transparency from the pop-up menu located at the bottom of the Optimize panel. Notice that the canvas color of the document has been added as the Matte color in the Optimize panel.

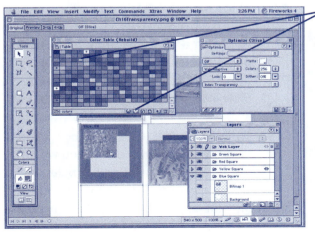

5. Choose Color Table from the Window menu, or click on the color palette icon located in the lower-right corner of the document window. Click on the pop-up menu (right arrow icon) and choose the Rebuild Color Table command. Click on a slice in the document window. Then, select a color in the Color Table panel. If you click on the Transparent button, that color will appear (or rather, disappear) when you export the file.

Modifying Transparency in the Export Preview Window

Select individual colors and make each one transparent. You can access this feature from either the Color Table panel or the Export Preview window. Before you can view a document's color table, a GIF, animated GIF, or PNG file format (or a PICT, TIF, or BMP file format) plus a color palette (such as Web Adaptive) must be selected in the Optimize panel.

Choose the Rebuild Color Table menu command to view the color palette for a document. Click on a slice object and then select a color to access the Edit Color, Transparent, Snap to Web Safe, Lock, or Add Color tools located at the bottom of the color table. The following steps show you how to make a color transparent in the Export Preview window.

1. Open a document that contains several image and slice objects.

2. Click on the File menu and choose the Export Preview menu command.

3. Click on the Preview check box located at the top of the Export Preview window if you want to view your changes in the right pane of the Export Preview window as you make them. Preview the document in the right pane of the Export Preview window.

4. Select a file format from the Format pop-up menu. In this example, I chose the GIF file format. The palette and color table will appear in the Options tab.

5. Type a number in the Color text box to set the number of colors you want to use for the document's color palette. Or, click and drag the slider control beside the text box to set the number of colors.

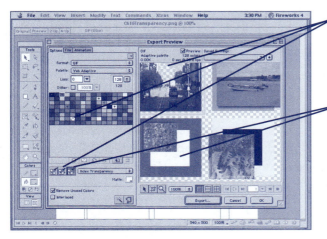

6. Click on the Plus Eyedropper Tool located below the color table. Then, click on a color in the preview pane. That color will become transparent.

7. Select the Minus Eyedropper Tool. Click on a color in the right pane of the window. In this example, I selected the white square. Even though that same color is part of the Index Transparency, the Minus Eyedropper Tool will remove the transparency setting for the selected object.

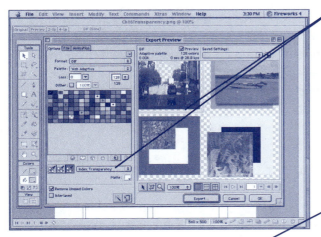

8. Choose Index Transparency from the pop-up menu located at the bottom of the Options tab. A gray-and-white checkerboard pattern will appear in the preview pane, indicating that the particular color is transparent. The Matte color well will show the index color used for the transparency. The colors for the document will appear in the Options tab of the Export Preview window.

9. Click on a color in the color table.

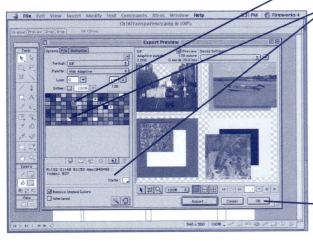

10. View the exact red, green, and blue RGB values for that color alongside its hexadecimal and index color values when you pass the cursor over the color. If you want that color to be transparent, click on the Transparent icon located below the color table. A gray-and-white checkerboard pattern will appear in place of the color if a particular color is marked as transparent.

11. Click on OK to save your changes. Or, click on Export to export the file to your hard drive.

Optimizing File Size and Image Quality

When you design Web graphics, try to select the highest quality images to import into Fireworks. I tend to keep vector objects as vectors, instead of converting them to bitmaps, so that I can continue to edit each object after I've exported some or all of the graphics to my Web server. After you've created the final layout for your Web page, you can begin optimizing the file size and quality of every aspect of the document. The previous sections showed you how to optimize individual slices and work with transparency settings. The next sections take a closer look at how to select a file format and change the quality of the Web graphics.

Choosing a File Format

The size of a Web page is determined primarily by the file size of each graphic contained in the page. Choosing a file format can either help or hurt optimization. For example, if you want to optimize a photo by choosing a GIF file format, the image quality might look terrible even though the file size might grow smaller. On the other hand, if you select a JPEG file format for that same picture, you'll probably retain all or most of the image quality and reduce the file size. The following sections show you how to optimize vector, JPEG, and animated GIF graphics.

Optimizing Vector Objects

The GIF file format works best with solid-colored objects, such as a closed path vector object with a solid fill color. If the document you want to optimize contains several areas of solid colors, consider saving that file as a GIF. The following steps show you how to view optimization settings for a GIF file.

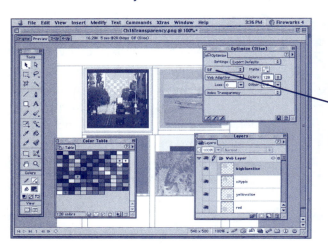

1. Select an object in the document window. Choose GIF from the left pop-up menu in the Optimize panel. The GIF file format enables you to store transparency settings, in addition to providing some file compression.

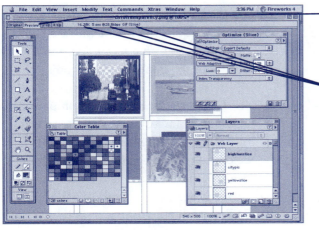

2. Click on the Preview tab to view the document as it will look when you export it.

3. View the file size and download time for a slice or for the entire document. The information in this example shows the download time for the selected slice. The entire file is 42.10K and would take 13 seconds to download at 28.8 kbps. The selected slice in the document is 16.28K and downloads in 5 seconds.

Optimizing Animation

If you've created an animation, you'll want to save it as an animated GIF file. Both Internet Explorer and Netscape Navigator have built-in support for displaying animated GIF files. Other animation file formats are not supported in either of these browsers. However, if file size and download time aren't critical for your target audience, you might want to consider creating the animation as a Flash file.

An animated GIF is a single file that contains two or more frames of animation. Each frame and object contributes to the file size and playback performance of the final animation. If you open an animated GIF file in Fireworks, a frame is automatically created for each frame of animation in the animated GIF file. The following steps show you to choose optimization settings for an animated GIF.

1. Open a document that contains two or more frames of animation. Select an animation object in the document window. Open the Optimize panel and choose Animated GIF in the left pop-up menu.

2. Select the Preview, 2-Up, or 4-Up tab in the document window.

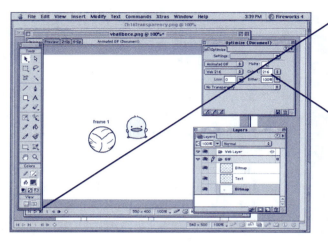

3. Click on the Play button to view the animation. You might want to step through each frame to compare the quality of the image in each frame.

4. Type a larger or smaller number of colors in the Colors text box. One way to reduce the file size is to remove colors to reduce the size of the color palette. In this example, I have not selected a preview pane. This file is 34.76K and takes 10 seconds to download at 28.8 kbps.

TIP

Empty canvas space can increase the file size of your document. Choose the Trim Canvas (Alt/Option + Ctrl/Command + T) command to remove any unused canvas space from the document.

Optimizing Bitmap Images

Digital photos and scanned images will most likely already be saved in the JPEG file format. JPEG offers a high or low level of compression without sacrificing the quality of the image. Of course, it helps to start with a high quality image before optimizing a JPEG file. However, depending on the number of colors in that image, you might also want to consider saving it as a GIF 126 or GIF 256 file, especially if you need to save that image with a transparent color. The following steps show you how to select the JPEG file format.

1. Open a document that contains several image objects. Choose JPEG from the left pop-up menu in the Optimize panel.

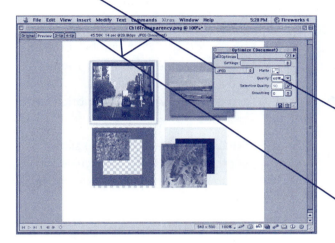

2. Click on the Preview, 2-Up, or 4-Up tab in the document window. Wait for Fireworks to create the preview image of the document.

3. Type a lower number in the Quality text box. This setting usually removes some image information from the file to create a lower-quality image.

4. View the file size and download time at the top of the document window.

Choosing a Compression Format

The key to reducing a file's size is to apply a compression algorithm. GIF, JPEG, and PNG all use a unique way of compressing image information. In general, compressing a file means that some information about that file is being removed. This may or may not affect the image quality of a file.

For example, you can reduce the number of colors available to a GIF file. Fireworks will try to remap any removed colors to the next closest color remaining in the newly defined color palette. However, the resulting picture may no longer be recognizable. The following sections provide a brief overview about how each file format works with its own special blend of compression.

GIF

GIF compression is ideal for solid-colored area images and graphics or images with transparency settings. You can adjust the color palette, number of colors, and loss and transparency settings for a GIF file. All these settings combined affect the way the final image is compressed.

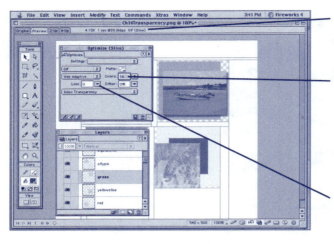

- **Size**. Choose a preview pane and view the file size for different color palettes and different numbers of colors.

- **Colors**. Type a number in the Colors text box to view the number of colors available to the document. Then, preview the file size and download times to see whether you notice any changes.

- **Quality**. Click and drag the slider control to adjust the Loss value for the image objects in the document.

JPEG

As mentioned in Chapter 8, a color table is not part of the JPEG specification, so you won't see one if you're working with a JPEG file in Fireworks. However, JPEG files probably provide the best loading time for photos and other complex image files due to this file format's ability to compress a file to a considerably small size. That's probably why almost all digital cameras use this file format to store image files.

The JPEG file format supports two different kinds of compression: lossless and lossy (pronounced loss-ee). Lossless compression reduces the file size without discarding any image information. The resulting file size might not be as small

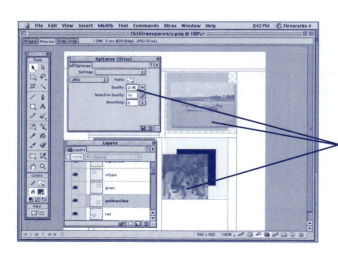

as a JPEG file created with lossy compression. However, the image quality will remain in a file saved with lossless compression. When you click and drag the Quality slider control, you are adjusting the lossy compression level for the selected slice or document.

- **Quality**. View the document in the preview pane to see whether the optimization settings downgrade the image quality.

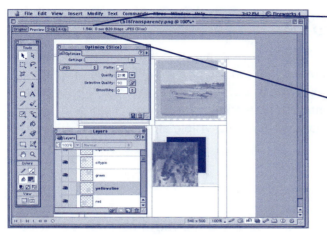

- **Size**. View the overall size of the document at the top of the document window (or the bottom-left area of a pane).

- **Performance**. View the download time for the document or selected slice. Try to keep the download time on the shorter side of a minute, unless you're sure that all your Web site visitors will be accessing your Web site with a broadband connection.

PNG

Choose between 8-, 24-, or 32-bit PNG file formats in the Export Preview window. Although PNG files are noticeably larger than GIF or JPEG images, they also provide the most dynamic support for Web graphics.

- **Size**. View the overall size of the document in the Export Preview window.

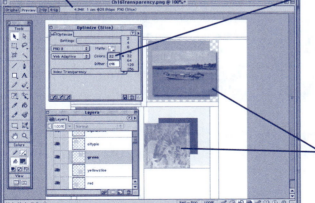

- **Colors**. The number of colors available to the document is displayed at the top of the Export Preview window, and can be changed in the Colors text box in the Optimize panel.

- **Interactivity**. Interactive behaviors, symbols, and instances are all stored in a PNG file.

- **Quality**. PNG files probably provide the best image quality of all three file formats supported by Fireworks.

- **Editability**. Continue to edit and update your Web graphics by always saving the final version of a Web page as a PNG file, or native Fireworks file.

Comparing Images

In some cases, a Web page won't require any optimization. For example, if you're creating a photo album for a Web site, you can use existing JPEG files to create individual Web pages and save each one as a JPEG file in Fireworks. You can view several different file formats along with different combinations of color and quality settings to see whether the changes will have any visible effect on the Web page.

Reducing Quality

You can reduce the quality of an image in several ways. The easiest way is to select a file format that supports fewer colors than the original graphic. Another way is to remove colors from the image. The following steps show you how to reduce the number of colors in a GIF and JPEG file.

1. Open a document that contains several image objects. Choose the 4-Up tab from the document window. Then, select the top-right pane. In this example, I selected a slice from the top-left pane.

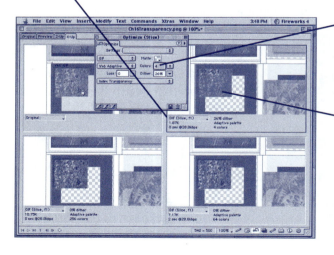

2. Choose GIF from the left pop-up menu in the Optimize panel. Then, type a number in the Colors text box. In this example, I typed the number 4.

3. Preview the resulting image in the right pane.

4. Select the lower-left pane in the 4-Up window.

5. Choose JPEG from the left pop-up menu in the Optimize panel.

6. Type a low number in the Quality text box. In this example, I typed 31.

7. Preview the low-resolution image in the preview pane. Compare it with its original image in the top-left pane.

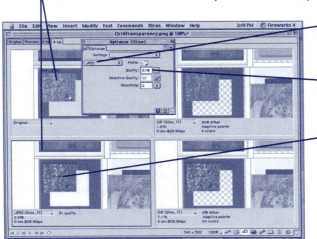

Reducing Size

One way to see how small you can make a graphic object is to choose a file format that generates the smallest possible file size. Preview changes as you make them, and compare the original with the smallest possible file to see whether you can tell any difference. The following steps show you how to reduce the file size for a GIF and JPEG file.

1. Select an object in the document window. Choose the 4-Up tab in the document window. Then, click on the lower-left pane.

2. Choose GIF from the left pop-up menu in the Optimize panel. Then, type a fairly low number of colors in the Colors text box.

3. Preview the file size in the lower-left corner of the preview pane.

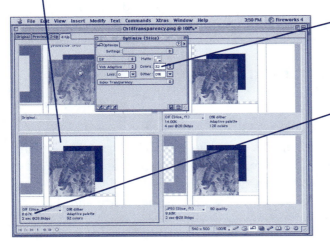

4. Select the lower-right pane of the 4-Up window.

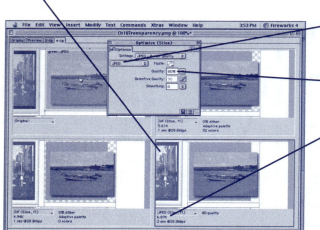

5. Choose JPEG from the left pop-up menu in the Optimize panel.

6. Click and drag the slider control to change the quality of the JPEG image.

7. View the file size in the lower-left corner of the preview pane. You might want to select a Quality setting that creates the same file size as the GIF image to compare the quality of the two images.

Choosing Colors

One of the last things to do before exporting a Web page is to choose the final color palette. There are a few things to keep in mind when choosing a color palette. Do you want a custom palette for a Windows- or Mac-specific computer, or is it better to optimize a color palette regardless of the computer platform that views the page? The following sections show you how to view, adjust, and preview colors in the Export Preview window.

Viewing Color Information in the Export Preview Window

You can choose from several types of color palettes in Fireworks. From the Optimize panel, choose from Adaptive, Web Adaptive, Web 216, Exact, Macintosh, Windows, Grayscale, Black & White, Uniform, or Custom palettes. Select different color palettes and compare the resulting images to optimize the colors for a document. The following steps show you how to select a color palette and view some of the settings you can change in the Export Preview window.

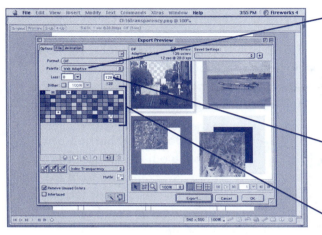

1. Open a document containing several image objects, then choose the Export Preview command from the File menu. Choose a file format and a color palette (if applicable) from the Options tab in the Export Preview window.

2. View the number of colors assigned to the image and compare it with the number of colors in the color table.

3. View the colors for the document in the color table. The small icon that appears in some color squares indicates that a setting from the tools located at the bottom of the color table has been applied to that particular color.

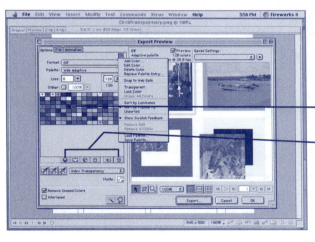

4. Select a color in the color table.

5. Set the color's transparency, snap its color to the nearest Web safe color, lock it, or delete it from the color table.

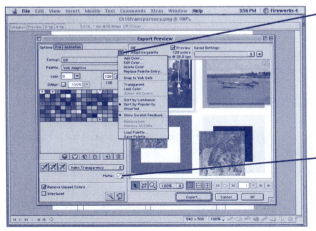

6. Click on the arrow button to view a list of menu commands, similar to the menu list for the Color Table panel. Select a menu command if you want to change the setting for a selected color, or if you want to re-sort or rebuild the color table.

7. View the matte color for the document in the Matte color well.

Previewing Colors for the Optimized Image

You can also preview a document in 2-Up or 4-Up modes in the Export Preview window. The Preview, 2-Up, and 4-Up buttons are located at the bottom of the Export Preview window, just above the Export button. The following steps show you how to preview two different file formats.

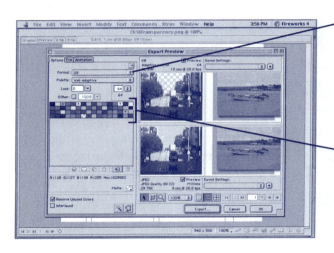

1. Open a document that contains several image objects. Then, select the Export Preview command from the File menu. Click on the Options tab and select the GIF file format from the Format pop-up menu.

2. View the number of colors for the document. Preview the image in the right pane of the Export Preview window.

3. Choose the 4-Up mode button located at the bottom of the Export Preview window. Click on the top-left preview pane and then select JPEG from the Format pop-up menu.

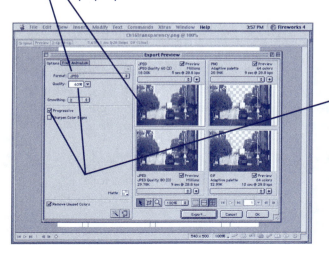

4. Type a different value in the Quality text box to compare the JPEG image to the GIF or PNG file. Check the Progressive check box if you want the JPEG file to load along with the rest of the Web page. The browser will progressively draw the JPEG as it loads in the browser window.

16

Exploring Automation and Updating Projects

Each task you perform in a Fireworks document is logged in the History panel. You can then use the History panel to select and replay steps, or to activate or even add more steps to a command. The Find and Replace panel and batch processing are other automation tools discussed in this overview of automating Fireworks.

In this chapter you'll learn how to:

- Automate tasks in the History panel
- Create JavaScript commands
- Use the Batch Process command
- Update files using the Find and Replace panel

Viewing Automation Panels

Use panels to automate repetitive tasks such as changing colors or text. The following sections show you how to use the History, Library, and Behaviors panels to automate tasks.

Navigating the History Panel

You can view, edit, or replay a task recorded in the History panel. However, the History panel only lists tasks completed while the document is open. When the document is closed, the History panel is cleared of data.

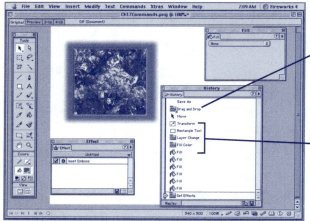

- **Tasks**. Effects, fills, stroke changes, and any tasks that can be "undone" are logged in the History panel. Click on any task in the History panel and click on Replay to repeat the task.

- **Commands**. Select multiple tasks in the History panel to create a custom command. View the commands you create in the Command menu.

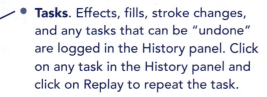

Using the Behaviors Panel

You can attach behaviors to objects in Fireworks. Click the Plus button to view behavior options in the Behaviors panel. Behaviors are created with JavaScript code.

- **Rollovers**. Add an object, symbol, hotspot, or slice and assign a rollover behavior to the graphic object.

- **Behaviors**. Create one or more behaviors for an object. Add or remove one or more rollovers to a symbol or instance on a Web page.

Using the Library Panel

Use the tools in the Library panel to add a button or graphic to a Web page. The Library panel works with the Button Editor window. (For more information on automating and making buttons, refer to the "Automating Button Creation" section later in this chapter or read Chapter 12.) Use the Library panel with the History panel to automate creation of buttons or image maps.

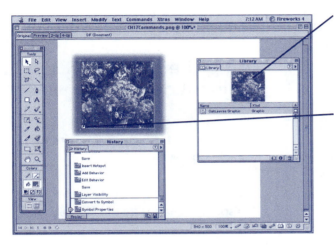

- **Symbol**. Drag a symbol stored in the Library panel to the document window. When the symbol is edited, any of its instances are also automatically updated.

- **Instance**. A small arrow in the lower-left corner of a selected object indicates that it is an instance of a symbol located in the Library panel.

Using the Find and Replace Panel

If you don't remember each color, URL, or line of text in a Web page, use the Find and Replace panel to locate and change items in the current document or across files. Click on the Options pop-up menu in the Find and Replace panel to assign backup behaviors to the Replace feature.

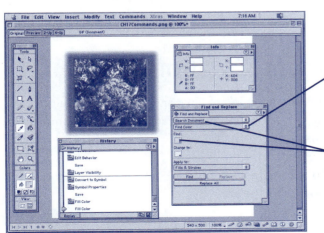

1. Click the second pop-up menu in the Find and Replace panel to select the item for which you want to search.

2. Fine-tune your search criteria by selecting the area in which you want to search from the first pop-up menu. In this example, I chose a color by typing its hexadecimal value in the color well.

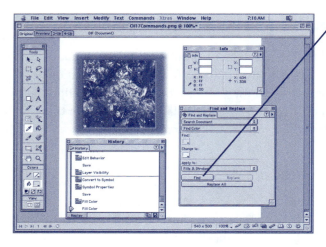

3. Click on Find. If any items are found, click on Replace or Replace All to apply the change.

4. After all the items have been changed, save your document.

Using the Project Log Panel

You can view a list of project files and the last date a file was updated in the Project Log panel.

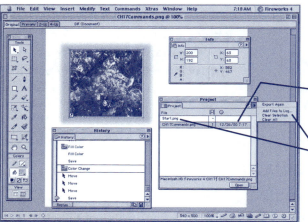

- **Last update**. The Project Log panel displays the last date the file was modified.

- **Project files**. Add one or several project files to the Project Log panel. Use the Project Log panel to identify any files that might have changed since the previous session.

Automating Element Creation

Buttons are as commonplace on Web pages as are links and anchors. If you plan to create several instances of the same button, you might want to create a command to help automate creating buttons.

You can also create commands to automate slice, hotspot, and pop-up menu creation. The following sections show you how.

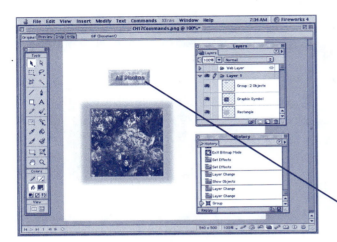

Automating Button Creation

Use the Library and Behaviors panels to help automate button creation. Each task used to create a button is logged in the History panel. The following steps show you how to create a command that adds a new copy of a button to the document window.

1. Create a button symbol and drag its instance to the document window.

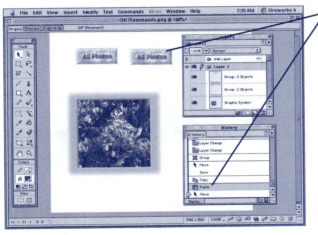

2. Select the button instance and then choose the Copy command from the Edit menu. The task will be recorded in the History panel. In this example, I've selected the Paste task in the History panel.

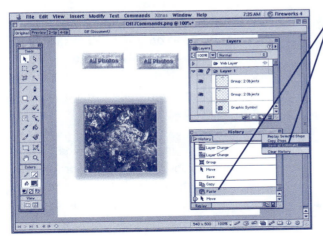

3. Select the Paste task from the History panel. Then, choose Save as Command from the panel's pop-up menu.

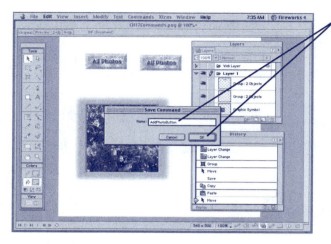

4. Type a name for the command in the Name text box. Then, click on the OK button.

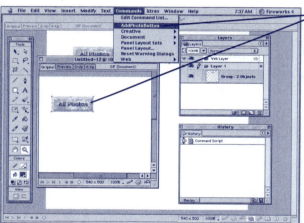

5. Select the command you just created from the Commands menu. A new copy of the button instance will appear in the document window.

Automating Slice Creation

Fireworks includes several image maps and buttons for navigation bars, making it easy to add navigation controls to a Web page. You might want to automate creating slices if you regularly create Web pages that will require slices, or if you're working on a large Web site that will use slices. The following steps show you how to use the History panel to create a command that inserts a slice into an image object.

1. Create an image object in the document window. Select the graphic object and then choose the Slice command from the Insert menu. A slice will appear over the selected graphic.

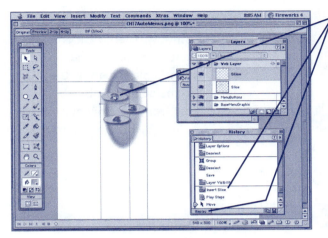

2. Select a second object in the document window. Then, click on the Insert Slice command in the History panel. Click on Replay to run the command.

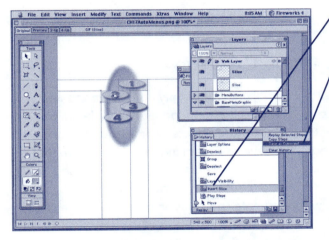

3. Click on the Insert Slice command in the History panel.

4. Choose the Save as Command item from the pop-up menu. Type a name for this command. Then, click on the OK button. The new command will appear in the Commands menu.

Automating Hotspot Creation

You can choose the Hotspot Tool in the toolbar, or develop a command to automate hotspot creation. The following steps show you how to use the History panel to create a command to insert a hotspot into an image object.

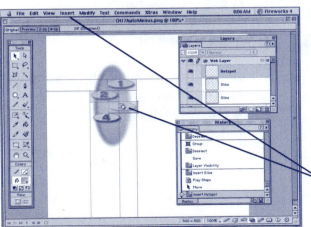

1. Select a third image object and then choose Insert Hotspot from the Insert menu.

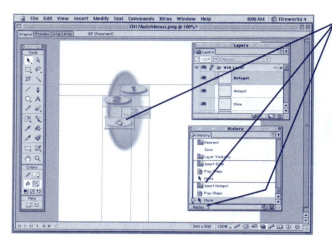

2. Choose a fourth image object in the document window. Then, click on the Insert Hotspot command in the History panel. Click on Replay to apply the command to the selected object. Repeat Step 4 from the previous section to create an Insert Hotspot command, if you want.

Automating Pop-Up Menu Creation

You've seen how easy it is to create a command. You simply hold down the Shift key and click on more than one command in the History panel, then select a new object and click on the Replay button to see if the selected commands perform the task you want. Then, you choose the Save as Command menu item from the pop-up menu in the History panel. As long as the selected steps are located between any divider lines in the History panel, you can create a command. The following steps show you how to automate the creation of a pop-up menu.

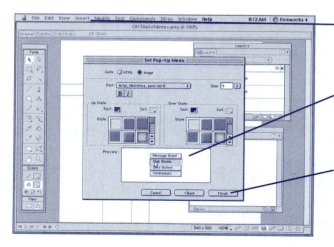

1. Select a slice covering a button symbol. Choose Insert Pop-up Menu from the Insert menu.

2. Type the menu items for the pop-up menu and then preview them in the Set Pop-Up Menu dialog box.

3. Click on Finish to save your changes.

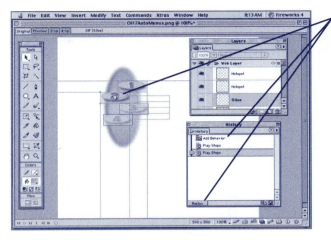

4. Select another button symbol slice and then select the Add Behavior command from the History panel. Then, click on the Replay button.

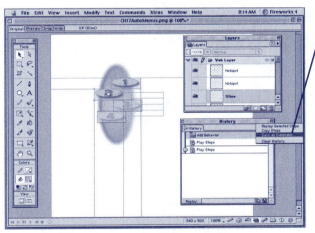

5. View the tasks in the History panel. Select the steps and choose Save as Command.

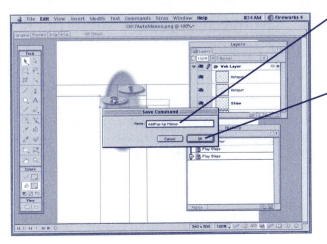

6. Type a name for the command in the Name text box of the Save Command dialog box.

7. Click on the OK button. The command will be created!

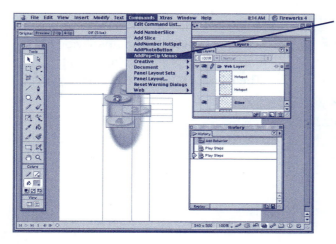

8. Click on the Commands menu to view the new command in the menu list.

Automating Tasks with the Find and Replace Panel

You can combine the power of the Find and Replace panel with the steps recorded in the History panel, and you can automate repetitive tasks using the search and replace feature.

Editing Objects with the Find and Replace Panel

As mentioned before, there are several different types of Web graphic elements for which you can search and replace in Fireworks. You can search for plain text, or for a specific font, font style, or font size. The following sections show you the diverse range of text settings you can search and replace in Fireworks.

Changing Text

Any vector text created with the Text Editor window can be searched for and found with the Find and Replace panel. Choose Find Text and then type the text you want to locate and its replacement text. The following steps show you how to search for the number 1.

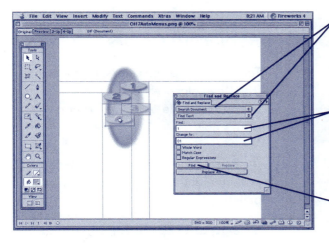

1. Click on the top pop-up menu in the Find and Replace panel to select the search criteria, then choose Find Text from the secondary pop-up menu.

2. Type the text for which you want to search in the Find text box. Then, type the replacement text in the Change To text box.

3. Click on the Find button to search the document or files. If a matching item is found, Fireworks will open the document and select the first matching item.

Updating or Replacing Fonts

You can also search for a wide range of font-related characteristics in one document or across several files. Select Find Font and select a font, style, and size to locate and replace.

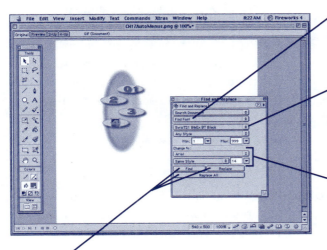

1. Choose Find Font from the secondary pop-up menu in the Find and Replace panel.

2. Click on the third pop-up menu and choose the font for which you want to search. Select a style or font size, too, if you want.

3. Enter the replacement font criteria in the Change To pop-up menus located at the bottom of the Find and Replace panel.

4. Click on Find, Replace, or Replace All to start the search.

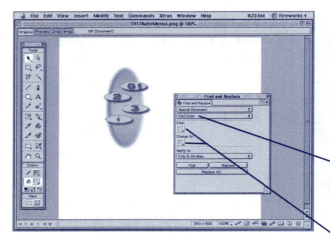

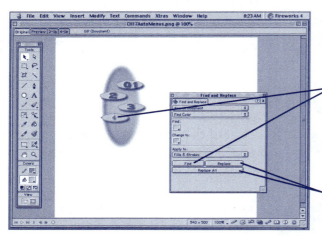

Finding and Replacing Colors

To find and replace colors, pick a color from the color well. Search and replace colors in one file or across several files. Here's how:

1. Select Find Color from the second pop-up menu in the Find and Replace panel.

2. Select a color for which you want to search from the Find color well. Then, pick the color to which you want to change it from the Change To color well.

3. Click on Find to search the document or files for the selected color. If a matching color is found, the matching item will be highlighted in the document window.

4. Click on Replace to change the selected color to the new color. Choose Replace All if you want to change all instances of the search item based on the search criteria defined by the first pop-up menu in the Find and Replace panel.

Searching for URLs

You can also search and replace URLs in Fireworks. Simply open the Find and Replace panel and type a URL you want to update. You can also search for a particular word in a URL. The following steps show you how.

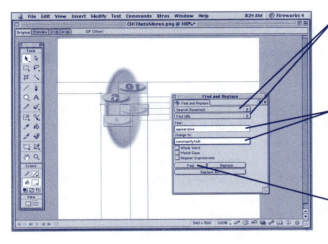

1. Click on the top pop-up menu in the Find and Replace panel to select the search criteria, then choose Find URL from the secondary pop-up menu.

2. Type the text for which you want to search in the Find text box. Then, type the replacement text in the Change To text box.

3. Click on the Find button to search the document or files. If a matching item is found, Fireworks will open the document and select the first matching item. Click on the Replace or Replace All buttons to update the matching items.

Non-Web 216

It's simple to search and replace colors that are not in the Web 216-color palette. Here's how:

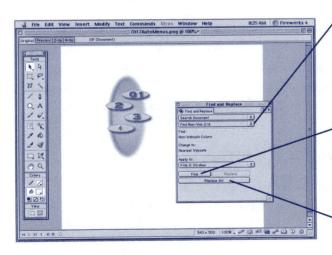

1. Click on the top pop-up menu in the Find and Replace panel to select the search criteria. Then, choose Find Non-Web 216 from the secondary pop-up menu.

2. Click on the Find button to search the document or files. If a matching item is found, Fireworks will open the document and select the first matching item.

3. Click on Replace All to update the colors.

Editing Web Pages

You can use the Find and Replace panel to edit multiple Web pages. You can even replace all occurrences of a found item in several files. Here's how:

1. From the top pop-up menu in the Find and Replace panel, select the files you want to search. Choose one of the following commands from the pop-up menu:

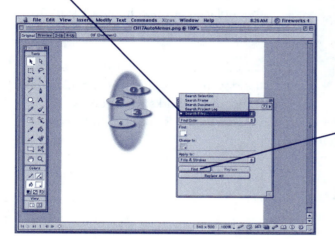

Search Selection, Search Frame, Search Document, Search Project Log, or Search Files. If you choose the Search Files command, hold down the Shift key and then select the files you want to include in the search.

2. Select the rest of the search criteria in the Find and Replace panel. Click on the Find button to see if any items in the selected files match the search criteria. Then, choose the replace settings for the matched items.

Working with Batch Processing

In addition to using panels, you can use the batch processing options to automate tasks. Fireworks is also Apple-scriptable. If you're familiar with JavaScript, you can write JavaScript scripts to control Fireworks within Dreamweaver 4.

Running a Batch Process Command

Turn any command into a batch process by replaying steps selected in the History panel. The following steps show you how to run the Add Pop-ups command as a batch process.

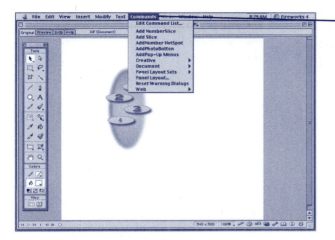

1. Click on the Commands menu to view a list of commands installed with Fireworks.

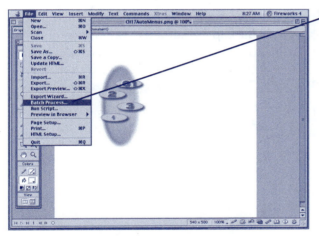

2. Choose the Batch Process menu command from the File menu.

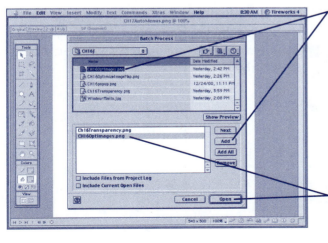

3. Select a file from the top window list in the Batch Process dialog box and then click on Add.

4. Pick a file from the bottom window list and then click on Open.

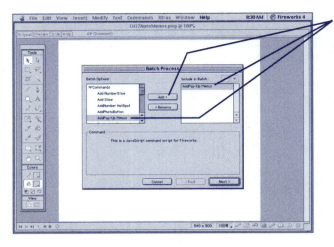

5. Select a command from the left window list and click on Add. The selected command will appear in the right window list. Click on Next.

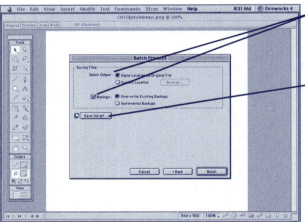

6. Choose the Batch Output and Backup file settings from the second page of the Batch Process window.

7. Click on Save Script to save the batch process criteria as a JavaScript file.

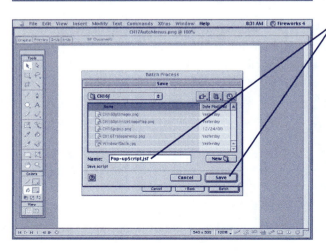

8. In the Save dialog box, type a name for the file in the Name text box, then click on Save. Fireworks will return to the Batch Process window.

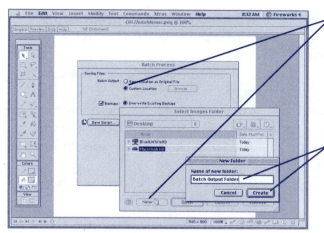

9. Click on the Custom Location button in the Saving Files, Batch Output section of the dialog box. If you need to create a new folder for the batch output, click on the New Folder button in the Select Images Folder dialog box.

10. Type a name for the folder in the New Folder dialog box and then click on Create.

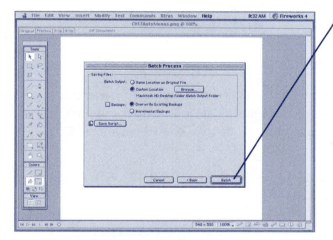

11. Click on Batch to run the batch process.

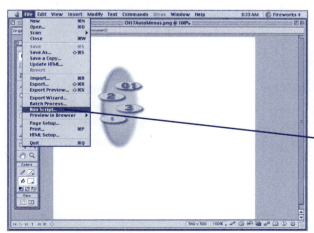

Running a Script

When you save a batch process command as JavaScript, you can run it by choosing the Run Script command from the File menu. Here's how:

1. Choose the Run Script command from the File menu.

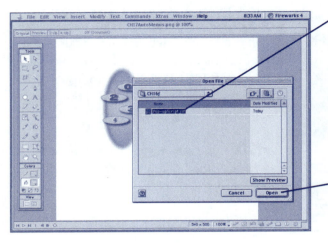

2. Select the JavaScript file for the batch command you want to run. You can also choose a file that has the JSF extension in its file name. For example, open the Commands folder in the Configuration folder of the Fireworks application folder. Each command is a JavaScript file stored on your hard drive.

3. Click on Open to run the selected script.

Updating a Project

Batch processing can be a great automation tool for making broad, general changes in a document or across a project. To create more detailed changes in a project or to automate a task such as a font or color change, create a one-step command.

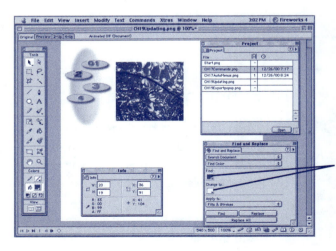

Finding and Replacing Colors

You can create a single command that replaces a particular color. Choose all or part of the task to create a command. Here's how:

1. Select the color you want to find from the pop-up menu in the Find and Replace panel. Then, select the color you want to use as a replacement color.

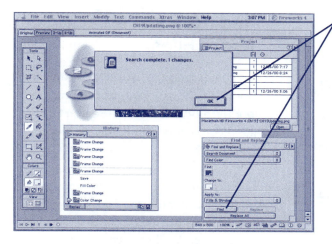

2. Click on Find. If any items are found, the Replace button will be enabled. Click on Replace or Replace All to complete the task.

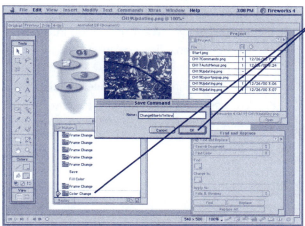

3. Click on a single step, or Ctrl/Command-click to select multiple individual steps, or Shift-click to select a group of steps that will comprise your command. Select Save as Command from the History Panel and type a name for the command in the Name text box. Then, click on the OK button to save the command.

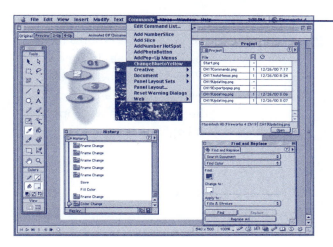

4. Select the Commands menu and view the new command in the menu list.

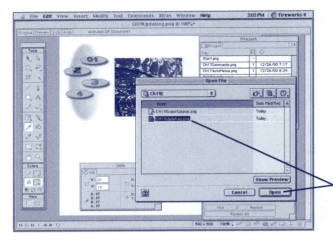

Finding and Replacing across Files

You can extend the search and replace capabilities to any Web documents on your hard drive using the Search Files menu command. The following steps show you how.

1. Click on a Search Files command from the pop-up menu in the Find Replace panel. Select the files you want to include in the search. A file selection window will open. Navigate your hard drive for the file or files you want to include in the search. Then, click on Open.

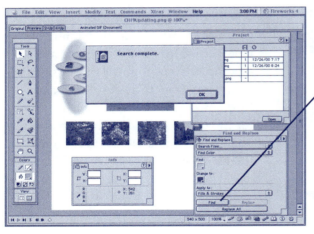

2. In the Find and Replace panel, choose the search criteria for the selected files and then click on Find.

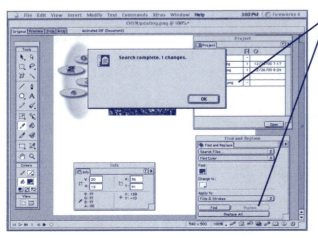

3. If you want to change the found item, click on the Replace button. Review the change in the document window. When you use the Find and Replace panel to modify an object, the name of the modified file will appear in the Project Log panel.

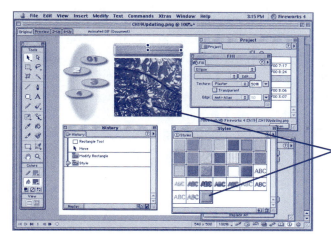

Changing Graphic and Text Styles

You can create a command to automate changes to a fill or stroke in either a graphic or text style. Here's how:

1. Apply a style to a selected object in the document window.

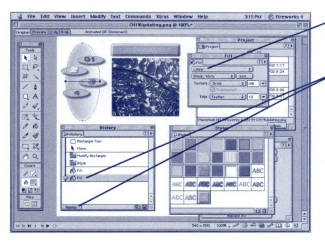

2. Choose the Fill panel and select a different fill for the object.

3. Go to the History panel and select the steps you want to automate. Click on Replay to rerun the steps on the same or a different object.

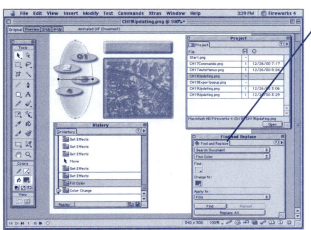

4. Use the Find and Replace panel to search for and replace a color in the selected object.

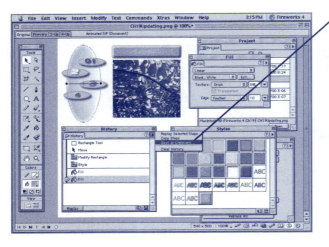

5. Choose the Save as Command from the History panel pop-up menu. Then, type a name for the command in the Save Document dialog box.

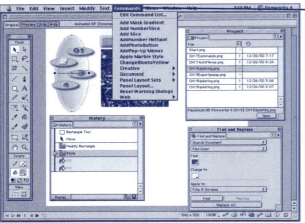

6. Click on the Commands menu and view the new command in the menu list.

Creating Commands for Live Effects

You can use the same effect to create a button or the base graphic for a nav bar. Consider automating settings with Live Effects when you first start a document or project. As you work, you can open the History panel and create commands for tasks you think you might eventually use again. If many of the images on a Web site share similar effects or settings for effects, it's probably a good idea to automate effect settings. The following steps show you how to turn a set effect task into a command.

1. Choose Effect from the Window menu or press Alt/Option + F7 to open the Effect panel.

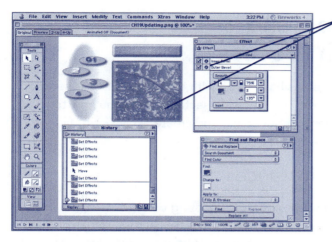

2. Double-click on the effect or choose the i button to view the settings for the effect. If desired, make any changes and then view the effect in the document window.

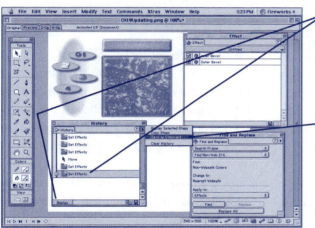

3. Choose a different image object that might use the same effect. Select the step in the History panel. Then, click on Replay to determine whether the selected steps change the effect settings.

4. If the effect is applied correctly and you want to save it as a command, choose Save as Command from the History panel's pop-up menu.

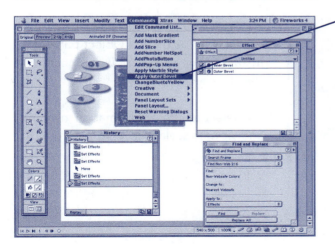

5. Click on the Commands menu and view the new command in the menu list.

Updating Symbols and Creating a Batch Process

What do symbols and batch processes have to do with each other? In this section, both are associated with commands. The following sections show you how to create commands for an animation symbol object and create a JavaScript file for a batch process.

Changing Animation Instances

A tedious task, perhaps more cumbersome than updating colors or text, is updating animation. Edit instances and run batch processes across frames or files to quickly update object elements in an animation.

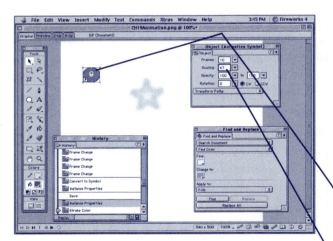

Instances are representations of symbols, which are created and stored in the Library panel. Edit an instance by editing its symbol. The following steps show you how to automate changing the scaling value in an animation symbol.

1. Open the Object panel. Then, select an animation instance in the document window.

2. Type a new scaling value in the Scaling text box in the Object panel. An Instance Properties task will appear in the History panel.

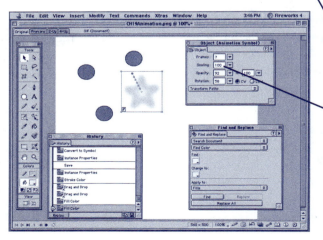

3. Select a different animation instance and view its scaling setting.

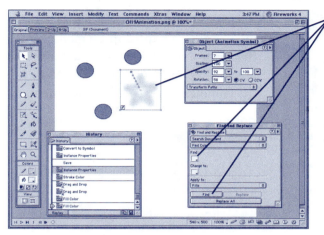

4. Open the Find and Replace Panel. Click in the color well and select a color for which you want to search. In this example, I've selected the color in one of the animation instances. Click on Find. The matching color will be found in the animation object.

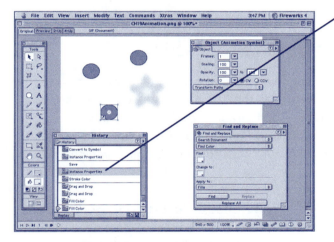

5. Click on the Instance Properties task created in Step 2.

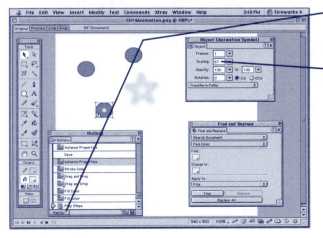

6. Select a new instance and click on Replay in the History panel.

The Object panel will display the newer Scaling setting.

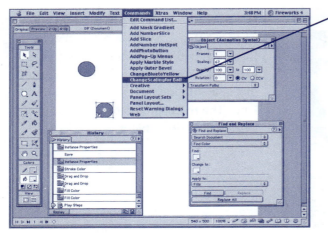

7. Choose the Save as Command menu item from the pop-up menu in the History panel. Type a name for the command and then click on OK. View the command in the Commands menu.

Saving Commands as Batch Processes

Fireworks has a few batch process commands that are preinstalled with the application. These commands are located in the Commands menu and are stored in the Command folder, located in the Configurations folder of the Fireworks application folder. Use the Batch a Command feature to turn a command into a batch process. The following steps show you how to save a single command as a batch process. However, you can select several commands, too.

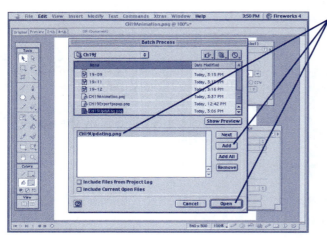

1. Choose the Batch Process command from the File menu. Select a file from the top window list in the Batch Process dialog box. Then, click on Add and click on Open.

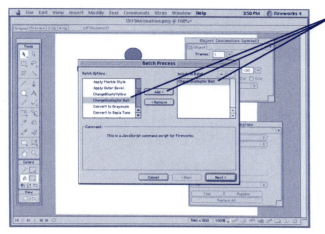

2. Choose a command from the Batch Options window list and click on Add. The selected command will appear in the Include in Batch window list. Click on Next.

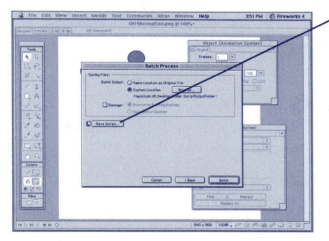

3. Click on Save Script.

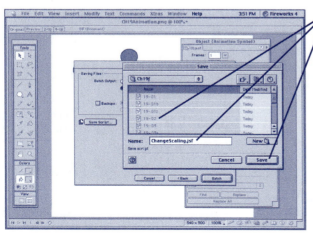

4. In the Save dialog box, type a name for the file in the Name text box. Navigate to a location where you want to store the file on your hard drive. Then, click on Save.

PART IV

Combining Web Graphics with Web Pages

The final phase of turning Fireworks Web graphics into a full-fledged Web page involves adding the final HTML code and JavaScript touches using an HTML editor. You can edit HTML code with a simple text editor such as Window's Notepad or the Mac's SimpleText. However, because Macromedia created both Fireworks and Dreamweaver, these appli-cations provide a level of integration to Fireworks Web page design. The examples in this section of the book specifically use Dreamweaver 4 with Firework 4.

17

Exporting Fireworks Files

Create a master copy of your Fireworks document by saving it as a PNG file. The PNG file format allows you to continue to edit those image objects after you export any optimized files and HTML code to be incorporated and uploaded to a Web server. When you save a document as a PNG file, Fireworks elements, such as layers, frames, and symbols, remain editable.

Fireworks enables you to export all or part of a document in a variety of file formats. For example, you can export a document as a Dreamweaver Library, CSS Layers (.htm), or Director (.htm) file. Or, you can export layers or frames to files. Fireworks also enables you to export Macromedia Flash (.swf), Adobe Illustrator 7 (.ai), Lotus Domino Designer, or Photoshop (.psd) file formats, in addition to any of the file formats that are available in the Optimize panel. You can also customize HTML code for Dreamweaver, FrontPage, or GoLive in the Export window. You can export HTML code independent of an image, or vice verse. In this chapter you'll learn how to:

- ● Use the Export Area Tool
- ● Export GIF, JPEG, and other kinds of image files
- ● Use the Export Wizard
- ● Export symbols and buttons

Exporting Pieces of a Web Page

Fireworks makes it easy to export a completed Fireworks document. You can choose either the Export command or the Export Preview command from the File menu. Fireworks enables you to export images and HTML, or only one of the two, in addition to giving you several other options. The following sections show you how to export an area or path from a Fireworks document.

Exporting an Area

Choose the Export Area Tool from the toolbox or press the J key on the keyboard. The Export Area Tool shares the same toolbox square as the Pointer Tool.

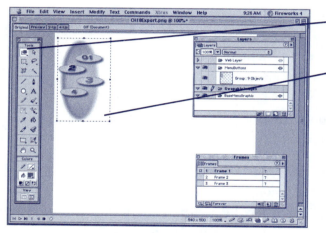

1. Select the Export Area Tool (J) from the toolbox.

2. Click and drag the cursor in an area of the document window that you want to export. Double-click inside the selected area to access the Export Preview window, and export the selected area of the document. Alternatively, you can choose the Export Preview command from the File menu.

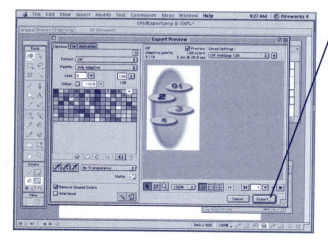

3. Preview the selected area in the Export Preview window. Click on the Export button to save the selected area as an image file.

Exporting Paths

Paths can be exported as vector objects. If you prefer to work with a custom set of vector drawing tools in another application, such as Adobe Illustrator, you can export a path from Fireworks, edit it in Illustrator, save it in Illustrator, and then import or open it in Fireworks. The following steps show you how to export an Illustrator file from Fireworks.

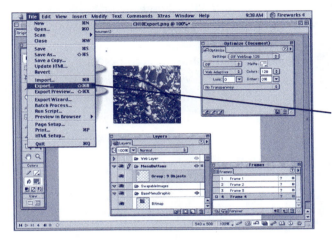

1. Click on a path in the document window. Select the Export command from the File menu.

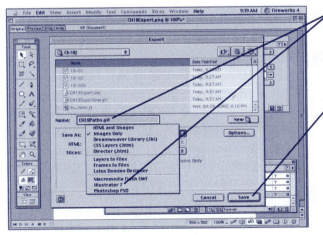

2. Choose Illustrator 7 from the Save As pop-up menu in the Export dialog box. Then, type a name for the file in the Name text box.

3. Click on Save.

Exporting Objects from Fireworks

If you are using Photoshop to create Web graphics, an image file might contain layers and masks, which you might also want to edit in Fireworks. To do this, you must save that file as a native Photoshop file, which is a PSD (Photoshop Document) file. Fireworks 4 enables you to import native Photoshop files, preserving layers and masks. This section shows you how to export different kinds of objects from Fireworks.

Exporting Mask Objects

Save a masked object as a native Photoshop file in the Export dialog box in Fireworks. If you want to share a mask with a Photoshop user, or if you use both applications to design Web graphics, the export settings might come in handy. The following steps show you how to export a Fireworks mask as a Photoshop file.

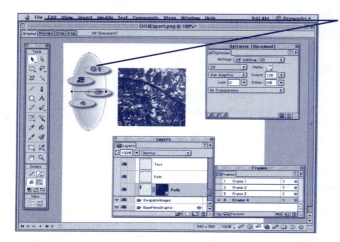

1. Select the masked object in the document window. Then, choose the Export command from the File menu.

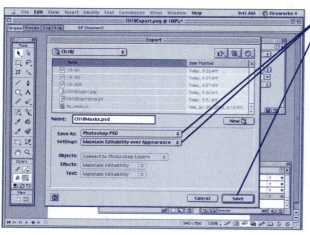

2. Click on the Save As pop-up menu in the Export dialog box and choose Photoshop PSD. Then, review the menu list in the Settings pop-up menu and choose a setting for the Photoshop file. In this example, I chose Maintain Editability over Appearance. Click on Save.

Exporting Slices

You can also export a single slice from a Fireworks document. The check box you need to check to export a single slice is located in the Export dialog box.

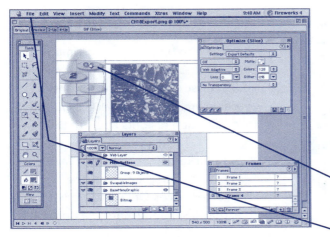

Alternatively, you can copy and paste an object to move it from one application to another. After you choose the Selected Slices Only check box in the Export dialog box, Fireworks will export the image covered by the selected slice in the document window. The following steps show you how to export a selected slice.

1. Select a slice object in the document window.

2. Select the Export command from the File menu.

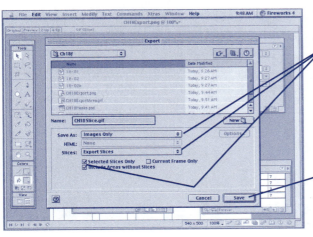

3. Choose Images only from the Save As pop-up menu. Then, select Export Slices from the Slices pop-up menu. Finally (this one's important!), make sure that the Selected Slices Only check box is selected.

4. Click on Save to export the slice.

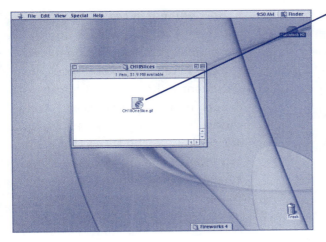

Fireworks will save the selected slice to its own file on your hard drive.

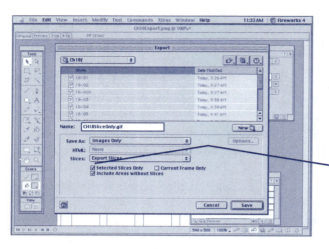

Slice Export Options

Use a slice to break up a large image map and help load a big image more quickly in your browser. Several slice options are available in the Export dialog box. The following list highlights a few of them.

- **Single slice**. Choose Export from the File menu and then check the Selected Slices Only check box to export a single slice from a document.

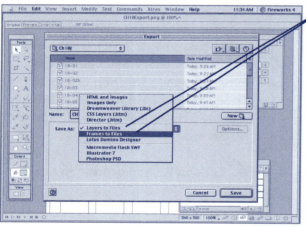

- **Layers or frames to files**. Export each frame or layer to separate files by choosing the Frames to Files or Layers to Files menu option from the Save As pop-up menu.

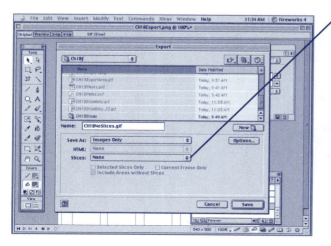

- **Export without slices**. If you decide you don't want to use slices or are just curious about comparing folder sizes of a Web site, export the document without slices. Choose Export from the File menu and then choose None from the Slices pop-up menu. However, be aware that if you export a document without its slices, it might be more difficult to reassemble in Web editor.

Exporting Images

Select an image, then optimize and preview it before exporting it to another Web application. The Export Preview window enables you to access all the same optimization controls that are located in the Optimize panel. But wait there's more; you can also optimize for file size, access the Export Wizard, or optimize each frame of animation from the Export Preview window. The following steps show you how to open the Export Preview window and export a file.

1. Select Export Preview from the File menu. Choose a file format from the Format pop-up menu of the Export Preview window.

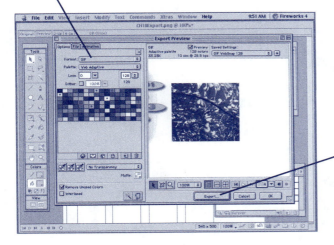

- **GIF**. Choose a GIF file format from the Format pop-up menu.

- **JPEG**. Choose a JPEG format to compare preview information.

- **PNG**. Notice the increase in file size if you select a PNG format.

2. Click on Export.

Exporting a Specific File Size

You can access the Export Preview window in several ways. The most obvious is to use the menu command in the File menu. However, you can also double-click on an area that was selected using the Export Area Tool, or choose any other Export menu.

1. Select Export Preview from the File menu.

2. Click on the Optimize to Size Wizard button.

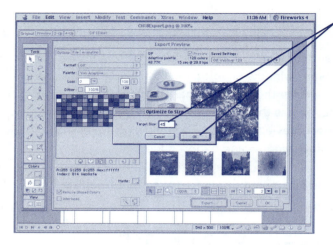

3. Type a number in the Target Size field in the Optimize to Size dialog box. Then, click on the OK button.

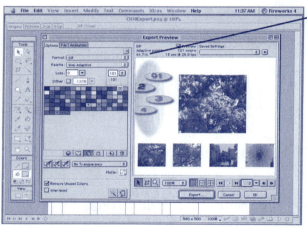

4. View the adjusted image and its file size in the Export Preview window.

Using the Export Wizard

The Export Wizard takes you step by step through the export process. Depending on what you want to export, the Wizard will analyze your selections and recommend export settings. You can access the Export Wizard command from the File menu, or by clicking on the Magic Wand icon in the Export Preview window. The following sections show you how to work with the Export Wizard.

Choosing an Export Format

If you're not sure how to export Web graphics, use the built-in Export Wizard to analyze and recommend export settings for selected items or an entire page. However, depending on the first selections you make in the Export Wizard, the following pages will change. The options shown in the steps in this section might not be available for all export options with this wizard. The following steps show you how to choose the first export format options in the Export Wizard.

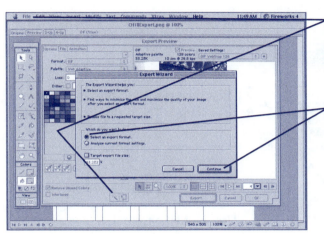

1. Choose the Export Wizard menu command from the File menu, or click on the Magic Wand icon at the bottom of the Export Preview window.

2. Click on a radio button in the first window of the Export Wizard. I've chosen Select an Export Format. Click on Continue to proceed.

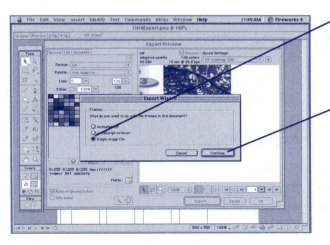

3. Three radio buttons appear in the second screen. Choose either Animated GIF, JavaScript Rollover, or Single Image File. I chose Single Image File.

4. Click on Continue.

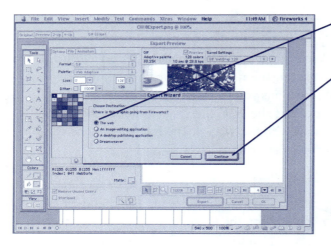

5. Choose a destination for the image file. In this example, I chose The Web.

6. Click on Continue.

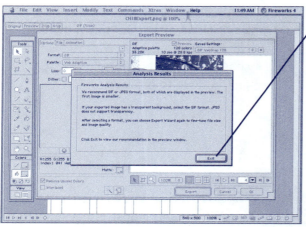

7. Read the results in the Analysis Results screen. Then, click on Exit.

NOTE

The Export Wizard can recommend file formats for exporting images. Use the Magnify Tool to take a closer look at image quality of the actual data to be exported, to see how closely it matches what you see in the preview windows.

Choosing an Export Destination

You can preview different file formats before you export a document or file from Fireworks. Use 2-Up or 4-Up modes to preview several different export options in the Export Preview window. When you're ready to save the exported file, navigate your hard drive to locate a folder where you want to save your files. The following steps show you how to select a place on your hard drive to save the files being exported.

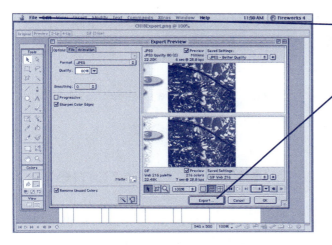

1. Choose the Export or Export Preview command from the File menu. Review the settings for the file.

2. Click on Export when you're ready to save the file.

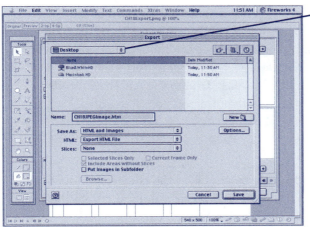

3. Choose Desktop from the pop-up menu located at the top of the Export dialog box. If you save your file to the desktop, it will be easily accessible and you won't have to remember a long path name to locate the file.

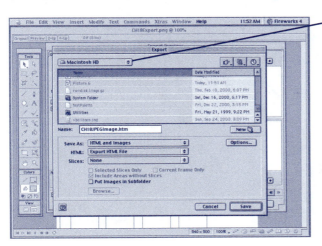

4. Select the root level of the hard drive if you don't want to clutter your desktop.

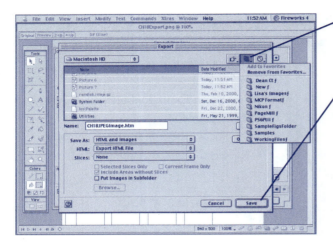

5. Click on the Favorites button if you've previously created a bookmark to a favorite folder.

6. Click on Save to save the file to your hard drive.

Exporting Frames

If you've designed an animation or created two or more frames within a Fireworks document, you can export each frame to a separate file. Similarly, if a document contains two or more layers, you can export each layer to a separate file. If you're familiar with HTML, you might want to export each layer as a Cascading Style Sheet. Although Fireworks layers are not the same as CSS layers in Dreamweaver, you can export each layer in Fireworks so that it can be used as a CSS layer in Dreamweaver. The following sections show you how to export one or several frames from Fireworks.

Exporting Frames to Files

Export a single frame or all frames to a file by choosing the corresponding export setting in the Export panel. If the pop-up menu does not seem to create the results you want, try using the Export Wizard.

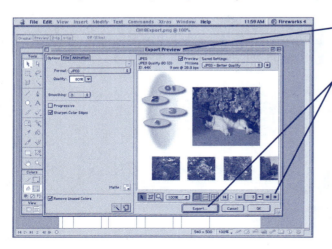

1. From the File menu, choose the Export Preview menu command.

2. Click on the step forward button to view each frame in the document. Then, click on Export.

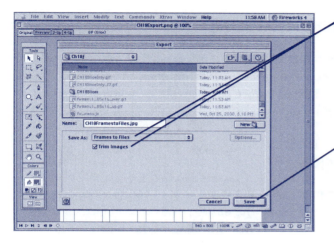

3. Select Frames to Files from the Save As pop-up menu to export the selected frame from the document. Select the Trim Images check box to format exported images to fit the objects on each frame.

4. Click on Save to save the files to your hard drive.

Exporting a Single Frame

If you've created a Fireworks document that contains more than one frame, you might only want to save the contents of a single frame as a separate file. Fireworks provides a check box in the Export dialog box, enabling you to only export the currently selected frame, which will be displayed in the document window. The following steps show you how to select this option in the Export dialog box.

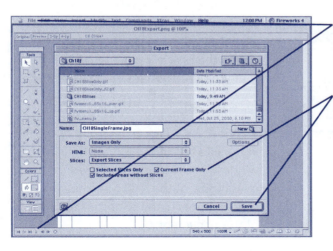

1. Select a frame you want to export from the Frames panel. Then, choose Export from the File menu.

2. Check the Current Frame Only check box in the Export dialog box. Click on Save to save the frame to a file.

Optimizing during Export

Although it's more efficient to optimize graphics before exporting, you can preview a page and any frames in the Export Preview window. This enables you to determine whether any settings should be adjusted before exporting. The following sections show you how to optimize a document, a specific file format, and an animation.

Optimizing Web Pages

You can optimize a Web page in many different ways, even if you're working with the settings in the Export Preview window. The easier pages to optimize are the ones with few image objects, or many objects with many similar colors. It's more difficult to choose precise optimization settings if there are several sophisticated photos or a rainbow of colors distributed around the document. The following steps are actually a brief list of things you can do to optimize a Web page.

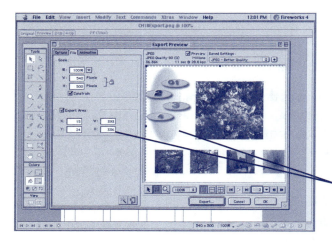

1. Click on the File tab in the Export Preview window and adjust the canvas area that will be exported. Check the file size in the preview pane to make sure that your changes are being executed correctly.

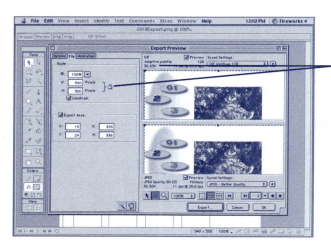

2. View the exact dimensions of the file in the File tab of the Export Preview window. You might want to reduce the overall size of the file to see how this change impacts the exported file size of the document.

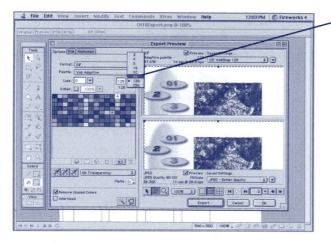

3. If you're working with a Web page that doesn't contain pictures, you might want to select a smaller set of colors for the color palette in the Options tab. Depending on the number of colors required for the document, you might be able to reduce the file size without affecting the image quality.

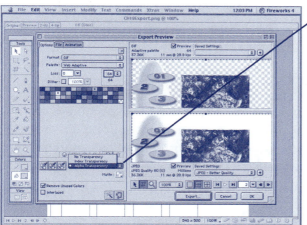

4. Check to see whether you have the right transparency setting selected for the document. The exported file size might shrink if the document doesn't need to display a color across a large area of the canvas.

Optimizing JPEG Settings

Although you can also optimize GIF and PNG files in Fireworks, this section is intended to compare optimizing a single file with an animation and a Web page. The following steps explore several optimization settings with which you can experiment on a JPEG file.

1. In the Export Preview window, select the Remove Unused Colors check box. If the image is fairly simple, you might want to convert some similar colors to share a single color.

2. Compare the image quality of the JPEG image with a GIF or JPEG file with a different quality setting.

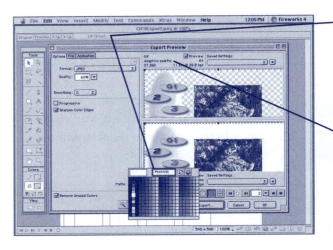

3. Choose a Matte color from the color well. The Matte color should match a solid-colored background image. It can help blend the edges of an image with its background color.

4. View the file size and its expected download time in the preview panes. If you cannot tell any difference in image quality between the two file types, choose the smaller file size.

Optimizing an Animation

Preview different color palettes and tweak frame delays in the Export Preview window for a file containing animation. You can choose from a single, 2-Up, or 4-Up preview mode and pick the best combination of settings before you export an animation. The following steps show you how to adjust some of the animation-related settings in the Export Preview window.

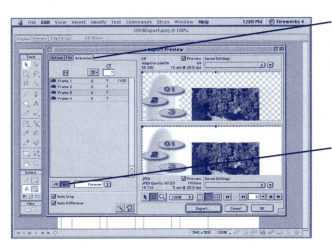

1. Open an animated GIF file. Choose the Export Preview command from the File menu. Click on the Animation tab to view the frame settings for the file. Preview different file format settings for the document.

2. Click on the Loop button if you want the animation to repeat its playback.

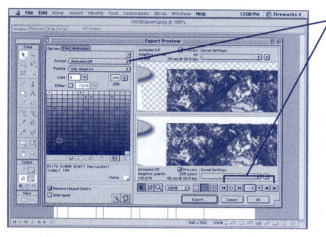

3. Choose Animated GIF from the Format pop-up menu in the Options tab. Use the Frame Controls to navigate through each frame of animation.

4. View the colors for the document. Try experimenting with different color palettes to see whether you can reduce the file size of the animated GIF.

Exporting Symbols and Instances

Animation, graphic, and button symbols created in the Library panel can be exported as a PNG file and shared between Fireworks applications and Fireworks documents. The Library panel stores the menu commands that enable you to export symbols from one Fireworks document and share them with another. In most cases, you will export the slice that covers an instance to export a symbol or instance from Fireworks.

You can export an animation, graphic, or button instance as a JPEG or GIF file. Choose a file format from the Optimize panel and then select the Export command from the File menu to export a document as a GIF, JPEG, or other supported file format. If you do not want to preserve the graphic, animation, or button information stored in a PNG file, you can only export a graphic file, such as a GIF or JPEG file, that converts the instance into a bitmap. The following sections show you how to export an instance as a single frame or slice.

Exporting an Instance in a Frame

The whole point of using a symbol to create graphics, buttons, or animation is to reduce the size of a file. If a document contains many instances of the same symbol, when you export the document each instance remains visible in the exported file. However, if you want to edit the exported file (I'm assuming you're using a JPEG or GIF file format), you'll discover that all the instances have been converted into bitmaps. So you can't really export a symbol or instance as anything other than a PNG file if you want to continue to modify it at some point in the future. However, you can export instances from a document as you would any other object, layer, or frame. Keep in mind, though, that although Dreamweaver and Director might be able to import and retain many unique features in Fireworks graphics and HTML files, other Web editors might not. The following steps show you how to export an instance by exporting a single frame to a file.

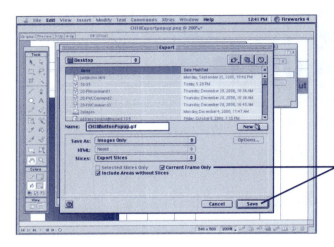

1. Create a new symbol in the Library panel and drag it into a document window. Copy and paste the instance into a new frame.

2. Choose the Export command from the File menu. Check the Current Frame Only check box, then click on the Save button.

Exporting a Button Instance as a Slice

Button symbols can contain frames representing each state. The proper way to export a button is by saving the slice and button instances as a PNG file that contains all the associated behaviors for the button symbol. If you only want to preserve the graphic image of a button, you can perform the following steps to export a button instance as a single slice.

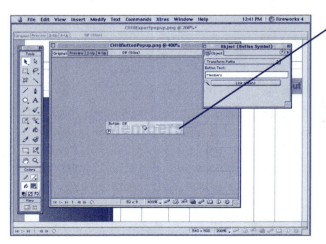

1. Select a button instance you want to export as a single slice. Copy and paste it into a new document window.

2. Choose the Export command from the File menu. Type a name for the file in the Name text box. Select Images Only from the Save As pop-up menu and then choose Export Slices from the Slices pop-up menu. Then, check the Selected Slices Only check box. Click on the Save button to export the button instance.

18

Working with Fireworks Files in Dreamweaver 4

If you've become familiar with the toolbox, document windows, and panels in Fireworks, you'll find a similar workspace in Dreamweaver 4. But wait, don't get too excited. Besides HTML, JavaScript code, commands, task history, and behaviors, Dreamweaver doesn't share many features with Fireworks. For example, Dreamweaver does not have any vector or bitmap drawing tools. However, many of the user interface elements in Fireworks 4, such as panels, menus, and floating tool windows are also available in Dreamweaver 4. This chapter explores the Dreamweaver workspace and shows you how to open and understand some of the graphics and HTML generated by Fireworks.

In this chapter you'll learn how to:

- Tour the Dreamweaver workspace
- Work with panels and preferences
- Define a site and open HTML files
- Create a Web photo album in Dreamweaver 4

Exploring the Dreamweaver Workspace

When you first start Dreamweaver, the workspace, tools, and menu commands can be intimidating. Although the panels in Dreamweaver might have different names and have a few different buttons and pop-up menu commands, some of the panel names are similar to those used in Fireworks 4. For example, the History and Behaviors panels are virtually identical, whereas the Layers and Frames panels are very different between the two applications. Dreamweaver can work with all the behaviors and commands created in Fireworks and can enable you to create a few that you can't create in Fireworks.

The menu names in Dreamweaver 4 are also almost identical to those in Fireworks 4 and Flash 5. But one click on any of them and you'll quickly realize the menu commands are much different in Dreamweaver than in Fireworks, or Flash 5 for that matter. Dreamweaver 4 is much more similar to UltraDev 4, Macromedia's HTML editor for database-backed Web sites.

Dreamweaver has a couple of additional panels that you won't find in Fireworks. The Properties panel enables you to define tables and table cells, or to format text or other visible HTML elements. Other features, such as Layers and Frames, share the same name, but are two totally different things in Dreamweaver and Fireworks. Layers in Fireworks are used to store and lay out image and Web objects. In contrast, layers in Dreamweaver are defined by the <div> tag and can store HTML page information. Frames in Fireworks can be used to create animation, while frames in Dreamweaver can be added to divide a Web page, enabling it to contain multiple groups of HTML code in one browser window. The Library panel in Fireworks is also different than the Library panel in Dreamweaver.

Before exploring the Dreamweaver workspace, there are several steps involved to move images and code from Fireworks to Dreamweaver. You can save a master copy of a Fireworks document as a PNG file before you export images and HTML. However, you will not be using the master PNG file in Dreamweaver, only exported image files, such as GIF, JPEG, or animated GIF files. The primary reason for using Dreamweaver is to add the Fireworks-generated HTML code to a Web page.

There are two different ways you can add Fireworks-generated HTML code into Dreamweaver. After you export image and HTML files from Fireworks, you can import or open a Fireworks-generated HTML file in Dreamweaver. Choose the Insert Fireworks HTML button (Fireworks icon) located in the Common category of the Objects panel to insert image-related HTML code into an existing Dreamweaver HTML file. As an alternative, you can choose Open to view, edit, or add more HTML code to your Web page.

Dreamweaver enables you to view HTML in two different views: Show Design View or Show Code View. In Show Design View, you can view the Web page as it will appear in a browser window, and edit the HTML elements as image objects. If you choose Show Code View, you can edit HTML and JavaScript code as text. Dreamweaver also has a third document view called Show Code and Design Views, enabling you to see the HTML code in the top part of the document window and the image objects in the bottom portion of the same window.

When you open a Fireworks-generated HTML file in Dreamweaver, you are viewing the JavaScript routines, HTML tags, and image map coordinates for the Web graphics you created in Fireworks. If the directory paths in the HTML code match the location of the image files for the open Web page, you will be able to view the image files in the Show Design View of the document window in Dreamweaver.

The following sections provide a brief tour of the panels, tools, commands, and document window features in Dreamweaver and UltraDev 4.

Navigating Panel Windows

When you first start Dreamweaver, the toolbox, panels, and Welcome windows will open. A complete list of panels is located in the Window menu. Take a tour of features in Dreamweaver from the Welcome panel, set HTML preferences from the CSS panel, or look up an HTML tag in the References panel. Add frames created or imported to a Web page using the Frames panel. Use the Object panel to select a particular frame format.

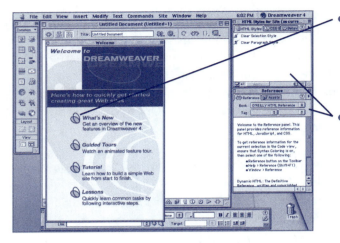

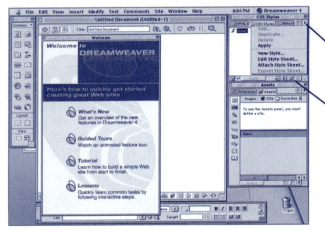

- **Welcome.** The items in the Welcome window provide a guided tour, tutorial, and lessons for Dreamweaver. Click on a dual-ellipse icon to select each item in the Welcome window.

- **Panels.** Like Fireworks, Dreamweaver has several panels in its workspace. You can view HTML Styles, CSS Styles, or Behaviors, or you can look up an HTML tag in the Reference panel. You can dock panels so that they share the same panel window, or undock them and place them anywhere you like in the Dreamweaver workspace.

- **Pop-up menus.** View a list of menu commands for the panel by clicking on the arrow button.

- **Shortcuts.** Some panels contain a group of icons in the lower-right corner. Each icon represents a shortcut for a menu command, enabling you to create or delete a file with a mouse click.

TIP

If a panel has a document icon at the bottom of its window, click on it to create a new element in that panel.

Accessing Tools in the Objects Panel

You can access a full bouquet of HTML tools from the Dreamweaver toolbox.

Although there's a full window of tools, you can choose from five additional sets of tools from the pop-up menu located at the top of the toolbox. You can also resize the toolbox in Dreamweaver. Simply click and drag the lower-right corner of the toolbox window to change its shape. The following list describes some of the toolbox tools in the Common category of the Objects panel.

- **Images**. You can embed an image file by choosing this button.

- **Categories**. View the list of categories for the Objects panel by clicking on the pop-up menu. Choose Characters, Common, Forms, Frames, Head, Invisibles, or Special from the categories pop-up menu.

- **Tables**. Add a table to a Web page to organize similar groups of Web data. You can store table data in rows and cells. Dreamweaver creates tables using the <table> tag, and creates table rows and cells using the <tr> and <td> tags.

- **Layers**. In Dreamweaver, a layer is a container that can hold HTML page information. Dreamweaver creates layers with the <div> tag. You can add one layer or multiple layers to a Web page. Fireworks enables you to export each layer as a CSS layer. However, when you export a document, layers are flattened in the resulting document.

- **Nav bar**. Click on the Nav Bar button to insert a nav bar object into the document. Create buttons and button states for your nav bar in the Insert Navigation Bar window.

- **Email link**. Add text and a link to an e-mail address by clicking on this button.

- **Flash**. Select this button if you want to embed a Flash object in your Web page. Macromedia Flash enables you to create animation and interactive motion graphics.

- **Fireworks**. Insert a Fireworks-generated HTML file by choosing the Insert Fireworks HTML button.

Finding Commands in Menus

The menus and menu commands in Dreamweaver enable you to create, insert, remove, edit, and automate Web page design. Most of the menu commands parallel the features you'll find in the different panels. The following list contains a brief summary of menus available in Dreamweaver.

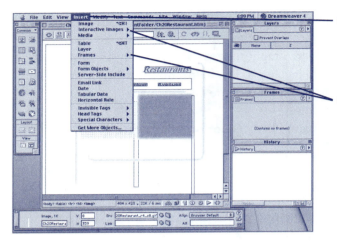

• **Menus**. The Dreamweaver menu bar consists of File, Edit, View, Insert, Modify, Text, Commands, Site, Window, and Help menus.

• **Submenus**. If an arrow appears to the right of a menu command, a submenu will appear whenever that menu command is selected. Submenus contain an additional menu list of commands for the selected menu item.

Examining the Document Window

You can view and edit HTML and JavaScript in the document window. Dreamweaver's document window contains its own toolbar, a document statistic section located at the bottom of the window, a group of shortcut icons, and the typical scrollbar and window controls. Use the Property Inspector window to view and edit Web objects, such as text or table cells. The following list highlights some of the more frequently used features in the document window.

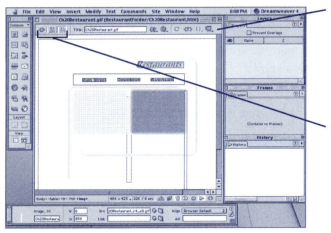

• **Toolbar**. Change the view of the document window, manage and preview files, or access the built-in reference and view options by clicking on a button in each document window's toolbar.

• **Viewing modes**. View a page in Design or Code view. Design View enables you to view and edit the Web page as if you were viewing it with a browser. In Code View, you can see all the HTML and JavaScript in the Web page. Choose the Show Code and Design Views button to display both views in a single document window.

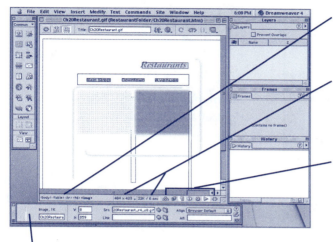

- **Tags**. Each tag used in the file appears in the lower-left corner of the document window.

- **Document statistics**. View the width and height of the document, along with its file size and download times, at the bottom of the document window.

- **Shortcuts**. Click on a shortcut icon to view a site, document assets, HTML styles, behaviors, CSS styles, document history, or the Code Inspector window.

- **Property Inspector window**. View, edit, or add object settings from this window. Select a table, table cell, text, frame, or layer from the document window to view or change its property settings.

Viewing a Document

In addition to all the tools, panels, and menus surrounding the document window, there are many ways you can view the Web page content, too. The following list shows you a few more tools that can make designing Web pages a little easier.

- **Standard view**. Choose between Standard and Layout views. You can insert tables in Standard View.

- **Layout view**. In Layout View, you can design the Web page layout using tables as the underlying structure. Use the Draw Layout Cell and Draw Layout Table buttons located in the Layout section of the Common category of the Objects panel to design your Web page layout.

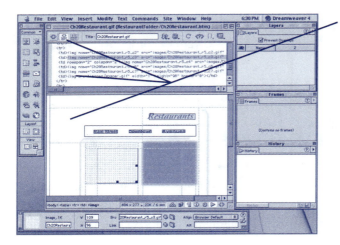

● **Code and Design views**. View your Web page source code in Code View, or preview it as you design in Design View. Or, you can view both Code and Design views in one window.

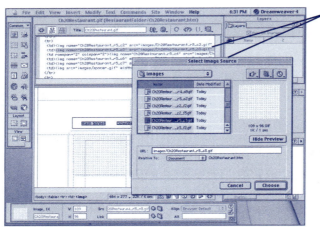

● **Viewing an image source**. Double-click on a table containing an image to view the source file for the image. Select a different image or use the one you've already selected.

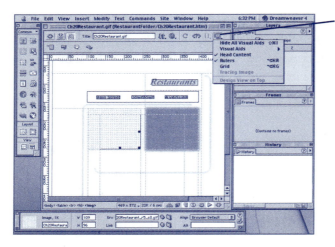

● **Layout options**. Access menu commands for rulers, grids, and visual aids from this pop-up menu.

Using Panels, Preferences, and the Launcher

Like Fireworks, Dreamweaver has several panels that provide instant access to a wide range of tools and commands. This section explains how to access and use the panels, preferences, and Launcher tools in Dreamweaver 4.

Viewing Object Information in the Objects Panel

You can insert specific HTML tags, such as table or image tags, or embed Flash, Shockwave, or Generator files into a Web page by choosing a button in the Objects panel. To insert an object into a document, first click in the location where you want to insert an object in the document window. Then, click on a button in the Objects panel to insert an object. The following list summarizes the categories and objects that live in the Objects panel.

- **Common**. View common objects in the Common category. The following buttons are located in the Common category: Insert Image, Insert Rollover Image, Insert Table, Insert Tabular Data, Draw Layer, Insert Navigation Bar, Insert Horizontal Rule, Insert Email Link, Insert Date, Insert Server-Side Include, Insert Fireworks HTML, Insert Flash, Insert Flash Button, Insert Flash Text, Insert Shockwave, and Insert Generator.

- **Forms**. If the Web site contains forms, add form-related items to the document by using tools in the Forms category. The Forms category consists of the following buttons: Insert Form, Insert Text Field, Insert Button, Insert Checkbox, Insert Radio Button, Insert List Menu, Insert File Field, Insert Image Field, Insert Hidden Field, and Insert Jump Menu.

- **Frames**. Choose from eight different types of frames in the Frames category: Insert Left Frame, Insert Right Frame, Insert Top, Insert Bottom, Insert Left Top-Left Corner and Top Frames, Insert Left and Nested Top Frame, Insert Top and Nested Left Frame, and Split Frame Center.

- **Head**. Define Web page <HEAD> info by choosing a button in the Head category. The following buttons are located in the Head category: Insert Meta, Insert Keyword, Insert Description, Insert Refresh, Insert Base, and Insert Link.

- **Invisibles**. Add an anchor, script, or comment to a Web page from the Invisibles category.

- **Special**. Insert an applet, plug-in, or Active X object by choosing its icon from the Special category of the Objects panel.

- **Character**. Add special characters to a Web page from the Character category in the Objects panel. The following buttons are located in the Character category: Insert Line Break, Insert Non-breaking Space, Insert Copyright, Insert Registered Trademark, Insert Trademark, Insert Pound, Insert Yen, Insert Euro, Insert Left-Quote, Insert Right-Quote, Insert Em-Dash, and Insert Other Character.

Creating Shortcuts in the Launcher Panel

You can quickly access panels, tools, and commands from the Launcher panel. Use the Preferences window to customize the items that appear in the Launcher. Choose the Preferences command from the Edit menu to open the Preferences window, then click on the Panels option to view the settings for the Launcher panel.

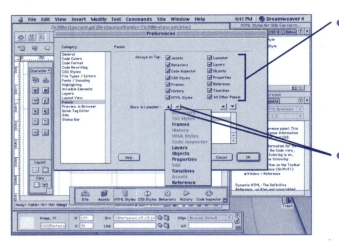

- **Panel options**. Click on a check box to select the tools you want to access from the Launcher panel.

- **Customize Launcher**. Add or remove items from the Launcher window by clicking the Plus or Minus buttons located above the Show in Launcher window list.

Customizing Dreamweaver Preferences

You can view or customize Dreamweaver preferences by choosing Preferences from the Edit menu. Click on a category in the left window list to view the preference settings in the right pane. Preference settings can be activated by selecting a radio button or by checking a check box. You can also select a preference from a pop-up menu, or by typing a value in a text box.

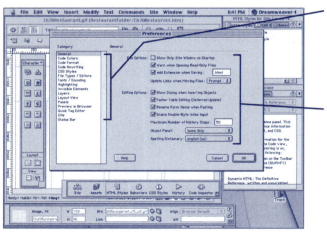

- **Categories**. Choose a Preference category from the left window list in the Preferences window. Each category in the list contains a unique set of preference settings.

- **Customize tasks**. Customize settings by choosing a check box or pop-up menu item from the Preferences window.

Creating Commands for Dreamweaver or Fireworks

Menus in Dreamweaver are organized in the same way as menus in Fireworks. However, Dreamweaver tools focus on Web editing and not on editing or creating Web graphics. Yet the History and Commands panels are nearly identical between the two applications. You can create commands and behaviors in Dreamweaver and share them with Fireworks.

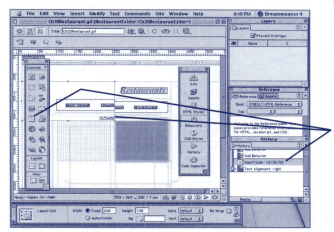

- **History panel**. The History panel logs many different tasks as you work on a document. Choose History from the Window menu, or press Shift + F10 to view the History panel.

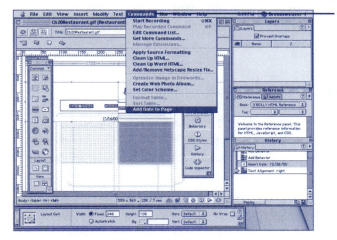

- **Commands menu**. The Commands menu contains a list of JavaScript files stored in the Commands folder of the Configuration folder of the Dreamweaver application folder. You can create commands in Dreamweaver and share them with Fireworks. Fireworks commands are located in the Configuration, Commands folder.

Exploring Web Site Design

As complex as a Web page can be, Web sites can be even more complex. When you create Web objects in Fireworks, they become table cells or rows in Dreamweaver. The following sections show you how to configure Dreamweaver and view some of the Web objects and behaviors imported from a Fireworks file.

Defining a Site

Navigate the image and Web files on your Web site with the Site window. Before you can start designing a Web site, you need to tell Dreamweaver where all its files are located on your hard drive. The following list shows you how to select a site in Dreamweaver.

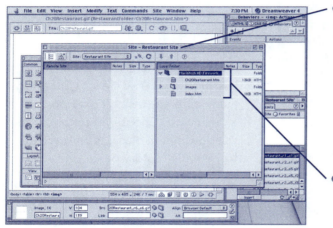

- **Site window**. Choose New Site from the Site menu. A Site Definition window will open. Select a category from the left window list and then complete any relevant information in the text fields located on the right side of the Site Definition window. In this example, I chose a local folder as my Web site directory.

- **Site files**. View the files and folders for the selected site in the Site window.

Working with Hotspots and Slices

The image maps and sliced objects designed in Fireworks change into table elements in Dreamweaver. If you have the resources to view the original Fireworks file while working on the HTML code in Dreamweaver, you can see how a hotspot or a slice translates from Fireworks to Dreamweaver. If you view the document in Design View, you can view a hotspot or slice object in a table in Dreamweaver and modify these objects as table cells or nested tables. The following list introduces you to Fireworks hotspot and slice objects as they appear in Dreamweaver.

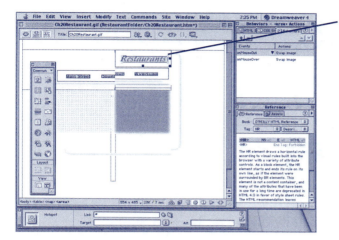

Table cells. If you've opened a Fireworks HTML file that contains a table to manage slices, click on an object in Design View to select a table cell. If the object is a hotspot, the Property Inspector window will display its object information. As an alternative, you can select the code between the <td> and /</td> tags in Code View.

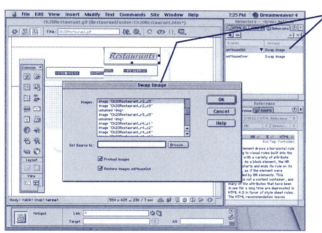

Assign a behavior. Click on the Plus button to view a list of behaviors for a selected object. Select a menu item to assign a behavior to the selected object.

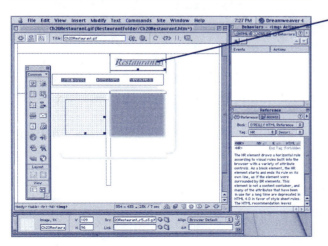

Select an image. Click on a table cell that contains an image file. The Property Inspector window will display the source location for the image, along with its width and height data. Click on the Align pop-up menu to adjust its alignment in the cell.

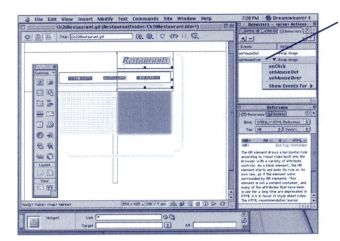

- **View events**. Select the Event pop-up menu for a behavior listed in the Behaviors panel. Choose a different event if you want.

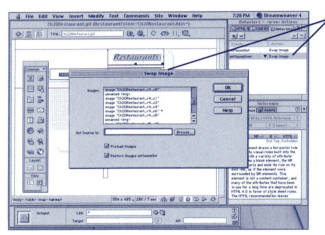

- **View behavior details**. Double-click on a behavior in the Behaviors panel to edit its behavior settings. Notice the Swap Image behavior settings in Dreamweaver are slightly different than those in Fireworks.

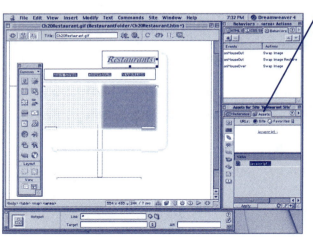

- **View assets**. Click on the Assets shortcut button located in the mini-launcher area of the document window to open the Assets panel. Select an object in the Design View of the document window and view its assets, such as JavaScript code, in the Assets panel. Use the Refresh button to update the contents of the Assets panel. Click on a button in the left side of the Assets panel. Then, click on an item in the Value window list to view that item's assets.

Assigning Behaviors

Creating a rollover in Dreamweaver is similar to creating a rollover in Fireworks. However, the drawing and editing tools are not available in Dreamweaver. Although the buttons and window list in the Behaviors panel in Dreamweaver are virtually identical to the Behaviors panel in Fireworks, Dreamweaver enables you to choose from a longer list of behaviors. The following list shows you the two basic concepts for creating a behavior in Dreamweaver.

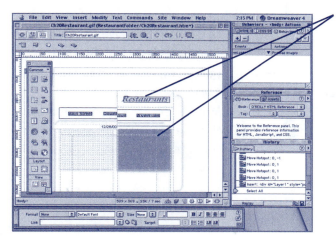

- **Select an object**. Click on a text, image, or Web object in the document window to select it. In this example, the window is in Design View. However, you can also select an object in Code View by highlighting the beginning and end tags in the HTML code displayed in the document window.

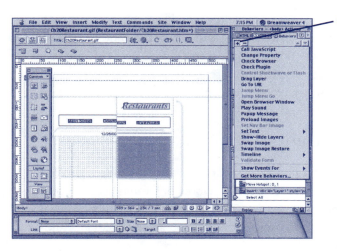

- **Assign a behavior**. Choose a rollover event from the Plus button pop-up menu in the Behaviors panel. This panel looks similar to the Behaviors panel in Fireworks. Click on the Show Events For item to select a specific browser for which the rollover should be tailored.

Working with Rollovers in Dreamweaver

Although you can view behaviors in the Behaviors panel and move objects in the Design View of the document window, the heart of a rollover is in the code and image files required to make an interactive Web task look real. The following list shows you how to view HTML and JavaScript code in the Show Code and Design Views window.

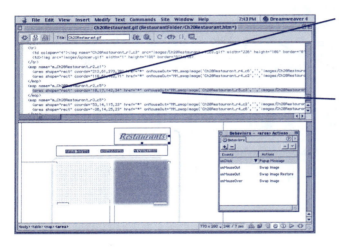

- **HTML code.** Tables, image maps, cells, rows, and JavaScript functions are all generated to use the Fireworks slices and create a rollover effect.

- **JavaScript functions.** Fireworks creates a standard Swap Image routine that can be called from the HTML code to create different rollover effects, such as onMouseOut or onMouseDown.

Working with Rollovers

Dreamweaver has a slightly different set of tools for working with rollovers than Fireworks does. There is a longer list of behaviors and a broader range of commands available in Dreamweaver. The following sections show you how to view the HTML code for rollovers, create and export a rollover from Fireworks, and then work with Dreamweaver and Fireworks in tandem to create interactive Web pages.

HTML Code and Rollovers

You can choose from a larger list of rollover behaviors to add to a hotspot or Web object in Dreamweaver 4. To create a rollover in Fireworks or Dreamweaver, you need to define a source and target image or text file. To create the rollover action, Dreamweaver uses a few JavaScript routines to identify and swap the source and target objects. Then it calls, or uses, those routines when the image is inserted into a table. The following list explains a few basic HTML elements used to create a rollover.

- **Tables**. There are several different HTML table-related tags that are used to create different kinds of tables in HTML. If you want to place an image object in a particular location on a Web page, you'll need to create a table with table rows

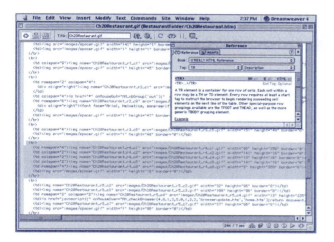

and cells so that a browser can figure out where to display a source image and its swapped image.

- **Image maps**. An image map works with table elements to tell a browser the coordinates of different image objects and where to display them in relation to a larger image file.

- **Image files**. An image file can be embedded as a background image or as a sliced file. Image files are usually GIF or JPEG files.

Modifying Rollovers in Fireworks

After you've exported image files that contain rollover behaviors, save the original source file as a PNG file. You can experiment with different export settings, create a backup of a particular rollover state, or use the PNG file to build a new design. The following list shows you how easily you can create a Swap Image behavior with the drag-and-drop handle in Fireworks.

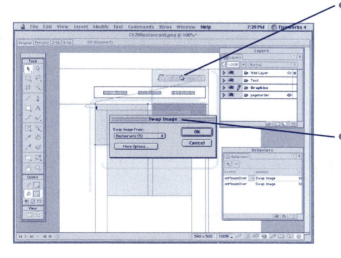

- **Drag-and-drop handle**. The easiest way to assign a behavior to a slice is by dragging and dropping the drag-and-drop handle. Click and drag the drag-and-drop handle to the target slice in the document window. The Swap Image dialog box will open.

- **Swap Image dialog box**. Choose a frame to complete the Swap Image behavior, or click on the Options button if you want to customize settings in the full-size Swap Image dialog box. Set up the Swap Image behaviors and then click on OK to save your changes.

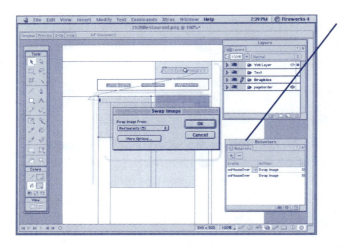

● **Behaviors panel**. The Swap Image behavior you've just created will appear in the Behaviors panel. Double-click on a behavior in the Behaviors window list to modify its settings. Or, select a behavior and click on the Minus button to delete it.

Exporting Rollovers to Dreamweaver 4

If you've assigned a behavior to a slice object or created a button symbol containing button states in Fireworks, you can export these objects and open them in Dreamweaver. You can continue to add more behaviors or modify the existing ones within Dreamweaver or another HTML editor. For best results, be sure to choose the right export setting for the HTML file from the HTML Setup dialog box before you export rollover-related files from Fireworks.

● **HTML Setup dialog box**. Before you export HTML from Fireworks, open the HTML Setup dialog box. Choose the HTML Setup command from the File menu. The HTML Setup dialog box will open. Click on the General tab.

● **HTML style**. Select Dreamweaver from the HTML Style pop-up menu. Then, click on the Insert Fireworks HTML button in the Common category of the Objects panel to open the Insert Fireworks HTML window and work with the Fireworks-generated HTML code in Dreamweaver.

Configuring Dreamweaver to Edit Images with Fireworks

You can continue to update Web graphics in Fireworks. However, you might have to update HTML as you update the Web graphics in Fireworks. Export an updated set of HTML and image files from Fireworks; Dreamweaver has a nifty Insert Fireworks HTML button in the Common category of the Objects panel to make importing HTML quick and easy. Click on this button to open the newer HTML code from Fireworks. Then, replace any of the older code in the larger Web page being designed in Dreamweaver.

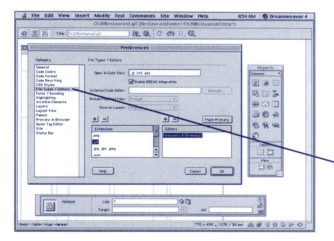

You can also configure Dreamweaver to automatically open Fireworks whenever you want to edit an image object embedded in an HTML file. The following list shows you a few different ways you can configure Dreamweaver to use Fireworks to edit image files.

- **File types and editors**. Open the Preferences window and select the File Types/Editors item from the Category window list. Select a file type from the Extensions window list. Then, add or select an editor application for the selected file type.

- **Optimize in Fireworks command**. You can also select an image object in a document and then choose the Optimize in Fireworks command from the Commands menu.

- **Edit With Fireworks 4 command**. If you're using a Mac, hold down the Control key; on a Windows computer, press the right mouse button. Then, click on an image object and choose the Edit With Fireworks 4 command.

Creating a Web Photo Album

If you have a digital camera or receive lots of digital images over e-mail, you can use Dreamweaver to create a Web photo album. The Web Photo Album menu item is a command that processes image files in Fireworks while generating HTML code in Dreamweaver. The command can take a folder full of image files and create a set of Web pages, enabling you to navigate the images in a browser window. The following list highlights the main steps involved in creating a Web photo album in Dreamweaver.

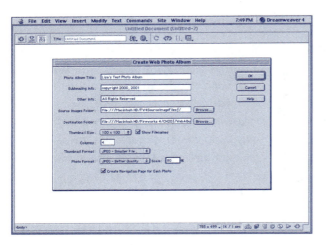

- **Create Web Photo Album command**. Choose this command and then select a folder full of files that you want to turn into a Web Photo album.

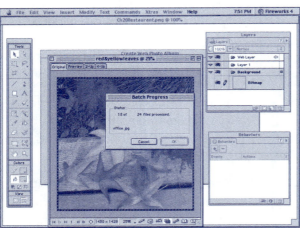

- **Batch Process**. Wait for the Create Web Photo Album Command to run. Dreamweaver will automatically start and process the image files in Fireworks. The amount of time it takes Fireworks to create the album depends on how large each image file is and how many files you've selected to be batch processed.

- **Browse photos**. When the script has completed, Dreamweaver will create a new Web page document containing the photo album

Configuring UltraDev 4

Adding and editing HTML and JavaScript code in UltraDev 4 is similar to the way you'd work with HTML and JavaScript in Dreamweaver 4. Both applications share the same HTML editing panels, tools, and commands. UltraDev 4 contains a few additional features that enable you to integrate your Fireworks graphics with a Web site that interacts with a database. The following list shows you how to configure the database mechanism for UltraDev 4. First, you'll need to install a database onto a Windows- or Linux-based system. Then, populate the database for any corresponding fields in your Web pages.

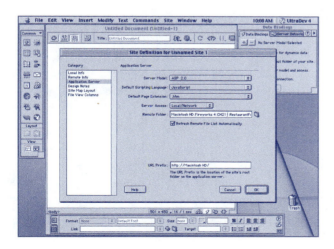

- **Database**. Select Define Sites from the Sites menu. Choose the New button to create a new site, or select the Edit button to modify an existing site. Then, click on the Application Server item from the Category window list. Choose a server model, a scripting language, the type of server access, and the folder location for your Web-related files from the site window.

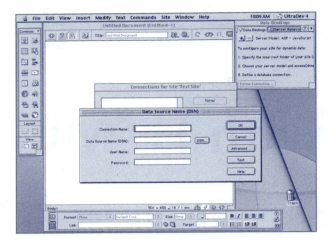

- **Connections**. Choose the Connections command from the Modify menu. Click on the New button to create a new data source.

- **Data source name**. Type a Connection Name, Data Source Name, User Name, and Password to define database access for UltraDev 4. Make sure that your computer is correctly connected to the same network as the computer server that's running the database.

19

Working with HTML and JavaScript Code

Designing Web graphics in Fireworks is easy partly because you don't have to hand-code the HTML and JavaScript that tells a browser how to handle buttons states and rollovers. You can actually design your Web graphics without touching any code. Export all or part of a Fireworks document as a Dreamweaver library (.lbi) file if you do not want to modify or create any of the HTML or JavaScript code generated by Fireworks. The Dreamweaver library is a file that can be embedded in a Web page along with any images you create. However, if you export a library, you won't be able to customize any of the HTML or JavaScript. For example, if you want to change the name of an image file in a Dreamweaver library, you'll need to make the change in Fireworks and export a new Dreamweaver library and image file. If you export HTML code for a Web page, you can type in the new file name, and edit the file name of the image in Windows or the Mac OS. This chapter shows you how to view, modify, and add HTML and JavaScript code generated by Fireworks in Dreamweaver 4. In this chapter, you'll learn how to:

- View HTML code generated by Fireworks in Dreamweaver
- Identify JavaScript functions and table tags in HTML code
- Modify a table in Dreamweaver and an HTML text editor
- Create a pop-up menu in Dreamweaver

Customizing JavaScript and HTML

You can change the code generated by Fireworks in many different ways. You can do something ambitious like replace or rewrite each JavaScript function to fit the behavior you want for your Web site. Or, you can make some relatively simple changes to update paths to files or change file names to be more recognizable. The following sections show you how to view and make some fairly easy changes to HTML and JavaScript code.

Viewing HTML for an Image Map

This first example doesn't really show you how to edit HTML code. Its intent is to familiarize you with what an image map looks like as HTML code. The most important elements of an image map are the image map name, the coordinates for the full image, and any behaviors and image files associated with each behavior. The following steps aren't actually steps to complete a task; they simply point out the different components of an image map.

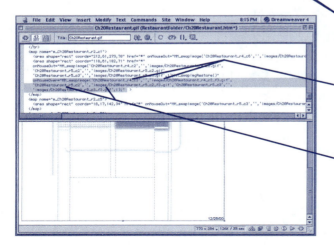

1. The image map information begins with the name of the image map, followed by the shape of the image map and its coordinates.

2. If the image map contains a rollover behavior, each behavior will appear within the image map tags.

3. For each behavior, the name of the slice file appears first, followed by the path to the file.

4. If the image map contains several slices, each slice is listed in the behavior definition, which begins and ends with a double quote character.

Updating File Locations

Fireworks creates paths for slice files based on the relative location of the HMTL file. If you plan to store image slices in a different folder on the Web server, or if you want to customize the location of all images for your Web site, you'll need to manually update the file locations for each image file in the HTML code. Here's how:

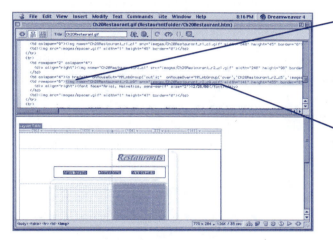

1. Locate the code containing the path you want to update.

2. Select the text for the directory path of the image file.

3. Type the new path name in the document window.

Changing the Title of a File

As you add or change images for a Web page, you might also need to change the HTML code to recognize a new file name. The following steps show you how to change the title of an HTML document.

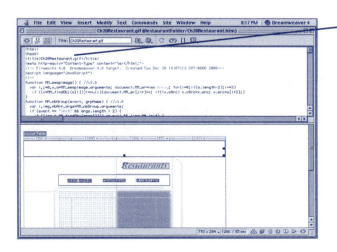

1. Locate the title tags in the document window.

2. Type a new file name in the document window.

3. Open the page in a browser. The title of the document will appear in the window title bar.

Examining JavaScript Functions

If you're familiar with scripting languages, such as Perl or AppleScript, some of the language elements in JavaScript might look familiar. JavaScript code consists of functions that can define a particular behavior, such as swapping images or preloading images. Each function has a name that can be called from another part of the HTML code. The following steps identify some of the core elements of a JavaScript function.

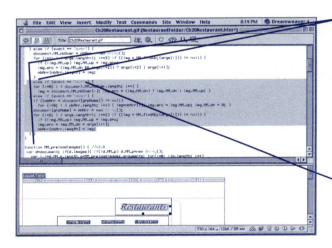

1. A function usually begins with the term "function" followed by the name of the function. In this example, I've selected an else if section of a function. If and else statements create conditional code. If the conditions defined in these statements are met, the code following it will be run.

2. An event is defined for the else if statement. In this example, the out event occurs when the cursor is moved away from an object containing a rollover behavior.

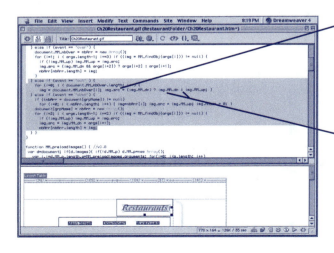

3. The image information for the else if statement is stored in a for loop. If the conditions of the for loop are met, then the image states defined in this function will be recognized by the browser.

4. The remainder of the else if statement tells the browser that if the over image is displayed, change it to the up image.

Viewing Table Tags

Fireworks creates a table to represent the canvas area of a document. Each slice is defined as a table row or cell in HTML code. The table tag in HTML is simply <table>. Table rows are <tr> and </tr>, and table cells are <td> and </td>. The tag </table> must be used to define the end of the table. The following steps show you the different table-related tags you'll find if you export an HTML file from Fireworks.

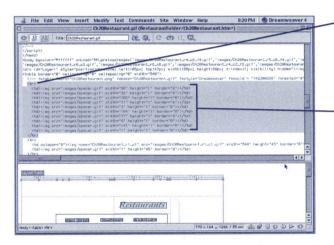

1. The <tr> tag defines the beginning of a table row. In this case, this table row contains a bunch of table cells that contain spacer, or empty, image files.

2. Each table cell is defined within the <td> and </td> tags.

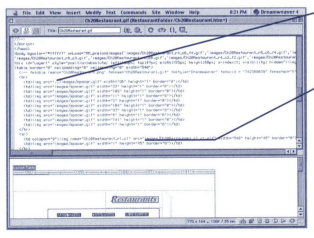

3. Type ../ to change the relative path from the images folder to the directory located above the images folder.

4. Change any other directory paths for any related files in the HTML code.

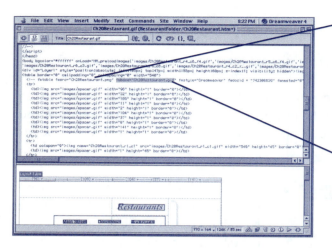

5. Comments are enclosed within <!-- and --> tags. Commented code is visible in an HTML editor window but will not appear in a browser window. This comment tells you the file name used to generate this HTML code.

6. The file name for the base image created for this HTML file is also included in this comment.

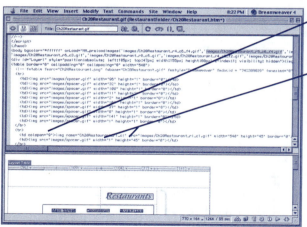

7. Each table cell can have a custom size. This table cell spans 9 columns.

8. Each object placed in a table cell can have a defined width or height. If no particular width or height is included with the image file, the cell size defaults to a default size, which may or may not display the entire image.

Customizing JavaScript Functions

You can modify JavaScript functions to create unique behaviors with Web objects. JavaScript functions and HTML code control most of the button states and pop-up menus created in Fireworks. All this code can be custom-tailored to create sophisticated or simple Web pages. The following steps show you the components that define a JavaScript behavior, and then show you how to customize the delay time for a pop-up menu.

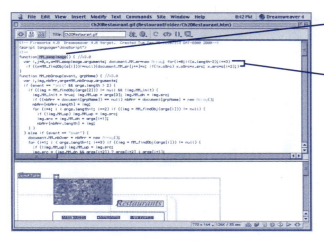

1. Select the name of the JavaScript function.

2. View the contents of the function to determine whether any of the subfunctions rely on a fixed function name.

3. View the place in the HTML code where the JavaScript function is called.

4. View the behavior or task that uses the JavaScript function. Locate any other instances in the HTML file that rely on the JavaScript function you want to modify.

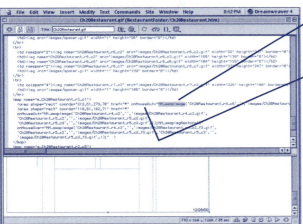

5. View the startTimeout function in the fw_menu.js file that Fireworks creates when you export a slice or hotspot that contains a pop-up menu.

6. Select the second value in the fwHideMenuTimer variable. Change the value from 1000 to a smaller value, such as 12.

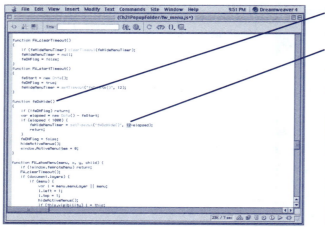

7. View the fwDoHide function.

8. Change the fwHideMenuTimer variable from 1000 to a smaller number, such as 12.

TIP

You can change the behavior for a rollover by adding or removing HTML or JavaScript code from a Web page. For example, if you want the target image to remain on the Web page when the mouse has moved off the button, you can change the image file that is displayed when the mouseOut routine is called.

Putting Together a Web Page

From a Zen standpoint, you only need a text editor, such as SimpleText (for Macs) or Notepad (for Windows) to create an HTML text file. However, if you've ever taken a look at all the JavaScript and HTML code created by Fireworks, you might want to take a good look at using a more sophisticated HTML editor application, such as BBEdit, FrontPage, or Dreamweaver. The main feature that's generally helpful in all these applications, is that different HTML and JavaScript language elements, such as tags, can appear in different colors, making it a little easier to figure out whether you forgot to add a closing tag or bracket. The following sections provide more information about assembling tables and adding HTML code using Dreamweaver 4.

Round-Trip Table Editing

Round-trip HTML editing and *round-trip table editing* describe Dreamweaver's ability to recognize table and HTML code created in other browser editors. On a Mac, you can configure Dreamweaver to work alongside BBEdit if you want to lay out a file in Dreamweaver and then tweak the HTML code in BBEdit. The following steps show you how an HTML file created in Fireworks appears in BBEdit.

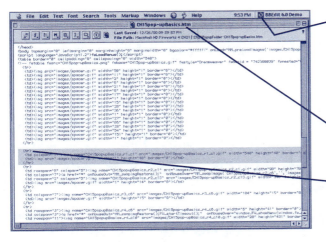

1. Double-click on the BBEdit application. This is a Mac-only application. If you have a Windows machine, you can work with Notepad or FrontPage alongside Dreamweaver.

2. Choose Open from the File menu and open an HTML file.

3. The table, table row, and table cell tags appear in the BBEdit window.

What Is a Table?

A table is an element of a Web page that can contain table rows and table cells. You can store text, images, and other embedded objects in a table. The following steps show you how to add tables to a Dreamweaver file.

1. Choose Reference from the Window menu (Shift + Ctrl/Command + F1). Select Table from the Tag pop-up menu. View the definition and usage information in the Reference panel.

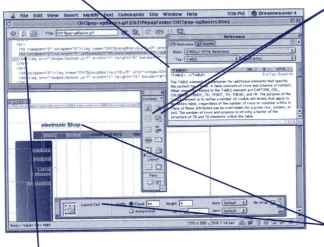

2. Open the Objects panel (Ctrl/Command +F2) and choose the Common category from the pop-up menu located at the top of the panel. Then, click on the Insert Table (or press Alt/Option + Ctrl/Command + T) or Insert Tabular Data button. Alternatively, you can choose the Table or Tabular Data commands from the Insert menu. Input the information you want to add to the file, then click on OK. A table or table with data will be added to the document window.

3. Select a table cell from the document window to view its settings in the Property Inspector window.

4. View the table content in the Code or Design views.

Viewing Tables Created in Fireworks

Table information generated from Fireworks will vary depending on the types of graphic objects you've created. The following steps show you how to view a table generated by Fireworks.

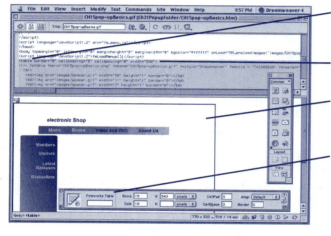

1. Look for the Table tag to find the beginning of the table.

2. View the width or height of the table.

3. Click on the table in the Design View to see how it will look in a browser.

4. View the settings for the table in the Property Inspector window.

Inserting a Rollover

Rollover behaviors are one of the more common elements stored in table cells. You can modify a table by inserting a rollover into it. The following steps show you how.

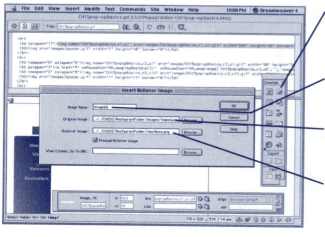

1. Choose the Insert Rollover Image button from the Common category in the Objects panel.

2. Type a name for the image in the Image Name text box.

3. Click on Browse and select the original image file.

4. Select the second Browse button and choose a rollover image file.

5. Click on OK to add the rollover and its code to the document.

Opening a File in another Directory

Here's another example of round-trip HTML editing. You can create or edit the file in an HTML editor application or in Dreamweaver. As long as the HTML editor does not modify any code you've modified manually, you should be able to open an HTML file in either application without having to worry about losing or modifying any additional code.

One of the changes you'll probably need to make is directory changes for the objects stored in tables. However, if you are able to create a local directory of your Web files that mirrors the directory paths on your Web server, you might not find yourself performing the following steps very often.

1. Select HTML code containing a path to an image file. You may need to scroll to see the actual code.

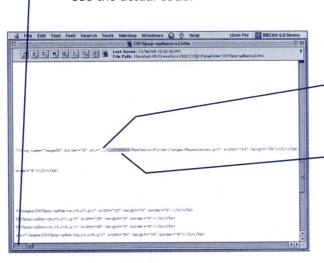

2. Each slash character indicates a folder in the path.

3. Each ../ indicates that the file or directory is located one level above the location of the current HTML file.

4. The folder name at the beginning of the path should exist in the path relative to the current file. You can also type an absolute path, such as a full URL, if you're not sure where the HTML file will be located on the Web server.

Viewing a Modified File in Dreamweaver

After you've modified the file in the HTML editor application, save it. Then, open that same file in Dreamweaver. If that file was originally created with Dreamweaver, you've just performed a round-trip HTML edit. The following steps show you how to open the file previously edited in BBEdit in Dreamweaver.

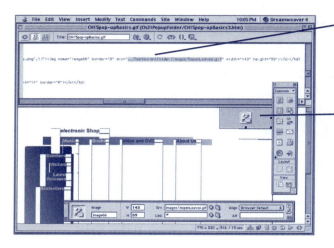

1. Choose Open from the File menu. Select the file and then click on the Open button. View the HTML code that was modified in the browser editor.

2. Select the object in the Design View to highlight its HTML code in the Code View section of the document window.

Adding HTML Code from Fireworks

You can choose the Insert Fireworks HTML button from the Common category of the Objects panel to add HTML code to a Dreamweaver file. I manually combined the code generated by Fireworks with existing code in my Web pages. The following steps show you how to add the Fireworks HTML code into an existing HTML file.

1. Open an existing Web page in Dreamweaver.

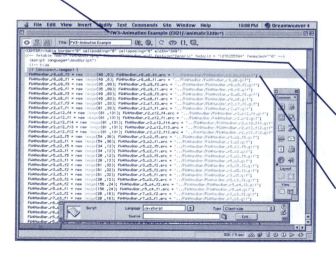

2. Select the JavaScript routines located at the beginning of the HTML file and copy and paste them into the <HEAD> section of the Web page.

3. Copy and paste the HTML code beginning with table tag down to the end of the image map code.

4. View the files and path names for each file in the HTML editor window. Modify any paths so that they contain the correct path to each image file.

Previewing with Design View

As you assemble the elements of your Web page, you might want to view the Web page layout in the Design View in Dreamweaver. Here's how:

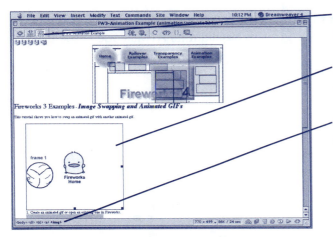

1. Click on the Show Design View button in the toolbar in the document window.

2. Select an image object and view its settings in the Property Inspector window.

3. View the tags used in the page at the bottom of the document window.

Locating and Organizing Image Files

After you've defined a site, Dreamweaver locates and organizes files as they appear on your hard drive. When you insert images in a Web page, Dreamweaver creates a new folder, titled Images, to store these files in a separate folder from your other HTML pages. The following steps show you where these folders are located on your hard drive.

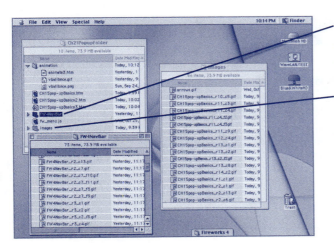

1. Double-click on a folder containing slice images. View the image files in the folder window.

2. Dreamweaver stores its image files in an Images folder. Double-click on this folder to view any image files for that Web site.

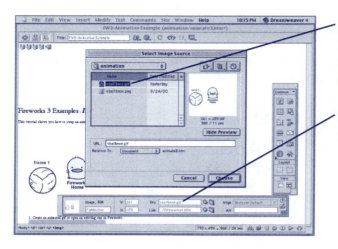

3. Double-click on an image object in Dreamweaver to open the Select Image Source dialog box. Select the image file, then click on Choose.

4. View the file name in the Property Instances window.

Adding Other Web Page Elements

In addition to viewing and modifying the HTML and JavaScript code created by Fireworks, you can add some new code using Dreamweaver Behaviors. Each behavior is stored in a JavaScript file in the Behavior folder, located in the Configuration folder of the Dreamweaver 4 application. The following sections show you how to add a few new behaviors to an HTML file created in Fireworks.

Adding JavaScript to Check for a Plug-In

If you're designing a Web page that will contain Flash files in addition to Fireworks-generated graphics, you might want to add code to the Web page to check the visitor's browser for the Flash plug-in. The following steps show you how.

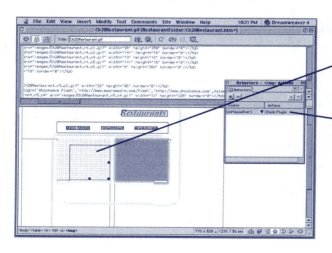

1. Select a table or table cell in the Design View.

2. Assign the Check Plugin rollover behavior to the selected object.

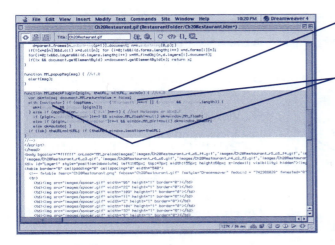

3. View the HTML code in Code View in the document window.

4. Locate the browsers defined to check for the Flash plug-in.

Adding JavaScript to Check for a Browser Version Number

You can assign a behavior to enable your Web page to check for a specific version of a browser. This can help you design Web pages that appear consistently in the browsers you've tested or browsers that you know support a specific version of HTML or JavaScript code. The following steps show you how to assign the Check Browser behavior to a table cell.

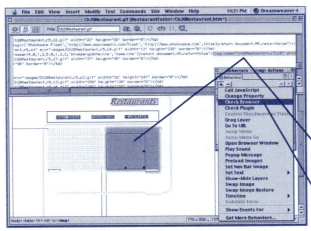

1. Select a table or table cell in the document window.

2. Select the Check Browser behavior from the Behaviors panel.

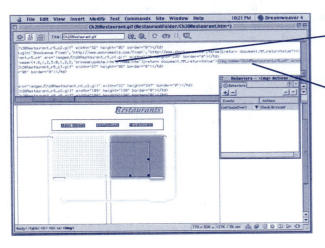

3. Change the document to show Code and Design views.

4. View the HTML code for the current document.

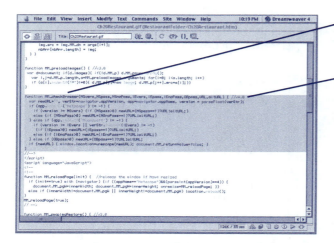

5. View the MM_checkBrowser function in the document window.

6. Look for the version numbers for which the function is checking.

Creating a Jump Menu

If you created pop-up menus in Fireworks, you'll be happy to know you can also create pop-up menus in Dreamweaver. Pop-up menus are called jump menus in Dreamweaver. The Insert Jump Menu window is organized a little differently than the Set Pop-Up menu window in Fireworks. Create a pop-up menu in both applications and compare them. The following steps show you how to create a jump menu.

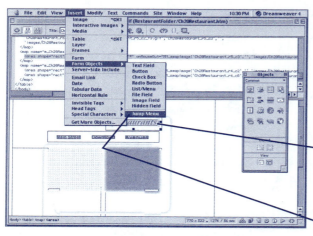

1. Click on an object to which you want to add a jump menu in the document window.

2. Choose Jump Menu from the Insert, Form Objects menu.

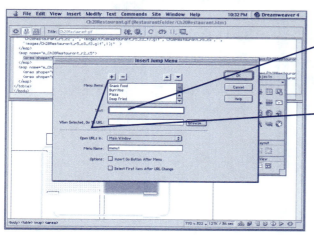

3. Type a menu item name in the Text field of the Insert Jump Menu dialog box.

4. Click on the Plus button to add the name to the window list.

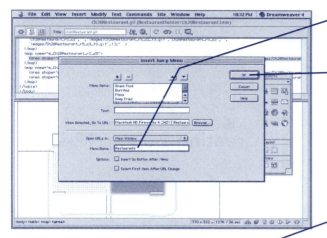

5. Type a menu name in the Menu Name text box.

6. Click on OK.

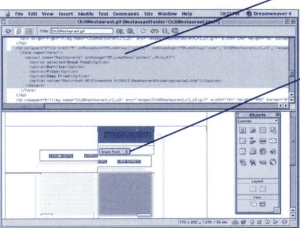

7. Look for the HTML code for the jump menu in Code View of the document window. The menu name and its menu items will appear in the selected table cell.

8. View the pop-up menu in the Design View of the document window.

Debugging JavaScript Code

I've got good news and bad news about this section. First the good news: You can debug JavaScript code in Dreamweaver 4. Now the bad news: You can only debug JavaScript on a Windows computer. Sorry, Macintosh folks! Go ahead and skip this section. The following steps show you how to invoke and view the JavaScript debug window.

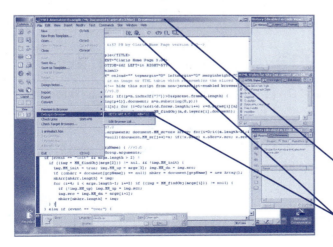

1. Open an HTML file that contains JavaScript code.

2. Choose Netscape or Internet Explorer from the File, Debug in Browser menu.

A dialog box will appear, asking you to save the current file before beginning the debug session.

3. Click on OK to continue, or click on Cancel if you don't want to start the debugger.

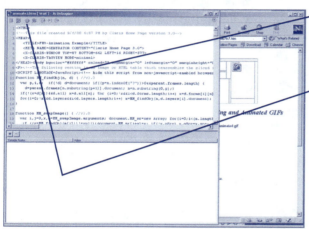

4. The JavaScript debugger window will open. Scroll through the HTML code and look for the JavaScript functions.

A set of control buttons is located in the upper-left corner of the debugger window.

Installing Dreamweaver Extension Files

If you purchased the Dreamweaver CD-ROM, you'll find several extensions located in the More Extensions folder on the root level of the CD. You can install these extensions and manage them with the Macromedia Extension Manager application. The following steps show you how to install a Dreamweaver extension using the Macromedia Extension Manager application.

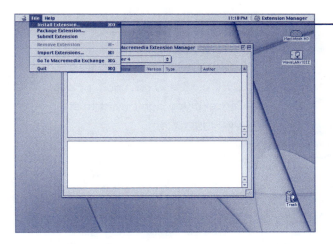

1. Choose the Install Extension command from the File menu.

2. Follow the onscreen instructions to select the extension and install it.

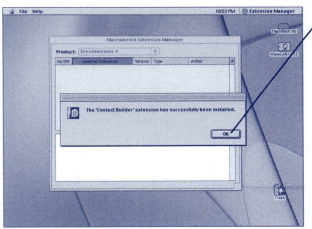

3. When the installation is complete, a dialog box will open. Click on OK.

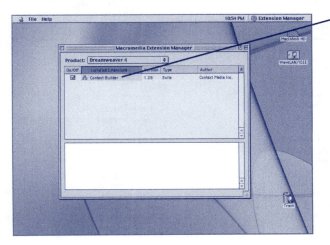

4. View the Dreamweaver extension file in the Macromedia Extension Manager window.

Index